Database Machines

International Workshop
Munich, September 1983

Edited by
H.-O. Leilich and M. Missikoff

With 140 figures and 2 tables

Springer-Verlag
Berlin Heidelberg New York Tokyo 1983

Editors

Prof. Dr. H.-O. Leilich
Institut für Datenverarbeitungsanlagen, TU Braunschweig
Hans-Sommer-Str. 66, 3300 Braunschweig, FRG

Dr. M. Missikoff
Consiglio Nazionale Delle Ricerche
– Instituto di Analisi dei Sistemi ed Informatica –
Via Manzoni 30, 00185 Roma, Italy

ISBN 3-540-12959-6 Springer-Verlag Berlin Heidelberg New York Tokyo
ISBN 0-387-12959-6 Springer-Verlag New York Heidelberg Berlin Tokyo

This work is subject to copyright. All rights are reserved, wether the whole or part of materials is concerned, specifically those of translation, reprinting, re-use of illustrations, broadcasting, reproduction by photocopying machine or similar means, and storage in data banks. Under § 54 of the German Copyright Law where copies are made for other than private use, a fee is payable to "Verwertungsgesellschaft Wort", Munich.

© Springer-Verlag Berlin Heidelberg 1983
Printed in Germany

The use of registered names, trademarks, etc. in this publication does not imply, even in the absence of a specific statement, that such names are exempt from the relevant protective laws and regulations and therefore free for general use.

Printing and binding: Beltz Offsetdruck, Hemsbach/Bergstr.
2145/3140-543210

Preface

The International Workshop on Database Machines in Munich is the third of its kind, preceeded by the meetings in Florence (Sept. 81) and San Diego (Sept. 82).

The workshop is aimed at providing an interchange of ideas and experience on computer systems designed to perform database operations more efficiently than general purpose computers with a software database management system. Many proposals have been published during the past 10 years, but now several systems have been built and practically implemented and some are even commercially available, so that confrontation with the real world is starting to occur.

The kinds of question which arise during this phase of coming to maturity are those involved with evaluation and measurement. The emphasis of the workshop is therefore on performance evaluation and the respective modelling techniques and methodology. Data flow and other new topics (including algorithms) are also treated with respect to performance and efficiency. We are glad to be able to include some papers on existing commercial products - from both the designer and the user viewpoints. We hope to encourage critical comments in this field and have arranged a session with the title "Where Database Machines Are Going" - to be followed by a panel discussion.

We would like to thank all those who are contributing to the workshop: the members of the programme and the organization committees and the authors themselves. Particular thanks are also due to Heinz Schweppe and Hans Christoph Zeidler for their initiative and endeavour which has made the meeting possible. We also would like to thank Dieter Schuett and the Siemens AG, Munich, for their assistance in local organization. The financing of the workshop would have caused great problems without the generous sponsorship of the Commission of the European Community and we would like to thank H. Fangmeyer of Ispra for his encouragement and help in this connection.

We hope that the workshop and its proceedings will constitute a valuable contribution to this fast growing class of computer architectures, database machines.

Braunschweig, July 1983   H.-O. Leilich
                                            M. Missikoff

CONTENTS

Dataflow and Database Machines

A Network-Oriented Dataflow Database System
    L. Bic, R.L. Hartmann...1

A Dataflow Retrieval Unit for a Relational Database Machine
    M. Glinz..20

A Concept for a Dataflow Database Machine - An Overview -
    R. Kubera, M. Malms...41

Modelling and Evaluation of Architectures

On a Specification and Performance Evaluation Model for
Multicomputer Database Machines
    G. Schiffner, P. Scheuermann, S. Seehusen, H. Weber.................46

Performance Modeling of the DBMAC Architecture
    S. Salza, M. Terranova, P. Velardi..................................74

Analysis of Filtering Efficiency in the Database Machine VERSO
    S. Gamerman, S. Salza, M. Scholl....................................91

Experiments in Benchmarking Relational Database Machines
    R. Bogdanowicz, M. Crocker, D.K. Hsiao,
    C. Ryder, V. Stone, P. Strawser....................................106

A Performance Study on Host-Backend Communication
    M. Drawin, H. Schweppe...135

On Selecting an Adequate Database Processor for
a Host-Backend Configuration
    P. Fuchs, D. Schuett...154

Where Database Machines are Going

Database Machines: An Idea Whose Time has Passed?
A Critique of the Future of Database Machines
    H. Boral, D.J. DeWitt..166

New Issues to Database Machines I

CID: A VLSI Device for Lists Intersection
    P. Bertolazzi, M. Missikoff, M. Terranova........................188

Data Handling and Dedicated Hardware for the Sort Problem
    W. Teich, H.Ch. Zeidler..205

Commercial Experiences

IDM-500 within a Mainframe Environment - Some first Experiences
    Ch. Riechmann..227

GEI's Experience with Britton-Lee's IDM
    G. Schumacher..233

New Issues to Database Machines II

A Message-Oriented Implementation of a Multi-Backend
Database System (MDBS)
    R.D. Boyne, D.K. Hsiao, D.S. Kerr, A. Orooji....................242

A Prolog Database Machine
    G. Berger Sabbatel, J.C. Ianeselli, G.T. Nguyen.................267

Data Structures and Algorithms

Performance Evaluation of Concurrency Control Algorithms
in the SABRE Database Computer
    J. Madelaine...277

Adaptive Segmentation Schemes for Large
Relational Database Machines
    Y. Tanaka...293

Querying and Filtering Formatted Files
    S. Abiteboul, M.-O. Cordier, S. Gamerman, A. Verroust..........319

On the Use of a Database Machine for Fuzzy Querying
    P. Bosc, A. Chauffaut, G. Hamon................................339

A NETWORK-ORIENTED DATAFLOW DATABASE SYSTEM

Lubomir Bic
Robert L. Hartmann
Department of Information and Computer Science
University of California

Irvine, California 92717

ABSTRACT: This paper presents a database model represented as a graph where each node is an active entity capable of receiving and processing data packages called tokens. This graph will be referred to as a dataflow graph. All requests are injected into the dataflow graph in the form of tokens which propagate through the graph by being replicated from one node to another. Thus computation proceeds in an asynchronous data-driven fashion.

This model permits a large number of independent processing elements to operate on the database simultaneously thus achieving a high degree of parallelism. Simulation results are included to demonstrate the system's behaviour in relationship to the number of existing processing elements and varying system loads.

1. Introduction

A typical database is an organized collection of data kept on some secondary storage media and accessed by a sequential stream of read/write operations. It is this single stream of operations, together with the relatively slow speed of secondary storage devices, that constitute the major limitations to database design. Exhaustive searches of large collections of data are prohibitively inefficient, and the use of indices, inverted files, and other auxilliary data structures must be introduced to achieve an acceptable level of performance. Even though such techniques are adequate for many database applications, their limitations are apparent. Especially in highly heterogenous information bases, with queries ranging over all possible attributes, the amount of auxilliary data structures necessary to support such queries may exceed the actual database size by a considerable factor. Furthermore, the low bandwidth of secondary storage devices, as compared to the speed of processing, renders most database applications highly I/O bound.

The steadily advancing LSI/VLSI technology is changing our perception of cost/size tradeoffs in memory utilization. Currently, 256 Kbit RAMs are available on a single chip and one megabit RAMs are expected in the late 1980's. Similarly, relatively powerful VLSI processors are available at a very low cost. The main focus of this paper is to investigate how this potential may be utilized in database technology; we will describe a scheme which permits the utilization of a very large number of RAM components accessed by a correspondingly large number of asynchronously operating processing elements. While such a scheme opens new dimensions to parallel processing by allowing simultaneous access to many parts of the database, and by decreasing the access time to individual elements, it is necessary to devise a new model of computation capable of
(1) exploiting such parallelism, and, at the same time
(2) solving problems common to all database systems, such as synchronization, reliability, back-up, etc.

This new model is based on the principles <u>dataflow systems</u> /Den75, AGP78/ which depart from the sequential, one-instruction-at-a-time concept of Von Neumann computers by enforcing data-driven functional computation. A dataflow program is a directed graph consisting of operators interconnected by arcs. Each operator is capable of receiving values arriving in the form of independent data tokens along its input arcs. After all inputs necessary to perform the desired operation have arrived the node produces an output value which is sent along its output arcs to subsequent operators. Thus, computation propagates asynchronously through the graph as values are being produced by individual operators, without the need for any centralized control.

As demonstrated in /BoDe81/ and /BiHe81/, dataflow principles can successfully be applied in relational database machines. In the system proposed in this paper a different approach is taken: instead of representing queries as dataflow programs, the database itself is represented as a dataflow graph, mapped onto a highly-parallel computer architecture. All requests are injected into the graph in the form of tokens and are propagated asynchronously from one node to another. We will show that such a model displays a high degree of parallelism within each request, in addition to allowing many requests to proceed concurrently.

The following sections present the model, its mapping onto an architecture, and simulation results which support the claims made throughout the paper.

2. The Model

2.1. Data Representation

To represent the database, we adopt the basic ideas of the entity-relationship model /Che76/ which perceives information as collections of entities and relationships. An entity-relationship diagram is used to describe a particular database. In this representation, entity sets and relationship sets are shown as rectangular and diamond shaped boxes, respectively; arcs are used to indicate the participation of entities in relationships. Attributes may be associated with both entities and relationships. They are defined as mappings between the entity or relationship sets and value sets. For example, Figure 1 shows a sample database describing relationships among sets of professors, courses, students, and dormitories.

The entity relationship model does not prescribe how sets and arcs are to be represented internally; For our system, we assumed a representation in which:

- all elements of an entity or relationship set are connected to a master node via arcs, and
- all arcs in the system are represented as bi-directional pointers.

A portion of the internal representation corresponding to the graph of Figure 1 is shown in Figure 2; it depicts the instances of 3 professors, 4 courses, and 5 students, interconnected via the corresponding relationships TEACH and ENROLL. (Heavy lines indicate the flow of tokens as will be explained in Section 2.3.)

2.2. A Dataflow View of Processing

The assumption implicit to most database systems is the existance of an outside agent -- a processor -- which accesses and manipulates the graph stored in secondary memory. Under this Von Neumann model of computation, adding more processors to the system becomes a very difficult task, primarily due to problems of synchronization. In order to overcome these difficulties, we adopt the dataflow point of view in which processing capabilities are incorporated into the graph itself. That is, each node is viewed as an active entity capable of receiving value tokens, traveling asynchronously along arcs, processing these independently of other nodes, and producing new tokens sent to other nodes.

Under this model of computation, all requests are injected into the graph in the form of tokens and their processing is governed by a data-driven propagation among nodes, as will be explained in the following section.

2.3. Execution of Requests

A data-processing language called CABLE (ChAin-Based LanguagE) has been proposed for the entity relationship model /Sho78/. In this language, each request against the database consists of navigational and _operational_ information. The navigational (or selection) information specifies a chain, or path, through the sets of entities and relationships. The operational information then chooses one set on the selected path and specifies which attibute values are to be output.*

For the dataflow database graph, we adopt a similar notion of navigation as in CABLE: A path through the graph is specified as follows,

$$S1/R1(S2/R2(...Sn/Rn)...)$$

where each Si is the name of an entity or relationship set and each Ri is a restriction of the form

$$\text{operand1 op operand2}$$

where op is a comparison operation (=, <, >, etc.), and each operand is an attribute value or a constant.

The intuitive meaning of the navigational information is as follows: Inject a token (carrying the navigational information) into those elements of set S1 which satisfy restriction R1. Each of these propagates a copy of the token along arcs connecting it to elements of set S2; each element of S2 that receives such a token and also satisfies restriction R2 will propagate the token into set S3, etc. This process is repeated until the final subset within Sn is selected. For example, a request may contain the following navigational information:

PROF/NAME="P2" (TEACH/all (COURSE/TITLE="ICS-1"
              (ENROLL/all (STUDENT/STATUS=GRAD"))))

which selects all graduate students enrolled in the ICS-1 course
----
* CABLE concentrates primarily on data retrieval operations;

taught by professor P2; (the keyword 'all' indicates that no restrictions were imposed on the relationships TEACH and ENROLL). The execution of the specified selection is carried out by propagating tokens from elements of PROF to elements of STUDENT via TEACH, COURSE, and ENROLL. Each token arriving at a node is propagated to the next set on the path, provided the node satisfies the corresponding restriction; otherwise, the token is discarded. Heavy lines in Figure 2 indicate the flow of tokens in response to the above query. Assuming that node C3 represents the course 'ICS-1' and nodes S1 and S2 are undergraduate students, the nodes selected as the final result are S4 and S5.

For a given request it is possible to specify more than one path converging onto the same set Sn. In this case, elements of Sn which satisfy restriction Rn and receive a token from all involved paths are selected. (In CABLE, this corresponds to selecting a set which is not at the end of a path.) For example, a request may involve the following navigational information:

PROF/NAME="P1" (ADVISE/all (STUDENT/all))
and
DORM/all (LIVE-IN/NO-OF-YEARS>2 (STUDENT/all))

which selects students advised by professor P1 who have lived in any of the dorms for more than two years. This selection involves two sets of tokens converging onto the set of students; elements of that set receiving both kinds of tokens then satisfy the selection criteria.

In addition to the navigational information, each request token injected into the graph carries the operation to be performed on each of the elements of the selected subset of entities or relationships. The following four basic operations are provided:

- Retrieve/attribute-list:

  retrieve specified attributes of the selected elements. (The physical transfer of data extracted from the graph to the outside of the system will be discussed in Section 3.3.)

- Modify/F,attribute-list:

  apply function F to specified attributes of the selected elements, i.e., modify their values.

- Delete:

  delete the selected elements. (This includes deletion of all arcs connecting the deleted element to the graph.)

- Insert/attribute-list/values-list:

  insert new element; in the case of an entity element, navigational information consists of the entity set name into which the element is to be inserted. In the case of a relationship element, navigational information consists of the two entity set names which participates in the relationship; the selected elements of both sets are joined via the new relationship element.

2.4. Concurrent Processing of Requests.

In order to introduce another degree of parallelism by allowing more than one request to be processed simultaneously, it is necessary to distinguish tokens belonging to different requests. This can be accomplished using a tagging scheme, similar to that introduced for general-purpose dataflow systems /AGP78/. In short, all tokens constituting one request carry the same tag.

A more serious problem introduced due to concurrent processing is the need to preserve data integrity. We define a transaction to be a sequence of one or more requests, each injected into the graph as a separate token. As in conventional systems, it is necessary to guarantee that all transactions are serializable, i.e., when processed concurrently they yield the same result as under serial execution.

We propose the following solution; all requests are initially submitted via a request processor which inspects their contents in order to determine the sets involved in each request. The request processor is also informed of the termination of all requests. If a request R is to perform a modification of set S, it will not be injected until all previous requests involving set S have terminated. Similarly, any subsequent request wishing to access elements of set S will be delayed until the modification request R is terminated. This rule permits requests to proceed simultaneously unless they involved the same set, and at least one of them performs a modification.

The additional burden placed on the request processor in the above scheme is to keep a simple trace of requests currently in progress. More complicated protocols may of course be envisioned; the purpose of this discussion was only to demonstrate that concurrent execution of requests is possible in the proposed system, while data integrity is maintained. Further details of the proposed model may be found in /BiHa83/.

3. Implementation

In the previous section, we have presented a rather abstract model of data processing in which all operators are injected into the dataflow database graph and propagate asynchronously by being replicated and forwarded by individual nodes. This section presents one possible implementation of such a model.

3.1. Architecture

We consider an architecture consisting of a two-dimensional array of

<u>processing elements</u> (PE) interconnected by horizontal and vertical communication rings. Thus, each PE is connected to its four nearest neighbors.* A large random access memory is associated with each PE. As will be discussed in Section 4, we have simulated arrays of up to 32x32 PEs. Assuming current technology, 0.5 MB of main memory may easily be accomodated with each PE. Hence, the entire system would comprise on the order of 500 MB of RAM -- a store large enough to hold a very large portion of any database. With further advancements of VLSI technology announced for the 1980's this number is expected to increase by an additional factor of 4. Furthermore, extrapolations of the obtained simulation curves show a very slow degradation in communication overhead as the array size is increased. Hence, it seems feasible to utilize more than the simulated 32x32 PEs.

The database graph is mapped onto the collection of individual memories in two steps:
First, a hashing function H is applied to the key k of each node, which yields an internal node number H(k). In a second step, a modulo n function MODN is applied to the number H(k), where n is the number of PEs constituting the architecture. The result MODN(H(k)) is then used as the PE number whose memory is to hold the corresponding node. In such a scheme, each PE may be viewed as the incarnation of all nodes mapped onto the PEs memory; for each of these nodes the PE must receive tokens, process these according to the node's contents, and produce results to be sent to other nodes.

By performing the mapping in two steps, the following advantages are achieved:
First, given a key value it is easy to determine the PE holding the

----
* Other interconnection schemes are being considered, however, at the time of writing, only the two-dimensional array has been simulated.

corresponding node by applying to it the hashing function H followed by the mudulo function MODN. On the other hand, an arc between two nodes k1 and k2 may be represented by recording the value H(k2) with the node k1 and the value H(k1) with the node k2, instead of having to record the key values k1 and k2 in their entirety. If the target range of the hashing function is relatively large compared to the number of existing PEs, the number of collisions to be maintained within each PE will be minimal.

The second advantage of using a two-step mapping is machine independence: in order to change the number of PEs constituting the architecture, only the modulo function MODN need to be adjusted; all internal node numbers H(k) remain constant.

3.2. Token Propagation

As mentioned above, arcs of the graph are represented as lists of internal node numbers kept with each node. These lists are segregated according to relationships in which they participate. This scheme permits n-to-m relationships to be implemented directly. Sending a token along an arc is then accomplished as follows; the PE holding the sending node determines the position (the i and j coordinates within the array) of the PE holding the receiving node. Based on that information and its own position within the array it determines which of its four neighbors has the shortest geometric distance to the destination PE, and sends the token into that direction. This operation is repeated by each PE receiving the token until the final destination is reached.

3.3 Data Input/Output

In order to inject request tokens into the system and conversely receive results generated by these requests, we assume that one or more PEs are connected to I/O processors. All input tokens enter the system via one of these PEs from which they propagate to their destinations in the way described in Section 3.2. The following paragraphs discuss how the initial token destinations are determined.

Consider again the navigational information introduced in Section 2.3. The first restriction R1 specifies the initial subset of S1 into which tokens must be injected. The techniques to locate elements of this subset may be based on (1) key values, (2) indexes, or (3) exhaustive search:

(1) If R1 specifies exactly one element based on its key, e.g., "Find the professor with employee#=X", then the hashing function, followed by the modulo n function, are used as discussed above; when applied to X they yield the number of the PE holding the corresponding element. The input token is then routed directly to that PE.

In a conventional network-based system such as DBTG /TaFr76/ this corresponds to the 'calculated location mode' of a record.

(2) As in conventional systems, indices may be maintained for certain attributes. We distinguish two levels of indices, referred as external and internal. For each attribute to be indexed, e.g. the rank of a professor, lists of PEs containing elements with the same attribute value are maintained (outside of the processor array). If the restriction R1 is based on such an attribute, e.g. "Find professors with rank='associate'", tokens are propagated to all PEs listed under the value 'associate'.

In addition to the external indices, each PE may keep its own indices pointing to individual nodes, in order to facilitate its memory management.

Maintaining external indices is profitable only if the lists of PEs are relatively short. If the number of PEs listed for a particular attribute value reaches a certain limit, it becomes more efficient to replicate the token to all PEs in the array using a 'flooding' mechanism described under point (3) below.

(3) If the restriction R1 is based on an attribute for which no external index is maintained, the request token is distributed to all PEs using a simple 'flooding' algorithm: the token is injected into an arbitrarily chosen PE from which it is replicated first in only one direction, say horizontally. Each PE in that row then replicates the token vertically along the corresponding column thus 'flooding' the entire PE array.

It should be noted that the third scheme is comparable in function to a sequential search in conventional systems. In the proposed system, however, the operation is distributed over a very large number of PEs and hence, its execution time is reduced to a fraction of time needed in a conventional system.

The above discussion described how tokens are injected into the PE array and routed to their initial destinations. In order to retrieve data extracted from the graph, it is necessary to guide output tokens to PEs equipped with I/O processors. This is accomplished by attaching to the navigational information of each request a destination component which maps onto such a PE. Thus, at the logical level I/O processors are viewed as nodes connected to the graph, to which tokens are routed in the same way as to other nodes. The only feature distinguishing I/O processors from regular nodes is their ability to act as sources and sinks for tokens.

For most database applications, it is not acceptable to output the sequence of results in a random order, rather sorting is required prior to output. Similarly, it may be necessary to perform accumulative operations on a sequence of results such as calculating their sum or finding the maximum value. To illustrate how such operations can be handled in the proposed distributed architecture consider the case of calculating the sum of selected values. Assume that the result is to be output via a PE located in row i and column j of the array. Normally, all final results are propagated horizontally and vertically until the geometric distance to the destination PE is reduced to zero. In the case of an accumulative operation, the following strategy is used: all results are propagated first in only one direction, say horizontally, until column j is reached. All PEs in that column calculate the partial sums of the received tokens. The total sum is then collected in a token which traverses column j, and is carried to the designated PE. Other accumulative operations as well as sorting can be handled in a similar manner, implying that more than one PE are utilized in performing such operations.

3.4. Reliability Issues and Back-up

Due to the large number of independent PEs and memory units the probability of a hardware failure is considerably higher than in conventional architectures. Thus, in addition to maintaining a back-up copy of the entire database, it is necessary to cope with failures of individual components. In particular, in the event of a PE failure, the associated memory must be accessible by another PE. Similarly, in the event of a memory failure, an up-to-date copy of its contents must exist.

We propose a scheme in which the memory of each PE is mapped onto an area of a non-volatile storage medium such as a disk. If a PE modifies a node in its RAM due to an update request, it is required to send a copy of the modified portion of the memory to the disk. Hence, the collection of all RAMs may be viewed as a 'write-through cache': read operations require access to only the RAM while write operations affect both the RAM and the corresponding image on the disk.

The communication between PEs and the disk is accomplished in a way similar to input/output processing described in Section 3.3, that is, via a set of I/O processors attached to one or a cluster of PEs.

The above scheme functions under the assumption that the total rate of updated records is less than or equal to the rate at which the disk is capable of accepting data. Data retrievals, on the other hand, which in most applications greatly exceed the number of update requests, are not subject to the above constraint and may be processed at the rate supported by the PE array.

Using the 'write-through' policy for all update oprations it is guaranteed that a current copy of each RAM is maintained on the disk. This copy may be used temporarily by the PE in the event of a memory failure. In order to cope with failures of the PE itself it is necessary to provide an alternate way of accessing information stored in the PEs memory. This is accomplished by connecting each PE to its own as well as to one of its neighbor's memory via a multiplexer/demultiplexer connection as shown in Figure 3. Under normal circumstances, each PE operates on its own memory. However, if PE_i detects PE_{i+1} to be inoperational, it switches the lines of MUX/DEMUX1, which enables it to alternately access the memories M_i and M_{i+1} using MUX/DEMUX2. Thus PE_i serves as a 'good samaritan' for PE_{i+1} until the failure is corrected.

4. Simulation Results

In order to demonstrate the feasibility of the proposed system, a series of simulations have been performed. While the main emphasis was on exploring the qualitative behaviour of the system, realistic values for the processing of each token (10 ms) and for sending a token from a PE to one of its neighbours (1 ms) were assumed. Each node of a set Si was assumed to be connected to an average of five other nodes of set Sj.

The first simulation series (Figure 4) shows the average request processing time depending on the array size which was varied from 1x1 to 32x32 PEs. The four curves correspond to requests generating a total of 73, 283, 423, and 493 tokens, respectively. Two important conclusions may be drawn from these results:

- There exists a minimal number of PEs necessary to process a request efficiently. If a substantially smaller number (a 20 to 1 reduction) is given, the response time grows exponentially. On the other hand, increasing the number past the minimum, results in only a minor degradation of response time caused by the longer communication paths among nodes.

- As more complex requests are processed, the optimal number of PEs increases. This, together with the relatively slow increase in response time, indicates that complex requests are capable of utilizing very large numbers of PEs.

While the above simulation series focuses on investigating parallelism within each request, the second series (Figure 5) studies the effects of parallelism achieved by concurrent execution of multiple requests.

Based on Figure 4, we assume the average processing time for an isolated request to be .18 seconds. Thus, the load factor of 1 is reached when a new request arrives every .18 seconds. Figure 5 shows the effects of gradually increasing the load factor of the system: with load factor of 2 the processing time of each request is doubled, however, the system is still capable of handling all requests, that is, the throughput has doubled as well. Only with the load factor approaching 3 does the system show a degradation in throughput, resulting in an exponentially increasing queue of unprocessed requests. In a conventional system, by comparison, such a queue begins to form as soon as the load factor approaches 1. This demonstrates great elasticity of the system and makes it capable of coping with large variations in the request arrival rate.

5. Conclusions

The main research contributions of this paper may be summarized as follows:

We have presented an extended view of a network-oriented database model by associating processing capabilities with each node of the network. The database is viewed as an 'active' dataflow graph, capable of processing and propagating request tokens asynchronously among its nodes, as opposed to being a static data structure operated on by an outside agent, the central processor.

As demonstrated by the simulation results, the dataflow point of view permits a large number of asynchronously operating processing elements to be employed in the machine architecture. Due to its highly parallel nature, the system seems particularly suited for applications which require extensive searches of non-indexed data collections, for example, in general information bases where queries are expected to range over all possible attributes.

References

/AGP78/ Arvind, Gostelow, K.P., Plouffe, W.: "An Asynchronous Programming Language and Computing Machine", <u>Advances in Computing Science and Technology</u> (ed. Ray Yeh), Prentice-Hall publ. 1978

/BiHa83/ Bic, L., Hartmann, R.: "The Active Graph Database Model", Proc. 2nd Int'l Conf. on Databases (ICOD-2), Cambridge, U.K., August 1983

/BiHe81/ Bic, L., Herendeen, M.: "An Architecture for a Relational Dataflow Database", Joint Proc. of SIGMOD Symp. on Small Systems and SIGMOD Workshop on Small Data Base Systems, Vol.7, No.2, Oct.81

/BoDe81/ Boral, H., DeWitt, D.J.: "Processor Allocation Strategies for Multiprocessor Database Machines", ACM Transactions on Database Systems, Vol.6, No.2, June 1981

/Che76/ Chen, P.P.: "The Entity-Relationship Model: Toward a Unified View of Data", ACM Trans. on Database Systems, Vol.1, No.1, March 1976

/Den75/ Dennis, J.B.: "First Version of a Dataflow Procedure Language", Mac Tech. Memorandum 61, M.I.T., Cambridge, 1975

/Sho78/ Shoshani, A.: "CABLE: A Language Based on the Entity-Relationship Model", Lawrence Berkeley Lab., Berkley, CA

/TaFr76/ Taylor, R.W., Frank, R.L.: "CODASYL Data Base Management Systems", ACM Computing Surveys, Vol.8, No.1, March 1976

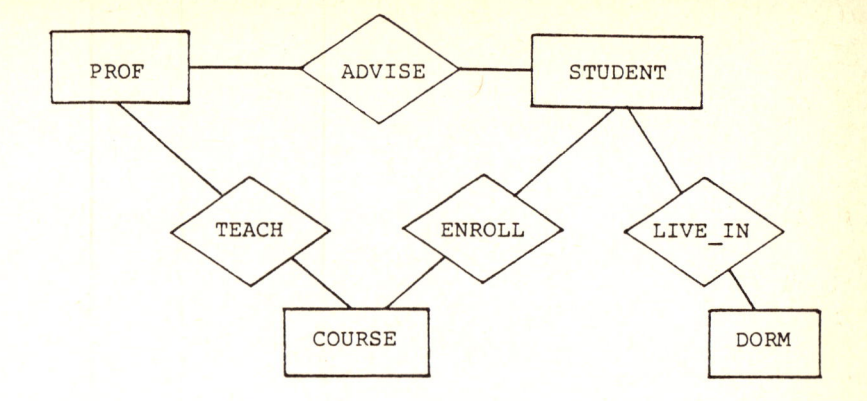

Figure 1

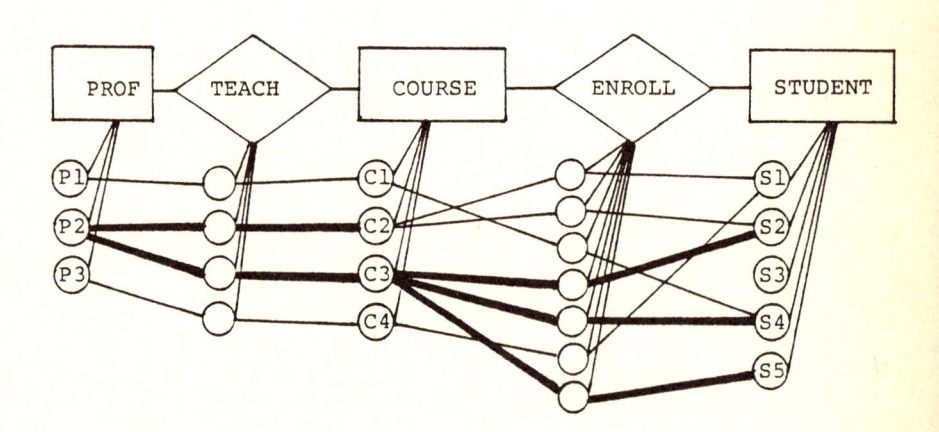

Figure 2

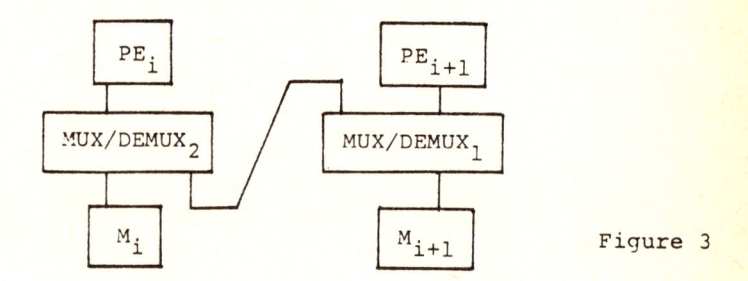

Figure 3

Figure 4

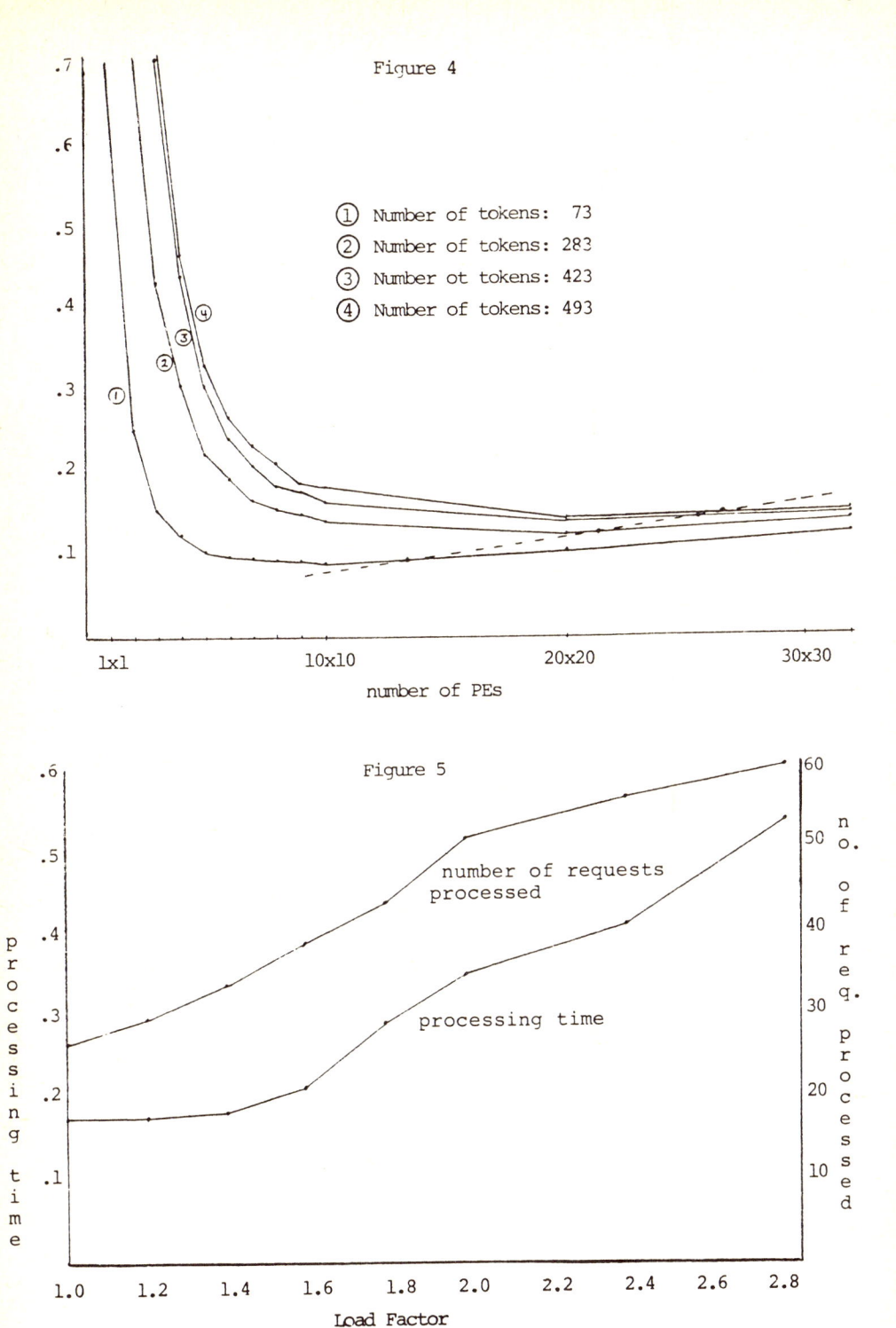

① Number of tokens: 73
② Number of tokens: 283
③ Number of tokens: 423
④ Number of tokens: 493

number of PEs

Figure 5

number of requests processed

processing time

processing time

no. of req. processed

Load Factor

A DATAFLOW RETRIEVAL UNIT FOR A RELATIONAL DATABASE MACHINE

Martin Glinz

Brown Boveri Research Center [*]
CH-5405 Baden, Switzerland

ABSTRACT

We present a dataflow retrieval unit for a relational database machine, consisting of an array of special data driven processors (with local networks connecting the processors of neighbouring rows) and some sorters.

The basis of our design is to interpret a query tree as a dataflow program, to map it directly onto hardware structures and to execute it under dataflow control, using pipelining and parallel processing.

We work with sorted relations and assume relations to be delivered from storage as sequential data streams.

In order to execute a query, we first assign a processor (with appropriate program) to every operation and a data path to every arc of the query tree. Then the relations needed are read and flow into the processor tree at the leaves. They traverse it on the preassigned data paths under dataflow control on byte level and are transformed by relational algebra operations in the processors they pass. All data streams are processed in pipelined fashion, parallel streams are processed in parallel.

Keywords: Relational Database Machines, Dataflow Retrieval Unit,
Dataflow Query Execution, Pipelining

---

[*] Work was carried out when the author was with Lehrstuhl für Betriebssysteme of Aachen Technical University in Aachen, Germany

1. INTRODUCTION

One of the most important problems in managing very large databases on general purpose computers is the retrieval of data. This is mainly due to the fact that computers with von-Neumann-architecture are not well suited to the task of data retrieval. With their processor-memory bottleneck and their strictly sequential principle of operation they are good for problems with complicated control structures, a small amount of data and no (or only a little) parallelism. Data retrieval however requires the processing of large amounts of data, whereas the operations are relatively simple and allow a high degree of parallelism. This contrast between processing requirements and available hardware led to the design and development of database machines.

Especially the relational database model (Codd 1970), a high level model that is an excellent model from the logical viewpoint but ignores the limitations of the von-Neumann-computer, needs a specialized hardware for efficient implementation. So nearly all database machines are designed to support the relational model.

Early designs (such as CASSM (Copeland, Lipovski, Su 1973), RAP (Schuster et al. 1978), RARES (Lin, Smith and Smith 1976), SURE (Leilich, Stiege, Zeidler 1978) and DBC (Banerjee, Hsiao, Kannan 1979)) addressed only one aspect of the problem, namely, the searching of large amounts of data on secondary storage devices.

DIRECT (DeWitt 1979) was the first database machine that was able to process all retrieval operations. Other designs followed, e.g. the dataflow database machine by Boral (1981) or RDBM by Auer, Hell, Leilich et al. (1980).

Boral and DeWitt were the first to analyze algorithms for retrieval operations and to point out that a query (formulated in Codd's relational algebra) could be interpreted as a dataflow program in a natural way.

The machine subsequently developed by Boral (1981) uses dataflow on a page level to control page distribution among the processors; the pages themselves are processed in von-Neumann-style. The decision to apply dataflow on page level resulted from a study (Boral and DeWitt 1980 and 1981), in which they analyzed the costs and benefits of distributing tuples, pages or relations and found the page solution to be best.

In this paper we propose a retrieval unit for a relational database machine that uses a "pure dataflow" approach, distributing every single byte with a dataflow mechanism. To avoid the communications and distribution overhead that led Boral and DeWitt to their page-level solution, we assign a processor to every operation in the query tree and connect the processors according to the paths in the tree <u>before</u> execution. This implies a loss of flexibility and a need for more hardware, but allows data driven connections between processors on byte level with nearly no communications overhead.

We use an array of processors with local connection networks able to connect the output lines of all the processors of a row to the input lines of all the processors in the next row (Fig. 2). The choice of several local switching networks instead of a single global one greatly reduces network complexity. From the conceptual viewpoint, the architecture allows the mapping of any query tree (up to a certain height and width) onto the processor array assigning a processor to every node and a connection path (via a switching network) to every arc. The relations involved in a query are read as sequential data streams from storage. Every stream is processed in pipelined fashion; independent streams are processed in parallel.

Our concept in this "pure" form has one major disadvantage: every processor must be able to execute complex operations (such as relational join). This problem is solved as follows: We assume all incoming relations to be sorted and attach some sorters to the processor array to sort relations having an unsuited sort order. This reduces the problem to the processing of sorted items, which can always be done by simple linear algorithms leaving the complexity in the sorters. So we have an array with many retrieval processors performing simple tasks and a small amount of sophisticated and complex sorters.

We assume data to be stored on conventional or on parallel-read disks with some high-speed channels from the storage unit to the retrieval unit. We do not consider here the problems of update or details of storage. These topics are discussed in Glinz (1982).

It is possible to use common microprocessors as retrieval processors and also to construct the sorters with von-Neumann-hardware. In our opinion however, a better solution is to use a specialized dataflow retrieval processor and to construct a pipelined sorter using these retrieval processors as the basic processing units.

The paper is organized in 6 sections: Section 1 gave an introduction and outlined our ideas. In section 2 we analyze the structure of retrieval queries and derive basic design decisions for a retrieval unit. In section 3 we discuss design considerations and present the architecture of a dataflow retrieval unit. Section 4 describes the processors of the retrieval unit. In section 5 we present a proposal for a database machine based on our retrieval unit and in section 6 we conclude with a discussion of some problems arising from our design.

2. ANALYSIS OF QUERY EXECUTION

In the relational model, all retrieval queries can be formulated by applying operations (or combinations of operations) of the relational algebra. The relational algebra consists of the operations SELECT, PROJECT, JOIN, UNION, INTERSECTION, DIFFERENCE, EXTENDED CARTESIAN PRODUCT and DIVIDE. A retrieval unit should support the first seven of these operations whereas DIVIDE is seldom needed and can be replaced by combining other operations. Additionally, some auxiliary operations such as SORT, COUNT, SUM or MAX should be provided.

Any relational algebra-query can be represented as a binary tree. An example is shown in Fig. 1.

Sample query (for a SUPPLIER-PART-database):

"Find the names of all suppliers that have supplied more than 100 pieces of part #1".

Query tree:

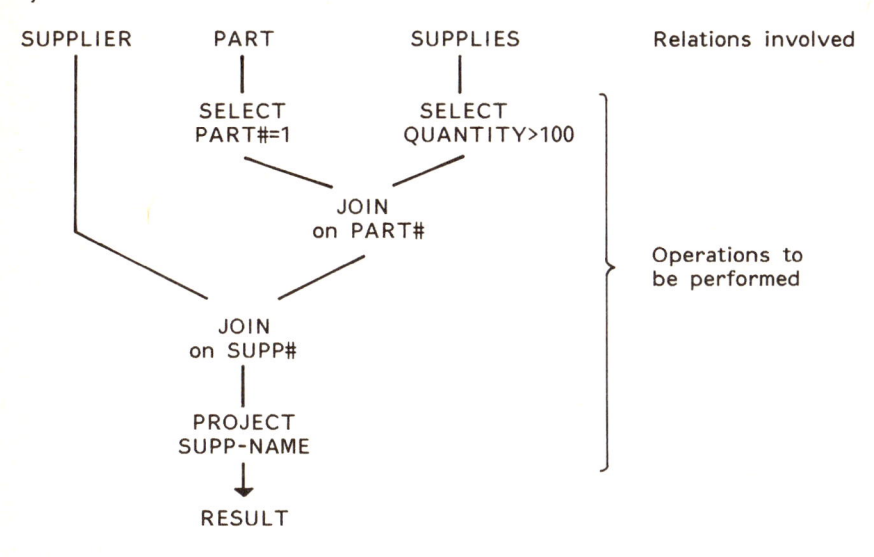

```
SUPPLIER      PART              SUPPLIES           Relations involved
               |                   |
              SELECT              SELECT
              PART#=1             QUANTITY>100
                   \             /
                    JOIN
                    on PART#
              \            /
               JOIN                                 Operations to
               on SUPP#                             be performed
                  |
               PROJECT
               SUPP-NAME
                  ↓
               RESULT
```

Fig. 1: Sample query tree

Our goal is to design an architecture for a retrieval unit that is adaptable to the structure of a query and thus allows a problem-oriented style of execution instead of the machine-oriented style on von-Neumann-architectures and many database machine designs.

To work out design objectives for such an architecture, we have to analyze what we believe to be the three main aspects of query execution:

- flow of data and control
- parallelism
- algorithms for the relational algebra-operations.

2.1 Interpretation of Queries as Dataflow Programs

A query is executed by executing the operations specified in the tree. Some of these operations depend on data of previous operations, but no operation depends on any control information of other operations. Thus we have no flow of control outside of the relational algebra-operations, but only flows of data.

In fact, a query tree can be interpreted as a dataflow program in a very natural and straightforward way: Take the nodes as operators, the arcs as data paths (from top to bottom) and the relations as input data. The data flows in at the leaves of the tree and activates (fires) the operators on the top level. These operators execute their operation and produce output data which flows to the next operators, activating these and so on. Finally, the root operator produces the desired result.

> We therefore decide to use dataflow as the operating principle for our retrieval unit.

As a relation normally consists of a large amount of data, we will see that the application of the "normal" dataflow activation (firing) rule is not optimal, because the operators have to wait until all their input data has arrived. In our case, this would mean that complete relations had to be available before an execution could start. However, a SELECT-operation, for example, can process a relation tuple by tuple in a pipelined fashion and does not need the complete relation before starting execution.

Moreover, when we consider that the secondary storage device delivers relations not all at once, but sequentially as data streams, we find that the application of the normal dataflow activation rule inhibits a possible parallel (i.e. pipelined) execution of operations and so slows down execution speed.

Therefore, we introduce the following <u>modified</u> activation rule: An operator is activated when at least one byte from every one of its input streams is available. Having processed these bytes, the operator will remain active if new input bytes have arrived in the meantime, otherwise the operator waits until the next set of bytes becomes available.

As relations may contain an arbitrary number of tuples, this kind of processing requires the introduction of a special control character, called RE (relation end) marking the end of a relation. An operator has completed its task and becomes inactive, when it has found an RE on all of its input lines and has terminated all its output lines by sending each an RE.

2.2 Parallelism in Query Execution

As we want to map the query structure onto the structure of the retrieval unit, we have to consider the possibilities for parallel execution inherent in a query structure.

In general, there are three possible kinds of parallelism (cf. Chang 1976):

1) parallel application of an operation on all data of a data set
2) pipelined application of an operation on a stream of consecutive data
3) parallel application of independent operations on different data

In the case of database query execution, parallelism of the third kind can be used for the execution of all operations being on the same level of the tree, e.g. the SELECT-operations in our example.

Parallelism of the first kind could theoretically be used in many cases, a SELECT-operation for example could be executed by as many processors as there are tuples in the relation. In reality however, relations are stored on an disk device that cannot supply all tuples in parallel. In the best case, a relation is delivered in a few parallel data streams. As the number of the streams is very small compared to the number of tuples, parallelism of the first kind cannot play an important role in query execution.

Instead, <u>pipelined</u> processing, the second kind of parallelism, becomes extremely important (cf. Smith and Chang 1975, Yao 1979). If we can find algorithms for the relational algebra operations that support pipelining, then we can use pipelining within the operations as well as for consecutive operations in the tree. If the processors executing the operations are fast enough, we thus can process the data streams coming in from disk without slowing them down.

> We therefore decide to execute independent operations in parallel and consecutive operations (whenever possible) in pipelining mode.

2.3 Algorithms for the Relational Algebra-Operations

Following the design decisions of the previous two paragraphs we need algorithms for the operations of the relational algebra that

- fit into a dataflow environment
- as far as possible, support pipelined processing of data streams.

The aim of processing the incoming data streams without slowing them down can never be completely reached, because of the existence of operations with non-linear complexity, where all input data may be required before a result can be produced (e.g. SORT). But we can try to reduce the number of such operations to a minimum.

Without any assumptions on the structure of the data we have:

Operations with linear complexity	SELECT, PROJECT (only when the projection contains a key), UNION (of results of previous selections on the same relation), auxiliary operations except SORT
operations with non-linear complexity	JOIN, PROJECT (in the general case), UNION (in the general case), INTERSECTION, DIFFERENCE, EXTENDED CARTESIAN PRODUCT, SORT.

But when we assume the input relations to be _sorted_, the picture dramatically changes: the only operations left with non-linear complexity are EXTENDED CARTESIAN PRODUCT and SORT. All other operations can now be processed in a simple, linear and _pipelined_ fashion.

The EXTENDED CARTESIAN PRODUCT is only seldom needed. Therefore, we take no measures to make it faster.

The SORT operation, however, must be very fast, because several sort operations may now be needed during execution of a query, even when we assume the stored relations to be properly sorted. The sort algorithm should meet four requirements:

- high speed, nearly linear time complexity
- suited for pipelined, dataflow controlled execution
- suited for external sorting
- able to remove duplicates during the sort process.

A merge-sort algorithm, working with n merge processors and buffer memories for totally 2^n tuples fulfills these requirements; relations with up to 2^n tuples are sorted with linear time complexity. The filling of the processor pipe needs $n+2^n$ time units; from then the sorter outputs a sorted tuple every time unit.

So we make the following design decisions: We assume all relations to be properly sorted; relations with a sort order that is unsuited for a specific operation have to be resorted before performing that operation. With the exception of the algorithm for EXTENDED CARTESIAN PRODUCT we can now use simple algorithms that are fully suited to dataflow controlled, pipelined execution and also support dataflow for the cooperation of operations. The algorithm for SORT also enables dataflow control and pipelining, but slows down the data streams that have to be sorted.

As an example, we give the algorithms for SELECT, JOIN and PROJECT (the SORT- algorithm is described in section 4.2).

SELECT: input: relation, attribute to be selected, selection operator (=, <, >, etc.), selection value

          action: for every tuple do:
                   compare value of attribute in the tuple with the selection value
                   if result = true then output tuple
                                    else delete tuple
                   end

JOIN: input: relations R1, R2, join-attributes A1, A2
                   R1 and R2 have to be sorted on A1 resp. A2; A2 must be a key in R2.

          action: set i = 1, j = 1
                   do until all tuples of R1 or R2 are processed:
                   compare values for A1, A2 in tuples t_i and t_j from R1 resp. R2
                   if result = "=" then join t_i and t_j, output result, set i = i+1
                            elseif result = "<" then delete t_i, set i = i+1
                                           else delete t_j, set j = j+1
                   end

PROJECT: input: relation, attribute list

           action: for every tuple do:
                     delete the values of all attributes not specified in the
                     attribute list, output this new tuple
                     end

                     If the attribute list contains no key, a REMOVE-DUPLI-
                     CATES operation has to be performed after the projection.

3. THE ARCHITECTURE OF A DATAFLOW RETRIEVAL UNIT

3.1 Design Considerations

The analysis of query execution led us to three basic design decisions for our retrieval unit:

(1) dataflow as the operating principle
(2) parallel execution of independent operations / pipelining of consecutive operations
(3) sorted relations / simple linear algorithms for most operations

Now we discuss the consequences of these decisions for the architecture of the retrieval unit.

Decision (2) has the strongest impact on the overall structure of the retrieval unit, because exploiting all parallelism requires a processor for every operation of a query and the possibility to connect these processors according to the arcs of the corresponding query tree.

The combination of (1) and (2) implies dataflow on at most tuple level; if we also want dataflow and pipelining in the processors themselves, we may even need dataflow on byte level. This low level of data communication inhibits any dynamic data routing, because the routing overhead becomes too high. We therefore have to assign static data paths prior to the execution of a query. This implies a loss of flexibility and a less efficient processor utilization (compared to dynamic routing), but on the other hand, the static method is stable (no dynamic scheduling or deadlock problems) and, more important, enables dataflow communication with nearly no overhead.

Decision (3) suggests the use of an array of many small processors for the operations with simple algorithms and a few complex and fast processors for sorting.

Before presenting our design, we have to discuss the problem of the processor connection network more thoroughly. The simplest solution is the arrangement of processors in a binary tree. But at closer examination, this solution proves inefficient, because the often used operations SELECT and PROJECT have only one predecessor in the tree, so actual query trees are always slimmer than a full binary tree. This means, that some of the high level processors in a binary tree network would nearly never be used. However, any network topology between the extremes of linear chain and full binary tree might lead to problems when mapping actual query tree structures onto the hardware.

Additionally, we would like a more flexible network, allowing the concurrent processing of more than one query or processing of one operation with more than one processor. On the other hand, we do not want a network with communication possibilities which are never used and only serve to increase network complexity.

When we look at the more global structures of a tree, we find the following characteristics: There are

- no connections between nodes of the same level and
- no connections between nodes of non-neighbouring levels.

In our approach, we will use a set of connection networks that retain these two global properties, but give up the local connection rule of having exactly one predecessor and up to two successors. Instead, we arrange the processors in an array (where the rows correspond to the tree levels) and connect all output lines of the processors of a row with all input lines of the processors in the neighbouring lower row. This gives us the desired flexibility without introducing useless connections. If we additionally connect the sorters to all row networks, we arrive at the final design as shown in the next section.

3.2 The Proposed Architecture

Fig. 2 shows the overall architecture of the dataflow retrieval unit we propose.

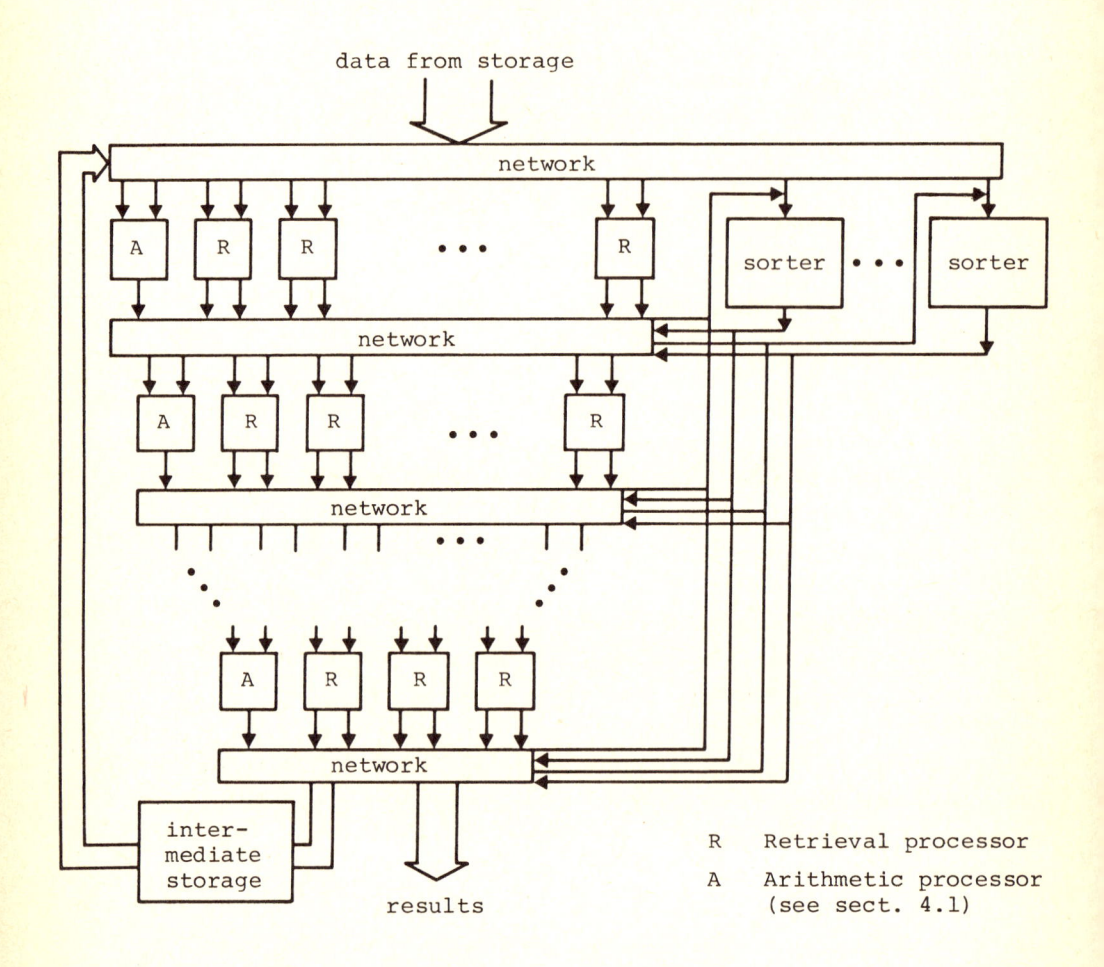

Fig. 2: The overall architecture of the retrieval unit

R   Retrieval processor
A   Arithmetic processor
    (see sect. 4.1)

The processors in the array perform all operations of the relational algebra and all auxiliary operations except SORT, which is done by the sorters. The number of processors per row diminishes from top to bottom corresponding to the tree structure of the queries to be executed in the array. More than one processor on the bottom level enables the concurrent execution of different queries. The networks consist of $9n^2$ unidirectional switches that enable the connection of any input line to any output line with the possibility of up to n concurrent, independent connections. The connections are unidirectional, because the flow of data is unidirectional.

Every connection consists of an eight bit parallel data line and a one bit control line. The latter is used to control the dataflow in the following way: Any processor that wishes to receive a byte on an input line, sets the corresponding control line to the high state, otherwise the control line is low. Any processor wanting to output a byte, transmits if the corresponding control line is high and waits if it is low. If more than one byte is to be transmitted, the sending processor waits a short time after transmission of each byte to see, whether the control line remains high or goes to low.

All data flows in at the top of the array and traverses it from top to bottom. Results are delivered at the bottom; intermediate results (e.g. when executing a GROUP BY-operation or a query that is too large to fit into the array) go to the intermediate store and are rerouted to the top of the array. There is no storage or iteration of data within the array; data is only buffered in the processors. Every processor in the array contains two buffers for one tuple each, the sorters contain buffers for up to one relation.

The internal structure of processors and sorters is discussed in section 4.

3.3 Query Execution

When a query is to be executed, we first assign to it the processors and data paths needed for execution. Then the relations to be processed are read from secondary store. The data find their processors automatically because of the preassigned fixed data paths; so no more control action is needed after starting the read. The query execution controls itself by the flow of data. We need no explicit program control, synchronization or process communication whatsoever.

Fig. 3 shows a possible mapping of the query from Fig. 1 onto the retrieval unit. The processing is delayed by a sort and a duplicate-removal. If we assume that all relations have n tuples and one time unit is the time to process one tuple, then the first result arrives at the earliest in $4+2*(n+ld\ n)$ time units after starting the execution and we have the last result in at most n time units later.

So we have a time complexity of $O(n)$ for the execution of queries that fit into the array and do not need intermediate storage on disk.

relations
123

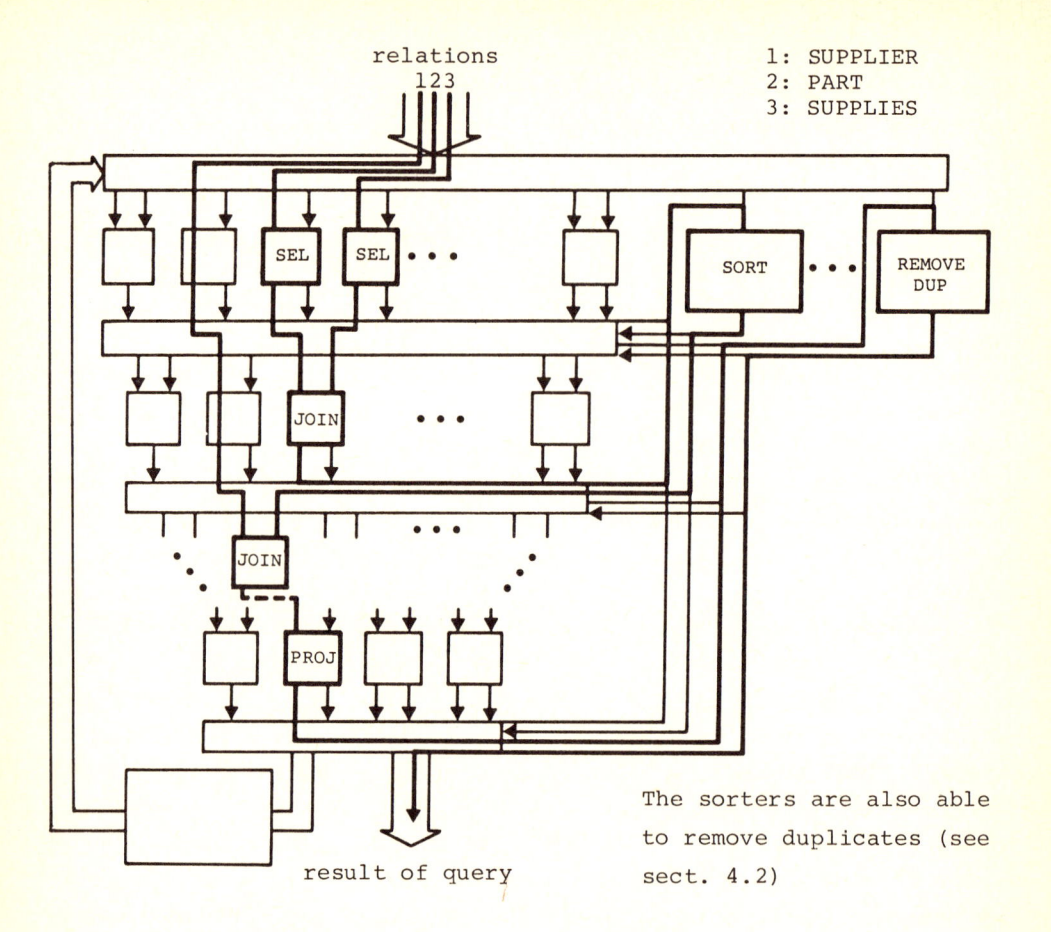

1: SUPPLIER
2: PART
3: SUPPLIES

The sorters are also able to remove duplicates (see sect. 4.2)

result of query

Fig. 3: Mapping of a query tree onto the retrieval unit

4. THE ARCHITECTURE OF RETRIEVAL PROCESSORS AND SORTERS

In this section we discuss the internal structure of the processors that the retrieval unit consists of. Although it is possible to use common microprocessors, we think it is better to use specially suited dataflow retrieval processors which are described below.

4.1 The Retrieval Processor

A retrieval processor consists of three modules (input, output and compare) and two one-tuple buffers. The modules cooperate by the same dataflow mechanism as described in sect. 3.2; additionally they exchange status information via three control lines. Internally, the modules are controlled by a data driven microprogram. A retrieval processor is programmed to perform a certain operation by loading three appropriate microprograms into the three modules. Fig. 4 shows the structure of a retrieval processor.

The _input_ module reads data from the proper input lines (depending on program and status) and routes them to the compare module and/or the buffers. As the compare module compares byte-pair by byte-pair, the input module synchronizes incoming tuples on the beginning of the values to be compared. The _compare_ module compares two tuples or two values from tuples, deletes the compared data and sends the result of the comparison to the output module. The _output_ module can output tuples, route them back to the input module or delete them. Further it can delete certain values within tuples (for projection) or concatenate tuples (e.g. for join). The auxiliary output line is needed for a few operations such as GROUP BY or SORT.

In conventional microprogramming, the micro-instruction to be executed next is selected by a micro-PC or by explicit specification in the previous micro-instruction. For the retrieval processor, we propose a different, _data_ driven microprogram execution that resembles to the execution rule of a turing machine. We define a _state_ of a module to consist of the availability of data at inputs, in registers, etc. and of the contents of some status bits. To perform an operation, we have to go through a well defined sequence of such states. To each of these states we assign a micro-instruction so that the execution of this instruction transforms the current state into the next state of the sequence and define the following execution rule: _A micro-instruction is executed, if the module is in the state that is assigned to the instruction._ As the actual state is mainly determined by the availability of data, we thus have a data driven microprogram execution.

To see how a retrieval processor operates, we describe the processing of a SELECT and of a JOIN operation (cf. Fig. 4):

SELECT: Before starting execution, buffer 2 is loaded with a pseudo tuple containing only the select value. Then the relation is routed tuple by tuple via I1 to buffer 1; the value to be compared goes to buffer 1 _and_ to the compare module. The select value is routed via RL2 back to buffer 2 and also to the compare module; the input module synchronizes the transmission, so that both values to be compared arrive synchronously. The compare module decides whether to select the tuple or not and signals the result to the output module. The latter reads the tuple from buffer 1 and outputs it or deletes it depending on the result of the comparison. Parallel to that, the next tuple comes in to the input module, the

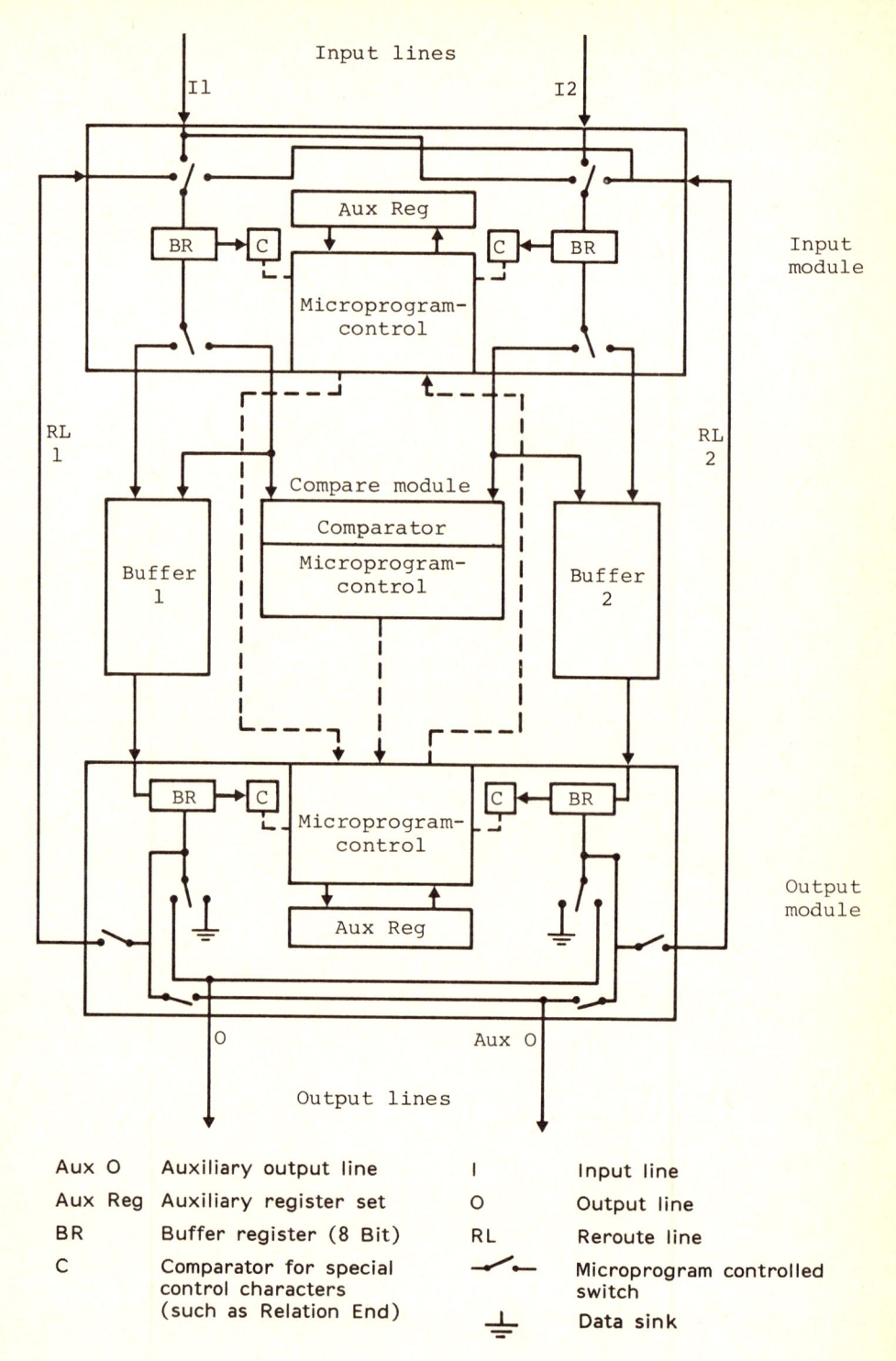

Aux O	Auxiliary output line	I	Input line
Aux Reg	Auxiliary register set	O	Output line
BR	Buffer register (8 Bit)	RL	Reroute line
C	Comparator for special control characters (such as Relation End)	—/—	Microprogram controlled switch
		⏚	Data sink

Fig. 4: The overall architecture of a retrieval processor

select value rotates again up to the input module and the next comparison starts. Thus we also have pipelined processing within the retrieval processor.

JOIN: Initially, a tuple from both relations is read and sent to the buffers, the join values also go to the compare module. In case of equality, the output module reads both tuples out of the buffers, concatenates and outputs them. Additionally, the contents of buffer 2 is rerouted to the input module for the next comparison. If the join values are not equal, the output module deletes the tuple with the lesser value and routes the other tuple back to the input module. In the next step, the input module reads the rerouted tuple and a new tuple from the other relation, sends them to the buffers, the join values are compared, a.s.o.

As the retrieval processor cannot perform any arithmetic operation (e.g. sum or average), we need an additional arithmetic processor (a microprocessor with data-flow interface) in every processor row of the retrieval unit.

For more details about the architecture of the retrieval processor and its programming, see Glinz (1982).

4.2 The Sorter

A sorter consists of a chain of retrieval processors as shown in Fig. 5. The retrieval processors are programmed as mergers; the i-th processor in the chain receives sorted sets of length $2^{(i-1)}$ on its input lines, merges them to sorted sets of length 2^i and outputs these sets alternately on its two output lines. Between the processors we have FIFO-Buffers with a capacity of 2^i tuples that store the first set (of the two sets needed for the next merge) while the second set is produced. (The first merger reads the relation from one input line and outputs ordered pairs alternately on its output lines).

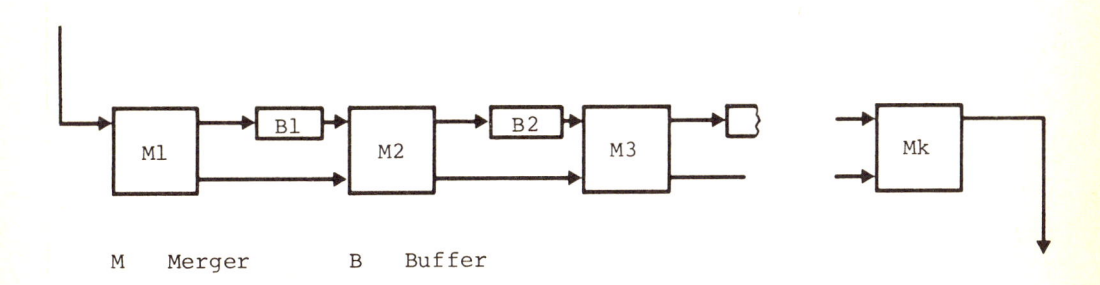

M   Merger   B   Buffer

Fig. 5: The architecture of a sorter

If we use k processors, we can sort relations with up to 2^k tuples in linear time. The problem of sorting larger relations is discussed in Glinz (1982).

To remove duplicates, the program of the mergers is slightly modified: if two compared tuples are equal, then the mergers output only one of them and delete the other one.

5. A PROPOSAL FOR A DATABASE MACHINE USING A DATAFLOW RETRIEVAL UNIT

In this section we sketch a database machine that uses a retrieval unit as described above. Such a machine consists of four units: a storage unit, a retrieval unit, a directory/update unit and an interface/control unit (Fig. 6).

The storage unit consists of disk drives and access control hardware that allows the output of data streams with the greatest speed possible. The retrieval unit performs all retrieval operations, whereas the update operations are executed in the directory/update unit. The latter also contains a memory with all directory information on the data stored in the storage unit. Finally, the interface/control (I/C) unit runs the host interface, manages all resources, analyzes incoming tasks and initiates task execution in the other units.

Data transmission between the four units is achieved using the same dataflow mechanism as found in the retrieval unit. Additional lines to the other three units are used to transmit orders from the I/C unit.

The interface/control unit does not control the other units directly. Instead, when a task comes in from the host, the I/C unit analyzes the task and schedules it if the required resources are available. For execution of the task, the I/C unit then gives orders to the other units, specifying the processors, memories and data paths to be used and the programs that are to be executed in the processors. The task execution is controlled by the executing units themselves, communication and coordination between different units is provided by dataflow. The I/C unit only becomes active again when the results arrive and have to be formatted and transmitted to the host.

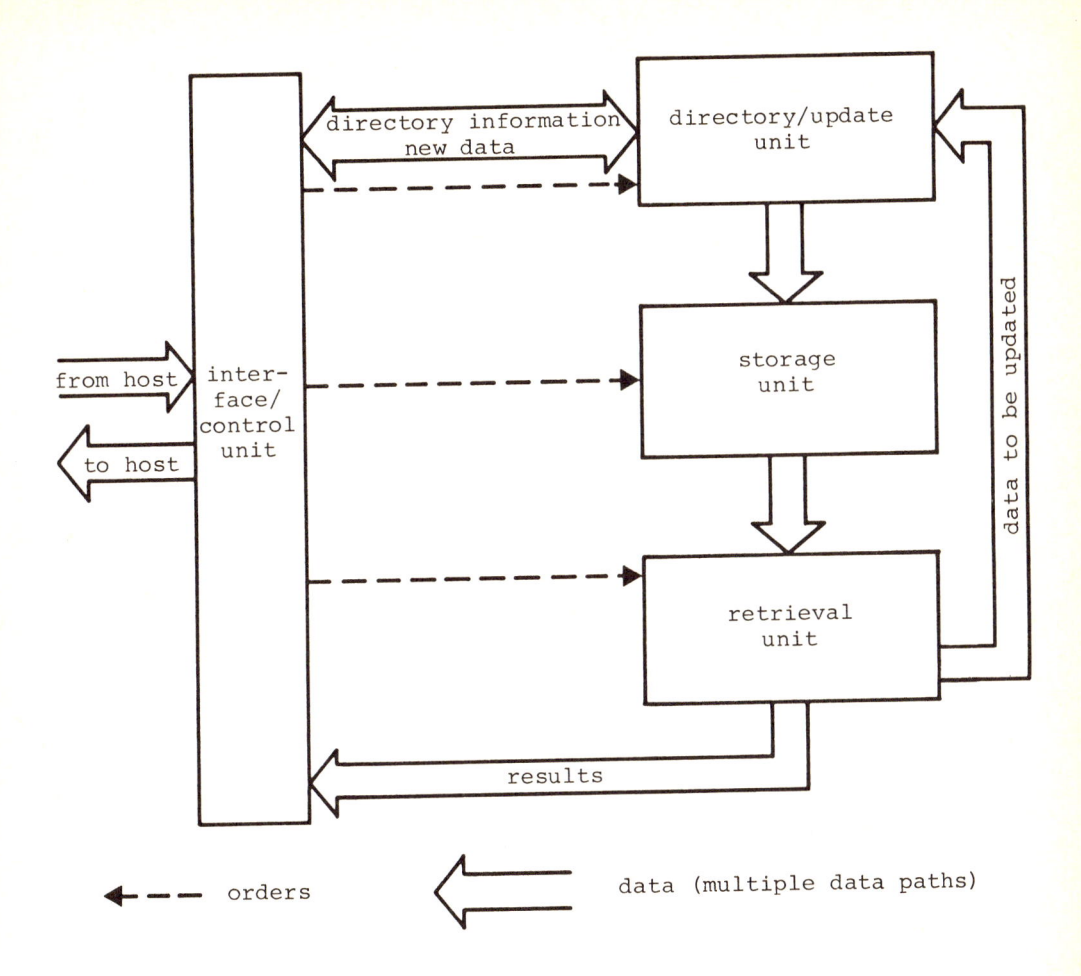

Fig. 6: Structure of a database machine employing the dataflow retrieval unit

6. DISCUSSION

Finally, we discuss some of the problems arising from our design and point out possible solutions and consequences.

- We did not carry out any quantitative performance measurements or evaluations. But we can make a qualitative statement on performance from architectural considerations (see paragraph 3.3). There we found that queries up to a certain size are executed with a time complexity of $O(n)$.

The crucial point with respect to performance, however, is whether intermediate results can be kept in internal buffers or must be stored on disk during query execution. In the first case we can achieve the theoretical speed also in practice; otherwise there might be heavy performance degradations caused by disk accesses.
As a consequence, the retrieval unit should be laid out in a size that matches with the average size of the expected queries and avoids intermediate buffering of data on disk.

- We have no index processing facility. We have omitted indices, because they introduce asymmetry into the data access process that has no correspondence in the data model. If required, an index pre-processing similar to that of DBC (Banerjee, Hsiao and Kannan 1979) could be used without altering our concept of query execution.

- Our concept may require too many sorters. This could be true if we have queries with many joins on relations with an unsuited sort order and many projections on non-key attributes. We may take the following two measures to reduce the number of required sortings:
  (1) We allow joins only on a few well defined attributes of a relation, as in the entity-relationship approach (Chen 1976) or in the functional approach (Glinz 1982). In this way we decrease the number of cases where a relation is sorted on an unsuited attribute.
  (2) We restructure queries before execution so that we can keep a key in the intermediate results and avoid unnecessary duplicate elimination. If cost considerations prevent a large enough number of sorters, a change of our concept with the aim of allowing dynamic allocation of sorters should be considered.

- Crossbar networks grow quadratically in complexity and cost. This is a big problem when using large networks. As we use several small ones, our networks remain within dimensions that we think to be manageable using crossbar switches.

- Queries can be larger than the processor array. In this case we must abandon the concept of fully self managing query execution. Instead the query has to be split up into parts that can be executed sequentially, with the intermediate results being stored between each step. This process must be controlled externally (e.g. by the I/C unit in our design). To avoid this case, the dimensions of the retrieval unit should be such that most expected queries fit into the array.

- All operations theoretically can be executed by more than one processor, so assigning a processor for every operation is not optimal. As we have already discussed in 2.2, data cannot be delivered from disk all in parallel, so we only have to consider a few parallel data streams.

The processing of relations in more than one stream is also possible in our concept, e.g. selections can be simply made in parallel; the results are collected with union-operations. When executing a <u>join</u> on more than one processor, the relations should be partitioned into blocks $a_1..a_n$ and $b_1..b_n$ so that any join value in block a_i of relation A is smaller than any join value in any block b_j of relation B with j>i and greater than any join value in any block b_k of relation B with i>k. Then the partial joins can be computed independently with processor k processing blocks k of relations A and B.

REFERENCES

AUER, H.; HELL, W.; LEILICH, H.-O. et al. (1980):
    RDBM - A Relational Data Base Machine.
    Informatik-Bericht Nr. 8005, Tech. Univ. Braunschweig 1980

BANERJEE J.; HSIAO, D.K.; KANNAN, K. (1979):
    DBC - A Database Computer for Very Large Databases.
    IEEE Transact. Comp. <u>C-28</u>,6(1979), pp. 414-429

BORAL, H.; DeWITT, D.J. (1980):
    Design Considerations for Data-Flow Database Machines.
    Proc. ACM-SIGMOD Conf. on Manag. of Data, Santa Monica, Ca. 1980
    pp. 94-104

BORAL, H.; DeWITT, D.J. (1981):
    Processor Allocation Strategies for Multiprocessor Database Machines.
    ACM TODS <u>6</u>,2(1981), pp. 227-254

BORAL, H. (1981):
    On the Use of Data-Flow Techniques in Database Machines.
    PhD-Thesis Comp. Sci. Dept. Univ. Wisconsin-Madison, TR #432,
    May 1981

CHANG, P. Y. (1976):
    Parallel Processing and Data Driven Implementation of a Relational Data Base System.
    Proc. ACM'76 Houston, Texas, Oct. 1976, pp. 314-318

CHEN, P.P.-S. (1976):
    The Entity-Relationship Model - Toward a Unified View of Data.
    ACM TODS <u>1</u>,1(1976), pp. 9-36

CODD, E.F. (1970):
    A Relational Model of Data for Large Shared Data Banks.
    CACM <u>13</u>,6(1970), pp. 377-387

COPELAND, G.P.; LIPOVSKI, G.J.; SU, S.Y.W. (1973):
    The Architecture of CASSM: A Cellular System for Non-Numeric Processing.
    Proc. 1st Symp. on Comp. Arch., Gainesville, Florida 1973, pp. 121-128

DeWITT, D.J. (1979):
    DIRECT - A Multiprocessor Organization for Supporting Relational Database Management Systems.
    IEEE Transact. Comp. C-28,6(1979), pp. 395-406

GLINZ, M. (1982):
    Eine datengesteuerte Datenbankmaschine auf der Grundlage eines funktionalen Datenbankmodells.
    Dissertation RWTH Aachen, 1982

LEILICH, H.-O.; STIEGE, G.; ZEIDLER, H.CH. (1978):
    A Search Processor for Data Base Management Systems.
    Proc. 4th Conf. VLDB, Berlin 1978, pp. 280-287

LIN, C.S.; SMITH, D.C.P.; SMITH, J.M. (1976):
    The Design of a Rotating Associative Memory for Relational Database Applications.
    ACM TODS 1,1(1976), pp. 53-65

SCHUSTER, S.A.; NGUYEN, H.B.; OZKARAHAN, E.A. et al. (1978):
    RAP.2 - An Associative Processor for Data Bases.
    5th Symp. on Comp. Arch. 1978, pp. 52-59

SMITH, J.M.; CHANG, P.Y.-T. (1975):
    Optimizing the Performance of a Relational Algebra Database Interface.
    CACM 18,10(1975), pp. 568-579

YAO, S.B. (1979):
    Optimization of Query Evaluation Algorithms.
    ACM TODS 4,2(1979), pp. 133-155

A CONCEPT FOR A DATAFLOW DATABASE MACHINE - AN OVERVIEW

R. Kubera , M. Malms
RWTH Aachen (W.- Germany)

Abstract : This short paper presents some architectural features of a database machine currently in its first design phase at the Aachen University (W.-Germany).

The main design goals for this database machine are:

1. the full support of the relational database concept
2. the effective exploitation of the parallelism inherent to the relational algebra queries.

Considering the usual organisation of relational queries in tree form, CHANG /1/ describes 3 basic levels of parallelism:

1. independent nodes can be processed in parallel
2. consecutive nodes may be processed in a pipeline
3. nodes may be split in several subnodes with each subnode operating on different input tuples.

Due to the similarity between a relational algebra query tree and an elementary data flow graph, the "data driven" computation concept is suggested by several papers /1-3/ as the most effective operational method for relational database machines. Of course the exploitation of the above mentioned levels 2 and 3 depends on various factors, i.e. the sort order of the involved domains, the type of operation (not all of them are suited to be pipelined or splitted) and the algorithms by which the operations are implemented on a multiprocessor system.

Our design proposes several dedicated processors ("Operational Units-OU",see fig.1) for the execution of the relational operations. These units - two of them have been realized in a prototype version (see /4/) - consist of a processor element operating on tuples stored in a content addressable local buffer or, if this unit is part of a pipeline, on one tuple in the register at a time. The microprogramable processor element also controls the data transfer between the node-inputs L and R and the output T. The buffer should be large enough to hold one or more tuple packets of a reasonable size (a relation is divided into several "tuple packets"). Here a

Operational Unit

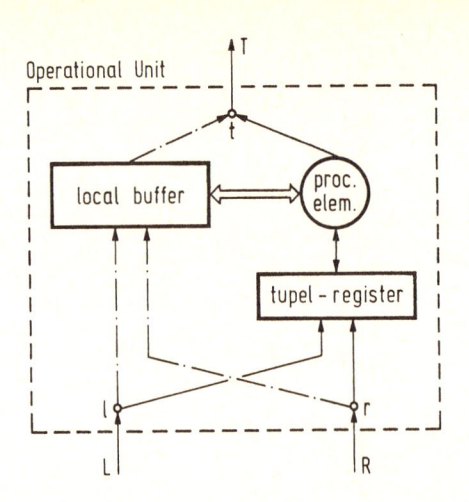

fig. 1

capacity of a few 100K bytes seems to be realistic.

In our preliminary design, up to 15 OU's may communicate with each other via a crossbar-like network (see fig.2). Each vertical branch of this network interconnects one transmitting to one or - in a broadcast mode - more units in a circuit-switching fashion. First-in first-out buffers are provided to balance the execution speed differences between communicating units. An additional computer module (CM, fig. 2) provides the facility to perform special functions on query results (e.g. statistical evaluations) within the database machine itself.

Starting a query processing, a central coordinator assigns a predefined number of idle units to the first executable operation after having received a query-packet from the host. Then the source relations are read from a central mass-storage and passed through an attribute-filter eliminating all those domains not involved in this particular query execution. The filtered tuples are loaded into the assigned OU's via a dedicated bus. The I/O-bandwidth of this bus and the storing-strategy of the source relations of course have a considerable impact on the degree of parallelism obtainable when processing tuples read from the mass-storage.

Generally the administrator assigns idle units to executable operations when the first input-tuples are available. Depending on the type of operation, more units can be added as soon as they become available (e.g. while processing a SELECTION or JOIN).

For each executable operation the allocation takes place by initializing the designated units and one communication controller with the necessary processparameters identifying the specific "role" each unit plays during the execution, and specifying the "partner-units", if the operation is spread over several units (node

fig.2

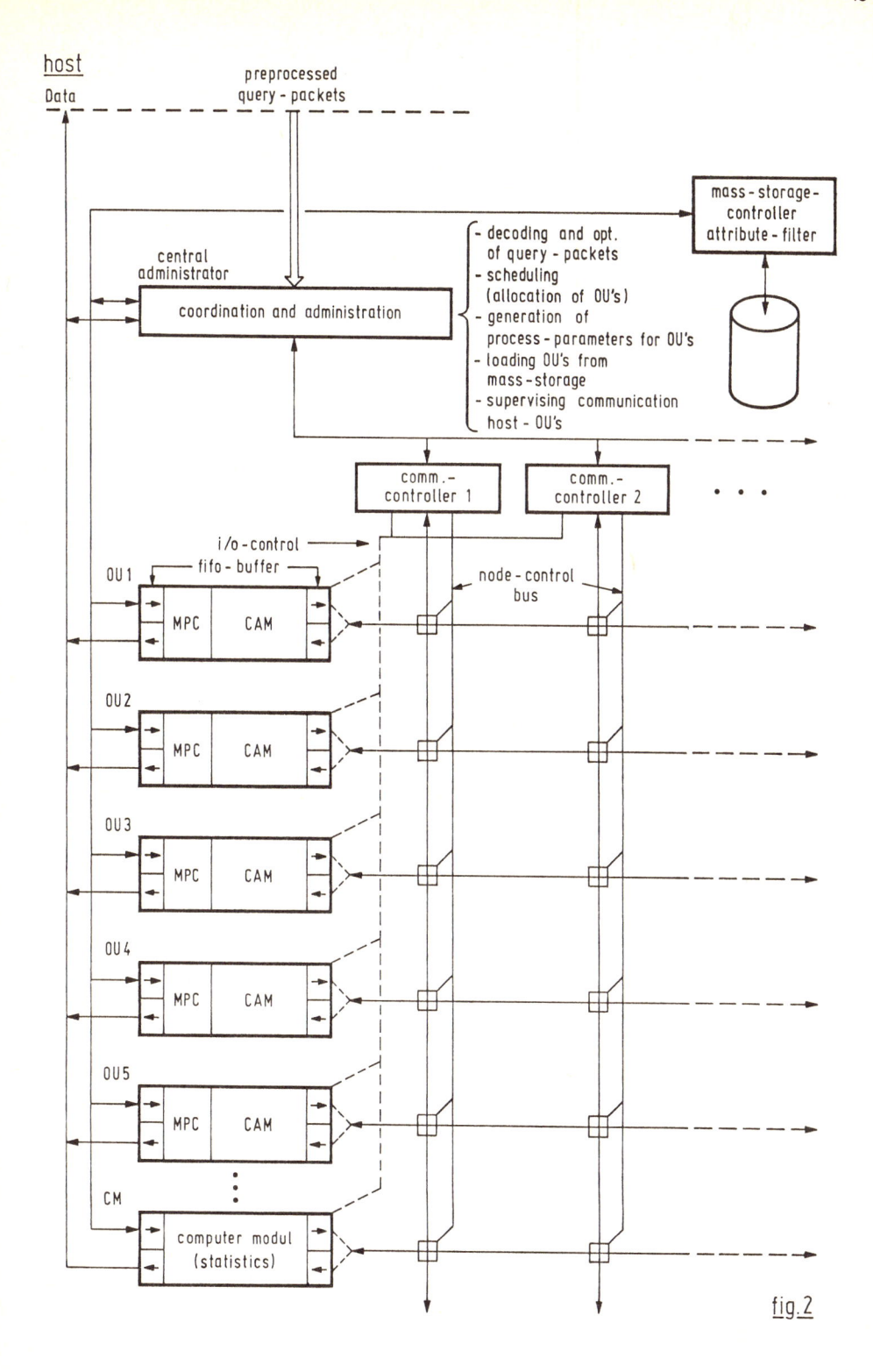

splitting). Intermediate relations are buffered in the OU's or output to the mass-storage when a buffer-overflow occurs.

In addition to the three levels of parallelism mentioned above /1/ the design of this database machine not only provides the facility to process consecutive nodes in a pipeline but also permits an operation to be pipelined within one node.

As an example it was examined to what extent this facility could accelerate the execution of the operation JOIN. This examination was based on two concepts:

1. single -OU- concept (SOC) the tuples of two relations are joined within one unit.
2. multi -OU- concept (MOC) there are at least three units needed for the execution of the operation JOIN in this concept. Each unit performs a specific part of this relatinal operation.

Both concepts lead to different times of execution t_{SOC} and t_{MOC} respectively, which are combined to a speed-up factor $S = t_{SOC}/t_{MOC}$. This means that the multi-OU-concept is S times faster than the single-OU-concept. The factor S depends significantly on the number n of bytes per tuple because the time to transfer one byte is different in the SOC and MOC. For each n a range for the value of S(n) as a function of several conditions can be specified. $S_b(n)$ -b stands for "best case"- will be the upper and $S_w(n)$ -w stands for "worst case"- the lower limit of this range. Since the number of bytes per tuple usually will exceed thirty (n > 30) it is obvious that the MOC works twice as fast as the SOC (see fig. 3).

At present our investigations concentrate on :

- the network and its communication principle
- the allocation mechanisms for the operational units
- the design of algorithms for the executing of the relational operations (including sorting),to be implemented on the units by microprograms. Algorithms must be provided which process whole relations as well as tuple packets.

fig. 3

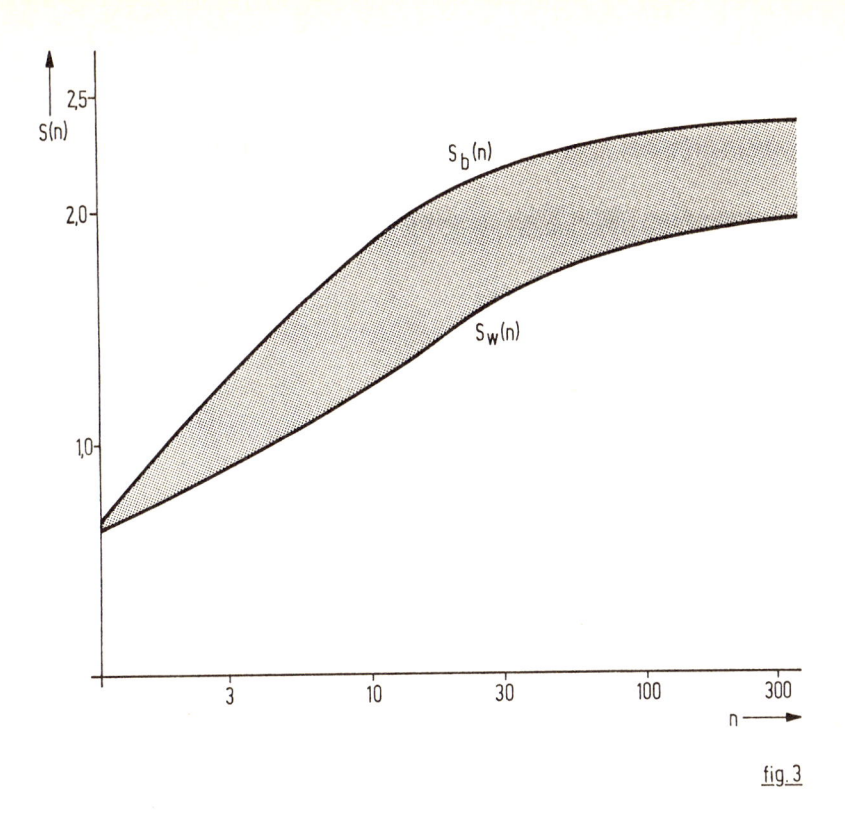

/1/ Chang, P.Y.
Parallel Processing and Data Driven Implementation of a
Relational Data Base System, Proc. of the 76 Conf. of the
ACM, p. 314-318

/2/ Boral, H. and DeWitt, J.
Processor Allocation Strategies for Multiprocessor Database
Machines, ACM Transactions on Database Systems, Vol.6, No.2
June 1981, p.227-254

/3/ Boral, H. and Dewitt, J.
Applying Data Flow Techniques to Data Base Machines
Computer (IEEE) Aug. 1982, p. 57-63

/4/ Malms, M.
Ein inhaltsadressierbares Speichersystem zur Unterstützung
zeitkritischer Prozesse der Informationswiedergewinnung in
Datenbanksystemen.
Fachberichte Informatik, Band 62, Springer Verlag, 1983

ON A SPECIFICATION AND PERFORMANCE EVALUATION MODEL FOR MULTICOMPUTER DATABASE MACHINES

G. Schiffner, P. Scheuermann[+], S. Seehusen and H. Weber

University of Bremen

Dept. of Mathematics &. Computer Science

2800 Bremen 33, W-Germany

[+]Northwestern University

Evanston, Ill. 60201, U.S.A.

Abstract

The paper outlines a concept for the design and performance evaluation of alternative database system and database machine architectures. The concept, therefore, integrates a software design method (such as modular design and specification) with performance prediction methods to produce a tool to uniformly predict the performance of software / hardware architectures.

1.0 Introduction

The past few years have witnessed the rapid development of database machines, i.e. software / hardware systems dedicated and tailored to perform some or all of the database management functions [SU80]. Many of theses proposals for database machines utilize specialized hardware to perform the retrieval and selection of records from secondary storage [BRA81]. While cost beneficial for simple retrieval operations, these designs do not address themselves appropriately to the other database functions, e.g. updates have to be performed in CASSM by the host [BAB79], the backup / recovery is not yet solved with cellular logic systems [STA79], etc. We further distinguish a category of database machines which employ general purpose processors to distribute some of the database functions. In this category are included DIRECT [DEW79] with its duplicated join processors and the DBC architecture [BAN78], which uses a series of pipelined processors for logical - address translation.

However, the advantages of introducing parallelism on a higher level, i.e. by pipelining or duplicating such functions as query preprocessing, directory search, consistency checking, have not been sufficiently studied [SWE82]. Equally important, it is not known under which general conditions a multiple computer system consisting of conventional processors is more advantegeous than a special purpose database machine.

In this paper we outline the design of a performance evaluation model for alternative database architectures. By integrating software design methods (such as modular design and specification techniques) with performance prediction methods we intend to produce a tool for uniformly predicting the performance of software / hardware architectures. This is particularly important in light of the fact that there are computer systems in existence and many others are becoming available, i.e. data flow machines which exploit parallelism at high level [HAY82].

Our performance evaluation model consists of a database system (DBS) model, a cost estimation model and a simulation model. In particular we concentrate our attention to the specification technique used to describe the mapping of a DBS to physical processors and correspondingly the mapping of logical execution schedules to physical execution schedules. Section 2 applies this specification technique for our architecture model and section 3 outlines the environment model which together comprise the DBS model. In section 4 we outline our cost evaluation model and show how the DBS model can be mapped into a simulation model based on Petri nets. Finally, in section 5 we present some experiments we carried out to quantify the effects of concurrent operations on two representative architectures.

2.0 The DBS Model

Although a number of performance evaluation studies have been carried out to compare the capabilities of a sample of database machines [DEW81, HAW82], no systematic methodology for the evaluation of alternative database machines has been previously available. Our model will allow a database designer to test for different granularities of parallelism in a database architecture, by specifying parameters at different levels of detail. In addition, our cost estimation model takes into account concurrent operations and computes a number of useful statistics, such as throughput, besides response time.

The proposed database machine evaluation model consists of three interrelated models as stated before. Thus it can be visualized as DBS (cost estimation model and simulation model). Furthermore the DBS model has two components; (architecture and environment model). We shall proceed now to elaborate more on the architecture model.

2.1 The Specification Technique for Database Architectures

Our specification technique for modelling database architectures employs the multilayer approach to represent the static and dynamic structure of the DBS functions and their successive mapping in a multiprocessor system. Such a multilevel approach allows for easier identification of different design parameters and permits one to examine trade-offs at different levels of detail.

The static structure of the DBS is specified at the highest level as a module hierarchy (MH) [WEB79]. We can specify how this module hierarchy is to be allocated to an abstract set of processors and furthermore how this abstract processor hierarchy (APH) is implemented in terms of concrete physical processors (PPH). This framework of design is illustrated on the left hand side of figure 1. Since only the static structure is visible in a module hierarchy, we associate another directed graph, denoted as the execution network, with the dynamic structure of the system.

At the highest level (see figure 1) we specify for each type of database operation, i.e. retrieval, update etc., a logical execution schedule (les) in terms of modules from MH. The union of these les comprises the logical execution network (LEN). At the concrete level,

Static Structure	Dynamic Structure

```
                                    ┌─────────────────────────────┐
                                    │   LOGICAL EXECUTION         │
                                    │  SCHEDULES (les) + LOGICAL  │
                                    │  EXECUTION NETWORK (LEN)    │
                                    └─────────────────────────────┘
   ┌──────────────────────┐                       │
   │ MODULES + MODULE     │                       │
   │ HIERARCHY ( M H )    │                       │
   └──────────────────────┘                       │
              │         ALLOCATE                  │
              ▼                                   ▼
   ┌──────────────────────┐         ┌──────────────────────┐
   │ ABSTRACT PROCESSORS  │         │   les^a  +  LEN^a    │
   │ + ABSTRACT PROCESSOR │         └──────────────────────┘
   │ HIERARCHY (A P H )   │
   └──────────────────────┘
              │         IMPLEMENT                 │
              ▼                                   ▼
   ┌──────────────────────┐         ┌─────────────────────────────┐
   │ PHYSICAL PROCESSORS  │         │   PHYSICAL EXECUTION        │
   │ + PHYSICAL PROCESSOR │         │  SCHEDULES (pes) + PHYSICAL │
   │ HIERARCHY (P P H)    │         │  EXECUTION NETWORK (PEN)    │
   └──────────────────────┘         └─────────────────────────────┘
```

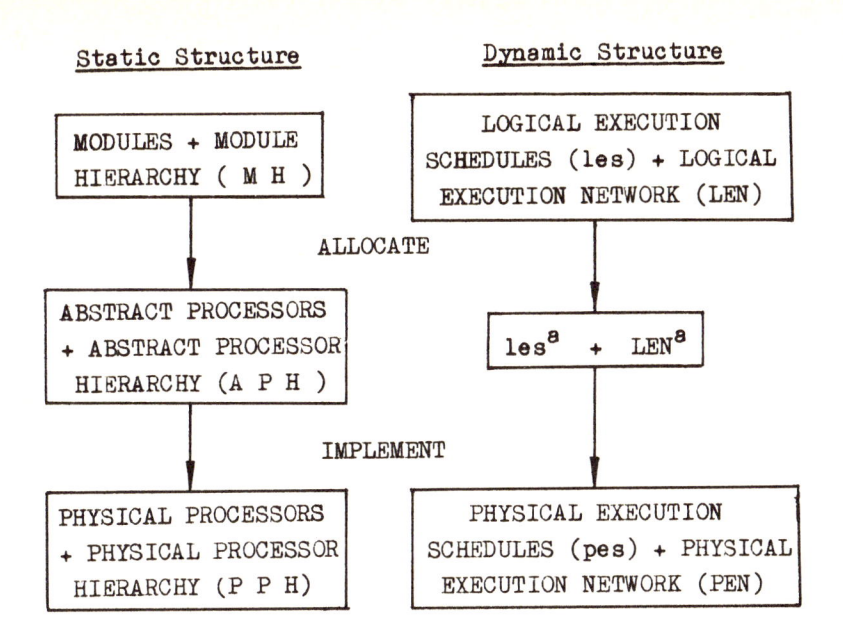

Figure 1: Multilevel specification of database architectures

this graph becomes the physical execution network (PEN).

To illustrate our specification technique we consider a simple version of a DBS. A functional decomposition of a DBS into a module hierarchy is illustrated in figure 2. In this hierarchy the edges represent the use relationship, i.e. an edge is directed from module A to module B if A calls B. Observe that not all paths are refined to the same level of detail, since we are interested basically in capturing those modules which affect mostly the performance in a multiprocessor architecture.

Under a global database module (DB) representing an unique access point we distinguish four components. The query preprocessor module (QP) supports user guidance to the system, a possible clarification dialogue and translation into a query language used by the system. The conceptual schema module (CS) is responsible for consistency and authorization checks and translates the query into an internal, executable form.

The actual execution of a query is under the control of the EXEC module which comprises two components. The control part of the execution is assigned to the Q^* - SCHED module, which is responsible for the scheduling of queries on multiple processors and for the

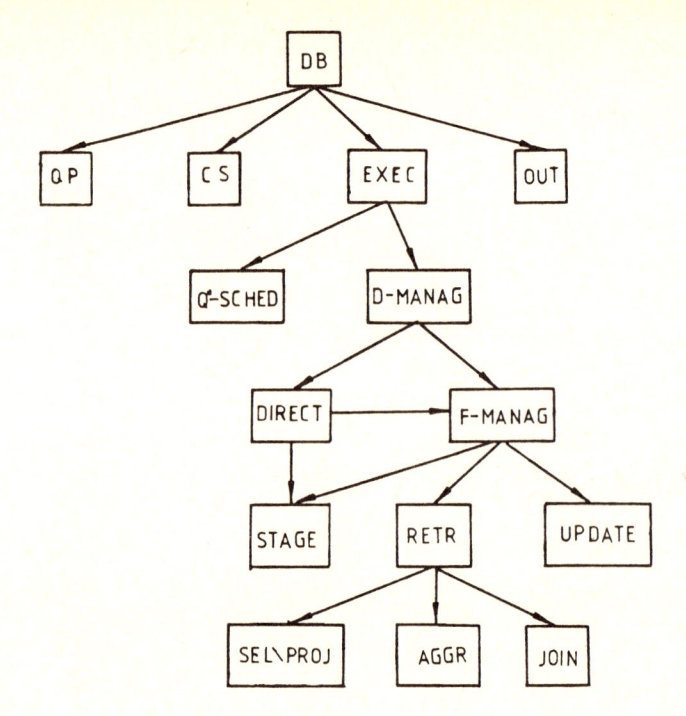

Figure 2: A module hierarchy representing DBS functions

synchronization of data accesses. The data accesses themselves are delegated to the D - MANAG module.

In the data manager (D -MANAG) manipulations of the actual data files are controlled by the file manager (F - MANAG) which may be supported by a directory search module (DIRECT) which accesses one or more indices. In either case the amount of data to be retrieved may be too large to be immediately processed and therefore one may require a staging mechanism (STAGE).

With regard to the file management operations we further distinguish between retrieval (RETR) and update (UPDATE) operations. This distinction is made in order to be able to quantify the effect of updates which have to be performed by the host, as in the case with specialized hardware designs. Under the RETR module we distinguish between the relational operators select, project, join and aggregate. Since most database machine designs are currently based on the relational data model, the above set of retrieval operations is comprehensive. The select and project operations are executed in one step, i.e. require a single scan of the data and are therefore modelled in one module (SEL/PROJ). In most systems the join and aggregate operations require intermediate steps, and in addition the aggregation may require the host intervention [STA79], hence these functions are modelled under the separate modules (JOIN) and (AGGR). A further refinement of the JOIN module to reflect the possible ways in which this operation may be excecuted in a multiprocessor environment [VAL82] may also be desirable, but is not shown in figure 2.

Finally, the completion of the user query, including formatting and error handling, is handled by the output module (OUT). The module hierarchy (MH) can be used to obtain some estimates on the time / cost associated with the different functions, but this is not sufficient. We would also like to express the sequence in which these modules may be executed and the number of times they are executed, in order to estimate better the above costs as well as the communication costs if the MH is mapped to a particular architecture. We observe further that for the purpose of performance evaluation it is not necessary to specify the execution sequence within a module, but only between modules.

For each query type, i.e. select, join etc., we thus define a directed graph, called a logical execution schedule (les). The nodes of the graph represent modules from MH, but the edges now show the potential execution sequence for this query type. The structure of a les is not just a subgraph of MH since edges may be added, to express a repetitive execution of a group of modules or to bypass optional functions. To allow for all these alternatives the nodes on paths of the directed graph must be marked correspondingly. Below are some of the alternative markings which have been identified:

  mandatory - the node is always executed (default)
  skipped   - the node is always omitted for this query type
  optional - based on some predicate this node may be executed or not
  on error - this node will be executed only if the previous module in
               sequence terminated unnormally
  in a loop - this node or group of nodes are executed several times

Figure 3 shows the logical execution schedule for a retrieval operation (no further distinction is made here, for simplicity, between types of retrieval). The marking of the graph is accomplished by using a representation similar to the one employed for regular expressions. The nodes of the graph are first numbered such that these numbers correspond to the hierarchical levels in the MH. In our notation from

$0 := (1, 4^o)^o, 2, 4^o, 3, 4$

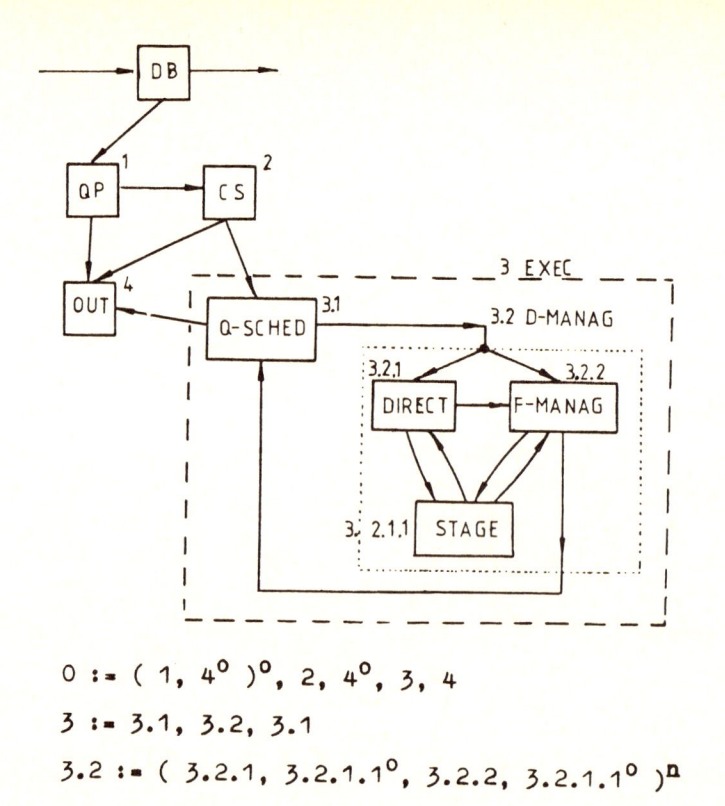

$3 := 3.1, 3.2, 3.1$

$3.2 := (3.2.1, 3.2.1.1^o, 3.2.2, 3.2.1.1^o)$

Figure 3: A logical execution schedule for a retrieval operation

figure 3 optional modules are indicated by an 'o', and loops are shown by enclosing the corresponding group of modules in brackets to which the label 'n' is attached. We are currently working to refine further this formal description.

By superimposing all the individual les's for the different query types we obtain the logical execution network (LEN) which encompasses all potential execution sequences. As we mentioned, the LEN provides us already with the opportunity to conduct a performance analysis at a high level of abstraction. A flow analysis of the graph can provide some information about the utilization of different components.

2.2 Mapping the Module Hierarchy to Abstract and Concrete Processors

As shown in figure 1 the modules and module hierarchy are mapped first to a gros architecture of abstract processors in order to be able to investigate different alternatives including multiple processors without considering any physical detail. The resultant structure at this level is called the abstract processor hierarchy (APH). In a further step, the abstract processors and APH are then mapped to (implemented by) actual physical processors, which can be described in a parametric fashion. The resultant graph structure at the physical level is called a physical processor hierarchy (PPH). The configuration of the actual hardware devices may restrict the number of available options (mappings) at the last level.

We can describe the successive mappings MH --> APH --> PPH by a process of graph labelling applied to MH and a sequence of graph transformations applied to this graph. The graph labelling proceeds as follows. Each node label denotes a processor - module pair, i.e. label 'k_x' means that module x is allocated to processor k. All edges emenating from a node 'k_x' are labelled 'k', i.e. bear the name of that processor. The initial labelled graph is obtained from MH by attaching the label 'u' (unspecified) to all nodes and edges to show that no allocation has been specified yet.

If each module x is assigned to a unique abstract processor k then the node label 'u_x' is replaced by 'k_x' (and similarly the edges labelled 'u' coming from 'u_x' are replaced by edges labelled 'k'. This describes a pipeline organisation with the characteristics of a multiple instructions, single data (MISD) machine.

On the other hand to achieve more parallelism the database designer may specify that a given module should be duplicated on a number of processors. Instead of attaching multiple labels to a node in the MH graph we opt to explicitly duplicate the module in question on separate nodes, each one corresponding to a distinct processor. This has the advantage that the communication lines between different processors are explicitly represented and allows for an easier estimation of the communication costs. In addition, since the duplicated module instances may operate concurrently, a new function which synchronizes these parallel processes is necessary. Thus for each duplicated module m a control module cm is created which becomes the only access point to the duplicated instances of m. The control module cm will be allocated to the same abstract processor where the duplicated module is called from so that no changes in the interface of the calling module occur. This situation is similar to the one we depicted in [SSW80], where a control module at a higher level of abstraction may have to be created in order to enforce update propagation among multiple views in a database system.

The graph transformations which we outlined above can be described formally in terms of graph rewriting rules [CLA79]. Due to the lack of space we restrict ourselves here to illustrate these transformations in a synthetic example. For more details about the formal mechanism the reader is directed to [SHI83]. Figure 4 represents the allocation of the module hierarchy containing x, y and z to 4 processors. The initial labelled graph without any allocation performed yet is illustrated in figure 4a. In figure 4b we allocate module x to processor 1 and change the corresponding labels. Step 4c illustrates the duplicated allocation of module y to processors 1 and 2 and the creation of a control module labelled 'l_cy'. Figure 4d shows how the graph depicted in figure 4b can be transformed by allocating first the module z to the processors 1 and 4. The difference is that in this case we know (from the allocation list) that z will be called from modules allocated to several processors. By the same argument as above this implies that the control module cz is to be duplicated by itself and accordingly allocated. The configuration in figure 4e is the one, after all three transformations have been applied. Notice that the order of applying these transformations is immaterial to the final result.

Finally, the abstract processor hierarchy (APH) is obtained by applying one more transformation to our labelled graph. All modules assigned to the same processor are aggregated into one node (shown by dotted lines in figure 4e) creating a hypergraph of the labelled graph. The remaining edges connecting the aggregated nodes can be interpreted as representing logical communication channels.

The last refinement of our static architecture assigns the APH to physical processors (see figure 1). The structure of the resultant PPH may differ from the structure of the APH in a number of ways: Since logical communication channels identify types of logical requests, at the physical level a number of logical channels could be assigned to the same physical channel. In addition at this level of description we specify a parametric definition of physical processor types, channel types and related cost figures. Finally, we observe that a number of additional mappings (which were not included in figure 1 in order not to obscure the picture) have to be specified at the physical processor level. In particular we have to identify how applications are

Allocation List:

        Processors 1 2 3 4
        Modules   x y y z

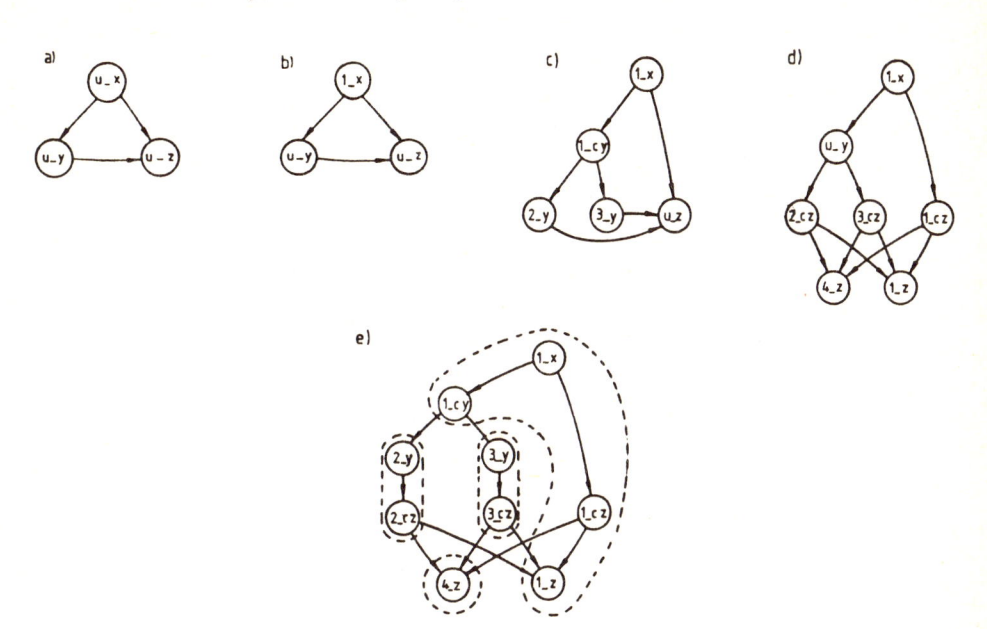

Figure 4: An example of a graph rewriting system

allocated to physical processors and how the different logical partitions of the database are stored on these processors.

3.0 The Environment Model

In order to evaluate the performance of a given DBS it is also necessary to consider the system workload under which it operates. Our environment model comprises two parts: the <u>database profile</u> and the <u>query profile.</u>

In the database profile we include the parameters which characterize the logical structure of a database. As we are dealing with a relational database the most important parameters which we consider are:

   (d1) the number of relations
   (d2) the cardinality of each relation and its tuple size

(d3) the number of indices (directory) and attributes indexed

In the query profile we include the external parameters characterizing the user's interaction with the system. The most important parameters which we distinguish here are subdivided into the following categories:

(q1) types of queries (and related selectivity factors)
(q2) query distribution function
(q3) query arrival rate

With regard to query types (q1), as a number of studies with naiv users have indicated [REI81], the clarification dialogue can be of considerable complexity and consume a relatively large share of the system resources. Hence in addition to the standard retrieval operations mentioned before (select, project, join, aggregate and update) we include a number of additional query types: user guidance, request for metadata (which is stored in the system's dictionary and conceptual schema) and existence check. We also associate with each retrieval operation an average selectivity factor, which is defined as the ratio of the number of records satisfying the query versus the number of records retrieved (or referenced by the query).

Unlike earlier performance evaluation studies of database machines [DEW81,HAW82] we intend to study the effects of different query profiles in a dynamic environment. Thus we do not consider only the effects of individual query types but also how they interact with each other in different query loads. In particular the query load is described by a query distribution function, which gives the frequency of occurence of each query type (q2), and by a query arrival rate (q3), another distribution function giving the time interval between any two arbitrary queries. In order to study realistically the gains of parallelism under concurrent operations we also assume that if a pipeline organization (suborganization) has only one CPU then this one is processing the requests in the queue in a round - robin fashion.

It is obvious that many distributions on range values can be fitted to the parameters discussed above (d1 -d3 and q1 - q3). To begin with we followed in our study the gros classification scheme proposed in [HAW81] and later expanded in [GOD81]. These authors distinguished the following characteristic types of applications (environments):

1. a bibliographic application with a medium size requiring long sweeps through the data,

2. a bussiness application represented by databases of various sizes and by queries with relatively small selectivity factors,

3. a statistical application employing a large database of large size which exhibits strong correlations among subsets of the data which are requested.

In our first experiments we varied the parameters in the environment model so as to encompass the application types described above.

4.0 The Cost Estimation Model and the Simulation Model

In addition to the modelling of different designs of database systems and their mappings to alternative database machine architectures we are now interested to evaluate the performance of alternate machine architectures. Up to now, most of the studies reported in the literature [DEW81, HAW82] focussed on the comparison of the response time as the only performance characterizing parameter. Some of the investigations also looked at the storage cost. Our goal is the development of a performance evaluation model that allows to incorporate other performance parameters to develop a more complete characterization of the performance of a given architecture. We will also present a simulation model that is based on an extended Petri Net concept. The model will be primarily used to model the effect of parallelism on the performance of the considered architectures.

4.1 Performance Measures

The execution of queries can be modelled by a token flow through a network of processors and associated queues. Since the behavior of each processor and its queue can be described as a queueing system, our performance measures can be defined using the terminology common to networks of queueing systems [KOB78].

Due to the fact that both processors and channels may be concurrently requested by tokens they will be both represented as servers in a queueing system, each one with its corresponding (input) queue. The stream of tokens arriving at each service station, is characterized by its arrival rate (AR) and service distribution (SD). From the latter we can derive the average service demand ($\overline{S}$) of the input tokens. Each server is restricted by its service capacity to perform not more than a certain work demand per time unit. The ratio $ST = \overline{S} / C$ is then called the <u>service time</u> (to complete one token) and its inverse $ASR = C / \overline{S}$ is called the <u>average service rate</u> (ASR) of the server [KOB78].

Our cost functions can be applied to the abstract level (les[a]) or to the physical processor level (pes), depending upon the level of detail required. In the following discussion we shall restrict ourselves to the physical processor level. Since the most important performance measure from the user's point of view is the response time we shall first elaborate on this performance measure.

In section 2 we have seen how we can specify for a certain operation its potential execution sequences in terms of a pes graph. Let p_i be the pes graph corresponding to a certain query q_i. The set of nodes in pes_i which we denote by $P_i = \{p_{i_1}, p_{i_2} \ldots p_{i_k}\}$ correspond to the distinct physical processors participating in the execution of q_i. The communication links allocated to channels between them are represented by the (set of) edges in pes_i which we denote by E_i. With each edge $e \in E_i$ we associate a capacity $c(e)$ representing the bandwith of the communication channel. Therefore the culmulative service time is composed of the service time $ST(p)$ at processor nodes and the service time $ST(e)$ at communication channels, which account for the time to transfer tokens between the processors. In addition, we have to add to the response time the waiting time (W) in front of each queue. Thus the response time (RT) can be expressed as:

$$RT(q_i, AR_r, SD_t) = \sum_{p_j \in P_i} ST(p_j) + \sum_{e_k \in E_i} ST(e_k) + \sum_{p_j \in P_i} W(p_j) + \sum_{e_k \in E_i} W(e_k) - \sum_{p_d = \text{disk controler}} OV(p_m, p_d)$$

The last term in this expression takes into account the potential overlap of some computations with memory transfer, treated as a special processor p_d.

Another class of performance evaluation measures estimate the congestion of the system. The simplest measure of congestion is given by the _traffic intensity_ (TI) which relates the arrival rate of tokens in front of a queueing network component to its average service rate: TI = AR / ASR. If a situation occurs where TI > 1, we say that the component is _saturated._

We have chosen the _utilization_ (UT) of a component as another performance parameter of interest to the development of a more general picture of the performance properties of a system.

$$UT = MIN(1, \frac{AR}{ASR})$$

The service rate of an element may be determined by first estimating the time consumption for the execution of all functions allocated to that element. It will then be finally determined by counting the number of invocations of all the functions weighted by their execution time. This measure then gives a first idea of the bottle-necks that can be expected in the system.

Furthermore, to quantify the effects of saturated components, we measure the _queue length distribution_ (Q) for each component in the network. Information concerning this measure can also be useful if one wishes to evaluate the amount of buffer storage required to accomodate waiting query tokens.

The above measure is tied together with the already mentioned _waiting time_ (W) of a token in a queue which can be computed as the ratio of the average queue length and the arrival rate using the result of a theorem [see KOB78].

In addtion to the above evaluation criteria, we feel it is important to measure the _throughput of the system_, i.e. the average number of query tokens completed per time unit. This measure is important to evaluate if we are processing a stream of different queries. Again, assuming a certain arrival rate of tokens AR_r and a service distribution SD_t of different service types, the throughput of a component relative to query q can be expressed as

$$TR(q_i, AR_r, SD_t) = ASR * UT = MIN(AR, ASR)$$

The throughput is equal to the arrival rate AR so far as AR is less than the service rate ASR. Beyond that point throughput equals the value of the service rate ASR. This maximal value is achieved if the server is continously busy, i.e. UT=1. With this definition the throughput of the system relative to a query can be determined from the processing element along the execution path of that query which performs at minimal throughput.

To compare the performance of different architectures we are interested in the behavior towards maximal throughput; in particular we like to measure how fast the system performance degrades under saturation of some elements. This influence can be expressed using the queue length distribution Q. One way to obtain a situation causing maximal throughput is to increase the arrival rate. Therefore we can refer to the gradient $Q' = d(Q)/dt$ during a fixed interval of time. This quantity denoted as congestion rate (CR), expresses the rate by which a queue grows relative to the arrival rate. Assuming a sufficient large interval of time CR will be zero or slightly above it as long no saturation of an element occurs. If the increased arrival rate leads to the saturation of a processing element, CR also grows until it reaches the gradient of the arrival rate which constitutes an upper bound. The increase within that interval may now be used as measure related to maximal throughput.

4.2 Simulation of Alternative Architectures Based on their Modelling by Function Nets

The simulation of alternative database systems and database machine architectures is primarily aimed at determining the impact of concurrent executions of database functions on multiprocessor systems. The modelling technique that is used to describe concurrently executing processing units closely resembles Petri Nets (PN). This technique has been chosen since it is well defined and provides means to formally verify important system properties like liveness and deadlock freeness. In addition it provides an expressive notation to present those systems.

The extended version of Petri Nets used in the modelling for the simulation experiments are called Function Nets (FN) [GOD80]. Similar to Petri Nets they are bi-partitite graphs consisting of two different types of nodes called agencies (i.e. transitions in PN) and channels (i.e. places in PN). A time consuming activity is associated with each agency representing the execution of some program. A storage unit is associated with each channel representing a queue of initialization requests for the activity associated with the agency subsequent to the respective channel. The dynamics of a system may then be modelled by a flow of tokens in FN through the firing of agencies under certain well defined conditions and by the temporary storage in the channels.

In the firing one token will be removed from all incoming channels of an agency (representing the initialization of the activity associated with an agency) and one token will be placed on each outgoing channel of an agency (representing the termination of the respective activity).

Alternately, the firing in the FN may be defined by the copying of one token from all input channels (instead of removing them from the input channels). In a further generalization the firing in the FN may be defined as an selective copying or removing of tokens from only one or some of the input channels and a selective writing to one or some of the output channels.

The delays in the token flow caused by the agencies may be defined in a number of ways as (I) a constant delay (II) a parameterized distribution or (III) any function composition of either predefined primitive functions or user defined primitive functions.

A number of additional primitive functions to determine the delay caused by some database system components were considered to be useful in addition to the existing repertoire of predefined primitive functions. Among those were, for example, primitive functions to compute the delay caused by an agency that schedule the input over different channels with different priorities. For more detail we refer to [SHI83].

Moreover, Function Nets differ from Petri Nets with respect to the meaning of tokens. While Petri Nets consider tokens as undistinguishable entities, Function Nets associate unique identifiers with tokens and possibly messages that can be interpreted and manipulated by the adjacent agencies during their firing.

5.0 Simulation Experiments

In the following experiments we do not attempt to model existing experimental machines but rather prototype systems that only resemble those systems as much as possible. We therefore model three types of architectures representing systems with conventional single data manipulation processors (CONV), like INGRES, with disk associated multiple data manipulation processors (ROT), like CAFS, and with cache associated multiple data manipulation processors (MEM), like DIRECT.

The analysed architectures are composed of two computer systems each one possibly consisting of multiple processors: a host system (HOST) and a backend system (BE) which are connected by an inter computer link (ICL) for a fast communication. To relieve the host we allocate the data access functions and, depending on the capabilities of the actual physical processors, the data management functions to the backend. For the same purpose we relocate functions which directly support an user dialogue from the host to an additional frontend system (FE), e.g. an intelligent terminal.

The Function Net of figure 5 gives an overview for this kind of a database machine architecture. Two elements which represent the user interface of the system have been added to the model: The 'query generation' agency produces a stochastic stream of query tokens of predefined types according to a particular application. Each query token is uniquely identified and carries with it the path information which is interpreted by the agencies. After the completion of a query its statistical data is analyzed by the 'statistic' agency. Only the major components of FE, HOST and BE which all share the ICL to exchange query tokens are visible on this abstract level.

The following figures visualize the stepwise refinements of the Function Net above. This process continues until that level of detail on which the functions that are subject to duplication can be modelled as separate agencies. As shown in figure 6 three functions, CSP, Q*-SCHED and D-MANAG, represent a first refinement of the HOST. These functions share a common CPU, denoted as CPU.HOST. The sharing of a resource can be precisely modelled in the Function Net by a channel with one initial token that will be removed to fire one of the agencies CSP, Q*-SCHED or D-MANAG and will be put back into the channel after its completion. To better visualize the token flow incoming edges are arranged on the left side and outgoing ones on the right side of an

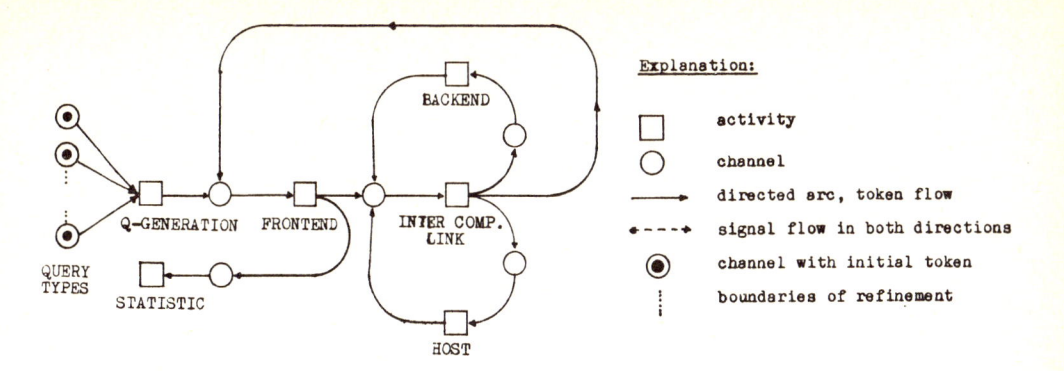

Figure 5: Overview of a DBM architecture

agency.

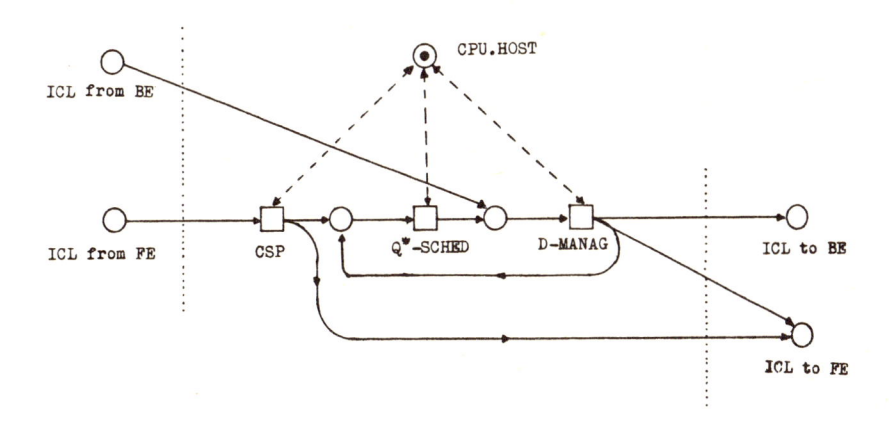

Figure 6: Refinement of a Host

In figure 7 the agency D-MANAG is further refined for the depiction of the detailed functions introduced in a previous section (see figure 2). Since the components of this agency may be executed in different orders we introduce a control agency to select one of the possible sequences. This approach has been chosen to keep the number of agencies as small as possible to avoid an explicit duplication of the agencies to represent different sequences. The control agency is assumed to have a minimal time consumption thus avoiding a critical congestion of tokens among several input lines.

The same modelling mechanism is employed to refine the agency representing the F-MANAG module of this Function Net. Without presenting further details we note that the refined agencies DAP (data access processor), AGG (aggregation) and COM (comparison) represent the modules SEL/PROJ, AGGREG and JOIN of figure 2.

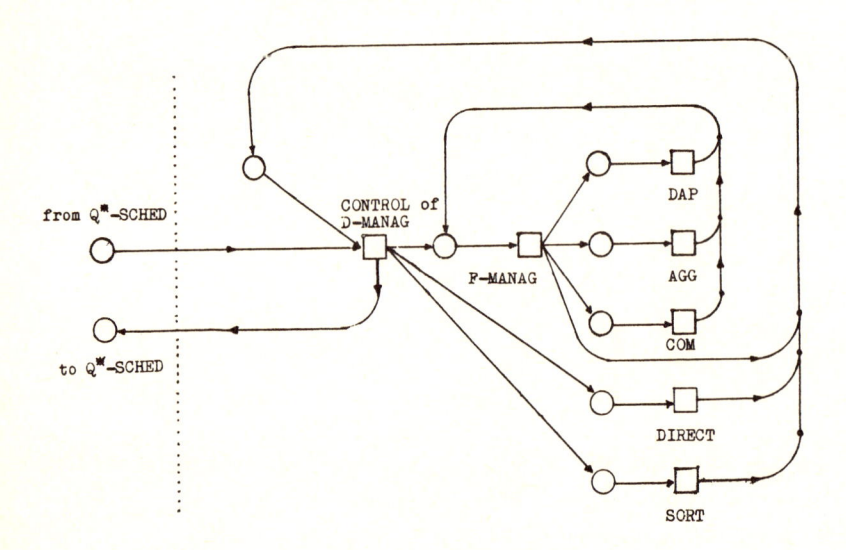

Figure 7: Refinement of the D-MANAG agency

To estimate the time consumption for each function we rely on data of a local area network system [KIE82], and on those reported in the database machine literature. Beeing aware of the difficulty to obtain detailed and compatible data we focussed on the relative importance of influencing parameters.

The presented experiments are confined to variations of the following variables (see also the appendix): Two representative architectures and different environment models distinguished by different query profiles and the size of the requested relations have been investigated so far. The total query load modification is modelled by changes of the arrival rate and the distribution of query types. Variations of the logical database organization, expressed by different selectivity factors of a query, have not been considered here.

5.1 Validation of the Simulation Model

The first set of experiments was conducted to validate the modelled architectures with the results obtained in other studies. Therefore the response time for only single queries was measured. The experiments were performed on the same relations to allow for a comparison of different query types. Additionally the size of the relation(s) was varied to measure the influence of the database size. The results of the CONV and the ROT architectures are presented in the diagramm of figure 8 which has one logarithmic scale to include values of a large range in one picture. The test results are shown to be similar to the results presented in the quoted literature: Complicated queries like join and aggregate, which require a decomposition into a considerable number of subqueries, strongly dominate all other ones. In our model, however, the response times are quantified more abstractly in terms of relation sizes and selectivity factors, and not only in terms of the number of disks accesses or similar measures. This permits us to express the performance of a system dependent on logical factors rather than on physical factors.

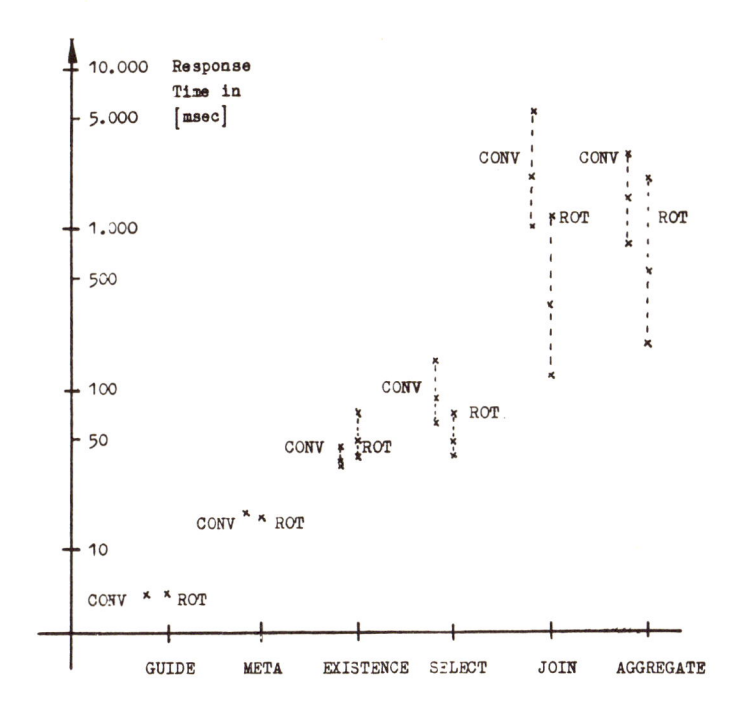

Figure 8: Response times of single queries with modified relation sizes

5.2 Performance of Multiple Queries

A stream of queries of different types is generated in the following experiments to simulate a more realistic load situation. In the beginning we fix the application characteristics and vary only the arrival rate of tokens to explore the effect of concurrent computations.

Since the simulation system optionally produces statistical material about utilization and token delays for each agency and channel, the disclosure of potential bottlenecks is readily visible as a first result of these tests. In the CONV model the loading and scanning of the memory buffer for complicated queries was identified to be critical whereas in the ROT model the large number of subqueries, each requiring a scan of the data, congested the associative disk device. Temporarily the inter computer link (ICL) was congested too, when large amounts of data were delivered to the host system. This applied particularly in the ROT model where the actual data search yields result tuples at much higher rate. The figures represent still an optimistic result because the ICL is exlusively used in our model for the database functions and not shared with other application tasks.

To present some results we refer now to the diagrams of the summarized results in figure 9. The curves in that figure refer to the simulation of the CONV model with a high percentage of complicated queries. The delay of tokens (W) in the queue of the most critical element, i.e. with the longest queue, is included in this diagram too. A comparison of this curve with the curve of the average response time (RT) indicates the performance degradation due to the critical component. In our example both curves exhibit a very similar shape and we conclude a single element dominating as bottleneck.

For the study of the performance under saturation, the arrival rate was increased until the queue(s) of the critical component(s) was (were) only growing. It seems to be reasonable to rather define a saturation interval than a saturation point for which we still get a sufficient performance of the system. This interval can be determined depending on several factors: (I) The throughput rate (TR) starts to increase only logarithmically with the increase of the arrival rate (AR); (II) the response time starts to increase highly exponentially with the arrival rate; (III) the congestion rate (CR) start to to grow above zero with the arrival rate.

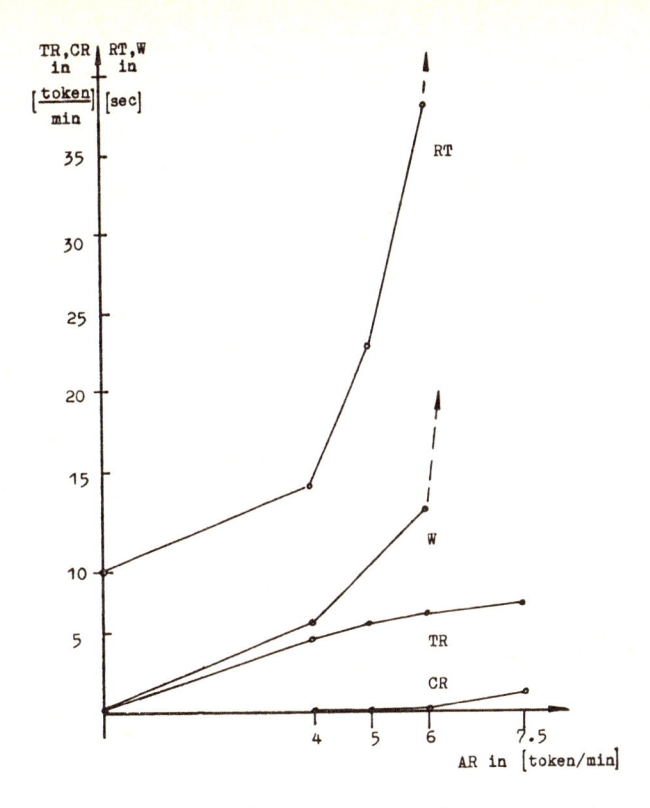

Figure 9: Performance towards saturation (CONV Model)

The shape of the characterizing curves for the performance of the system under saturation within that interval (see figure 9) reveals some important information on the behaviour of the system. This analysis could be refined by also determining the utilization of the system for the found interval. The gradient of the increase of the utilization within that interval is a measure for the rate with which the congestion increases up to a total blockage of the system. For the example depicted in figure 9 the utilization increases from 91% up to 97% for that interval. This indicates a rather smooth congestion increase.

The difference in the shape of the curves to other known results can be explained as follows: The unfitted shape of the curves representing the simulation results may be attributed to the probabilistic nature of the token generation process and to the statistical analysis performed at the end of an experiment that considers only fully completed queries, .i.e. those which left the net, thus neglecting tokens still remaining in the net. However, an extended simulation time would further smooth the curves shown in the diagram.

5.3 Performance in Different Profile Experiments

Experiments to explore the impact of different application profiles vary the distribution of query types. The load expressed by the arrival rate will be kept fixed. To allow for a direct comparison the results of different architectures we fix the arrival rate to such a value that the least performing architecture, in our simulation this is the CONV model, still operates in a stable manner, i.e. below saturation at approximately 85% utilization.

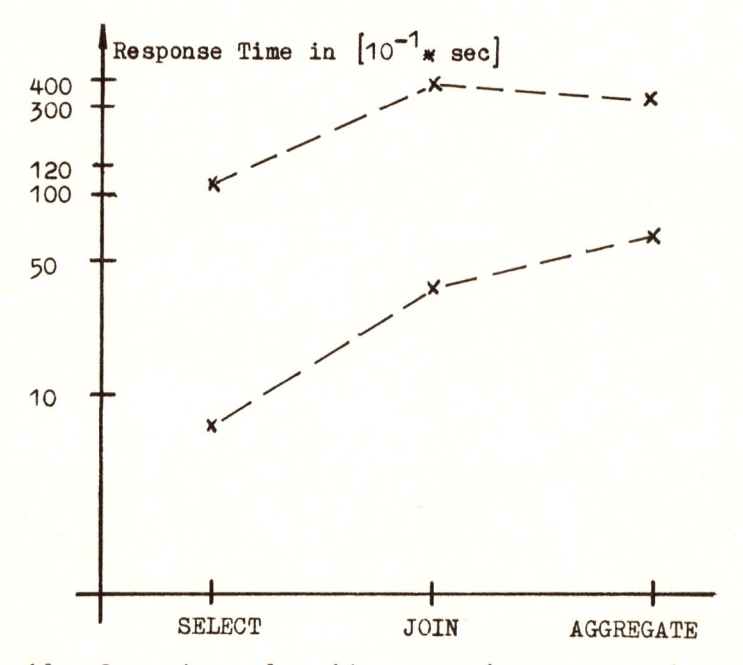

Figure 10: Comparison of architectures by response time

Three different query types on two different architectures have been investigated in the experiment. The performance has been measured in terms of the response time for the query types. Figure 10 shows the results of the simulation for a low percentage of complicated queries. These experiments confirm the principal results obtained in the first experiments. In addition the modelling concept and the simulation allow to draw some conclusion based on the parameterization of the query mix: For the example presented in figure 10 the number of select queries was ten times higher than the number of join queries and sixteen times higher than the number of aggregate queries. The results indicate that both join and aggregate queries were still dominating. The query mix that causes a critical congestion would be found in a factorial analysis based on a series of similar simulation results.

The results also allow to compare the different architectures. A significant difference in the performance of the two architectures can be observed for the given arrival rate and query mix. We therefore use again a logarithmic scale to fit both curves in one diagram. The differences between the two architectures would somewhat diminuish at a lower arrival rate since the different degree of system utilization (CONV at 87%, ROT at 37%) would then diminuish correspondingly.

Conclusion

The paper presents a uniform method for the specification of the design and the performance prediction of software / hardware systems. It is especially aimed at analyzing the impact of multicomputer architectures. The method allows the investigation of the effect of function duplication by duplicating processing units upon the overall performance of the system. The method has been successfully employed in the analysis of the performance of multi computer database machines.

A number of features of the proposed method seem to be of particular importance:

(I) With its modular specification and design concept it provides a powerful instrument to flexibly alter software / hardware architectures for the analysis of their relative advantages and drawbacks.

(II) The performance prediction is not only based on one performance measure but the method allows for the determination of several different parameters all expressing different performance aspects of the system under investigation.

(III) The performance prediction model can be based on the well defined formal model of Petri Nets, thus providing an even richer instrument for the evaluation of other properties of software / hardware systems.

The method, therefore, represents a general tool for the uniform design and performance evaluation of different database systems and database machine architectures.

Appendix

Relationsizes: R1   5 000 / 10 000 / 20 000 tuples
               R2   500 / 1 000 / 2 000 tuples
Tuplesize: 100 byte
total DB-size: 0.25 - 1 Megabyte

Physical Characteristics

Specification of the data store: Ampex 9200 disk drive and CCD -cells as in [HAW82],
Specification of the ICL: According to the UNIVAC bus used in [KIE82,SHI82]; (gros capacity 1 megabit/sec; fixed packages of 800 bytes assumed),
Specification of physical organization of the data: According to [HAW82] such that 1 page - 1 phys. block.

Application Characteristics

The query types Select, Join and Aggregate are used as in [HAW82,BRA81]. Additionally we introduce:

GUIDE : requests answered by the QA module,
META : requests answered by the CS module,
EX   : existence requests answered by the DIRECT module or, if not present, by the SEL/PROJ module.

The application profiles are based on the results of [GOD80, LEH79, HAW81]. So far we simulated three profiles which distinguish (I) a high percentage (more then 40%) of simple queries, i.e. of types GUIDE, META, EX and SELECT, (II) data intensive and multirelational queries, i.e. of type JOIN, and (III) data intensive queries with additional built-in functions, i.e. of type AGGR.

Simulation Characteristics

Size of the Model:

FN elements \ Model	CONV	ROT
No. of Agencies	16	10
No. of channels	33	25
No. of arcs	89	57

Only about half of the channels represent queues which load the system. The other ones merely model external input parameters, e.g. selectivity factor, relationsize etc.

Performance of the Simulation

Results \ Model	CONV	ROT
Simulation Interval (min)	20 - 180	10 - 70
Arrival Rate (token/min)	3.3 - 30	8.5 - 67
CPU Consumption on a IBM-370/VM (sec)	90 - 135	60 - 90

Bibliography

[BAB79] Babb E.:
    Implementing a relational database by means of specialized hardware.
    ACM TODS Vol 4, No. 1, March 1979, pp 1-29

[BAN78] Banerjee J., Baum R., Hsiao D.:
    Concepts and capabilities of a database computer
    ACM TODS Vol. 3, No. 4, Dec. 1978

[BRA81] Bray Olin H., Freeman Harvey A.:
    Data base computers.
    Lexington books, 1981.

[CLA79] Claus K., Ehrig H., Rozenberg G. (eds):
Graph grammars and their application to computer science and biology.
Lecture Notes in Computer Science, Vol. 73, Springer Verlag Berlin 1979.

[DEW79] DeWitt D. J.:
DIRECT - a multiprocessor organization for supporting relational database management systems.
IEEE TOC, Vol. C-28, No. 6, 1979.

[DEW81] DeWitt D. J., Hawthorn P.:
A performance evaluation of database machine architectures.
in: Proc VLDB, 1981

[GOD80] Godbersen H. P., Meyer B.E.:
A net simulation language.
Proceedings Summer Computer Simulation Conference, Seattle, WA., Aug. 1980, AFIPS Press, 1980. pp.188-193.

[GOD81] Godbersen H.P., Munz R., Schneider H.-J., Schiele F., Steyer F.:
A distribute DBS on a minicomputer network, VDN.
(in german). Final project report, German Ministery of Research and Technology, Grant
No. 081-5011 A,1981.

[HAW82] Hawthorne P., DeWitt D.:
Performance analysis of alternative database machine architectures.
IEEE TOSE Vol. SE-8, No. 1, Jan. 1982, pp.61-75.

[HAW81] Hawthorne P.:
The effect of target applications on the design of database machines.
ACM SIGMOD 1981, pp. 188-197.

[HAY82] Haynes L.S., Lau R.L., Sewiorek D.P., Mizzel D.W.:
A survey of highly parallel computing.
Computer, Vol 15, No. 1, 1982

[KIE82] Kiel F., Creutz G., Huelsewiede H.-D., Kleist H., Seyferth A., Schmid E.H.:
A local area network for an information system supporting broad-band communication and a very large number of users (in german).
NTG Fachberichte, Vol. 80, 1982.

[KOB78] Kobayashi H.:
Modelling and analysis: An introduction to system performance evaluation methodology.
Addison Wesley 1978.

[LEH79] Lehmann H., Blaser A.:
Query languages in database systems.
IBM, Technical Report TR 79.07.004, Heidelberg Scientific Center, 1979.

[PET77] Peterson J.L.:
Petri Nets.
ACM Computing Surveys, Vol. 9, No. 3, 1977.

[REI81] Reisner, Phyllis:
Human factor studies of database query languages: a survey and assessment.
ACM Computing Surveys, Vol. 13, No. 1, 1981.

[SHI83]   Schiffner G.:
A specification and performance evaluation model for multicomputer database machines.
University of Bremen, Forthcoming Dissertation, 1983.

[SSW80]   Scheuermann P., Schiffner G., Weber H.:
Abstraction capabilities and invariant properties modelling within the Entity - Relationship approach.
in: Entity - Relationship approach to system analysis and design, P.P. Chen (ed.), North Holland Publ. Comp., 1980, pp. 121-140.

[STA79]   Stanley Y.W.S., Nguyen L.H., Emam A., Lipovski G.J.:
The architectural features and implementation techniques of the multicell CASSM.
IEEE TOC Vol. C-28, No. 6, 1979, pp. 430-445.

[SU80]   Su S.Y., Chang H., Copeland G., Fisher P., Lowenthal E., Schuster S.:
Database machines and some issues on DBMS standards.
Proc. NCC, 1980, pp.191-208.

[SWE82]   Schweppe H., Stiege G.:
Database machines - a state of the art report.
Technical University Braunschweig, Technical Report, 1982.

[VAL82]   Valduriez P., Gardarin G.:
Multiprocessor join algorithms of relations.
in: Improving database usability and responsiveness, P.Scheuermann (ed.), Academic Press, 1982, pp. 219-236.

[WEB79]   Weber H.:
Modularity in database system design: a software engineering view of data base systems.
in: issues in data base management, H. Weber, A.I. Wasserman (eds.) North-Holland Publishing Company, 1979, pp. 65-91.

PERFORMANCE MODELING OF THE DBMAC ARCHITECTURE

S. Salza[*], M. Terranova[*], P. Velardi[**]

[*] IASI - CNR, Viale Manzoni, 30 - 00185 Roma, Italy
[**] Fondazione U. Bordoni, Viale Europa, 126 - 00147 Roma, Italy

ABSTRACT

In this paper we present a performance analysis study of the data base machine DBMAC. A two level hierarchical model is used to represent both the details of the internal structure and the interactions between the system and the environment. This approach allowed to characterize the global performance of the database machine and to compare different design alternatives at the phisical architecture level.

1. INTRODUCTION

Since research activity began in the early 70s in the Data Base Machine field, several DBMs were designed and implemented. Recently some of them became available on the market as potential competitors of traditional data base management systems. Such a situation stresses the need of a more precise evaluation of their performance both to compare the available systems and to guide the design of new ones.

According to that a considerable modeling effort has been performed during the design of the DBMAC database machine developed under funding of Italian National Reseach Council [MIS82B]. This allowed to verify the basic choices of the system design. In fact, a quantitive analysis was necessary to evaluate the impact of the logical architecture and in particular of the data organization on the system performance [MIS82A], [CES82B].

In this paper we present a modeling approach, based on product form queueing networks, to characterize the overall performance of the database machine as a function of the system configuration and of the workload profile. More specifically we focused on the interconnection between the processing units and the mass storage.

We are indeed convinced that this is a crucial issue in a multi-processor database machine. In fact, due to the high amount of data transfers, this interconnection may easily become the system bottleneck and finally determine the global performance.

In the next section we describe the main points of the DBMAC architecture. The following sections present a two level hierarchical model of the system and its solution. In particular section 4 deals with the workload characterization, and section 5 and 6 with DBM internal analysis. Finally section 7 presents the aggregate model that allows to obtain the global performance indices.

2. THE DBMAC SYSTEM

DBMAC is a data base machine based on a modular parallel multiprocessor architecture (fig. 1). The main elements of the system are the Processing Units (PU), that run the Database Machine Management System, and Intelligent Disk Devices (IDD) storing the relational data base. The PUs are single board computers that operate in multiprogramming. They work most of the time on the local memory without interfering each other, moreover a Global Bus (G-Bus) allows both interprocessor communication and access to the Global Memory (G-RAM) where the main data structures of the distrubuited operating system EXMAC are stored.

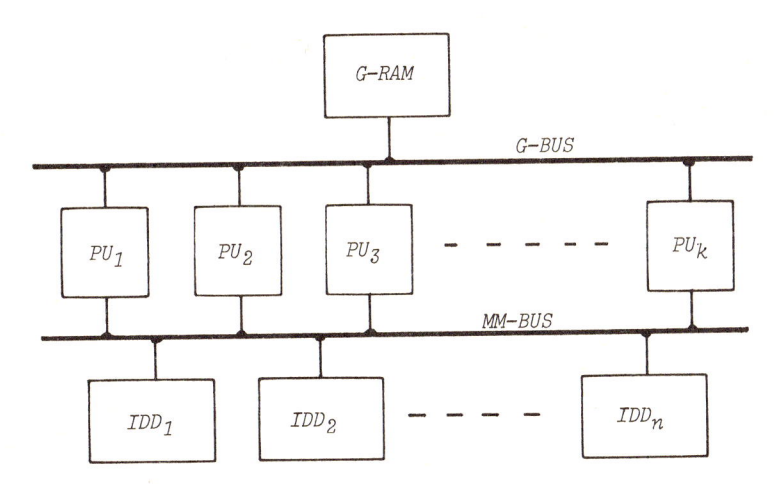

Fig. 1 - DBMAC architecture

An interconnection structure (MM-BUS) connects the PUs and the IDDs. Every IDD is a substystem composed by a mass storage device, a control CPU and a large memory buffer. Data are stored in 10k pages. The PUs issue requests to read (write) a page. Requests are queued and scheduled (at every IDD) by the control CPU that manages the DMA transfers between the disk and the buffer. Finally the page is sent to the PU through the MM-BUS.

The buffering capabilities at the IDDs allow an asynchronous coupling between IDDs and PUs and therefore a better utilization of the MM-BUS. Moreover a further improvement of the disks performance can be attained by a simple pepaging technique.

The basic system task is transaction processing. Every transaction is executed activating, possibly on different PUs, several parallel elementary processes. Every elementary process operates on a single data page and includes the page transfer from/to the IDDs. The homogeneity of the architecture (any process can run on every available PU), allows load balancing and therefore good PU utilization.

Due to large amount of data transfered between the PUs and the IDDs, the crucial part of the architecture is indeed the MM-BUS. Therefore the decision was made to initially concentrate on modeling this part of the architecture.

Two different architectures were considered for the MM-BUS. The first one, called Single-Bus (SB) architecture, is based on a single high speed parallel bus (fig. 2) to carry both large data messages (data pages) and short control messages (requests and acknoledges). Due to the large ratio between the two kind of messages (10^2), the transmission on the bus in performed by packets to avoid the short messages to be penalized.

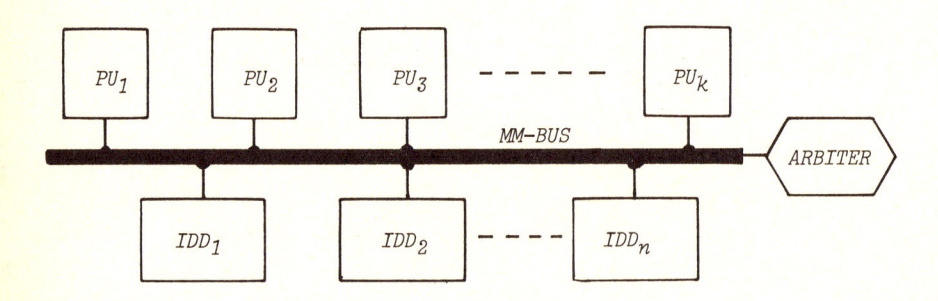

Fig. 2 - The Single Bus architecture

The second architecture, called Multiple-Bus (MB), provides every IDD with a dedicated bus for data transfers. Every PU can connect to every data bus through a multiplexing logic, and holds the bus during a whole data page transfer. Furthermore a common bus connecting all the devices is devoted to the control messages. All the busses are implemented with high speed serial connections which provide a sufficient bandwidth for a single IDD throughput.

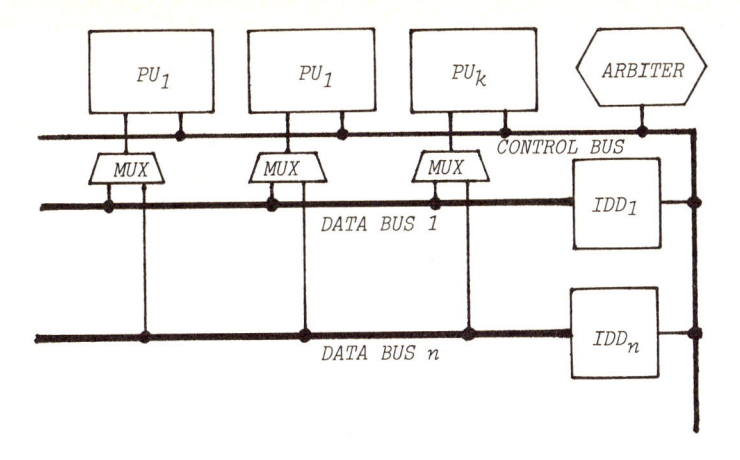

Fig. 3 - The Multiple Bus architecture

The main advantage of the MB architecture is to provide a data transfer capability that grows with the system, i.e. with the number of PUs and IDDs. On the contrary the Single Bus has a fixed bandwidth and for large system configuration may become the bottleneck. Indeed one of the purposes of this study is to compare the two solutions and to determine in quantitative terms the limit to the expansion of the SB architecture.

3. THE DBMAC PERFORMANCE ANALYSIS

The main goal of our analysis is to characterize the global performance of the database machine, that is the overall utilization and the transaction response time. To achieve this goal we set up a two level hierarchical model that allows to deal with the complexity of the task.

At the first level we analize the internal DBM operation in a stationary condition, i.e. with fixed load and multiprogramming level, to get both the device utilizations and the DBM throughput. This step allows also to understand and quantify how the system performance depends on the device characteristics and on the system configuration and internal structure, notably the PU-IDD interconnection.

An higher level model is then considered to include the whole system surrounding the DBM (Front-end or local network) where the transactions originate. At this level the DBM is represented as a single service facility having, for a given workload and configuration, the service rate (throughput) that the previous step allowed to compute.

As far as the modeling methodology is concerned models at both levels are simple product form queueing networks [BASK75]. This is in line with the purpose of our study, to compare different architectures and predict performance during the system design and early implementation. In fact analytical models (compared to simulators) have a very low computational cost, that makes possible an extensive parametric analysis.

4. WORKLOAD REPRESENTATION

We can consider the "external world" surrounding the database machine simply as a source of transactions (fig. 4) that arrive to the DBM to be processed and finally join a sink (get back to the outside world when processing is completed). The time T a transaction takes to go through the DBM is called transaction response time and is one of the the most important performance indices we are considering in our study.

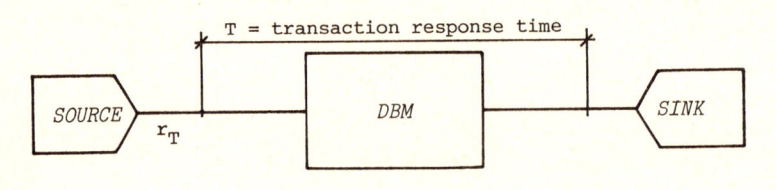

Fig. 4

Actually T depends not only on the system configuration (number and type of PUs and IDDs) and on the interconnection architecture we are considering, but also on the workload characteristics. Therefore any performance prediction or measure has to refer to a given workload. We need then to measure and characterize the workload itself.

We decide to represent the whole workload with a limited set of transactions $Z = \{z_k, k = 1,...,K\}$, and to assume that a mix of them arrive to the DBM with an overall rate r_T. In particular identical instances of transaction z_k arrive at rate $r_k = r_T \cdot p_k$, where p_k is said *relative frequency*.

Every transaction of the set is defined in terms of *relational primitives* by an *execution graph* (fig. 5), where, referring to the Data Pool organization [MIS82A], [CES82A] used in DBMAC, the nodes represent Data Pool primitives that operate on the database domains.

The execution graph evidentiate a first level of parallelism, but a more relevant one lies inside the primitives. In fact we assume that the domains are stored in the mass memory (IDDs) in 10K *pages*, and that every page can be processed indipendently (elementary process).

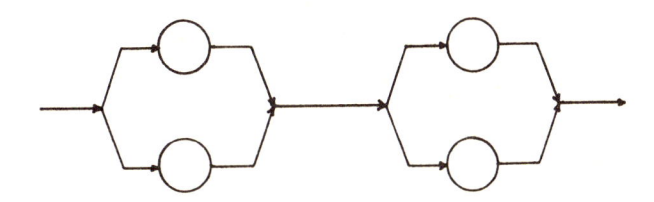

Fig. 5 - Execution graph.

More formally, for every transaction z_k in Z we call H_{ki} the set of primitives in its execution graph, and for every primitive $h_k \in H_k$ we define:

- W_{ki}: number of elementary processes in h_{ki} that write a page in the IDDs.
- R_{ki}: number of elementary processes in h_{ki} that read a page from the IDDs.
- I_{ki}: average number of instructions executed for every elementary process in h_{ki}.

Note that the total number of elementary processes in h_{ki}, that is $W_{ki} + R_{ki}$, depends on the database domain on which the primitive operates, while the number of instructions executed depends on the primitive type and on the statistical characteristics of the database. Moreover we assume that I_{ki} includes all the processing overhead needed to start the process and to link the results.

From this stil too detailed description we can then get global parameters to represent the *workload profile*. In fact we can define an *average elementary process*, which syntetizes the workload character istics and has an average number of instructions executed given by:

$$I = \sum_{k=1}^{K} p_k \sum_{h_{ki} \in H_k} I_{ki} \qquad (1)$$

and a probability to read (or write) a page during its execution equal to:

$$p_R = \frac{\sum_{k=1}^{K} p_k \sum_{h_{ki} \in H_k} R_{ki}}{\sum_{k=1}^{K} p_k \sum_{h_{ki} \in H_k} R_{ki}+W_{ki}} \quad , \quad p_W = 1-p_R \tag{2}$$

The average elementary process is indeed considered as the workload basic component when modeling the DBM operation. Furthermore the individual transaction types z_k are characterized by the number of average elementary processes they require to execute:

$$N_k = \sum_{h_{ki} \in H_k} R_{ki}+W_{ki} \tag{3}$$

In our study we considered a sample data base with 5 relations, which in the Data Pool organization are stored as 13 domains with a size ranging from 110k to 2880k for a total of 7570K. A set of 10 transactions was selected to represent the workload. The transactions have four different topologies (execution graphs) and a number of elementary process executions N_k ranging from 20 to 426. Moreover the number of instructions executed by the elementary processes (including overhead) I_{ki} ranges from 30000 to 36000.

5. INTERNAL ANALYSIS OF THE DBM

We now consider the DBM in stationary conditions, that is with a fixed population of *average elementary processes*. Actually a process disappears as soon as its execution terminates, but we assume that it is immediately replaced by another one with (statistically) identical characteristics.

This situation can be modeled with a classical queueing network to represent the resource contention between the processes that are executed in parallel, and to compute the utilizations of the relevant resources, PUs, IDDs and busses.

The model for the SB architecture, represented in fig. 6 in the simple case of 2 PUs and 2 IDDs, is a closed queueing network with a fixed population of customers circulating in it. The customers represent the average elementary processes that are currently executed, and are divided in *routing chains* (one for every PU) i.e. subsets of customers each representing the m processes that are multiprogrammed on the same PU.

Every customer cycles around in the network, starting at the PU queue and visiting (one or more times) the other queues before to come back. In fact every cycle represents the execution of an average elementary process that is composed by a PU processing phase plus a mass memory access (read or write), which in turn includes the IDD access and the bus services according to the communication protocol.

The routing is probabilistic, that is when leaving a queue the next one is selected according to fixed probabilities. For instance, when leaving the PU, the different paths corresponding to a read or write access to the mass memory are selected according the the probabilities p_W and p_R computed in sect. 4 for the average process. In turn the probabilities p_{Ri} and p_{Wi} to perform the access on a given IDD depend on the database allocation and on the access ratios of the files storing the domains.

Finally the probability p_H takes into account the advantages of the prepaging policy that consists in reading several contigous pages per access. Clearly p_H depends on the paging factor q, i.e. the number of pages read per access, and for large IDD buffers and large domain size can be expressed as:

$$p_H = \frac{q-1}{q} \qquad (4)$$

Whith the exception of the PUs, all the resources are shared by customers of different routing chains. In fact every queue has several *classes*, both to keep apart customers of different routing chains, and to represent services at the same queue with different service times: for instance short and long messages going through the bus.

The average service times are computed according to the workload profile (sect. 4) and the device characteristics:

- t_p , average service time at the PU queue:

$$t_p = \frac{I}{r_p} \qquad (5)$$

where r_p is the execution rate of the PU.

- t_D , average service time at the IDD queue:

$$t_d = t_a + q \cdot t_t \qquad (6)$$

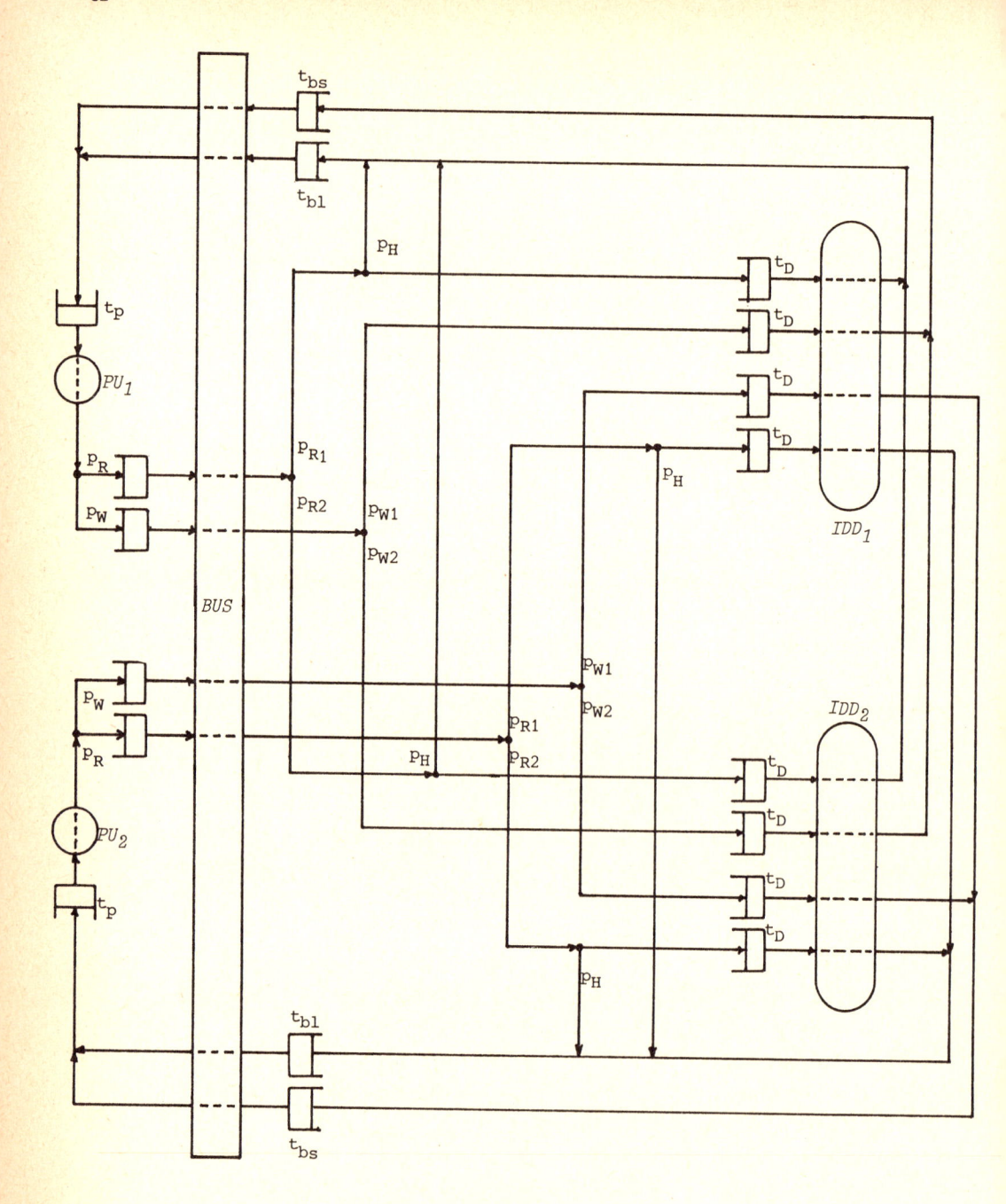

Fig. 6 - Queueing network model for the SB architecture.

where t_a is the average access time and t_t is the transfer time for a single page.

- t_{bs} and t_{bl}, average bus service times for long and short messages:

$$t_{bs} = \frac{l_s}{r_b} \qquad t_{bl} = \frac{l_l}{r_b} \qquad (7)$$

where l_s and l_l are the message lengths and r_b is the Bus transfer rate (including arbitration overhead).

As far as the queueing disciplines are concerned we adopted FCFS (First Come First Served) with exponential service times for the Disk queues, and PS (Processor Sharting), which is the limit case of the Round Robin, for the PUs and the bus. In fact for the PUs PS allows to represent the RR scheduling policy and for the Bus the arbitration mechanism that sends messages by packets. Furthermore with PS we can assume general service time distributions.

In a quite similar way we can also define a model for the MB architecture. Fig. 7 depicts the case of 2 PUs and 2 IDDs. The main difference is that a private bus (and then a bus queue) is provided for every IDD. Moreover all messages are sent in one packet (FCFS queueing discipline), and control messages are not represented.

Both models can be solved without noticeable computational problems, despite of the apparent complexity (10 chains, 30 queues and 90 classes for the MB model with 10 PUs and 10 IDDs). In fact, due to the assumptions we have made on the routing, the queueing discipline and the service time distribution, they are easily solved as product form networks [REIS78,CHAN80].

Numerical results are shown in fig. 8 for the two architectures and for a configuration of 4 PUs and 3 IDDs. We assumed a balanced load situation, in which all PUs have the same multiprogramming level and all the IDDs the same probability to be referenced. Moreover a prepaging with level q = 4 is assumed.

The figure depicts the behaviour of the throughput C_p of the single PU expressed in cycles (average elementary process executions) per second, versus the multiprogramming level m.

According to these results a reasonable value for m ranges between 4 and 7. For lower values the PU throughput C_p sharply decreases, while higher values would give a modest improvement in front of larger memory requirements to accomodate the processes.

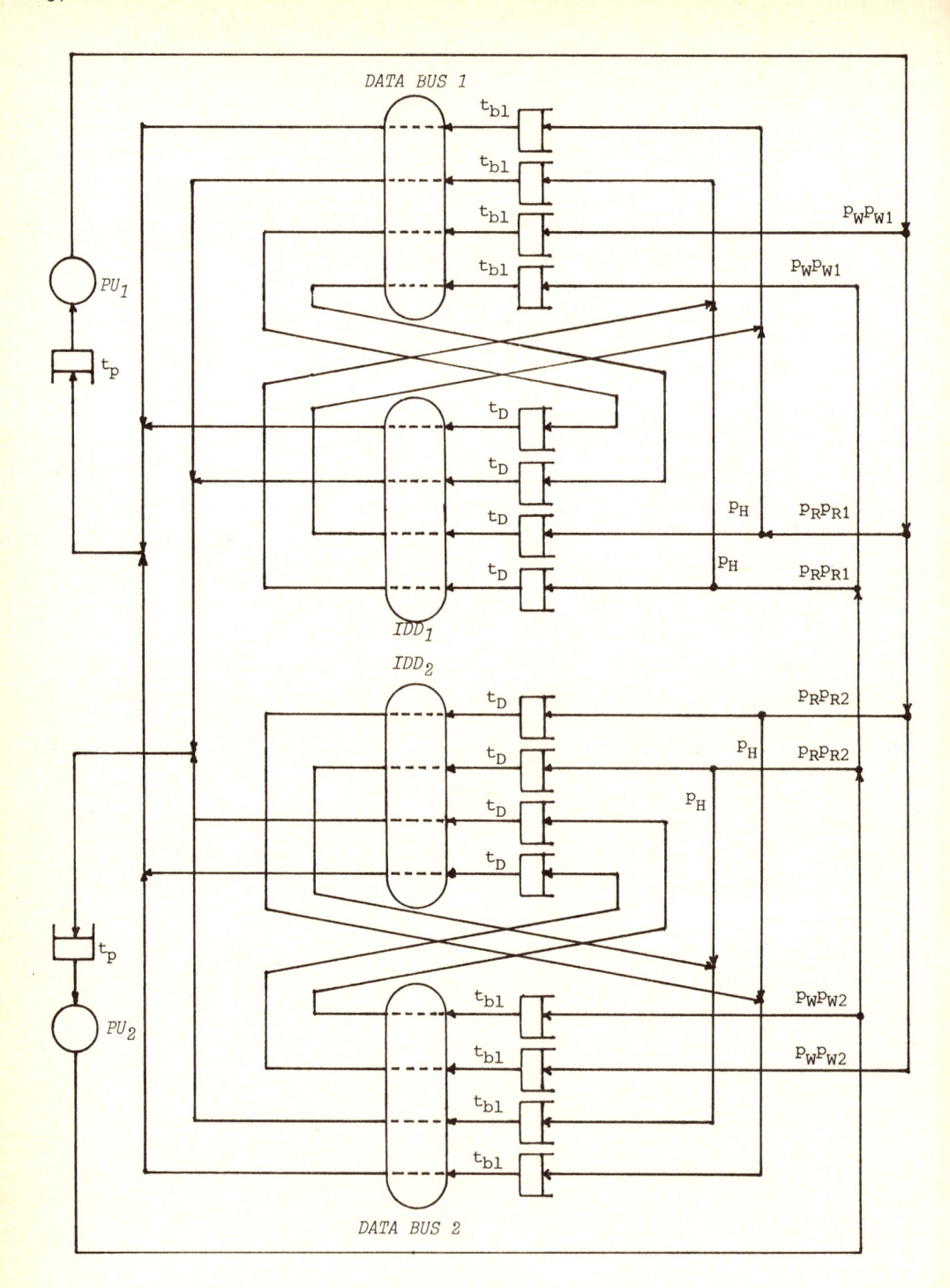

Fig. 7 - Queueing network model for the MB architecture.

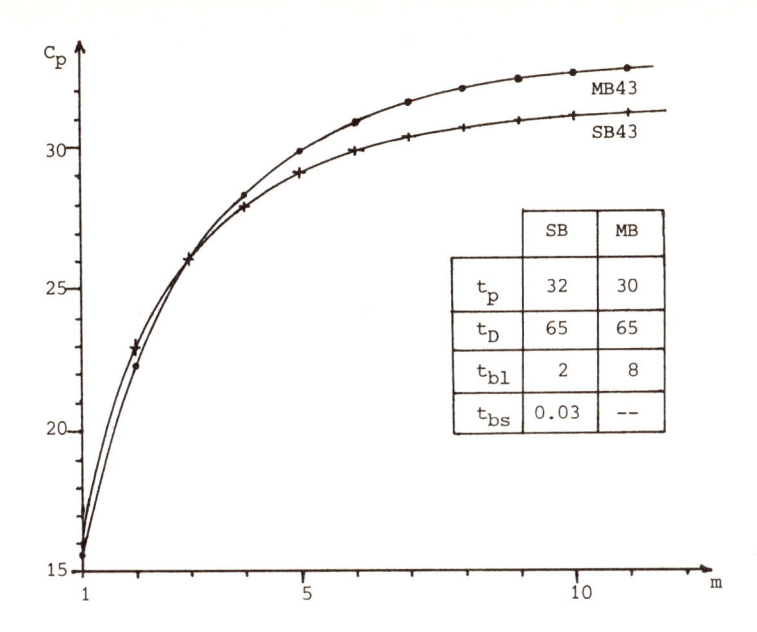

Fig. 8 - Chain throughput vs. multiprogramming level.

One should notice the better performance of the SB architecture for low multiprogramming levels, due to the larger bus service time which results in a shorter queueing time at low congestion levels.

On the other hand the SB has poorer performance for large values of m because of the interference in the accesses to the PU local memory during data pag page transfers. In fact the low transfer rate of the serial data bus allows interleaved memory accesses in the MB architecture, while the high speed Single-Bus requires to stop the PU operation during data transfers. This has been represented in the model with an increase of the PU service time.

6. DEVICE UTILIZATION AND SYSTEM CONFIGURATION

Although we need to solve the queueing networks defined in the previous section to get throughput and the resource utilizations, very useful information for system configuration can be obtained directly from the network topology and the expected service times.

Let us consider a totally symmetric situation of balanced load, equal service time for resources of the same type and identical routing probabilities for all the chains. In these conditions, based on well known results for closed networks, while resource utilizations vary with the chain population m, their ratios are constant. More precisely for every couple of resources a and b the ratio of the utlizations is given by:

$$\frac{u_a}{u_b} = \frac{v_a}{v_b} \frac{t_a}{r_b} \qquad (8)$$

where v_a/v_b is the *visit ratio*, i.e. the number of visits a customer makes on the average to resource a for every visit to resource b, and t_a and t_b are the expected service times.

We can then easily express the ratio between PU and IDD utilizations in the general case of n_p PUs and n_d IDDs. In fact for every PU and every IDD we can write:

$$\frac{u_d}{u_p} = \frac{v_d}{v_p}\frac{t_d}{t_p} = \frac{n_p}{n_d}(p_W + p_R(1-p_H))\frac{t_d}{t_p} = \frac{n_p}{n_d}(1-p_R p_H)\frac{t_d}{t_p} \qquad (9)$$

where the visit ratio (which is the same for both architectures) takes into account both the configuration (n_p, n_d) and the routing probabilities (p_W, p_R, p_H).

Note the effect of the prepaging ($p_H > 0$). One may also explicitely consider the relation between t_d and p_H (4),(6), and express the utilization ratio as a function of the prepaging factor q:

$$\frac{u_d}{u_p} = \frac{n_p}{n_d}(1 - \frac{p_R(q-1)}{q})\frac{t_a+qt_t}{t_p} \qquad (10)$$

Similar expressions can be derived for bus and PU utilizations. In the SB architecture, considering that for every visit to the PU two bus services are required (short and long message), and that all the PUs are utilizing the same bus:

$$\frac{u_p}{u_p} = n_p \frac{t_p}{t_{bs}+t_{bl}} \qquad (11)$$

Instead for the MB architecture one bus is provided for every IDD, and then:

$$\frac{u_d}{u_p} = \frac{n_p}{n_d}\frac{t_p}{t_{bl}} \qquad (12)$$

Equations (9) to (12) are useful for a preliminary step in system configuration. In fact, for given devices characteristics and workload profile, they allow to select the system the ratio between the number of PUs and IDDs, and the prepaging factor that correspond to the desired utilization ratio.

Moreover this kind of analysis allows to identify the system bottleneck, i.e. the resource with the largest (relative) utilization, that determines the maximum throughput of the system.

In particular from equation (11) we can determine the limit in the expansion of the SB architecture. In fact, with the values we considered in sect. 4 and a sufficient number of IDDs, the Bus becomes the system bottleneck for n_p = 15, and then there is no use to increase the number of PUs over this limit. One should note that this is a theoretical bound. Actually a more reasonable limit for the SB architecture is n_p = 6 which corresponds to a Bus utilization of about 30% when the PU utilization is around 90%.

7. GLOBAL PERFORMANCE ANALYSIS

As we announced in section 3, based on the result of the internal analysis we can define an higher level model in which the DBM is represented as a part of a more complex system.

According with the workload description (sec. 4) we assume (fig.9) that a Poisson stream of transactions is arriving to the DBM with an overall rate of r_t. Moreover each of the K transaction types is characterized by arrival frequency p_k and by the work demand N_k, expressed in elementary process executions.

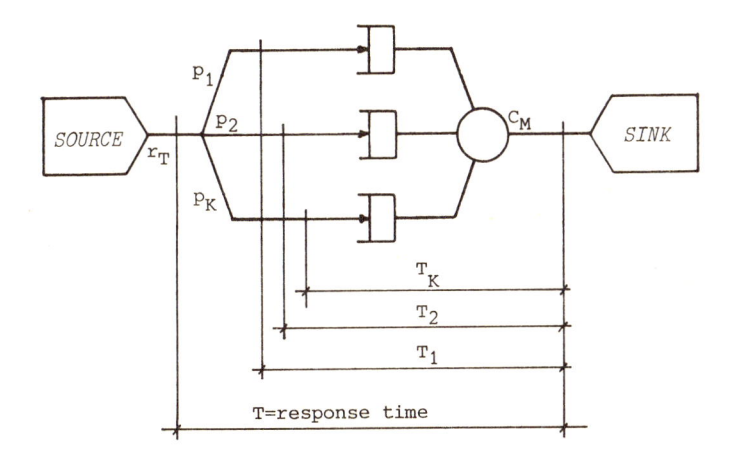

Fig. 9 - The aggregate model.

The DBM is then represented as single service station with fixed service rate C_M expressed by:

$$C_M = n_p C_p \qquad (13)$$

That is the total throughput in elementary processes executed per unit of time.

Note that C_p (and then C_M) depends on the multiprogramming level m. Actually we assume to set a maximum value m_o for m, and that, when at least a transaction is being processed, every PU is working exactly at level m_o. This obviously requires a minimum number of active elementary processes of $m_o \cdot n_p$. This assumption is indeed quite reasonable because of the high parallelism that can be found both at execution graph level and inside the primitives (parallel processing of the pages of the same domain). Moreover the homogeneous multiprocessor architecture allows both to distribute the load to the processors in a balanced way and the sharing of the resources among all the transactions that are executed in parallel.

According to this the model is a classical M/G/1 queue, with PS discipline and K customer classes, and can be easily solved for the transaction respons time:

$$T = \frac{N}{C_M - r_T N} \qquad (14)$$

where N is the average work demand, i.e. the average number of processes executed per transaction:

$$N = \sum_{k=1}^{K} p_k N_k \qquad (15)$$

In fig. 10 the expected transaction response time T is plotted versus the transaction arrival rate r_T for two configurations of the SB architecture. Note the asymptotes corresponding to the *DBM capacity* r_M, i.e. the maximum transaction arrival rate that can be handled by the system:

$$r_M = \frac{C_M}{N} \qquad (16)$$

Aside the expected transaction response time T for the whole transaction mix, we can also compute the expected response time for each transaction type z_k, which, due to the PS discipline is proportional to work demand:

$$T_K = \frac{N_k}{C_M - r_T N} \qquad (17)$$

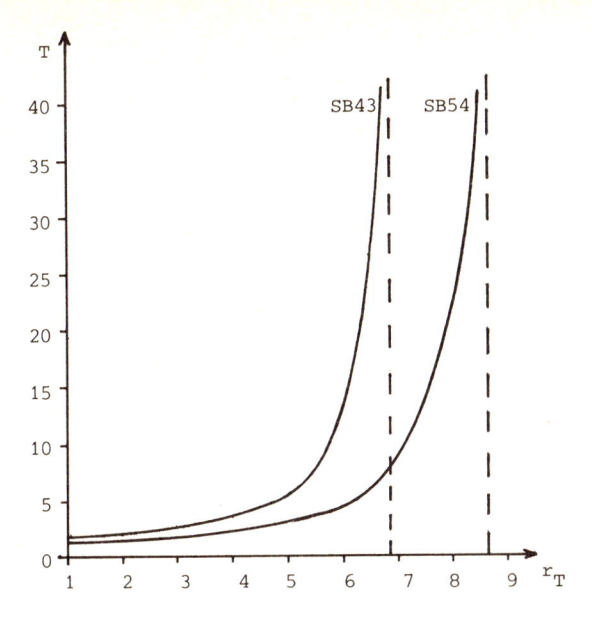

Fig. 10 - Expected transaction response time.

8. CONCLUSIONS

In this paper we have presented a modeling analysis of the performance of the multiprocessor database machine DBMAC.

The study is based on a two level hierarchical model. In the lower level we characterize in a quite detailed way the internal operation of the DBM. This allows both to compare different design alternatives and to obtain quantitative criteria for system configuration.

At the higher level, in a more schematic model, the interaction between the DBM and the environment is represented. We can then get global indices, like transaction response time, to investigate on the relationship between the overall system performance and the workload characteristics.

As far as the modeling methodology is concerned, the result of this study convinced us that analytical models, due to their simple structure and low computational cost, are the most suitable tool for a global analysis of the system structure.

REFERENCES

[BASK75] F. BASKETT, K.M. CHANDY, R.R. MUNTZ and F. PALACIOS-GOMEZ: *Open Closed and Mixed Networks of Queues with Different Classes of Customers*, JACM 22, 2 (Apr. 1975).

[CES82A] F. CESARINI, G. SODA: *An Analysis of the Processes Activated by the Relational Primitives in DBMAC*, DATANET/DBMAC Tech. Rep. 10, 1982.

[CES82B] F. CESARINI, D. DELUCA, G. SODA: *An Assesment of DBMAC Query Processing*, Proc. of II IWDM, San Diego 1982.

[CHAN80] K.M. CHANDY and C.H. SAUER: *Computational Algorithms for Product Form Queueing Networks*, CACM 23, 10 (Oct. 1980).

[MIS82A] M. MISSIKOFF: *A Domain Based Internal Schema for Relational Database Machines*, 1982 ACM/SIGMOD int. Conf. on Data Management Sysyem.

[MIS82B] M. MISSIKOFF, M. TERRANOVA: *The Architecture of DBMAC, a Relational Database Computer*, Proc. of II IWDM, San Diego 1982.

[REIS78] M. REISER and C.H. SAUER: *Queueing Networks Models: Methods of Solution and their Program Implementation*, in K.M.Chandy and R.T.Yen eds., "Current Trends in Programming Methodology", vol. III, Prentice-Hall 1978.

ANALYSIS OF FILTERING EFFICIENCY
IN THE DATABASE MACHINE VERSO

S. Gamerman[*,+], S. Salza[**], M. Scholl[+]

ABSTRACT

The Relational Database Machine VERSO uses a hardware mechanism wich filters data upon its transfer from mass memory to main memory. This paper studies the efficiency of this Filter. A probabilistic modelling approach for evaluating the Filter utilization is introduced. In order to illustrate this approach we perform the analysis for the Union operation under a simple algorithm. The modelling methodology we propose is indeed general and will be used in further studies to analyze the Filter performance on other operations, and in particular Join, which is the most critical one in a relational system.

1. - INTRODUCTION

Access to large amounts of data stored on mass memory is known to be a time consuming task of Database Management Systems (DBMS). In order to ease the problem and improve system performance, the Relational Database Machine VERSO [1] uses an hardware mechanism which filters data upon its transfer from mass storage to main memory. Such a mechanism does not directly save on access and transfer times, but takes advantage of these times for processing data. Therefore processing power is saved as well as channel capacity, since the filtered data volume is much smaller than source data. More precisely the VERSO Filter is a programmable device capable of performing on elementary data blocks of 16 K bytes, not only the unary operations of the Relational Algebra [3] (selection, projection as well as insertion and deletion), but also the binary operations as long as relations are sorted (union, intersection, join, etc.).

The objective of the study reported in this paper is to evaluate and quantify the VERSO Filter's efficiency which for a given operation to be performed, depends both on the architectural choices and on the strategy choosen for implementing the operation.

---

[*] Université Paris Sud, Orsay, France
[**] IASI-CNR, via Buonarroti 12, 00185 Roma, Italia
[+] INRIA, 78153 Le Chesnay Cedex, France

The probalistic modelling approach presented below should allow the VERSO designer to improve the system architecture and should help him in choosing the "best" algorithm for implementing each of the operations listed above.

By "best" algorithm we mean the one which maximizes the filter utilization. Indeed in such I/O bound architectures, the filtering mechanism is much faster than the I/O device (moving head disk). Therefore one should expect the Filter to be idle part of the time. A good algorithm should decrease the Filter idleness and therefore increase its throughput.

The main objective of this paper is to illustrate on the Union operation how one can evaluate the VERSO Filter utilization. One simple algorithm has been choosen for implementing the Union operation. It has been analyzed on the VERSO architecture.

Further studies should apply the same modelling approach to other operations and in particular Join which is the most critical operation of relational systems in terms of performance.

2. - THE VERSO ARCHITECTURE

The VERSO DBM basically includes the following components :

(i) a 68000 processor in charge of the high level DBMS functions; it sends to the controller C, elementary blocks commands (data transfers and filtering operations) and is in charge of the dialogue with the outside world (front-end computer or local network) not represented on the figure :

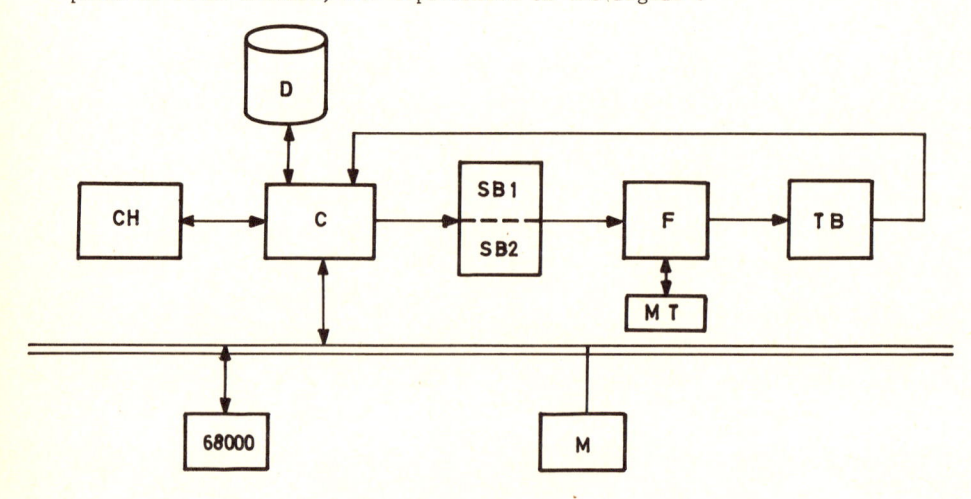

Figure 1 : VERSO architecture

(ii) RAM memory M

(iii) a special purpose controller C (AMD microprogrammable bit slice processor) which controls the filtering process, interfaces the disk and is in charge of all data transfers.

(iv) a hardware Filter F and its memory MT.

(v) a dynamic RAM called Cache (CH) of size 512 K bytes (or possibly 1 M bytes).

(vi) a 300 M bytes moving head Disk storing the database.

(vii) a 32 K bytes Source Buffer SB, and

(viii) a 16 K bytes Target Buffer TB.

For more details on the architecture, the reader is referred to [2].

The data path represented on figure 1 is illustrated by taking the example of selection/projection. In order to perform this operation, the following steps are necessary :

(1) Load into the Filter memory, the program corresponding to the request.

(2) Load from the Disk D into the Source Buffer SB, one block of the relation to be filtered.

(3) The Finite state automaton like Filter scans SB one byte at a time and eventually writes onto TB, the relevant bytes. After SB has been scanned (one single pass), the filtered data are available in TB.

The average filtering cycle time τ (time to read a byte, analyze it and possibly write it onto TB) is 400 ns. The Cache access time is 400 ns while it takes 800 ns to transfer a byte from the Disk to SB.

The Filter does not have to wait until SB is full of data loaded from D, before starting filtering. Its "on the fly" capability allows him to start filtering as soon as a few bytes have been written from D onto SB. Three events may then happen :(a) Either, the Filter stops because the end of the relation is encountered, or (b) SB has been totally scanned, then start again steps 2 and 3, or (c) TB is full of data filtered, then execute step (4) :

(4) TB is emptied either on the Disk (the target relation TR is a new Database relation), or on the Cache (TR is an intermediate result) or, on the 68000 processor RAM memory M (final result to be sent to the user).

Once TB has been emptied, filtering can be resumed (step 2 and 3).

Observe that the source relation to be filtered may be an intermediate result stored on the Cache, then in step 2 the source buffer SB is loaded from the Cache. If the Cache happens to be full, then some space is freed by emptying part of the Cache content onto the disk.

For performing a binary operation such as Union, Join, etc. SB is divided into two Source Buffers SB1 and SB2 of size 16 K into which the two input relations are loaded. The following section precisely describes which algorithm has been choosen for Union.

3. - THE UNION ALGORITHM

We want to perform the Union between two Base Relations R1 and R2, initially stored on the Disk, and assume the Target Relation R3 is also to be stored on the Disk.

We choose to divide the Cache into two parts C1 and C2 of fixed size and to initially load C2 with part of Source Relation R2, while C1 stores the Target Relation. If during the operation C1 becomes full, it is emptied onto the Disk. If C2 becomes empty it is loaded again from the Disk.

Moreover, to deaden the negative impact of the access times (seek+latency), we also decide that all the data transfers from/to the Disk are performed block by block where a block is the content of a Disk track, of size 16 K bytes.

While performing the Union the Filter is either idle or in one of the two following phases :

a) Working on the fly with the Cache : i.e. filtering while SB2 is loaded from C2.
b) Working on the fly with the Disk : i.e. filtering while SB1 is loaded from the Disk.

Such active phases end when one of the following events happens, and triggers the appropriate data transfers to start a new active phase :

(i)   TB becomes full

   - If SB1 is still under loading from the Disk, then continue the transfer until the end of the block.
   - Empty TB onto C1 (this possibly requires first to unload C1 onto the disk).
   - Start phase a.

(ii) SB1 becomes empty

- Start an access on the Disk to get the following block of relation R1. In parallel unload TB and, if time is left, load SB2 from C2.
- When access time is over, start phase b.

(iii) SB2 becomes empty

- If SB1 is still under loading, finish up loading.
- Then start phase a.

4. - THE FILTER UTILIZATION

While performing Union, during every cycle (of duration τ=400 ns) of its busy period, the Filter reads one byte from SB1 and one byte from SB2, compares them and writes the smallest in TB. If, say, the smallest byte comes from SB1 during the following cycle the Filter will have to read again the same byte from SB2 and compare it with the following byte of SB1.

Let us now denote by q the probability that the two bytes compared by the Filter are equal, q is a statistical characteristic of the couple of relations R1 and R2. We assume q is always the same for every comparison. Then, during every cycle, with probability q one byte is read from both sources, with probability (1-q)/2 one byte is read from SB1 only, and with probability (1-q)/2 one byte is read from SB2 only. In all cases one byte per cycle is written onto TB.

Such a byte level description is, in fact, too detailed for our purpose and, as we shall see later, would lead to computationally untractable models. Therefore we decide to decrease the granularity of the representation and to consider a group of m bytes, that we call a page, as the elementary unit. Then we extend to the page level the statistical description we gave above. The time too is then divided into slots of size σ=m.τ, where a slot is the time needed to transfer a page from C2 to SB2 (or from TB to C1), while it takes two slots to transfer a page from (to) the Disk.

Now if we assume that the two Source Relations R1 and R2 have the same size of N blocks and that n is the granularity, i.e. the number of pages in a block, then according to the above discussion, the expected size of the Target Relation is N*(2-q)*n pages, and the expected time the Filter is busy during the Union operation is :

$$E[t_f] = N*(2-q)*n*\sigma \qquad (1)$$

However a significant additional time is spent loading from and unloading onto the Disk the Buffers and the Cache and performing accesses on the Disk. The actual execution time of the operation t_u is then significantly larger than t_f. Note that, while t_f depends only on the size N of the input relations, t_u largely depends on the algorithm utilized to perform the operation.

Therefore we introduce the Filter utilization :

$$\alpha = \frac{E[t_f]}{E[t_u]} \qquad (2)$$

as a performance index to measure the effectiveness of the algorithm.

Assuming null access times on the Disk and infinite Buffers sizes, the utilization α is always bounded by the transfer rate of the Disk, where the relations are coming from (and finally going to). Therefore for all algorithms, an upper bound of α is :

$$\alpha_{MAX} = \frac{(2-q)*N}{4*N+2*(2-q)*N} = \frac{2-q}{2*(4-q)} \qquad (3)$$

where, the denominator represents the time to read the two Source Relations from the Disk, while filtering on the fly (the unit of time being the time needed to filter a block) and to write back the target relation while the numerator is the net filtering time (1). Therefore, depending on the value of q, α_{MAX} is ranging between 1/4 and 1/6.

The utilization is considerably improved if we assume the operation is performed on intermediate relations originally stored in the Cache, and that the Target Relation is also to be written onto the Cache. In this case an upper bound for α is :

$$\alpha'_{MAX} = \frac{(2-q)*N}{2*N+(2-q)*N} = \frac{2-q}{4-q} \qquad (4)$$

which gives 1/2 for q=0 and 1/3 for q=1.

5. - THE PROBALISTIC PERFORMANCE MODEL

In order to evaluate the Filter utilization α for the algorithm we proposed in section 3 we need to compute the expectation of the execution time, $E[t_u]$. t_u can be seen as a sequence of phases of the following kinds (figure 2) :

(a) D→Cache : C2 is loaded from the Disk with N2 blocks of R2. This phase occurs every time C2 becomes empty (C2' content has been totally loaded in SB and filtered).

b) **Cache→D** : every time C1 is full (N1 blocks of the target relation have been produced by the Filter), its content is moved to the Disk.

c) **Processing** : in between the two phases a and b processing can resume, i.e. blocks are loaded both from C2 and the Disk respectively into SB2 and SB1, filtering is performed and periodically TB is unloaded into C1.

```
--| D→C2 | Processing | C1→D | Processing | D→C2
  |------|------------|------|------------|------
```

Figure 2 : Filtering phases

Then, grouping all the phases of the same kind together, we can write :

$$E[t_u] = N*T_D + N*(2-q)*T_D + E[t_p] + (n_a + n_b)*E[t_a] \quad (5)$$

where $T_D = n*2*\sigma$ is the time needed to transfer a block from/to the Disk, and t_a is the Disk access time (seek+latency).

The first two terms in (5) represent the total time needed to transfer the Source Relation R2 and the Target Relation between the Disk and the Cache (phase a and b). The fourth term accounts for all the access times performed during phase a and b, where n_a and n_b denote the number of times phases a and b are repeated :

$$n_a = \frac{N}{N2} \qquad n_b = \frac{N*(2-q)}{N1} \quad (6)$$

Finally $E[t_p]$ represents the total time spent in the processing phase, and can be expressed as :

$$E[t_p] = \frac{N*(2-q)*n}{\lambda} \quad (7)$$

where λ is the Filter average processing rate, i.e. the average number of pages written into TB per unit of time during the processing phase (recall the unit of time is the time needed to transfer a page from the Cache to SB2 $\sigma = m.\tau$).

5.1. - The infinite Cache model

To compute the average processing rate λ we can consider a simplified model with an infinite Cache, initially loaded with the Source Relation R2, and where the Target Relation can entirely be stored. Under these assumptions phases a and b (C1→D and D→C2) of figure 2 vanish and the Filter is always in the processing phase.

We can then give an analytical solution to such a model under stationary conditions, i.e. we assume relations of infinite size are filtered and we represent the Filter operation through a suitable stochastic process which allows us to compute λ.

We define the state $s=(n_1,n_2,n_3)$ of the system as having the following three components (see figure 3) :

- n_1 : number of pages still to be read by the Filter in SB1.
- n_2 : number of pages still to be read by the Filter in SB2.
- n_3 : number of pages written into TB.

In order to simplify the structure of the process we observe the system (the Filter and the Buffers) only at particular time instants τ_i i=0,1,..., where one of the following events happens :

(i) The Filter starts working on the fly with the Disk
(ii) The Filter starts working on the fly with the Cache.

According to the previous assumptions, the states s_i form a stochastic process $\mathcal{P} = \{s_i; i=1,2,...\}$ with state space S. More precisely $\mathcal{P}$ is a Markov Renewal Process [4], since it may be proved that :

1) The transition probabilities p_{sr} to have a transition from the state s to the state r only depend on the current state.

2) The sojourn time t_{sr}, i.e. the time spent in state s before a transition to state r occurs, has a distribution depending only on the current state and the next state.

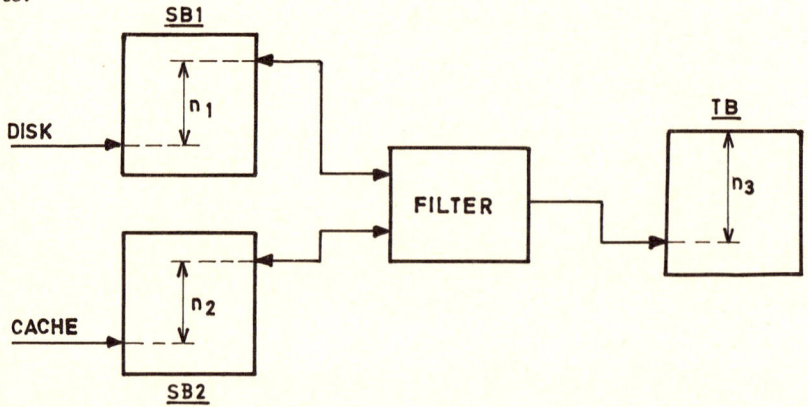

Figure 3 : State of the system : $s = (n_1,n_2,n_3)$

These conditions are indeed verified in our case because of the structure itself of our model, and the simplifying assumptions we have made, as we shall see in the following section.

5.2. - The State Space and the transition probabilities

From the above definition one can easily understand that the number of states quickly grows with the granularity n, i.e. as the number of pages per block increases. This is indeed the main reason we had to decrease the granularity from the byte level to the page level. Such an approximation is however justified by the numerical results which show a very fast convergence with n (see sect. 6).

A first obvious bound to the number of states in n^3, but with the additional hypothesis that the Disk access time can be assumed deterministic and equal to n slots, the number of states is reduced to :

$$card(S) = n^2 + 2n - 1 \qquad (8)$$

In fact the state space S is divided into two subsets of states that correspond to the above mentioned events (i) and (ii) (see previous page).

- **Disk States** : These are the states where the Filter starts working on the fly with the Disk, and the Target Buffer TB has been completely emptied during the Disk access time ($t_a = n*\sigma$). Therefore we just have n states according to the following constraints on the state components :

$$n_1 = n_3 = 0 \qquad 0 < n_2 <= n \qquad (9)$$

- **Cache States** : The Filter just starts working on the fly with the Cache. This may happen either because TB became full and was previously emptied, or because SB2 became empty while the Filter was working on the fly with the Disk. The total number of such states in $n^2 + n-1$ according to the following inequalities, that can be proved considering the way the process is entering the Cache states :

$$\begin{array}{ll} 0 < n_1 <= n \;, & 0 <= n_2 < n \\ 0 \leq n_3 \leq n \;, & n_2 * n_3 = 0 \\ n_1 + n_2 <= n \;, & \text{if } n_3 <> 0 \text{ then } n_1 + n_3 >= n \end{array} \qquad (10)$$

To compute the transition probabilities a transition tree is then built for every state i S, to represent all the possible "histories" i.e. all the evolutions of the Buffers that can take place during a stay of the process in state i before the next transition occurs.

The root of the tree is state i. After one time slot, several events may occur (one page has been read from SB1 or from SB2 or from both). To each event corresponds one edge from the root to an internal node, the probability of the event being attached to the edge (resp. $(1-q)/2$, $(1-q)/2$ or q). Then the process starts again until a state $j \in S$ is reached : the leaves of the tree correspond to all states j that can be reached from state i in one transition. To each transition $i \rightarrow j$ corresponds a path in the tree of lengh t_{ij} time slots where t_{ij} is the sojourn time in state i given a transition occurs into j. The corresponding transition probability p_{ij} can be computed as the product of the probabilities attached to each edge in the path.

According to the previous outline a simple recursive procedure has been built that generates for a given granularity the two matrices :

$$P = \{p_{ij}\} \qquad T = \{t_{ij}\} \qquad i,j \in S \tag{11}$$

of the transition probabilities and the sojourn times.

Moreover within the same algorithm a third matrix is computed :

$$B = \{b_{ij}\} \qquad i,j \in S \tag{12}$$

whose elements b_{ij} represent the number of pages filtered (i.e. written into TB) during the transition from i to j.

5.3. - The Average Processing rate

We can now solve the process $\mathcal{P}$ for the relative number of visits v_i to state $i \in S$, which is defined as the probability that the next transition occurs into a state i. The v_i are just the equilibrium probabilities of the Embedded Markov Chain of the process $\mathcal{P}$, i.e. a discrete time chain with the same space S and the same transition matrix P than the process $\mathcal{P}$.
Therefore the v_i can be simply computed as the solution of the redundant system of linear equations :

$$\begin{cases} v_i = \Sigma_j v_j * p_{ji} & i \in S \\ \Sigma_i v_i = 1 \end{cases} \tag{13}$$

Once the relative number of visits is known we can finally compute the average processing rate :

$$\lambda = \frac{\Sigma_i v_i * b_i}{\Sigma_i v_i * t_i} \qquad (14)$$

as the ratio between the expected number of pages filtered during the sojourn time in a state, and the expected sojourn time, where :

$$b_i = \Sigma_j p_{ij} * b_{ij} \qquad i \in S \qquad (15)$$

is the expected number of pages filtered during a visit to the state i, and :

$$t_i = \Sigma_j p_{ij} * t_{ij} \qquad i \in S \qquad (16)$$

is the expected sojourn time in state i.

6. - DISCUSSION

6.1. - Infinite Cache model

The computation of the average processing rate is possible as long as the granularity n is not too large. As a matter of fact the basic complexity lies in the solution of the system of linear equations (13) which has the order equal to the cardinality of state space (8).

Table 1 gives λ for different values of the probability q and of the number n of pages in a block.

n \ q	0	.25	.5	.75
2	.382	.342	.309	.280
4	.370	.338	.307	.281
8	.367	.337	.305	.279

Table 1 : Average processing rate λ as a function of q for various values of n

One should note that, mostly for high values of q, λ converges extremely quickly with n. As a matter of fact n=8 proves to be already satisfactory in every case. This keeps the cardinality of the state space under 80, and therefore makes the system (13) solvable with any classical numerical method.

The average processing rate λ is also plotted in figure 4 as a function of q for a granularity of n=8. As one should expect λ decreases as q increases, because a larger value of q implies on the average more pages are read from the Source Buffers SB1 and SB2 for every page written into the Target Buffer TB, and half of the pages are coming from the Disk. Therefore both the Disk access times and the transfer rate at a speed which is half that of the Filter bring λ down.

The minimum value $\lambda=1/4$ is attained for q=1. In this case the Filter, according to the algorithm of sect. 3, is cyclically performing the following phases :

(i)   Filter on the fly with the Disk (2n slots)
(ii) Unload TB (n slots)
(iii) Load SB2 from the Cache (n slots).

At the end of the first phase a block is written onto TB and the contents of SB1 and SB2 are completely consumed. Then a Disk access has to be started. It takes one revolution of the Disk. So there is time to unload TB and load SB2, then phase (i) can resume. Thus because one block is obtained every four slots, the Filter actually works 1/4 of the time.

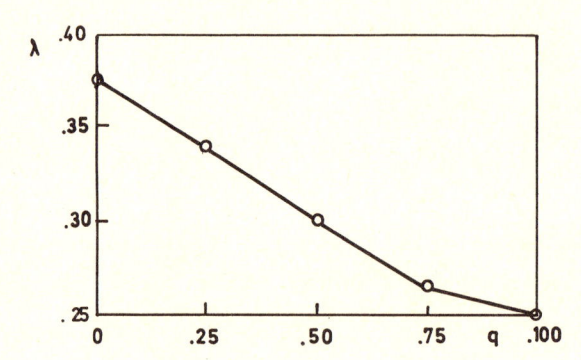

Figure 4 : Average processing rate versus q

The maximum value of $\lambda=.37$ is reached for q=0, and is still rather low. In fact, due to the finite size of the Buffers and to the transfer speed of the Disk, almost two thirds of the time is spent emptying TB into the Cache and filling SB1, while the Filter is idle. One should anyway notice that λ has an upper bound of 1/2, due to the fact that also in the infinite Cache model one Relation is coming from the Disk.

In summary the analysis suggests improvements to the architecture. A larger parallelism between data transfers would subtantially increase λ.

6.2. - Filter Utilization

Figure 6 depicts the behaviour of the Filter utilization which, as we pointed out in sect. 4, is the main performance measure to evaluate both the system configuration and the algorithm.

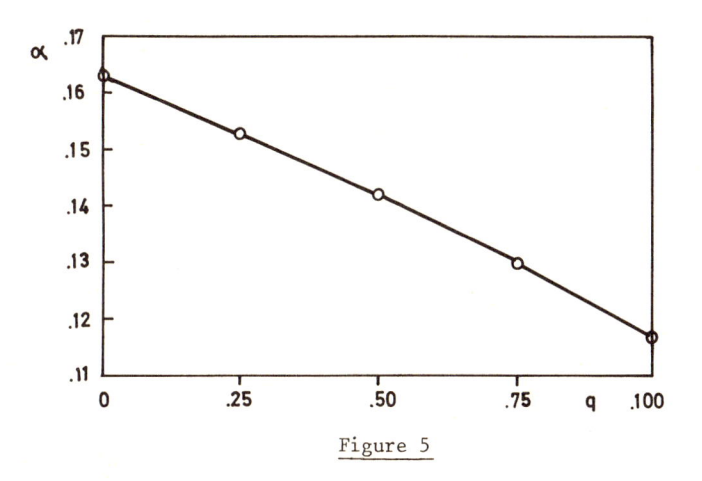

Figure 5

The results refer to the case of a Cache of size M=512 KB. The size N1 and N2 of the two parts of the Cache C1 and C2 where computed, for every value of q, in order to minimize the expression (see (6)) :

$$n_a + n_b = \left\lceil \frac{N}{N_1} \right\rceil + \left\lceil \frac{N*(2-q)}{M-N_1} \right\rceil \tag{14}$$

Moreover the Disk access time $E[t_a]$ is 30 ms (23.5 ms for seek and 6.5 ms for latency). This time is assumed for the accesses due to Cache loading/unloading. Instead, within the infinite Cache model, according to the hypothesis of sect. 5, the access time is considered to be deterministic and equal to n slots :

$$E[t_a] = n*\sigma = 16K*\tau = 6.5 \text{ ms} \tag{15}$$

which in turn is equal to the latency time. This makes this assumption quite reasonable, because during the processing phase two consecutive blocks of Relation R1 accessed on the Disk are very likely to be on the same cylinder.

Figure 6 illustrates the Filter utilization as a function of the Cache size. A larger Cache obviously improves the utilization because it decreases the number of transfers between the Cache and the Disk. The improvement on Filter utilization is negligible after a given Cache size (in our case, between .5 MB and 1 MB) has been reached.

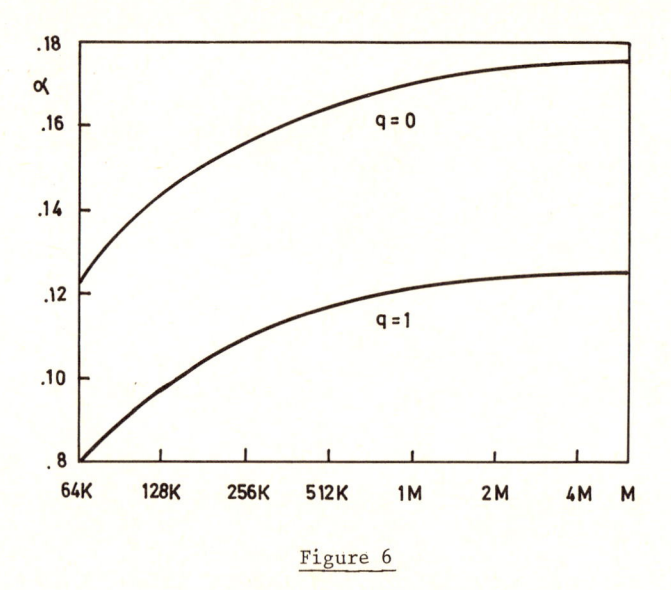

Figure 6

According to these results the Filter utilization is indeed very low : the Filter is idle almost 80 % of the time. However this is mostly due to the architectural constraints and, with regard to the bound (3) of sect. 4, we can conclude that the proposed algorithm is performing relatively well.

7. - SUMMARY

We studied in this paper the efficiency of the hardware Filter in the Relational DBM VERSO. The main objective of this study was to introduce a modelling approach for evaluating the Filter's throughput rate or utilization α. In order to illustrate this approach we chose to evaluate α for the Union operation. The maximum achievable throughput rate for this operation was shown to be less than 1/2. A simple algorithm for Union was analyzed under this approach. The Filter' utilization with this algorithm turned out to be low ($\alpha < 20$ %). Although one should not expect a significant improvement with better Union algorithms, this should be proved by applying the same modelling approach on other algorithms. Such a modelling approach will also be used in further studies for evaluating the Filter'utilization for other operations than Union and in particular Join wich is the most critical operation of relational systems.

REFERENCES

[1] F. Bancilhon and M. Scholl, "Design of a Backend Processor for a Database Machine", Proceedings of the ACM-SIGMOD Conference, Santa Monica, California, May 14-16, 1980.

[2] F. Bancilhon, D. Fortin, S. Gamerman, J.M. Laubin, P. Richard, M. Scholl, D. Tusera and A. Verroust, "A Relational Back-end Database Machine", Proceedings of the International Workshop on Database Machine, San Diego, California, September 1982.

[3] J.D. Ullman, "Principles of Database Systems", Computer Science Press, New York, 1980.

[4] E. Cinlar, "Introduction to Stochastic Processes", Prentice-hall, Englewood Cliffs, N.J., 1975.

EXPERIMENTS IN BENCHMARKING RELATIONAL DATABASE MACHINES

Robert Bogdanowicz, Michael Crocker, David K. Hsiao,
Curtis Ryder, Vincent Stone, and Paula Strawser
Naval Postgraduate School
Monterey, CA 93940

ABSTRACT

The goal of the work reported here is to develop a machine-independent methodology for benchmarking database machines. As an initial step, performance measurement experiments are being conducted on a relational database machine. The experimental environment is described. Results from an application of the methodology are reported. The results not only are indicative of the machine performance, but also characterize the methodology for benchmarking.

1. INTRODUCTION

With the advent of database machines, there is a new field of application for benchmarks. One application is the comparative evaluation of alternative database machine architectures. It is this application which interests us. We are currently conducting research with the goal of developing a methodology for benchmarking database machines.

As a part of our research, we have been experimenting with a relational database machine. Our goal in these experiments is not to make a definitive pronouncement on the performance of the machine, but to learn how to design benchmarks and interpret measurements. We have programmed a database generation tool to build artificial relations. We have designed and run benchmark experiments using artificial databases.

In the remainder of this section, we discuss the design goals for a methodology for benchmarking database machines. In the next section of this paper, we briefly describe our proposed methodology. In the remaining sections, we discuss our experience in benchmarking a relational database machine.

1.1. Design Decisions for Database Machine Benchmarks

The essence of benchmarking is the construction of the workload model. Historically, workload models have been constructed either by selecting portions of the real workload, or by designing an

---

The work reported here was supported Contract N00015-75-C-0573 from the Office of Naval Research, by the Naval Postgraduate School, Monterey, California, and by DPSCWEST, Pacific Missile Test Center, Pt. Mugu, California.

artificial workload model based on observed characteristics of the real workload. This practice results in benchmarks which are machine-specific and application-specific.

Some researchers [Knut71, Flyn74] have proposed workload models which attempt to characterize a "typical" workload in terms of a mix of statements in some high-level language. The characterization of a "typical" workload is again based on observations of existing applications. By constructing the model in a high-level language, we achieve machine independence. However, whether the workload is "typical" is hard to measure.

The characterization of workload for a database machine is a two-dimensional problem. We must model the database as well as the applications. Also, it is likely that neither a typical database nor a standard set of applications which we wish to benchmark will exist.

Since our goal is comparative evaluation of alternative machine architectures, our methodology must be machine-independent. The methodology must also be database-independent and application-independent, so that it can be used to benchmark machines with or without existing databases and applications.

1.1.1. Machine-Independence

First let us restrict the class of database machine architectures which we expect to benchmark. We exclude from our study those special-purpose architectures designed to support specific types of applications, such as text retrieval. We are interested in those architectures which support a variety of database management applications.

We will also restrict the scope of the research to the relational database machines. There are two very pragmatic reasons for this restriction. First, the problem is difficult without the complication of translation between data models. Second, there is a long list of proposed architectures for database machines based on the relational model. This list includes RAP, RARES, CASSM, DIRECT, CAFS, LEECH, DBMAC, VERSO, RDBM, SABRE, and ICL.

The machines on the list above represent a variety of proposed architectures. But we require that our methodology be machine-independent. Haynes [Hayn82] suggests that database machines are a special case of high-level language computers. The database machine implements the data definition and data manipulation primitives of the query language. In order to avoid biasing the benchmark toward a particular hardware architecture, we will design our benchmark programs for a <u>virtual relational database machine</u>, with operations defined by the query language.

1.1.2. Application-Independence

The workload will be modeled as a collection of statements or queries in a relational data manipulation language. The <u>benchmark kernals</u> will include retrieve, update, insert, and delete operations, each with an implicit restriction operation. Retrieve operations may also be combined with projection and join operations. The usual aggregation operations, sum, average, min, and max, as well as operations which effect partition and ordering are included.

Sets of queries will be designed to measure the effects of controlled variance of workload parameters. These parameters reflect not only the operations being performed, but also information about the underlying relations. Parameters such as the number of predicates used to express a restriction reflect work which must be done by the database processor(s). Parameters which express information about the underlying relations, for example the proportion of the relation which must be examined and the proportion which is actually used in constructing the reply, reflect the work which must be done in accessing the database.

2. A BENCHMARKING EXPERIMENT

A series of measurement experiments is being conducted on a relational database machine. The object of the experiments is to learn how to design benchmark programs for relational database machines and to learn how to interpret the benchmark measurements. First we describe the environment in which the experiments are being conducted. We then describe our database model.

2.1. The Environment

The tools available for constructing benchmark experiments are those provided by the host software interface and the host operating system. The implementation of the benchmark experiments is restricted to those tools available. Here we describe the environment in which our experiments were conducted. We first describe the backend database machine. We then discuss the host software interface and the available measurement tools.

2.1.1. A Relational Database Machine Architecture

Figure 1 shows a typical microprocessor-based database computer organized around a high-speed bus. The major database processor, which is microprocessor-based, supervises command execution, manages system resources, and performs those database management functions not assigned to the auxiliary processor. The auxiliary database processor, built from special-purpose hardware, performs a restricted subset of the database management functions. It can process data at disk transfer rates. It can operate as a filter or as an auxiliary processor.

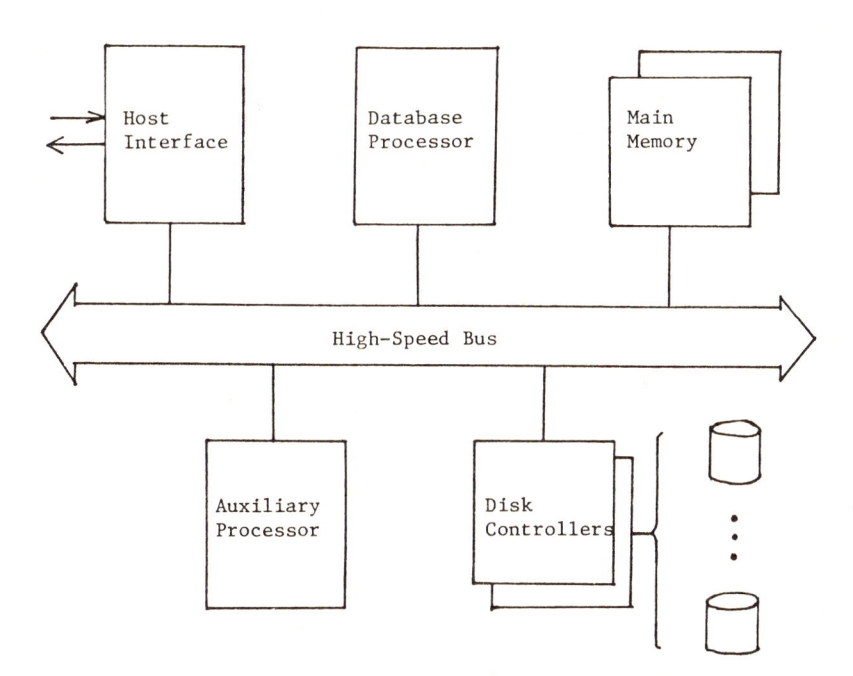

Figure 1: The Basic Configurarion of a Relational Database Machine

The machine with which we have been experimenting has the same basic organization. It is configured with one disk controller and two 600 Mbyte disks. The amount of memory has varied from .5 Mbytes to 2 Mbytes. We have also experimented with configurations with and without the auxiliary processor.

2.1.2. The Host Software Interface

Database machine technology is still in the early stages of development. There are certain tools, such as high-level language interfaces, report writers, and accounting packages, which one expects to find in a finished product. However, in the experimental stages, these tools may not be available. Such was the case in our environment.

The only tool available when we began designing our experiments was the interactive query language interface. We were limited to running query scripts at terminals. An operating system facility allowed us to use pre-defined terminal scripts, eliminating the variability of terminal think time. We were able to eliminate most of the parse-time variability by using pre-parsed commands, stored in the database. Some variability is introduced by the query post-processor, which formats data for display on the screen. This variability is not significant within query sets.

2.1.3. The Measurement Tools

The performance index which we chose for these experiments is response time. The host operating system provided no facility to interactively access the host system clock. We were therefore limited to measuring elapsed time from the database machine clock, which has a resolution of 1/60th second. No software probes were available to monitor CPU and I/O activities in the database machine. Hardware probes also were not available to us.

We are interested in learning about the effect of varying certain parameters on database machine performance, not in absolute performance measurement. By calculating the mean response time over a number of trials, we can increase the precision of our measurements. We therefore conclude that the rough measurements are adequate for our purposes.

2.2. The Database Characteristics

Three sets of parameters must be considered in modeling the database. The first set of parameters relates to database size. The number of relations in the database, the widths of the tuples, and the number of tuples per relation determine database size. The second set of parameters relates to the structure of the data within the database. The number and types of attribute values in a tuple and the distributions of attribute values partially determine the database structure. The third set of parameters relates both to database size and to database structure. This is the set of indices in the database.

We have built a database generation tool which is used to generate relations based on the first two sets of parameters. The index structure will be varied dynamically during the execution of the benchmark programs. The database generation tool and the database built for the benchmark experiments are described in the following sections.

2.2.1. The Database Generation Tool

The prototype database generation tool supports integer and character-string data types. Through an interactive interface, the user can request the generation of an arbitrary number of tuples of fixed length and fixed format. The user defines the format attribute-by-attribute in response to prompts.

The user may choose from several alternative methods of value generation. Integer values may be generated sequentially or randomly within a specified range. Uniqueness of random values may be assured. Character strings in collating sequence may also be chosen. Values may be chosen from enumerated domains randomly or according to a discrete distribution specified by the user. For the prototype, discrete distributions are limited to multiples of 5%.

The prototype was designed and implemented with a limited set of alternatives. However, the tool is modular, so that adding alternatives such as exponential or normal distributions would be simple. We expect, however, that the set of alternatives supplied in the prototype is sufficient to model the proportions required for our benchmarks.

2.2.2. The Experimental Database

Using the database generator, we generated artificial relations for use in our experiments. First we chose tuple lengths. We assume that the unit of disk access is a block in some multiple of 1K-bytes. We selected tuple lengths of 2000, 1000, 200, and 100 bytes. The idea is that contrasting the same operations performed on relations with different numbers of tuples per block would give some measure of processor overhead versus I/O time. For the particular machine used in these experiments, a unit of disk access is a 2K-byte block, so that the tuple sizes provide a range of 1 to 20 tuples per block.

The choice of number of tuples was arbitrary. We defined a "small" relation as one containing 500 tuples. A "large" relation we defined as containing 10,000 tuples. As intermediate sizes, we chose 1000, 2500, and 5000 tuples/relation.

A standard template was designed for each tuple size. A portion of each template is also standard. Figure 2 illustrates the standard tuple templates.

100-byte tuple width		200-byte tuple width		1000-byte tuple width		2000-byte tuple width	
ATTRIBUTE NAME	TYPE	ATTRIBUTE NAME	TYPE	ATTRIBUTE NAME	TYPE	ATTRIBUTE NAME	TYPE
key	i4	key	i4	key	i4	key	i4
mirror	c11	mirror	c11	mirror	c11	mirror	c11
rand	i4	rand	i4	rand	i4	rand	i4
uniqrand	i4	uniqrand	i4	chars	c63	chars	c79
chars	c4	chars	c4	p5	c9	p5	c9
letter	c1	letter	c1	p10	c9	p10	c9
p5	c9	p5	c9	p20	c9	p20	c9
p10	c9	p10	c9	p25	c9	p25	c9
p20	c9	p20	c9	p30	c9	p30	c9
p25	c9	p25	c9	p35	c9	p40	c9
p35	c9	p30	c9	p40	c9	p50	c9
p50	c9	p35	c9	p45	c9	p60	c9
p75	c9	p40	c9	p50	c9	p70	c9
p80	c9	p45	c9	p60	c9	p75	c9
		p50	c9	p65	c9	p80	c9
		p55	c9	p70	c9	p90	c9
		p60	c9	p75	c9	p100	c9
		p65	c9	p80	c9	up10	uc255
		p70	c9	p85	c9	up20	uc255
		p75	c9	p90	c9	up25	uc255
		p80	c9	p100	c9	up50	uc255
		p85	c9	up10	uc255	up75	uc255
		p90	c9	up25	uc255	up80	uc255
		p100	c9	up50	uc255	up100	uc255

Figure 2: Standard Tuple Templates for the Database

Each template contains a sequential integer attribute, a random integer attribute, and a unique random integer attribute. The sequential and random integer attributes can be used to enforce different orderings of the same data. Each template also contains attributes specified with values in a specified discrete distribution over a number of enumerated values.

As an example of the discrete distribution, consider the "P5" attribute shown in each tuple template in Figure 2. The "P5" attribute values are generated with uniform distribution over twenty (20) enumerated values. A retrieval with a restriction consisting of an equality predicate on one of those attribute values will return 5% of the tuples in the relation. If the values are generated in blocks and an index is built on those values, the number of blocks of data accessed from the disk can also be accurately predicted. Discrete distributions can be used to approximate other distributions, such as the normal or exponential.

2.3. The Benchmark Query Sets

Our initial approach to defining benchmark queries was to concentrate on a set of operations. Given the set of operations, we generated questions about how varying a given factor or factors would affect performance.

As an example, consider retrieve operations with projection. How much work is involved in projection; is it less than the savings realized by transmitting fewer data to the host? All other things being constant, is the amount of work involved in projection more closely related to the number of attributes being projected or the volume of data being projected? How does permuting the order of attributes in the target list affect response times?

Generating the benchmark queries, then, is a process of considering how to use the structure of the relations in the database to answer these questions. By contrasting retrieval operations that retrieve the entire tuple with retrieval operations that project on the same tuples, we can answer the first question. Queries that project certain proportions of the tuple based on number and length of attributes can be formulated to provide answers to the second question. Some regular strategy, such as rotating the order of the attributes in the target list, can be adopted to gather information relating to the third question.

In the next section of the paper, we describe some of the benchmark experiments conducted and give an interpretation of the results.

3. EXPERIMENTAL RESULTS

In the sections which follow, we report the results of some benchmark experiments and supply interpretations of the results. Except as noted, the results reported here are from tests on the system configured with 2-megabyte main memory and the optional auxiliary processor. The tests were run at non-prime times in order to reduce variability due to host system workload.

3.1. Selection and Projection Experiments

3.1.1. Varying the Volume of Data Retrieved

Simple queries to select 5% of the tuples of the relation were run against twenty relations with various tuple widths and relation sizes. No indices were built, so in each case the entire relation was accessed from the disk. Figure 3 shows the results. The response time increase is nearly linear as the relation size increases.

Figure 4 shows the same results, with additional interpretation. Each of the three horizontal lines is marked with the number of blocks of data accessed from the disk. The response times are the same where the numbers of blocks accessed are the same, regardless of tuple width. This indicates that the simple retrieves are processed at disk transfer rates.

3.1.2. Varying Volume of Data Accessed - The Effect of Indices

The volume of data accessed from the disk may be reduced through the use of indices. The indices themselves are stored in the database, and must be accessed and searched to determine the addresses of the relevant tuples. When the relation is small, the time required to access and search the index may offset the gain afforded by accessing fewer blocks of the relation. For larger relations, however, we expect to see an improvement in response time for queries qualified on indexed attributes.

Recall that Figure 4 shows the response times for simple queries to select 5% of the data in the relation processed against relations with no index structure. Using the same database, dense

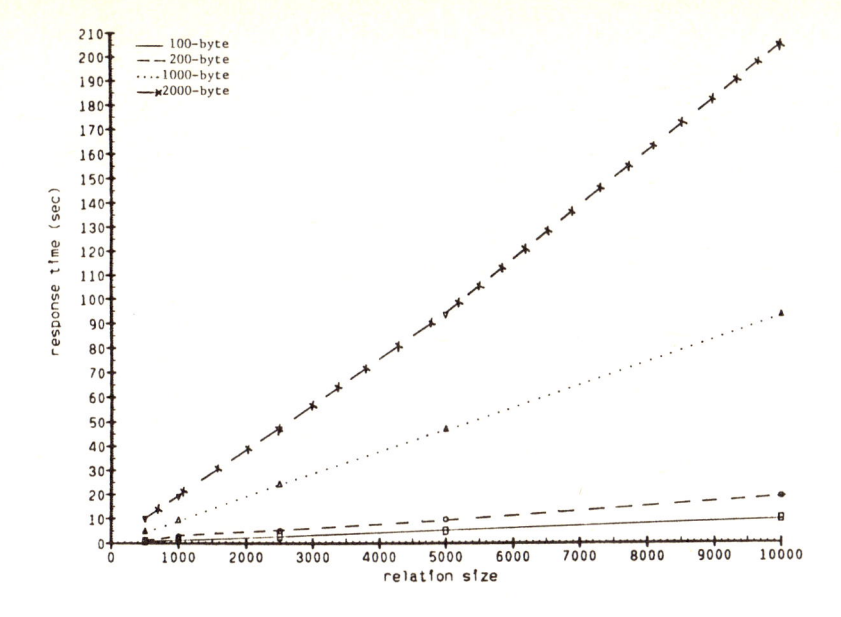

Figure 3: Simple Selects with No Indices

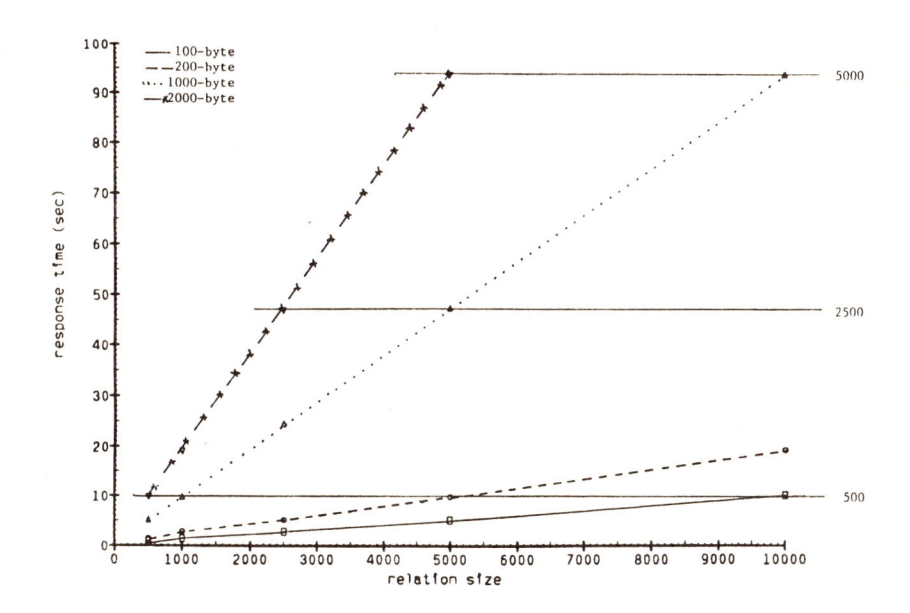

Figure 4: Simple Selects with No Indices - Blocks Accessed

indices were built on the attribute values corresponding to the query qualifications. The queries used in the simple selection experiments described in Section 3.1.1 were rerun. Figure 5 shows the response times for these queries. The response times again increase linearly as the relation size increases.

Figure 6 illustrates the response time improvement afforded by the index. The vertical axis of the graph is the ratio of response time without index to response time with index. The tuples were stored in an order that results in limiting the number of blocks accessed to 5% of the total number of blocks in the relation when an index is available. Even for "small" relations, i.e. 500 tuples, there is some improvement. This is the improvement even when a dense index is used. Some small additional advantage could be expected for a nondense index.

Compare the response time improvement for the queries against the 1000-tuple relation with 100-byte tuple width to the response time for the queries against the 500-tuple relation with 200-byte tuple width. Both require that 10 blocks of data be accessed from the disk, plus the number of blocks required for the index. Recall from Figure 4 that response times for simple selection depend on the number of blocks accessed from disk. We can say, then, that the difference in response times between the two queries is the time required to access and process the index data. We note that the response time improvement ratio in Figure 5 suggests that the index volume is the dominating factor.

Another interesting observation is that the shapes of the curves indicate that the improvement ratio approaches a finite upper bound. In these experiments an absolute upper bound can be derived as follows. Let t be the time required to retrieve all the n tuples of a relation. We have shown that response times for simple retrieves are a linear function of the number of blocks of data accessed from the disk. Taking the best case, a query to retrieve 5% of the tuples of the relation will require 5% of the blocks of the relation to be accessed from the disk, with a response time of $.05t$. The improvement ratio is then $t/.05t = 20$. All ratios will be strictly less than 20, since the index must be accessed and searched.

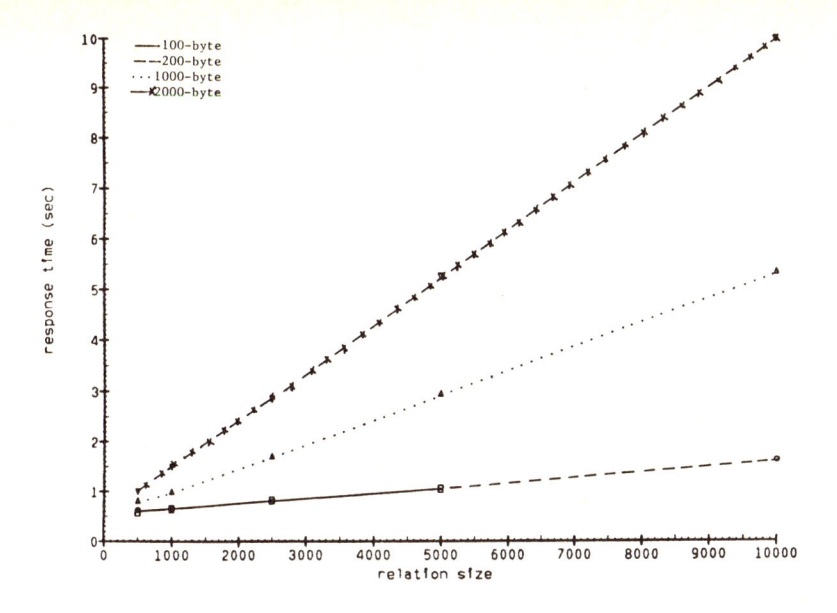

Figure 5: Simple Selects with Dense Index

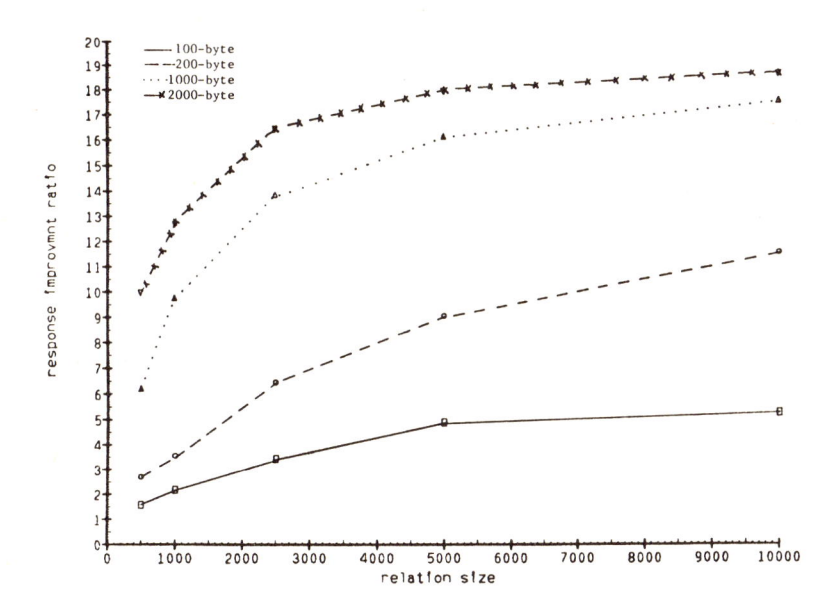

Figure 6: Response Time Improvement with Dense Index

3.1.3. Varying Volume of Data Accessed — The Effect of Data Compression

Another technique used to reduce the volume of data accessed from the disk is data compression. Character string attribute values may be stored without trailing blanks. Numeric attribute values may be stored without leading zeros. The savings in disk space is dependent on the actual values stored in the database. There is a tradeoff of disk space saved vs. time required to compress and decompress the data. Figure 7 shows the results of two sets of experiments contrasting identical queries run against a relation in stored with data compression and the same relation stored in uncompressed form. In the case of the 100-byte tuple relations, the storage requirement is reduced by approximately 50% through data compression. For the 2000-byte tuples, the reduction is approximately 90%.

The results suggest that there is some overhead in setting up parameters for decompressing attribute values. This is clearly illustrated in the case of the relations with 2000-byte tuple width. Here, the improvement approaches the absolute upper bound of 90%, the degree of compression. This upper bound is derived in a manner similar to that in the last section. However, there is some per-tuple processing cost also, as the results for the relations with 100-byte tuples suggest. The improvement is close to 30% for the 10,000-tuple relation, while the absolute upper bound is 50%.

3.1.4. Varying the Order of the Data Retrieved

Figure 8 shows response times for queries which retrieve all tuples in a relation, requiring that data returned be ordered on the key field. The queries were run against relations with 100-byte tuple width. Three identical relations were created for each relation size. One relation had no associated index. A second relation had a dense index on the key field. A third index had a nondense index on the key field.

The differences in response times are not significant. It is interesting to note, however, that the sort process does not use the nondense index to advantage. The nondense index implies that the tuples of the relation have been stored physically in order. However, response times for the relations with the nondense indices are uniformly higher.

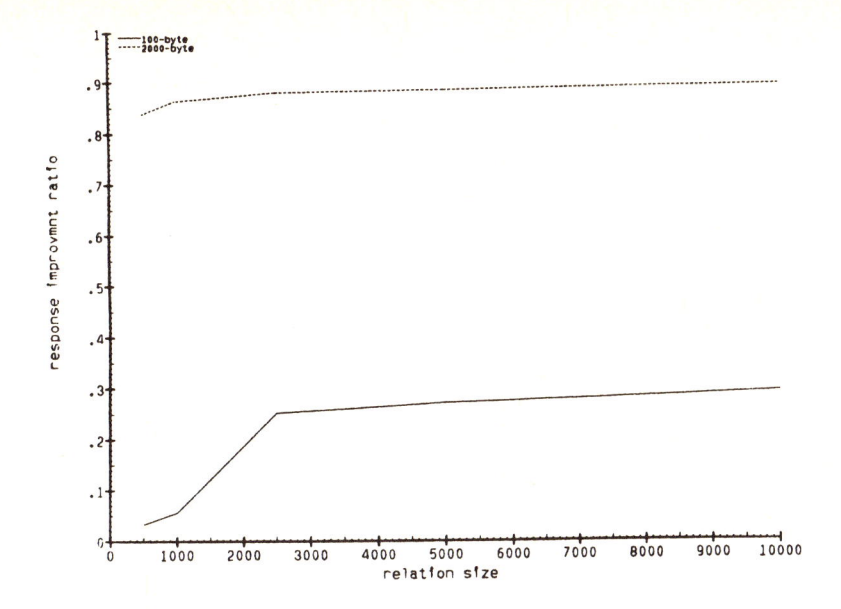

Figure 7: Effects of Data Compression

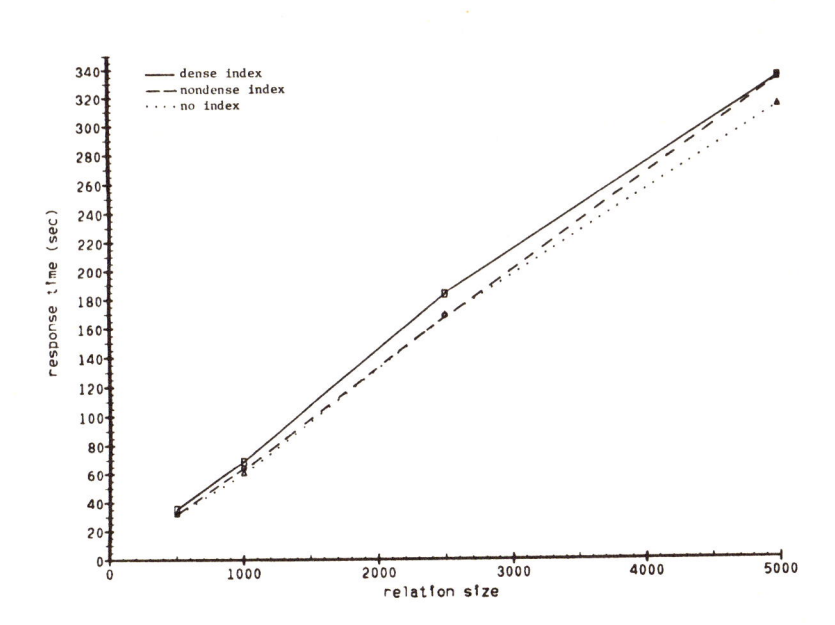

Figure 8: Ordered Retrieves with Indices on Key

Figure 9 shows a rough comparison of the sorting capabilities of the host machine to those of the backend machine. Two batch programs were used in these experiments. The first retrieved the tuples in order from the backend. The second retrieved the tuples from the backend, and invoked an external sort at the host. The backend compares favorably with the host for the range for these tuple widths and relation sizes.

3.1.5. Varying the Number of Attributes Projected

Figures 10, 11, and 12 show the response times for projecting 25%, 50%, and 75% of the attribute values of the tuples of various relations. Note that although the magnitude of the measurements varies with the percentage of attribute values projected, the shapes of the curves are similar. For the 100-byte and 200-byte tuples, the curves are relatively flat. The curve for the 1000-byte tuples is relatively flat up to 1000 tuples. The curve for the 2000-byte tuples rises steeply from the first point. The determining factor seems to be the volume of data in the source relation. Where the relation size exceeds the main memory size, response times increase sharply.

Figures 13, 14, 15 and 16 contrast response times for returning all attribute values and the response times for projecting various percentages of the attribute values. Where the tuple width is small and the number of tuples per block is greater, the work involved in the projection causes the response times for projections to be greater than the response times for retrieving all attribute values. Where the number of tuples per block is small and the main memory size exceeds the relation size, it is cheaper to project attribute values than to retrieve all attribute values. However, when the relation size exceeds the main memory size, it is again cheaper to retrieve all attribute values.

3.2. Join Experiments

3.2.1. Varying the Relation Size and the Tuple Width

Figure 17 shows the results of some join experiments where relation size and tuple width are varied. All joins are equijoins on the key field, with no further qualification. In each case the relations being joined had identical tuples widths. Results are shown for tuple widths of 100, 200, 1000, and 2000 bytes. A relation of 500 tuples is joined with a relation of 1000 tuples; the

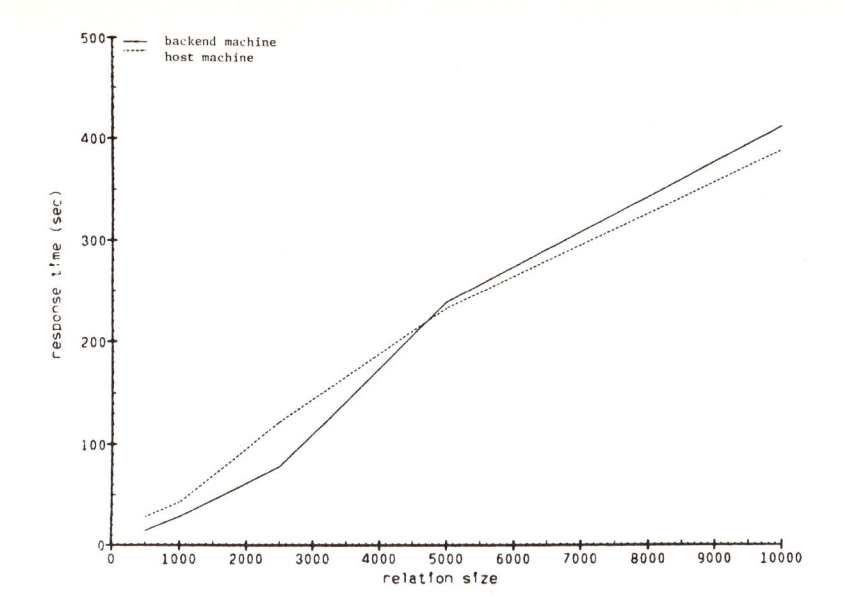

Figure 9: A Comparison of Host's and Backends Ordering Capabilities

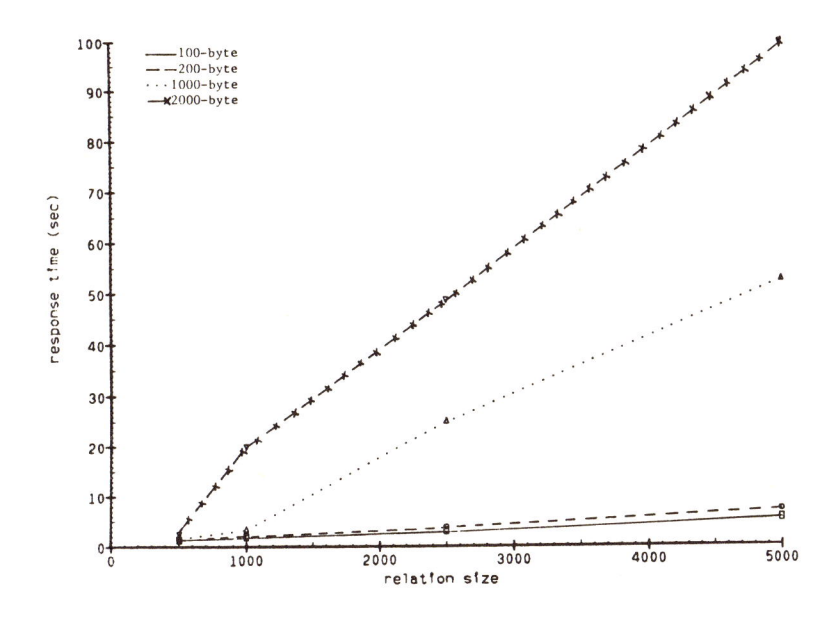

Figure 10: 25% Projections on 5% Selections

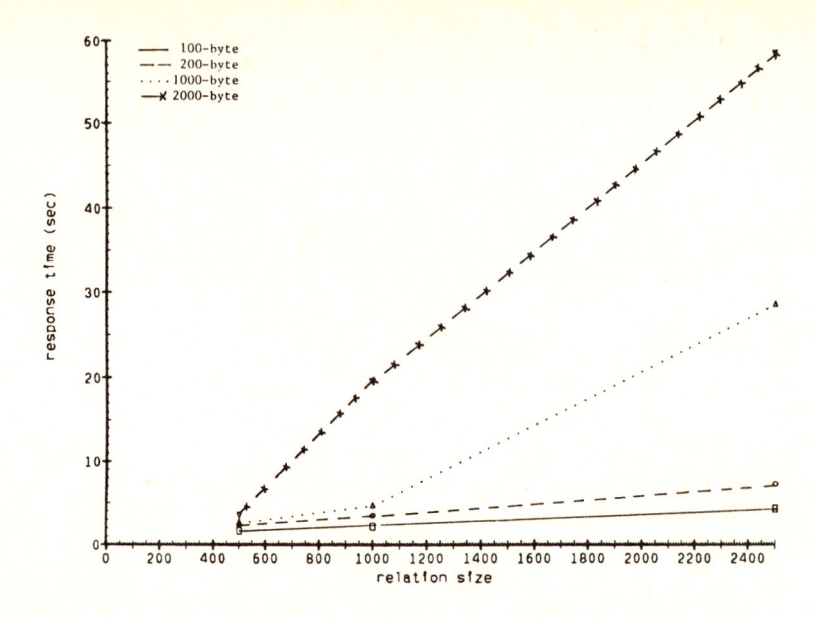

Figure 11: 50% Projections on 5% Selections

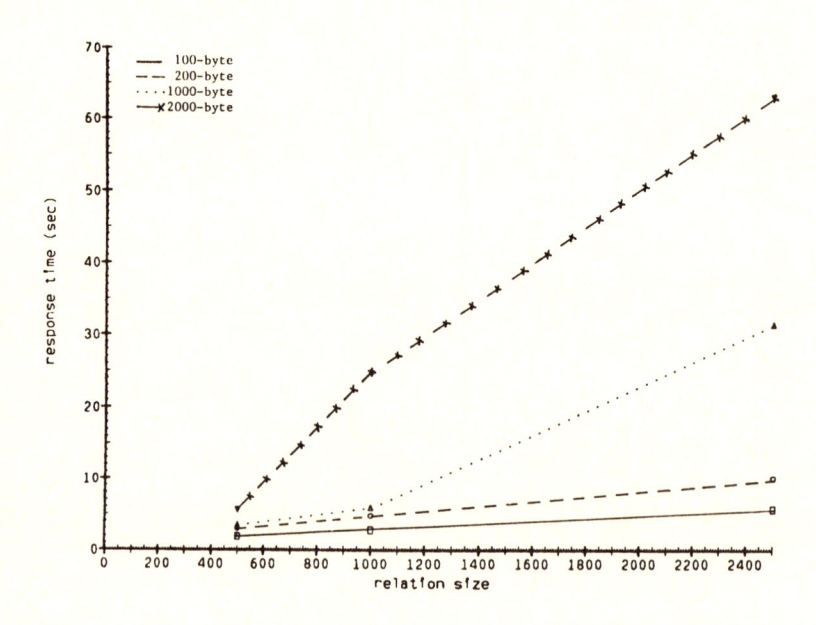

Figure 12: 75% Projections on 5% Selections

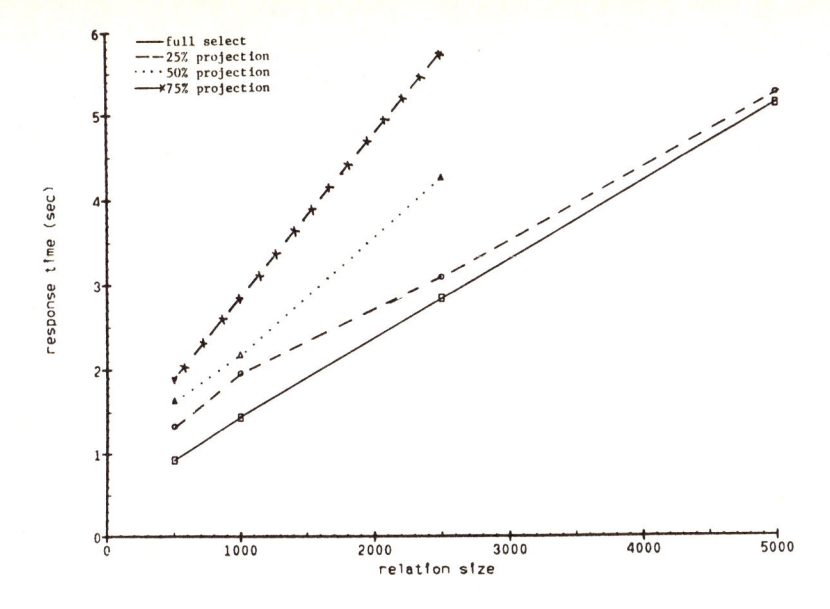

Figure 13: Comparison of Projection and Selection for 100-byte Tuples

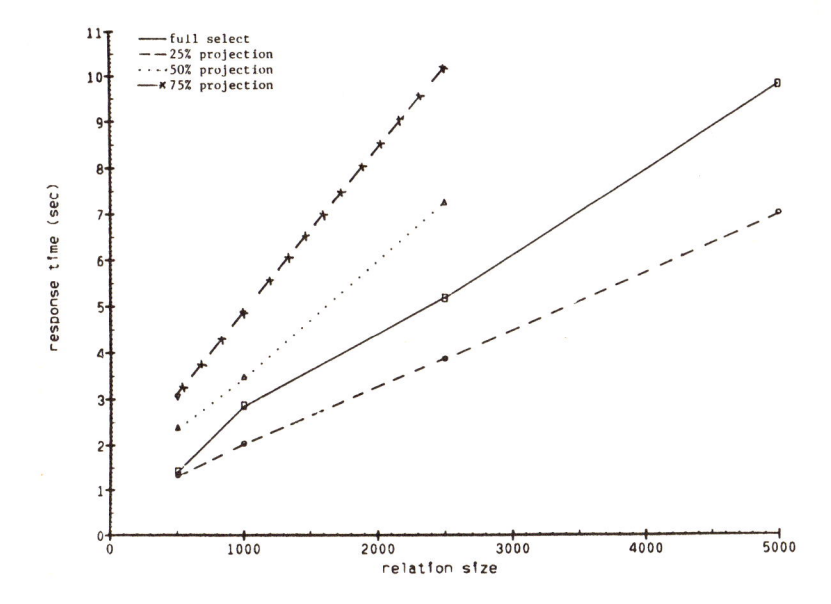

Figure 14: Comparison of Projection and Selection for 200-byte Tuples

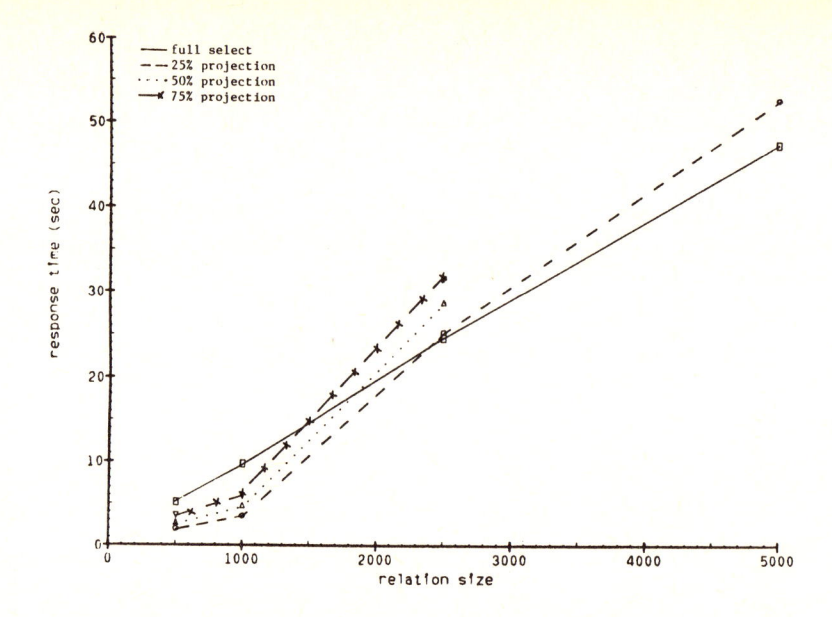

Figure 15: Comparison of Projection and Selection for 1000-byte Tuples

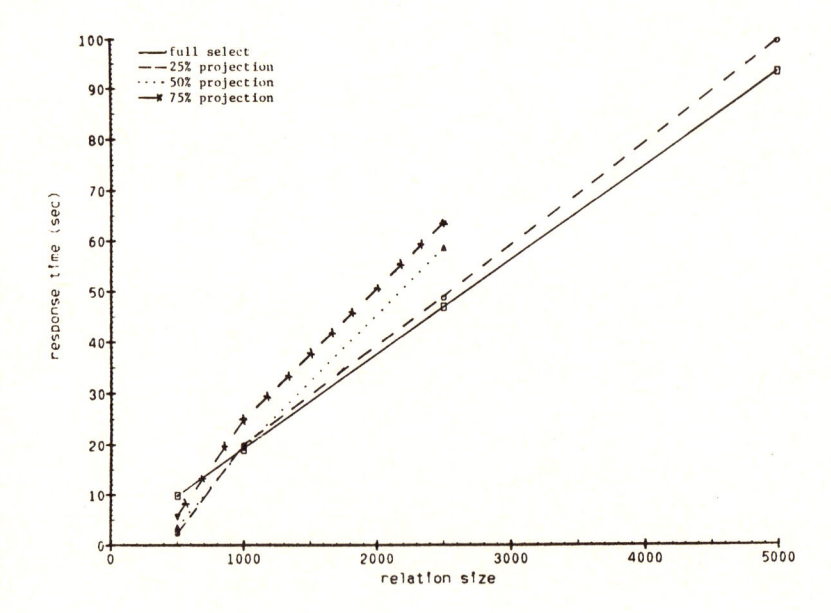

Figure 16: Comparison of Projections and Selection for 2000-byte Tuples

resulting relation has 500 tuples. Similarly, a second join involves relations of 2500 and 5000 tuples, and a third join involves relations of 5000 and 10000 tuples.

Figure 17 shows the effect of varying relation size. Response times increase linearly with the number of tuples in the relations. The increase is more rapid for the larger tuple sizes, indicating that the volume of the data involved in the join is a significant factor. Figure 18 shows the effect of varying tuple width. Where the number of tuples being compared is equal, the response times are greater for the larger tuple widths. This again suggests that the volume of the data is the significant factor in these response times.

Figure 19 shows the mean response times for all tuple sizes, graphed agains the number of tuples accessed. It is evident that the overhead of setting up the join is being absorbed as the size (in number of tuples) of the relations being joined increases. The mean response time for a given tuple width will approach some asymptotic lower bound.

3.2.2. Varying the Database Size

Figure 20 contrasts response time for similar joins in different databases. The NPSTEST database contains 48 user relations, and occupies 31,350 blocks on the disk. The three small databases contain 2 user relations each. NPS4, NPS5, and NPS6 occupy 150, 750, and 1500 blocks respectively. Neither the size of the database nor the number of objects in the database significantly affects the response times.

3.2.3. Varying the Physical Organization

A series of tests was planned to identify the optimum disk placement for joins. We planned to compare joins between relations on separate disks with joins of relations on the same disk to measure the effect of disk contention. The capability to assign a specific relation to a specific disk was not available. However, we were able to spread the allocation for a database across multiple disks. The placement of the relations within the allocation is controlled by the backend system.

The results in Figure 21 show joins for relations on the same disk and relations spread across two disks. In the database which

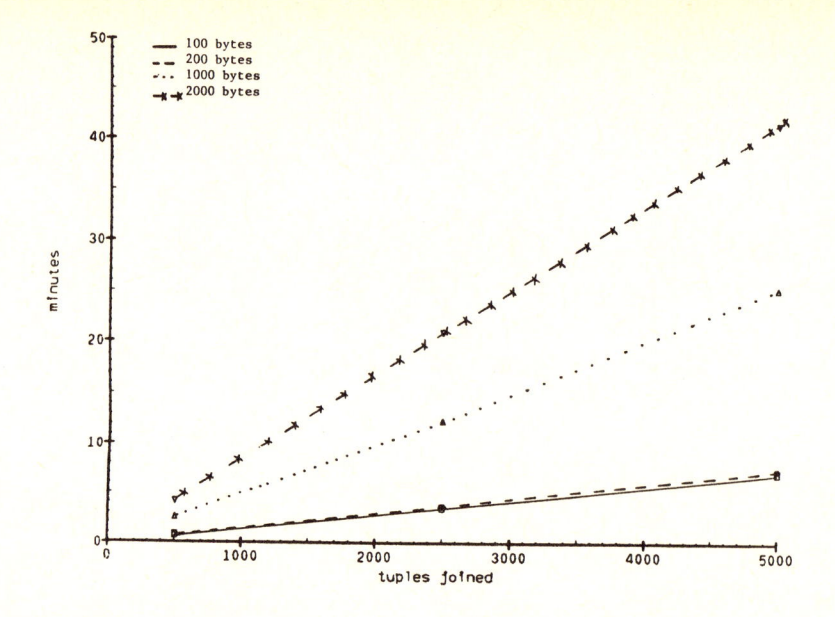

Figure 17: Equijoins as Relation Size Varies

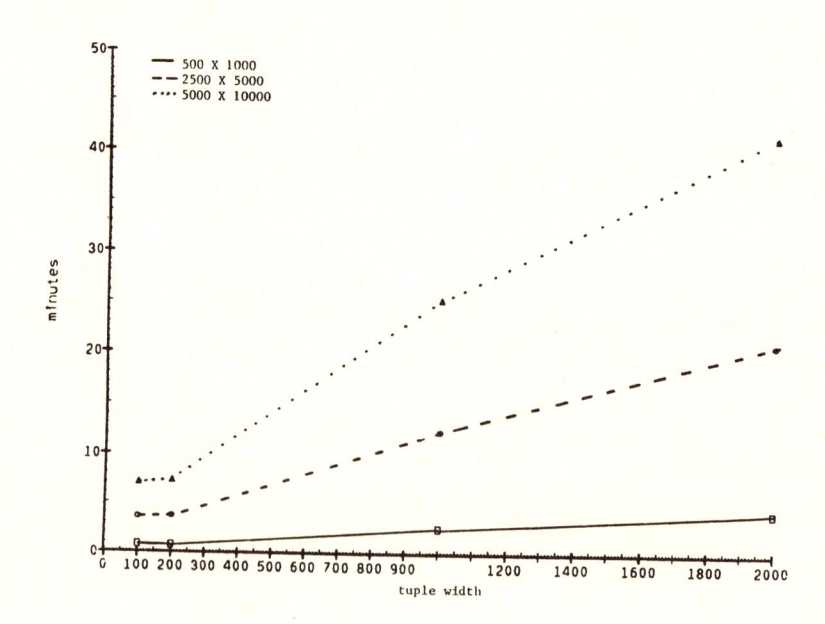

Figure 18: Equijoins as Tuple Width Varies

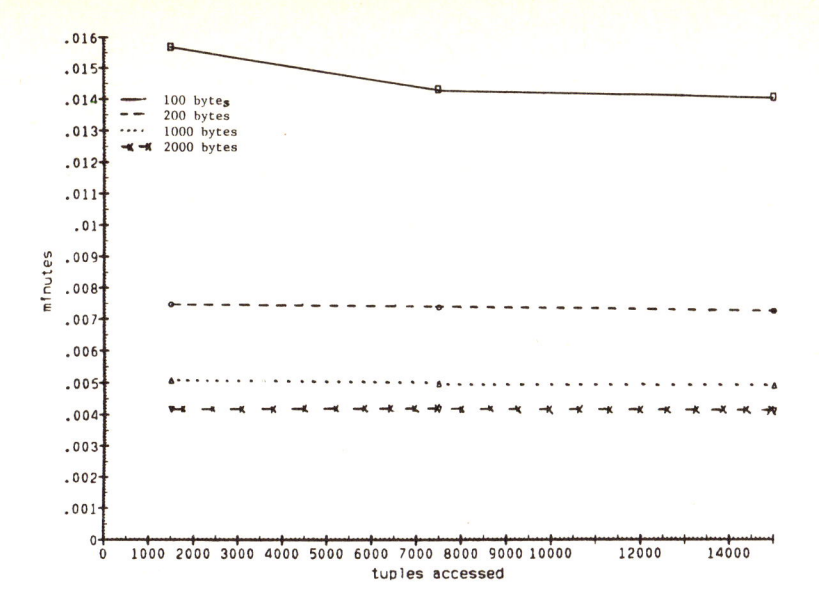

Figure 19: Mean Response Times for Equijoins

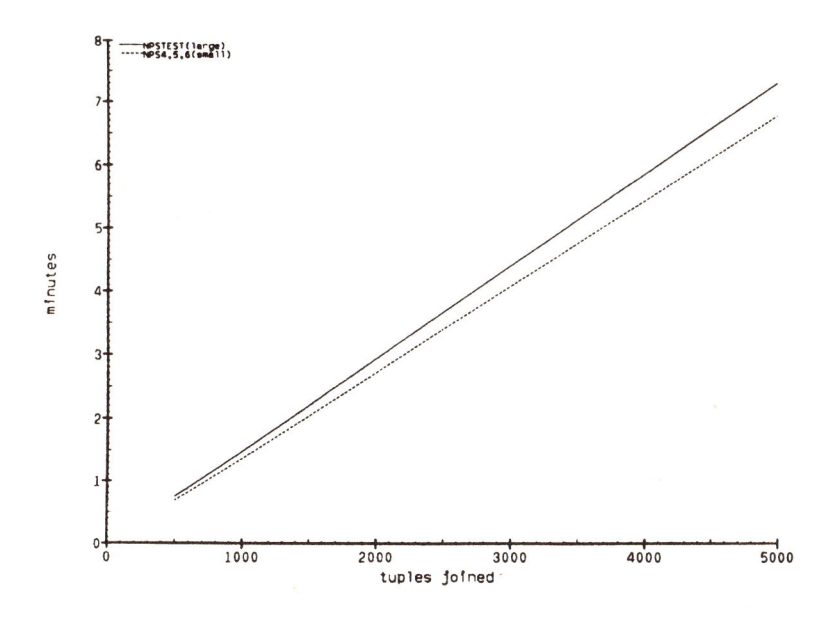

Figure 20: Equijoins Where Database Size Varies

was spread across disks, the relations being joined were not on separate disks, but were spread according to the loading algorithm of the machine across both disks. The results do not indicate a significant difference in the joins.

3.2.4. Varying the Index Structure

Figure 22 illustrates how indices improve response times for joins. As expected, the response times for joins where the join attribute is indexed are lower than the response times for joins with no index. An unexpected result is that there is little difference between response times where the index is a dense index and where the index is nondense.

When a nondense index is available, the equality join can be reduced to a simple merge. This is not the case for the dense index, since no ordering of the tuples is implied. It is the case here that the tuples of the relations with dense indices were actually stored in key order. That the backend machine detected this is one possible explanation.

3.2.5. Varying the Selectivities

First, Figure 23 shows the results of an experiment run to test whether the backend machine bases join strategies on relation size. One set of joins named the smaller relation first in the qualification; the other set of joins named the larger relation first. Reversing the order in which the relations were named in the equality predicate had no effect on response times. We therefore conclude that the backend machine does use relation size when selecting join strategies.

Figures 24 and 25 show the response times for a set of experiments where a restriction was added for one of the relations in the join. It is evident from the results that the restriction is applied before the join is performed.

3.2.6. Varying the Machine Configuration

Figure 26 shows response times for identical joins performed under three different machine configurations. The three configurations are 1/2-megabyte main memory with an auxiliary processor, 2-megabyte main memory with no auxiliary processor, and 2-megabyte main memory with an auxiliary processor. The joins were per-

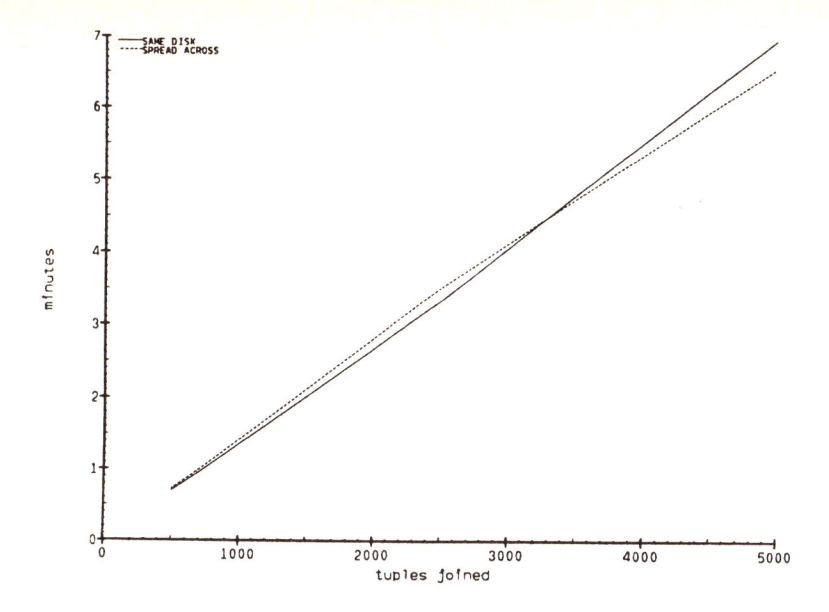

Figure 21: Equijoins where Physical Organization Varies

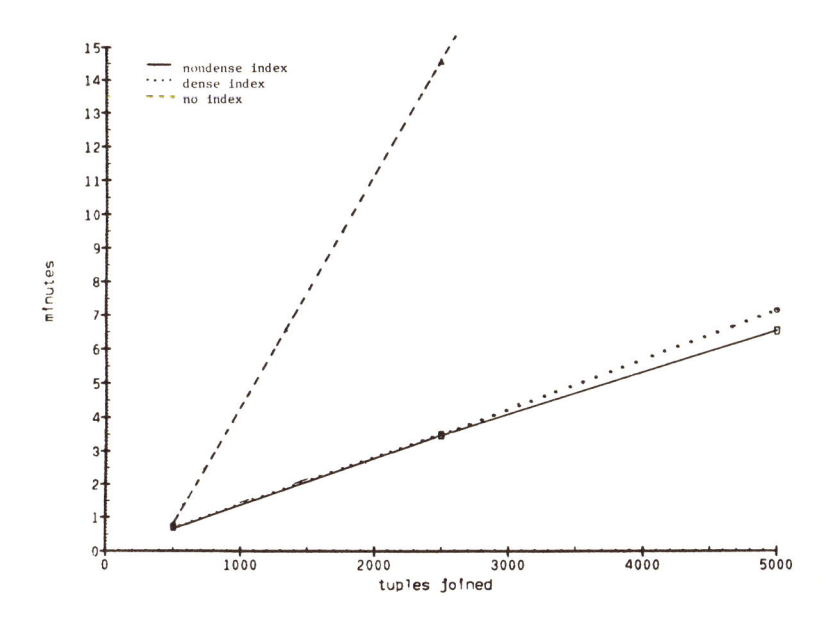

Figure 22: Equijoins where Index Structure Varies

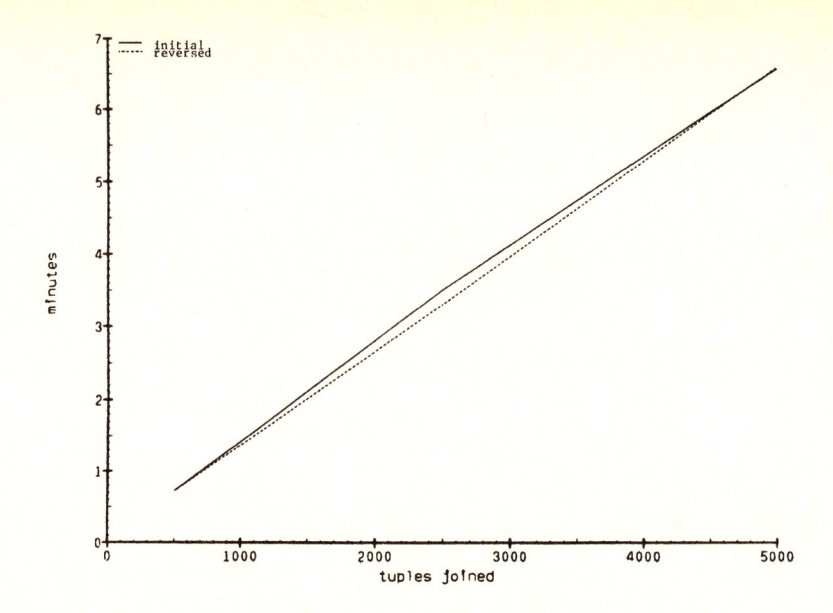

Figure 23: Equijoins where Predicates are Reversed

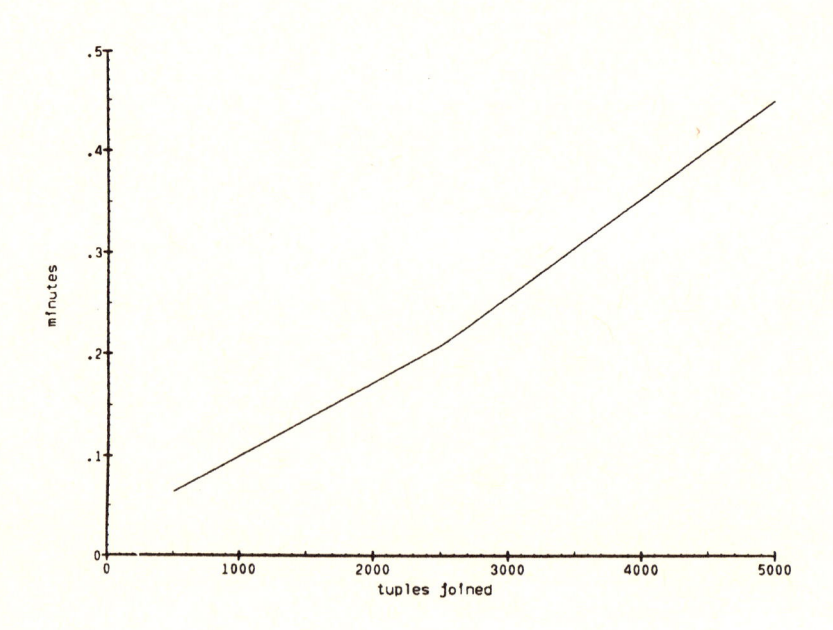

Figure 24: Equijoins with 5% Restriction

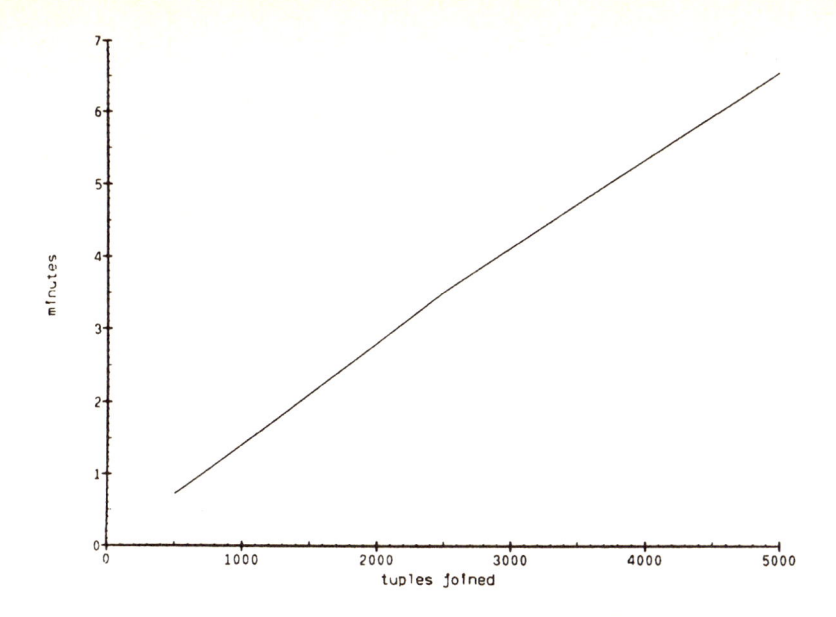

Figure 25: Equijoins with No Restriction

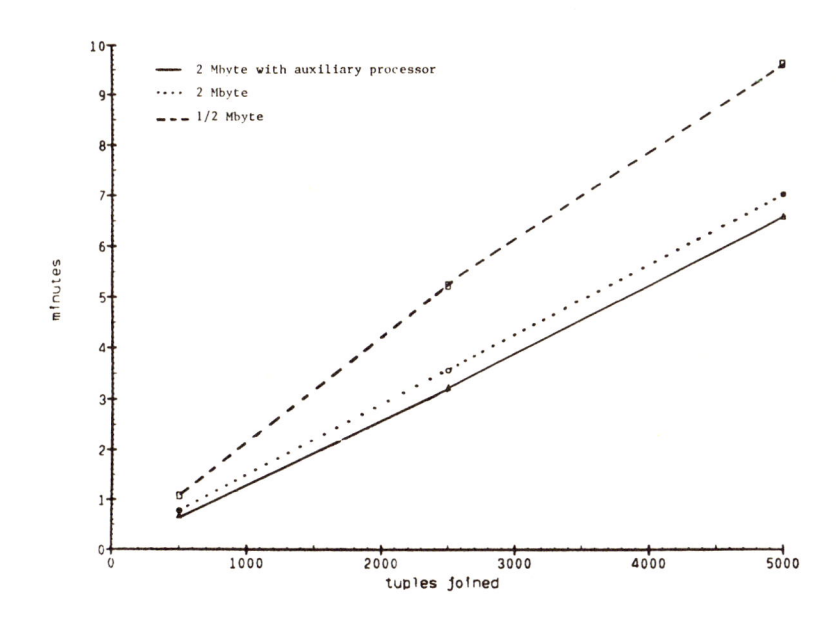

Figure 26: Equijoins with Varying Machine Configurations

formed over relations with a 100-byte tuple width. The increase in main memory size from 1/2 to 2 megabytes resulted in a 27% to 31% improvement. The addition of the auxiliary processor improved response times only 6% to 12%. This seems to indicate that the size of the available main memory is a more important factor in performing joins than the presence or absence of the auxiliary processor.

4. CONCLUSIONS

Our goal is to develop a machine-independent, application-independent methodology for benchmarking relational database machines. The methodology is based on the relational operations at the query language level to provide machine independence. Artificial databases and sets of queries designed to measure the effects of varying workload parameters contribute to application-independence. We have applied the methodology to a particular relational database machine. Results for sets of experiments on the selection, projection, and join operations are reported.

Selection experiments reveal that the response times for selections increase linearly with the volume of data accessed. That the response times are proportional to the volume of data accessed from disk is supported by the results of the data compression experiments. Where the degree of compression is high, there is significant improvement. The use of indices on the qualification attributes results in improvement even for small relations. Selections with an ordering specification show that database machine performance for ordering is competitive with the particular host machine tested. However, the ordering algorithms may not be taking advantage of nondense indices.

Projection experiments show that where tuple width is small and the number of tuples per block is large, the work involved in projection causes response times to be greater than response times for retrieving entire tuples. The results also suggest that when the relation size exceeds the main memory size, it is cheaper to retrieve entire tuples.

Equijoin experiments on two relations again exhibit response times which increase linearly with the volume of data accessed. The size of the database, i.e. the number of objects in the database, does not appear to be a significant factor. As in selection, indices on the join attributes result in a significant improvement in response times. There is, however, no significant difference between the use of dense and nondense indices. The same experiments run with different machine configurations suggest that the main memory capacity is a more significant factor in performance for joins that the presence of the auxiliary processor.

The results reported in this paper represent only a portion of full set of benchmarks. They do, however, show that a set of simple experiments with controlled variation of workload parameters provide useful results.

REFERENCES

[Bogd83] Bogdanowicz, Robert A., *Benchmarking the Selection and Projection Operations, and Ordering Capabilities of Relational Database Machines*, M.S. Thesis, Naval Postgraduate School, Monterey, CA, June 1983.

[Croc83] Crocker, Michael D., *Benchmarking the Join Operation of a Relational Database Machine*, M.S. Thesis, Naval Postgraduate School, Monterey, CA, June 1983.

[Ferr78] Ferrari, Domenico, *Computer Systems Performance Evaluation*, Prentice-Hall, Inc., 1978.

[Flyn74] Flynn, M. J., "Trends and Problems in Computer Organizations", *Proceedings IFIP Congress 1974*, North-Holland, Amsterdam.

[Hawt79] Hawthorn, Paula and Michael Stonebraker, "Performance Analysis of a Relational Data Base Management System", *Proceedings of the ACM SIGMOD Conference*, 1979.

[Hawt81a] Hawthorn, Paula, "The Effect of Target Applications on the Design of Database Machines", *Proceedings of the ACM SIGMOD Conference*, 1981.

[Hawt81b] Hawthorn, Paula and David J.DeWitt, "Performance Analysis of Alternative Database Machine Architectures", *IEEE Transactions on Software Engineering*, Vol., SE-8, No. 1, January, 1982, pp. 61-75.

[Hayn82] Haynes, Leonard S., "Database Machines Viewed as High Level Language Computers", *Proceedings of the International Workshop on High-Level Language Computer Architecture*, 1982.

[Knut71] Knuth, D. E., "An Empirical Study of FORTRAN Programs", *Software -- Practice and Experience*, Volume 1.

[Ryde83] Ryder, Curtis J., *Benchmarking Relational Database Machines - Capabilities in Supporting the Database Administrators' Functions and Responsibilities*, M.S. Thesis, Naval Postgraduate School, Monterey, CA, June 1983.

[Ston83] Stone, Vincent C., *Design of Relational Database Benchmarks*, M.S. Thesis, Naval Postgraduate School, Monterey, CA, June 1983.

A Performance Study on Host-Backend Communication

M. DRAWIN
H. SCHWEPPE

Technische Universität Braunschweig
Inst.f.Theor.u.Prakt.Informatik
Gausstr. 11
D-3300 Braunschweig
W-Germany

Abstract

This paper discusses the interface between host computers and database backends. The logical interface (single tuple vs set transfer) and the communication characteristics (data rate, overhead) together with their effects on throughput, response time and host CPU offload are investigated in a simulation model.

In addition, the relationship between query characteristics (number of I/O transfers, internal processing time) and throughput and offload effect is also studied.

1. Introduction

The most important objective of research and development into database machines (DBM) is that of increasing the performance of database systems (DBS). If the host machine is relieved of the data management tasks and if the CPU is a critical resource in the system, total throughput can be assumed to be higher. Response time may be decreased if the DBM offers architectural support for time-consuming non-numerical operations. Even when only a software backend is employed, i.e. a conventional computer running only the DBS and no other applications, the response time may be diminished if the additional overhead caused by the general purpose operating system is reduced by employing a streamlined database operating system.

Most work on DBM evaluation deals with the pros and cons of the backend (BE) architecture itself, i.e. it is investigated how efficiently certain classes of queries can be executed on particular DBMs.

Offloading the DBS, however, leads in consequence to additional I/O operations, i.e. at least two for each DBS call from an application program. Furthermore, communication between host and backend (BE) is more expensive than disk I/O. This is due to the protocol processing which is necessary to synchronize the independent host and backend systems. The situation is similar to distributed database processing where communication overhead is a major problem in processing nonlocal references.

In this paper we will discuss the communication problem in host-backend configurations for database processing. Two aspects are investigated:

   a) how does the logical interface between host and BE effect the performance of the overall system?

   b) to what extent does the data transfer rate on the one hand and protocol overhead on the other influence the effectiveness of the configuration?

The first question concerns the protocol between host and backend from a DBS point of view: a tuple-at-a-time interface and the transfer of tuple sets from the backend to the host are the extreme solutions. (We will not consider configurations where physical pages are transferred, since in this case most of the DB processing has to be done in the host; this solution tends to be very ineffective.)

Obviously, both issues are related and both have to be investigated in order to give a reliable evaluation of host-backend (H/BE) configurations.

In /SEKI 82/ some calculations have been made on the basis of a typical query in order to evaluate the different reasonable logical H/BE interfaces. The problem of balancing the host and backend capacity has been studied in /SCHF 82/.

In /MAWA 76/ a detailed analysis has been performed, which deals with
the question as to whether system data (dictionary, schema) are to be
placed in the host or BE. Only CODASYL-type systems are considered. Our
approach is simpler in this respect and does not differentiate between
schema and database processing. However, the processing environment,
e.g. operating system overheads and non DB workload, has been simulated
in more detail.

The query processing model used in the simulation of H/BE systems is
described in the following chapter, followed by a discussion of the
different logical interfaces. The simulation model is presented in
chapter 3. The results will be discussed in chapter 4, with respect to
the question mentioned above.

2. A Model of Queries and Query Processing

The entities of interaction between application programs and a DBS are
queries passed to the DBS and data sets made available to the
application programs in a communication buffer. In the simulation model
the queries and the result sets are represented by a set of parameters
which describes the load of the resources with respect to this query
(unless otherwise stated, both read and write requests are called
queries)

Processing of a query is done in a basic cycle of the DBS:

- query preprocessing, e.g. query compilation (if necessary),
  analyzing the query control blocks, checking coherence with
  the DB description (schema) etc. It is assumed that no I/O is
  needed during this step.

- access to secondary storage (page fetch), using the operating
  system I/O facilities

- processing the accessed data, e.g. fetching the record(s) to
  be processed from the accessed page (we assume a linear page
  address space which is mapped onto page slots of the devices)

- transferring data to the application program if qualified

In general, steps 2 to 4 are repeated several times; the number of iterations depends on the query and the DB characteristics.

As a rule the principal parameters which are used to describe a query are the number of tuples in the DB, the average tuple length, the page size and the query selectivity, i.e. the fraction of the DB which satisfies the query.
The most significant aspects of query execution in a simulation model are processing time and the number of I/Os. However, they cannot be directly derived from the above parameters. The implementation of the particular database (= access path, strategy of query execution etc.) has an influence on both the number of I/Os and processing time.

A query is characterized by:

s   = total number of tuples to be examined

card = result set cardinality

clu = number of tuples to be examined per page

sel = number of tuples to be examined per
       result tuple

In addition, the length l of result tuples is given.

sel is a negative exponentially distributed random variable, l and card are normally distributed and clu is derived from l and the pagesize. Clearly, the parameters are related: s = sel*card and s/clu = number of pages to be accessed (if mean values are used. If a parameter is said to have a certain value in the following, we always mean the expected value for the case where the parameter constitutes a randomly distributed variable).

It is easy to see how to relate this parameter set to different classes of queries. For example, if s is equal to the cardinality of the relation and clu is pagesize divided by l, this corresponds to sequential processing. (The page size is assumed to be 4k bytes.)

The other extreme is s = card and clu = 1. It can be interpreted as primary key access with negligible probability of finding more than one result tuple on one page.

Disregarding the H/BE communication overheads, the query execution algorithm is modelled as follows:

```
REPEAT
   take query from queue
   preprocess query
   WHILE tuples left to be processed
       IF page NOT in buffer
       THEN start I/O
            release CPU during I/O
       FI
       check tuple qualification
       IF qualified THEN put tuple in result set
       FI
   END-WHILE
END
```

All tests are performed using the parameter set of the query. For example, the tuple qualification check will be positive after sel-1 (pseudo)tuples have passed by. Start I/O is explicitly taken into consideration, since I/O needs much more CPU time than most of the operations on records in main storage (4000-6000 instructions in some operating systems).

A preemptive policy is assumed, where several time slices may be necessary to process a query. The time slice is a further system parameter.

In a host-backend configuration things are complicated by the need for message transfer between the two computers, regardless of whether the DB processor has a conventional or special purpose architecture. (Shared memory is excluded from this study, since it is a solution only suited to tightly coupled systems, but not to network configurations which are increasingly gaining in importance.) Since protocol overhead and transfer time are principal factors which influence throughput, both are considered in the model.

However, the communication overhead is not only determined by the technical parameters but also by the logical interface between host and backend. Two versions will be considered:

V1: <u>single-tuple interface</u>

Application programs send requests (queries) for one tuple to the backend. The query is executed by the backend according to the procedure in a centralized system. The result tuple is immediately returned via the communicaton interface to the application program which is now able to continue (e.g. send a further request to the DB backend). This is a typical interaction of application programs and CODASYL-type systems.

The one-record-at-a-time logic, however, is not limited to CODASYL systems. DBS with an external set interface nearly always implement set processing by an internal single record interface which can be used as the logical H/BE interface. On the other hand, some CODASYL DBS have a set-oriented external interface and thus allow for a different type of communication interface than just one record at-a-time.

V2: <u>set interface</u>

Result sets are transferred in larger portions (e.g. physical blocks containing multiple tuples). This leads to a need for a more sophisticated communication manager on the host side. The user working areas which contain intermediate and result data sets for each user which are managed by the DBS have to be subdivided between host and backend, if tuple sets are transferred. A tuple request from an application program using e.g. SQL's FETCH command is first directed to the communication manager which then checks whether there is a tuple of the requested data set in its buffer. If not, it will send a request for a block of records to the backend. A single tuple is then transferred into the address space of the application program.

It is obvious that the communication manager has to execute a number of non-trivial and time-consuming tasks, e.g. buffer management, cursor administration and data set management for each active user, analyzing the opcode for each query (since FETCH commands are to be interpreted locally by the communication manager on the host) etc.

3. The Simulation Model

The simulation model for the H/BE versions V1 and V2 is depicted in Fig.1.
The conventional DBS configuration used for comparison consists only of the host processor and the attached disk storage subsystem.

The host computer has two queues of tasks which apply to the CPU. They have different priorities. System tasks, i.e. operating system services, have the highest priority (I) and queries -no matter whether requested from a terminal or from an application program- are serviced with lower priority (II). That part of the load of the host which is not caused by service requests of the DBS is modelled by an additional source of batch jobs (1) with lower priority.

The same holds for the backend, but there is no queue of DBS-independent low priority tasks. The disk subsystem consists of several units. The number is a system parameter which has been set to 8 in the experiments. Accesses are uniformly distributed over the units. The I/O subsystem has been modelled rather roughly (no channel contention, no conflicts on common data paths etc.). This is, however, justified by the fact that the I/O-subsystem (but not the CPU activity caused by I/O requests!) is independent of the configurations mentioned above. If it turns out to be a bottleneck, it will be a bottleneck in all configurations.
Host and backend are connected by two message queues, one in each direction (III,IV). The corresponding service stations in the model represent the physical transfer of data in duplex mode.

Let us now persue a query through the system. First, as soon as the CPU has been received, preprocessing is done. In case of request for an operating system service, a task is scheduled for high priority processing. This happens in two situations: disk I/O is requested (2) or a message transfer (in either direction) is to be started or finished (3,4). This is because the communication manager (CM) is assumed to be a high priority operating system process. When a query is to be passed to the BE, it will enter queue III for transfer, after the start-message routines of the CM have been processed by the host CPU. The backend CPU is now requested in order to receive the message on the

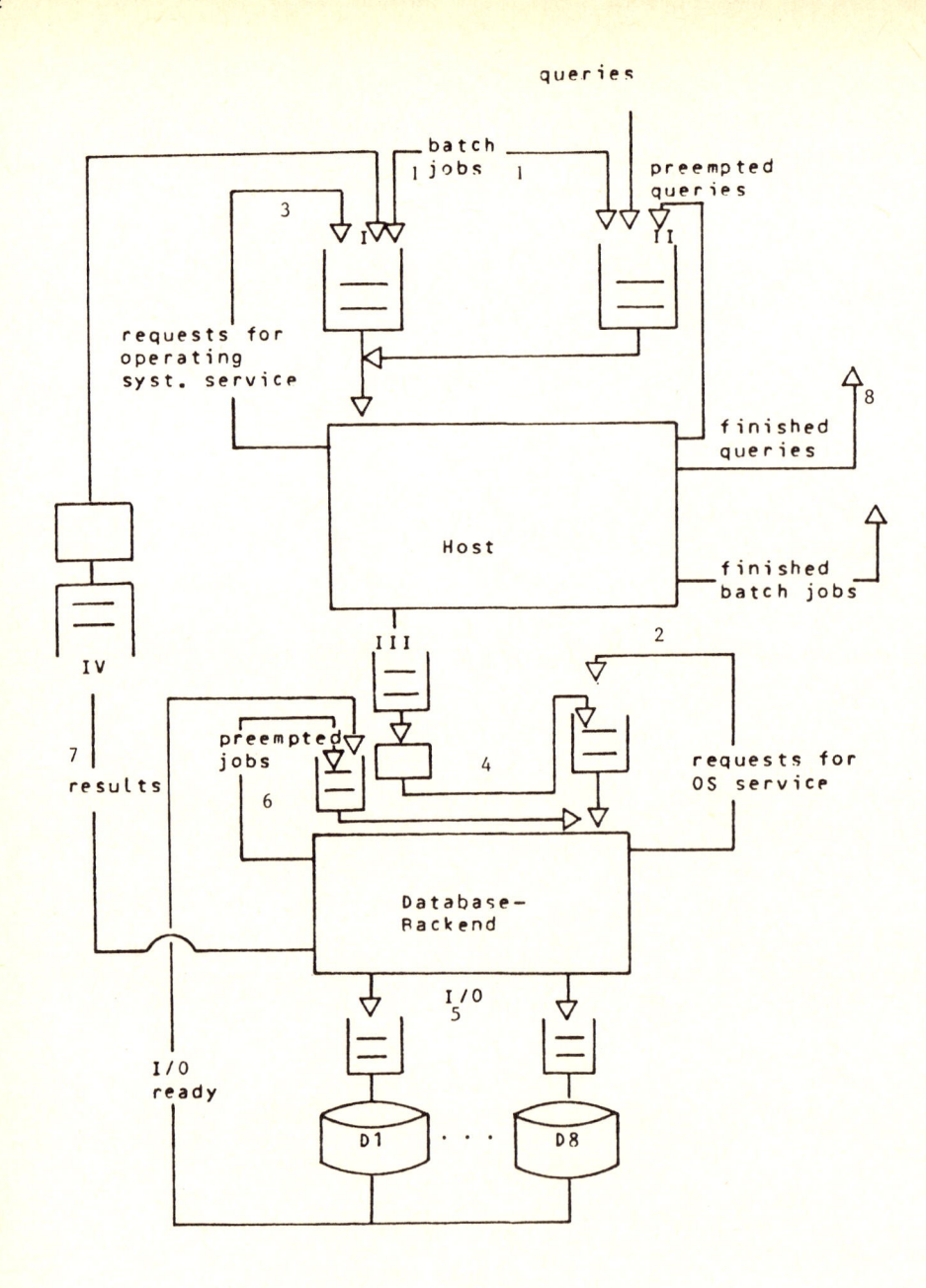

Fig. 1. The Simulation Model

BE side (4). The query is processed along the lines described in the preceeding chapter. I/O (5) as well as BE-CPU service (6) is needed for query evaluation. In case of the bidirectional, single tuple record interface, the result data (one tuple) is immediately returned to the host (7). Some post-processing by the application program which issued the query is simulated in the model before it leaves the system (8).

All processes are preempted, when their time-slice runs out. In this case they reenter the corresponding queue.

4. Experiments and Results

As in most computer systems, throughput and response time are among the most interesting indicators which characterize the performance of H/BE configurations. It is necessary to pay attention to these indicators when varying the parameters of interest, such as communication delays, since unexpected situations may arise. It is no surprise, for example, that response time may increase if the application programs and the DBS are running on different processors, but it is, for example, not obvious that the throughput may be decreased when the database management routines are offloaded from the host.

In all experiments, the service time for the various system components has been adjusted to the average disk access time. For example, the start I/O-time has been set to about 10% of the access time, while the location and processing of one tuple in a page has been assumed to be less than 1% of the I/O. Since absolute units of time, such as milliseconds, may be misleading in a simulation model, a relative measure is used. However, a time unit (tu) of the model is of the order of magnitude of a msec.

4.1. Result Set Cardinality

It is obvious that an increase in the cardinality of the result set will increase the response time of a query. More interesting is the relationship between the cardinality and CPU utilization. There is a significant difference between the single tuple (V1) and the set interface (V2) as far as the overhead per tuple is concerned (Fig.2). The

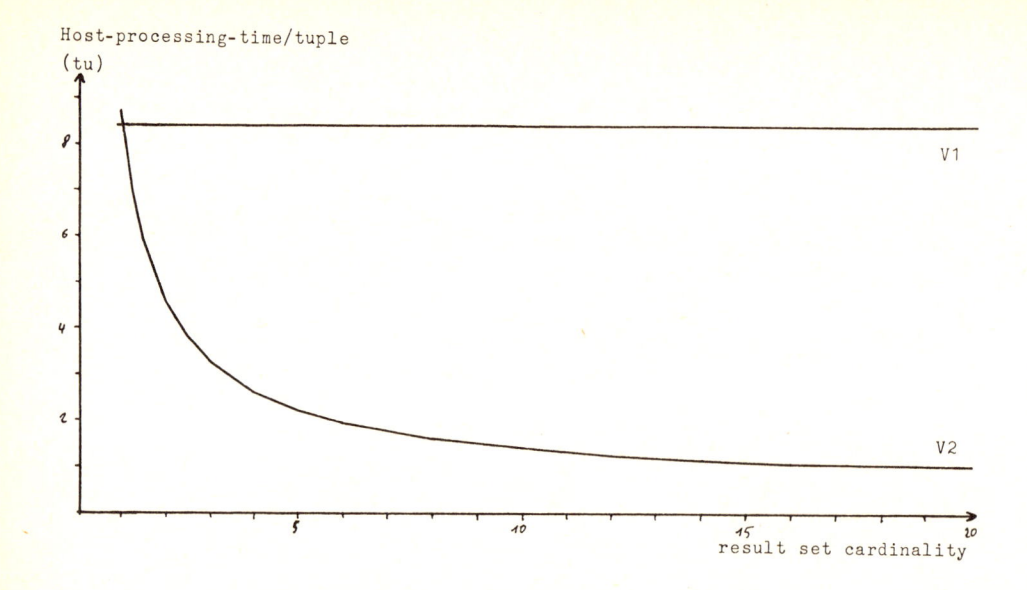

Fig. 2. Influence of Result Set Cardinality

set interface will be less effective if the result set contains no more than one element. This is due to the additional overhead for set management on the host side.

The influence of the result set cardinality is similar for the backend.

In the following experiments a constant cardinality (four tuples) will be assumed.

4.2. Data Transfer Rate between Host and Backend

In this experiment the influence of the data transfer rate on response time and throughput is investigated. Four rates have been used: 12 b/tu and 24 b/tu for slow, serial connections, 48 b/tu for simulation of medium scale packet switching nets and 1.5 kb/tu for channel-to-channel connections. The overhead has been left constant with a mean value of 4 time units which is equal to the start I/O overhead of the disk transfer. The remaining parameters, such as the number of records of the result set, have also been fixed.

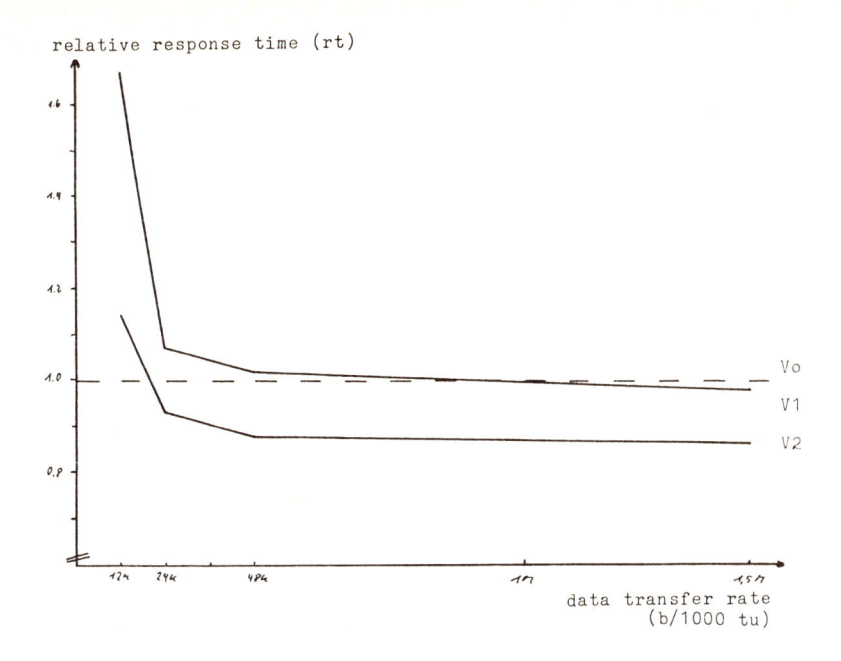

Fig. 3. Relative Response Time / Data Transfer Rate

Figure 3 shows the effects on the response time, which has been normalized by the response time of the host-only system (rt := r(Vi) / r(Vo), with r(Vi) = response time in version i).

There is no effect on the response time beyond transfer of more than 40 b/tu, but an exponential increase occurs for lower rates. This is due to queueing effects in the communication channel.

Furthermore, there is no significant difference between single tuple and set transfer (V1 and V2, respectively), except for a nearly constant difference in the response time in favour of V2.

The response time is lower in the set transfer version than in the host-only system. This result contradicts the performance predictions for database machines made by many authors, e.g. /DATE 83/. The effect can be explained by the workload which has been assumed constant. Therefore the waiting times caused by queueing effects will be shorter in the H/BE configuration than in the host-only system. The H/BE system, however, has twice the CPU performance (assuming a backend with the same capacity as the host). Increases in the workload will deteriorate response time.

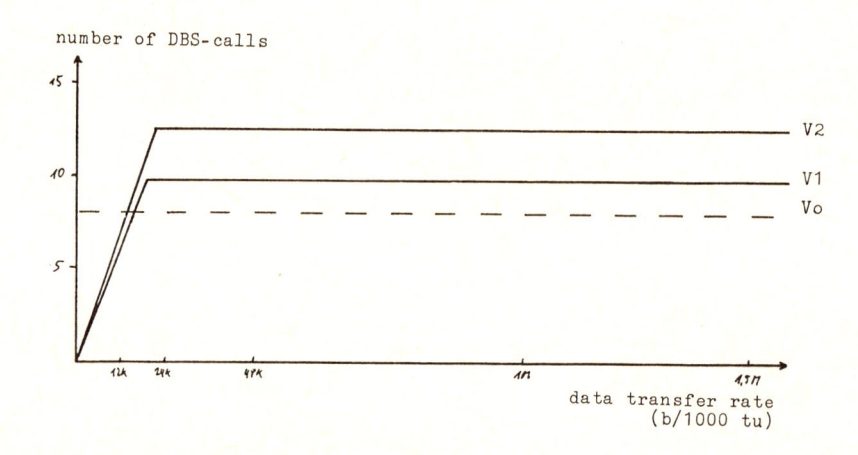

Fig. 4. Throughput / Data Rate

Fig.4 shows how throughput is affected:

Below a certain transfer rate (18 b/tu under the assumptions of the model), the throughput is less than in the host-only system (Vo). Line speed is the limiting factor in this case. The limiting transfer rate depends on other parameters such as the average tuple length.

With increasing transfer rate, throughput will become larger than in the Vo system, provided the backend is powerful enough to take over the CPU workload caused by the database tasks. Regardless of this, the backend CPU will cause a bottleneck when the line speed exceeds a limit (24 b/tu with the parameters chosen). Thus the transfer rate has an influence on throughput only in the low speed range.

The result corresponds with those reported in /MAWA 76/. No qualitative difference has been perceived between set and single tuple transfer.

4.3. Communication Overhead

In general, transfer of messages is a CPU-intensive operation due to the protocol processing, switching of process context etc. In our model, both the sender and the receiver of a message spend a certain amount of time for message handling. In the second experiment, the influence of CPU overhead used for message transfer is studied.

We assume an implementation that requires the processing of only one interrupt when a message has been transferred. This is an optimistic assumption, since in some existing H/BE systems several interrupts occur. The overhead has been related to the start I/O time (stio) for disk access: x * stio with x = 0.1, 0.5, 1 and 2, i.e. the message transfer is assumed to be in the range from a tenth to double that of the I/O channel. The transfer rate is 48 b/tu for all runs.

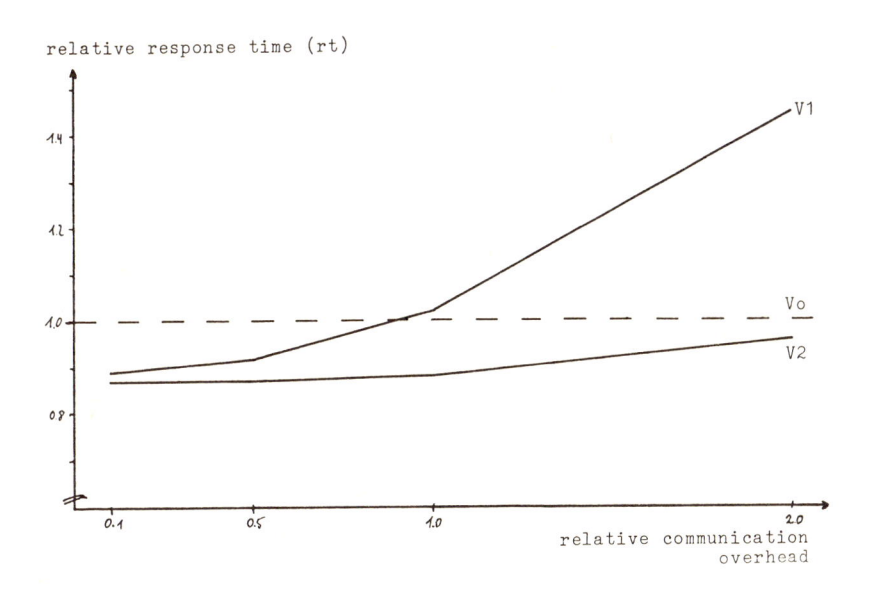

Fig. 5. Relative Response time / Communication Overhead

Figures 5 and 6 show the response time and maximal throughput depending on the overhead.

number of DBS-calls

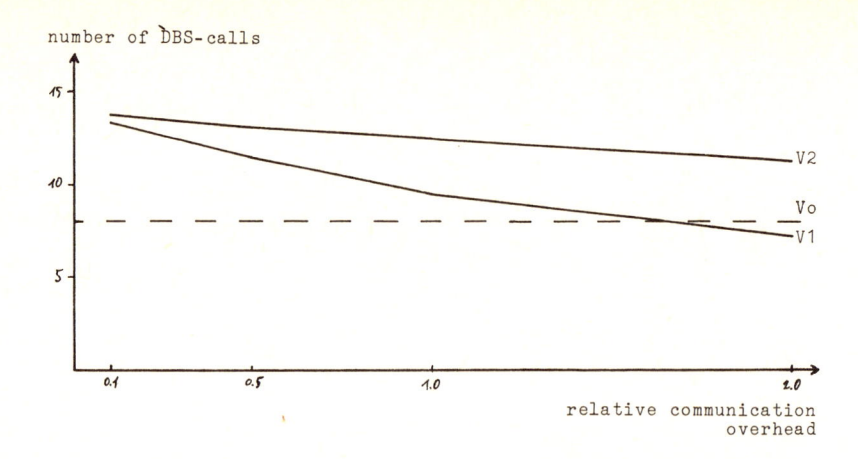

[Figure: graph with curves V2, Vo (dashed), V1 vs relative communication overhead, axis 0.1, 0.5, 1.0, 2.0; vertical axis 5, 10, 15]

Fig. 6. Throughput / Communication Overhead

The effect of communication overhead as determined in the simulation model is less than assumed. Both response time and throughput turn out to be superior than the conventional implementation Vo if V2 (set transfer) is chosen as the logical interface. This holds even if the overhead is twice the start I/O time. In the case of a single tuple interface (V1), things get worse. Response time increases markedly and throughput becomes less than in the host-only system. The maximum throughput is determined in both cases by the CPU capacity of the backend.

A more instructive approach than throughput and response time is to study the net offloading effect on the host. The workload of the system is characterized by the percentage of CPU utilization incurred by non-DBS tasks (R) and the percentage of utilization by DBS tasks (both derived from the task interarrival times). Let A(o) be the CPU utilization incurred by the DBS tasks of the host-only system and A(i) the utilization after offloading (i=1 : single tuple interface, i=2 : set interface). The <u>offloading factor</u> ofl(i) is defined as:

$$ofl(i) := (A(o)-A(i))/A(o)$$

It shows the offloading effect independent of the non-DBS workload R. Considering Fig.7 it is obvious that offloading is significantly affected by the communication overhead, in particular when data trans-

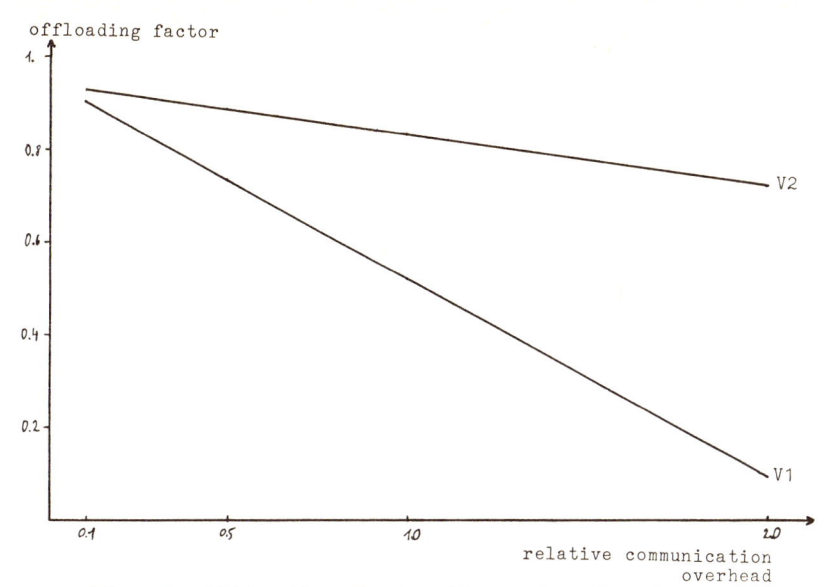

Fig. 7. Offloading Factor/Communication Overhead

fer is implemented one tuple at a time.

In this case, no more than a 10% gain in host CPU capacity will be achieved if the communication overhead is large.

4.4. Different Types of Queries

As far as system performance is concerned, queries may be classified according to the CPU processing and the number of I/O transfers required. As discussed in 2, the parameters sel and clu provide good indicators of the I/O and CPU service required by a particular type of query.

It should be remembered that a high value for sel implies a high amount of internal processing. Sel tuples have to be checked per result tuple. Clu represents the number of tuples which need to be processed and stored in one page. Thus the number of disk accesses depends on this parameter (and of course on sel and the cardinality of the result set).

The first problem to be studied is the relationship between query types and the offloading factor. Given a certain application profile, how much can be gained by offloading the DBS?

The experiment is performed as follows: initially, the different query types (represented by clu, sel), are simulated on the host-only system in order to obtain the response time for each query type. The simulation of the H/BE configurations V1 and V2 gives the offloading factor ofl for each version.

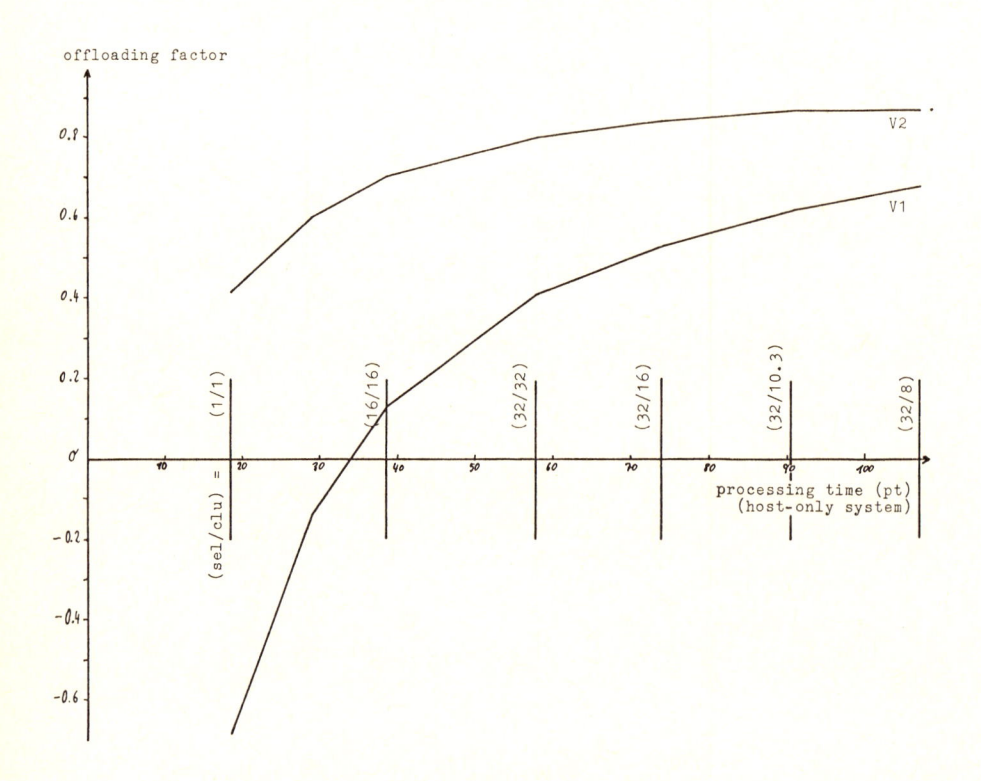

Fig. 8. Offload Effect for Different Query Types

Figure 8 shows the dependency between the processing time of a query (in a conventional system) and ofl. Processing time (pt) is defined as response time minus waiting time because of queueing effects. The relation between query type and process time is indicated on the x-axis.

It is important to note that the result set cardinality has been assumed to be constant for all query types. Thus the communication overhead is also constant.

The transformation $x = 1/pt$ shows that offloading factor is inversly proportional to the processing time.

The next aspect to be investigated is the influence of the query types on the workload R which is not caused by DB tasks. This can split down into two subproblems:

a) how much can R be increased in a H/BE system before the host becomes a bottleneck, under the assumption that the backend has maximal throughput?

b) what is the minimum value of R which does not cause a throughput reduction in a H/BE system?

Both subproblems are related to the communication overhead in a H/BE system. The backend throughput determines the host CPU utilization as far as communication and DBS application program processing is concerned. If R is increased above a certain level, the host CPU capacity will become a bottleneck and thus reduce the throughput of DBS tasks.

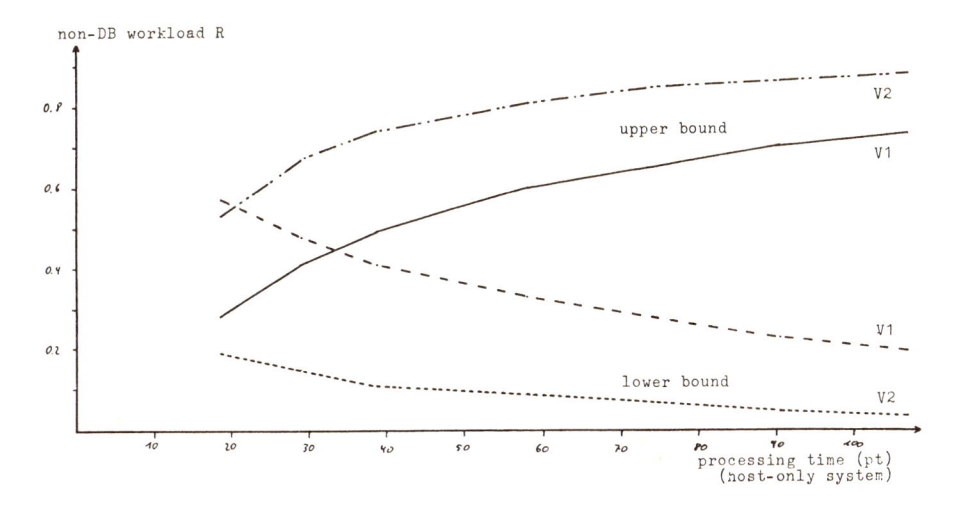

Fig. 9. Minimal and Maximal non-DB Workload

Fig. 9 shows the dependency of the limiting value for R (upper bound) on the response time and on the query types.

The second problem is surprising at the first glance. Suppose the fraction A(Vo)=100-R is offloaded from the host. If R is less than the fraction which is needed for communication handling by the backend, throughput will be less than in the host-only system (assuming host and backend have the same CPU capacity). The lower bound is also shown in Fig.9.

5. Conclusion

The simulation experiments showed clearly that the communication between host and backend has a strong influence on the performance of the overall system. In nearly all situations the set interface between host and backend is superior to the single tuple interface. Data transfer rate has less influence than communication overhead, which is caused by operating system services (process context switching, message handling, driver software). This is because the host or backend CPU, but not the transmission line, will become the bottleneck if the workload is increased and the transfer rate exeeds a certain limit.

The net offloading effect is in many situations less than might be expected if CPU capacity is doubled by installing a backend. There are even situations where throughput decreases in the H/BE system as compared to a host-only system. The offloading of the DB workload to a backend will be the more effective the more processing time is required for typical queries.

The decision whether to upgrade the host system or to install a backend has to be made on the basis of a careful analysis of the overall workload including the fraction of non-DB tasks and of the system costs. The optimization of the cost/performance ratio is beyond the scope of this paper.

We presume that the utilization of a special purpose database machine which significantly reduces query processing times will make H/BE configurations more attractive. Furthermore, loosely coupled host processors and database servers are likely to become more significant than tightly coupled H/BE systems.

6. References

/DATE 83/
        Date, C.: <u>An Introduction to Database Systems</u>, Volume II, Addison Wesley, Reading 1983

/SCHF 83/
        Schuett, D.; Fuchs, P.: On Selecting an Adequate Database Processor for a Host-Backend Configuration, this volume

/MAWA 76/
        Mariansky, F.; Wallentine, V.: A Simulation Model of a Back-End Data Base Management System
        Proc. Pittsburgh Conf. on Modelling and Simulation, 1976

/SEKI 82/
        Sekino, A. et al.: Design Considerations for an Information Query Computer
        Proc. Int. Workshop on Database Machines, San Diego, 1982

ON SELECTING AN ADEQUATE DATABASE PROCESSOR FOR A HOST-BACKEND
CONFIGURATION

P. Fuchs and D. Schütt
Siemens AG
8000 München 83

Abstract.
The paper discusses criteria for selecting an optimally sized
database processor for a host-backend configuration with
predefined database workloads.

Furthermore, the impact on transaction rates and response times
by off-loading database activities is investigated.

Introduction.
Off-loading the database management system (DBMS) from a mainframe
into an attached backend processor can have several motivations:

- Attaching a dedicated processor to an existing mainframe may be
  more expensive (in terms of hardware costs) than upgrading of a
  large mainframe.

- A backend processor can be shared by several hosts. Thus concurrent
  access to a database even from nonhomogeneous hosts is possible.

- Disengagement of the DBMS frees the host for concentration on
  application programs.

- An increase in performance (transactions per seconds) can be
  achieved by concurrent operation of the host with the backend
  processor and secondary storage devices (provided that
  the communication overhead is not crucial).

- The isolation of the DBMS permits easier maintenance, better
  tuning and testing. Furthermore, data security problems are
  easier to manage, i.e. for application programs it is almost
  impossible to access sensitive data.

- Database nodes in a network will play a significant role in
  the future.

In addition, a host-backend configuration can bridge a performance
gap between two successive members of a computer family and add
fault-tolerant capabilities, i.e. it can serve as a reliable
member in the computer family.

In [1] interface problems between host and backend are attacked.
Simulation experiments showed that a set interface is superior
to a tuple-at-a-time interface.

In [2] different logical host-backend interfaces are evaluated
by means of calculations on the basis of a typical query.

In this paper the issue of balancing workloads of a host and an
attached software backend is investigated.

Throughout this paper the following assumptions are made:

1) The operating system load is assumed to be proportional to
   application loads and therefore will not be considered.

2) The effects on response time and throughput by attaching a
   database backend to a mainframe are discussed separately.

Definitions:

k_{DB} = portion of processor load used for database activities

k_{DBMS} = portion of processor load used by the DBMS

k_A = portion of processor load used by database application programs, terminal software, and TP monitor

k_{NDB} = portion of processor load used for non-database activities

Obviously, $k_{DB} = k_A + k_{DBMS}$ and

$k_{DB} + k_{NDB} = 1$ (no idle time is assumed).

$\alpha = \dfrac{k_{DBMS}}{k_{DB}}$ = DBMS portion of database activities

q_{BE-H} = quotient of KOPS ratings of backend and host (hardware power ratio)

$f_H = \dfrac{1}{1-k_{DBMS}+c}$ = maximum increase in host activities possible by off-loading the DBMS where c is the portion of processor load caused by the host-backend communication

$f_{BE} = \dfrac{q_{BE-H}}{k_{DBMS}+c}$ = maximum increase in DBMS activities possible after having off-loaded the DBMS into a backend

I. $k_{NDB} = 0$

The host-only system is not used for non-database activities.

We assume that $k_{DB} = k_A + k_{DBMS} = 1$ and $\dfrac{k_A}{k_{DBMS}} = $ const.

When off-loading the DBMS from the host into an attached backend the host is freed for additional database application programs. Thus k_A can be increased provided that

- the backend can accept the corresponding DBMS load
  (i.e. q_{BE-H} is adequate)

- the host-backend communication is not a bottleneck
  (i.e. the free processor load of both backend and host
  is not consumed by the communication).

I.1 $c = 0$

The following table and figures give some support for selecting a backend of optimal size for different KOPS ratios of host and backend.

k_{DBMS}	f_H	\multicolumn{6}{c}{f_{BE} for $q_{BE-H} =$}
		0.25	0.33	0.50	0.67	1.00	2.00
0.25	1.33	1.00	<u>1.33</u>	2.00	2.66	4.00	8.00
0.33	1.50	0.75	1.00	<u>1.50</u>	2.00	3.00	6.00
0.50	2.00	0.50	0.67	1.00	1.33	<u>2.00</u>	4.00
0.67	3.00	0.38	0.50	0.75	1.00	1.50	<u>3.00</u>
0.75	4.00	0.33	0.44	0.67	0.89	1.33	2.67

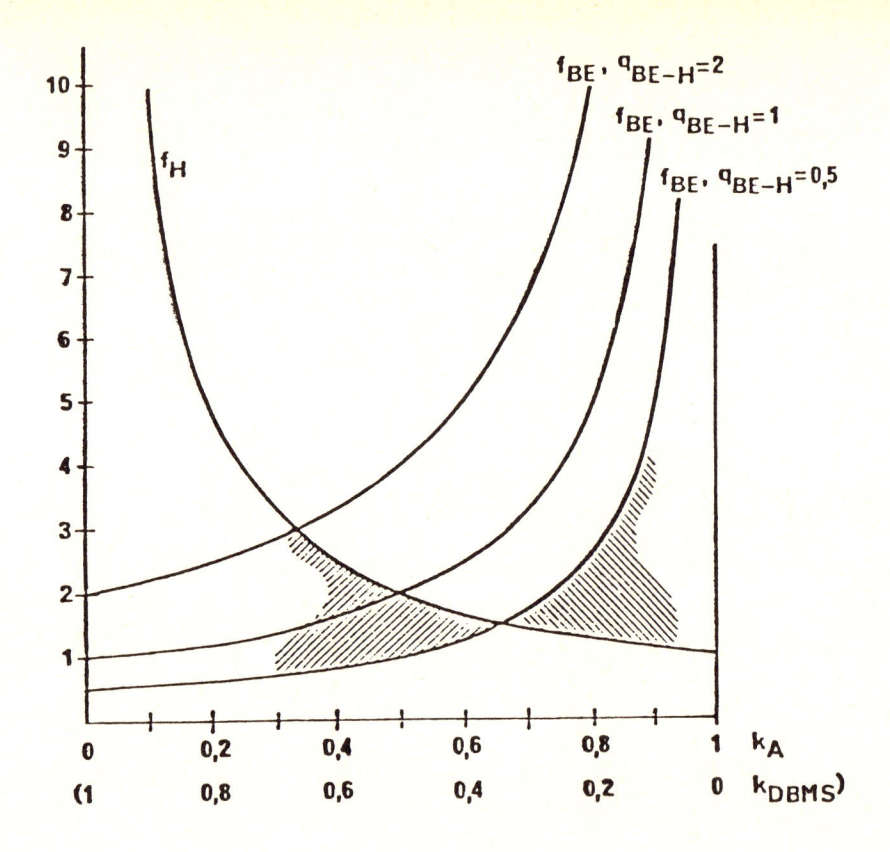

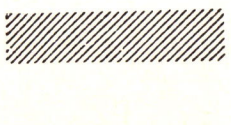

////////// backend cpu time occupied but free host cpu time

////////// host cpu time occupied but free backend cpu time

Obviously, the KOPS rating of the backend should exceed k_{DBMS}. Otherwise, a slowdown of database operations would occur ($f_{BE} < 1$).

If $q_{BE-H} = k_{DBMS}$ the freed host computer time can only be used for non-database activities. Hence, no higher transaction rate can be achieved.

On the other hand, f_{BE} should not exceed f_H. Otherwiese, the host cannot make full usage of the backend.

If $f_{BE} = f_H$ then the optimum operating point of the host-backend configuration is achieved (all underlined values in the foregoing table).

I.2 $c \neq 0$

Let us consider the following example:

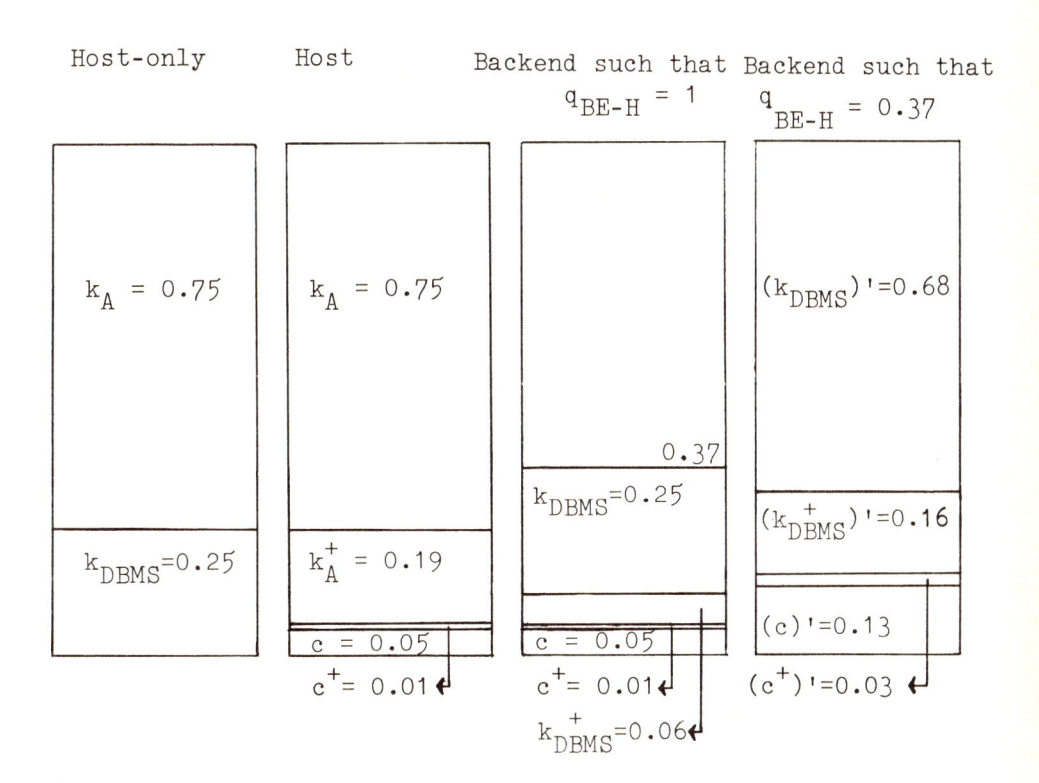

Host-only	Host	Backend such that $q_{BE-H} = 1$	Backend such that $q_{BE-H} = 0.37$
$k_A = 0.75$	$k_A = 0.75$		$(k_{DBMS})' = 0.68$
$k_{DBMS} = 0.25$	$k_A^+ = 0.19$	0.37 $k_{DBMS} = 0.25$	$(k_{DBMS}^+)' = 0.16$
	$c = 0.05$	$c = 0.05$	$(c)' = 0.13$
	$c^+ = 0.01$	$c^+ = 0.01$ $k_{DBMS}^+ = 0.06$	$(c^+)' = 0.03$

where

$k_A^+ = (1-k_A-c) \dfrac{k_A}{k_A+c}$ is the increase in k_A after having off-loaded the DBMS

$c^+ = (1-k_A-c) \dfrac{c}{k_A+c}$ same for c

$k_{DBMS}^+ = \dfrac{k_A^+}{k_A} k_{DBMS}$ same for k_{DBMS}

$(\ )'$ denotes division by q_{BE-H}.

Obvidously, $k_A + k_A^+ + c + c^+ = 1$ and $k_{DBMS} + k_{DBMS}^+ + c + c^+$ must be the 'optimum' q_{BE-H}.

Thus the optimum operating point for a host-backend configuration is defined by

$$q_{BE-H} = k_{DBMS} \dfrac{(k_{DBMS}-c)\, k_{DBMS}}{1-k_{DBMS}+c} + c + \dfrac{(k_{DBMS}-c)\, c}{1-k_{DBMS}+c}$$

$$= \dfrac{k_{DBMS}+c}{1-k_{DBMS}+c},$$

i.e. $f_{BE} = f_H$.

The next table computes optimum q_{BE-H} and f_{BE} (= f_H) values for given values of k_{DBMS} and c.

k_{DBMS}	c/k_{DBMS} 0,0	0,1	0,2	0,4	0,6	0,8	1,0	
0,25	0,33	0,35	0,38	0,41	0,44	0,47	0,50	q_{BE-H}
	1,33	1,29	1,27	1,17	1,10	1,04	1,00	f_{BE}
0,33	0,50	0,52	0,55	0,58	0,61	0,64	0,67	
	1,50	1,41	1,38	1,24	1,14	1,07	1,00	
0,50	1,00	1,00	1,00	1,00	1,00	1,00	1,00	
	2,00	1,82	1,67	1,43	1,25	1,11	1,00	
0,67	2,00	1,83	1,71	1,56	1,45	1,38	1,33	
	3,00	2,50	2,14	1,67	1,36	1,15	1,00	
0,75	3,00	2,54	2,25	1,91	1,71	1,59	1,50	
	4,00	3,08	2,50	1,82	1,43	1,18	1,00	

For $k_{DBMS} < 0,5$ and increasing c the ratio q_{BE-H} also increases.

For $k_{DBMS} > 0,5$ and increasing c the ratio q_{BE-H} decreases.

For $k_{DBMS} = 0,5$ the ratio $q_{BE-H} = 1$ for all c.

Note that c^+ only depends on k_{DBMS} while

k_{DBMS} depends on $\dfrac{k_A}{k_{DBMS}}$ which is $\begin{Bmatrix} > 1 \\ < 1 \end{Bmatrix}$ if k_{DBMS} $\begin{Bmatrix} < 0,5 \\ > 0,5 \end{Bmatrix}$.

Now we compute the transaction rate T_{H-BE} for an optimum host-backend configuration.

Let T_H denote the transaction rate for the host-only system.

Then $T_{H-BE} = T_H \cdot f_{BE} = T_H \dfrac{q_{BE-H}}{k_{DBMS}+c}$.

Example: Let $k_{DBMS} = 0.33$ and $c = 0.2\ k_{DBMS}$.

Then $q_{BE-H} = 0.55$ and $T_{H-BE} = 1.38\ T_H$.

Denote by

t_H, t_{BE} the response time required for the execution of a database transaction in a single processor system (host or backend)

t_{H-BE} the response time required for the execution of a database transaction in a host-backend configuration

t_c the data communication time for the exectuion of a database transaction in a host-backend configuration.

Then $t_{H-BE} = t_{BE} + t_c$.

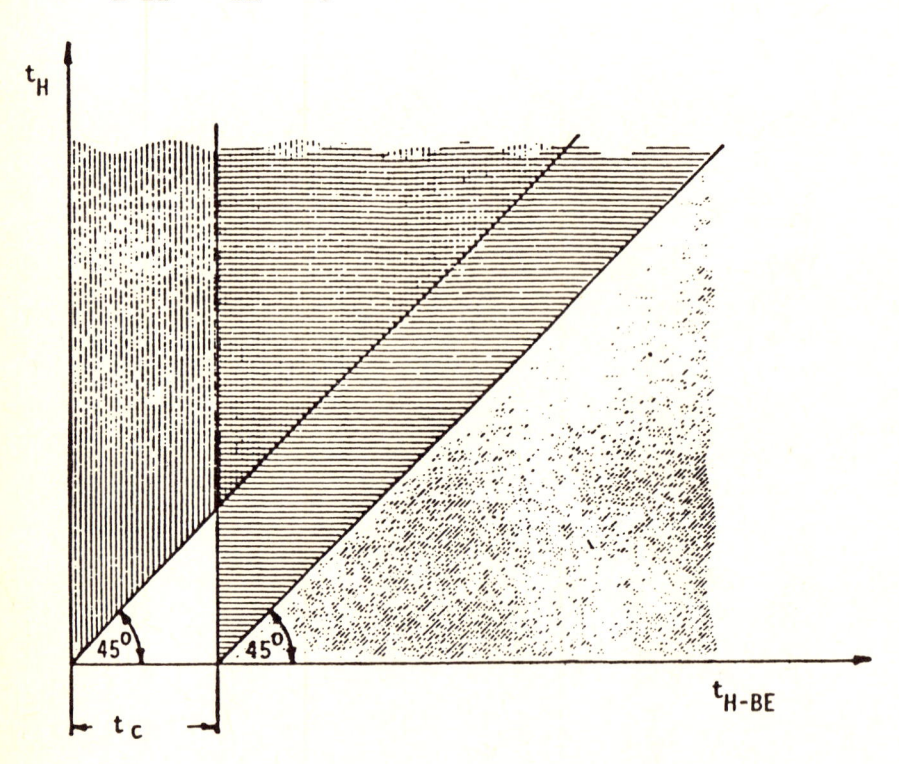

When using a host-backend configuration for database activities $t_{H-BE} \leq t_H$ would be desirable.

Suppose that $t_{H-BE} \approx \dfrac{1}{f_{BE}} t_H + t_c$.

Then $\dfrac{1}{f_{BE}} t_H + t_c \leq t_H$, i.e. $\dfrac{k_{DBMS} \cdot t_H}{t_H - t_c} \leq q_{BE-H}$.

II. $k_{NDB} \neq 0$

When having off-loaded the DBMS into a backend the freed host cpu time is spent for additional database and non-database activities such that $\dfrac{k_{NDB}}{k_{DB}}$ remains constant.
The backend is assumed to be adequately sized.

Furthermore, $c = 0$ is assumed in order to emphasize on the relation between k_{DB}, α and the increase in k_{NDB} after having off-loaded the DBMS.

Example:

Host-only	Host	Backend such that $q_{BE-H} = 0.67$
$k_{NDB} = 0.20$	$k_{NDB} = 0.20$	$(k_{DBMS}^{+})' = 0.40$
	$k_{NDB}^{+} = 0.13$	
$k_{DBMS} = 0.40$	$k_{A}^{+} = 0.27$	
$k_{A} = 0.40$	$k_{A} = 0.40$	$(k_{DBMS})' = 0.60$

Where

$$k_{A}^{+} = k_{DBMS} \dfrac{k_A}{1 - k_{DBMS}}$$

$$k_{NDB}^{+} = k_{DBMS} \dfrac{k_{NDB}}{1 - k_{UDS}}$$

Obviously, $k_{NDB} + k_{NDB}^+ = k_{NDB} (1 + \frac{k_{DBMS}}{1-k_{DBMS}}) = k_{NDB} \cdot f_H =: y$

$k_A + k_A^+ = k_A \cdot f_H$

$k_A \cdot f_H + k_{NDB} \cdot f_H = 1.$

Now we investigate $k_{NDB} \cdot f_H = y$ as a function of k_{DB} and

$\alpha = \frac{k_{DBMS}}{k_{DB}}$

(The term $k_A \cdot f_H$ could be investigated similiarly).

$y = \frac{1 - k_{DB}}{1 - k_{DBMS}} = \frac{k_{DB} - 1}{\alpha \cdot k_{DB} - 1}$ ($0 \leq y \leq 1$)

For $\alpha = 0.5$ we get the following hyperbola:

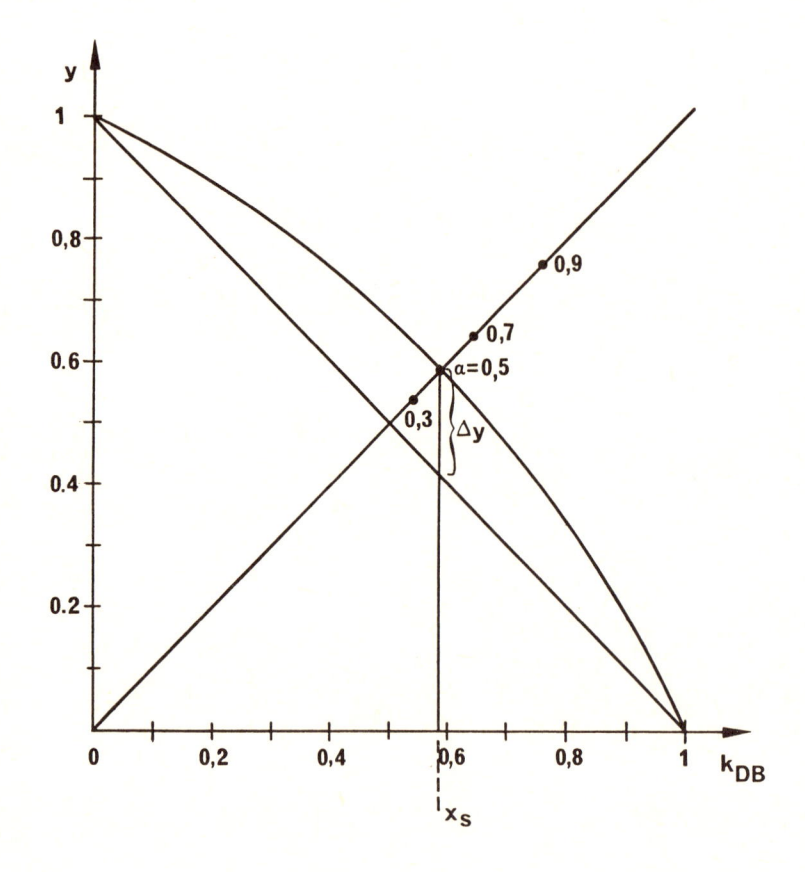

This results in:

$$x_s = \frac{1}{\alpha}(1 - \sqrt{1-\alpha})$$ where x_s denotes the x-coordinate of the vertex

$$\lim_{\alpha \to 0} x_s = 0,5$$

$$\Delta y = 2x_s - 1$$

$$k_{NDB}^+ \leq \Delta y$$

For a given α, Δy represents a limit for the increase in non-database activities.

Example:

Let $\alpha = 0.5$ and $k_{NDB}^+ = 0.13$.

Then $x_s = 0.59$ and $\Delta y = 0.17$.

Conclusion.

This paper has discussed some effects when off-loading database activities from a mainframe to an attached backend. For given workloads consisting of database-only activities criteria for selecting an optimally sized backend are derived.

For workloads including non-database activities some first results are presented.

References:

1. Drawin M., Schweppe H.: A Performance Study on Host-Backend Communication, IWDM Proceedings, München, 1983

2. Sekino A. et al: Design Considerations for an Information Query Computer, IWDM Proceedings, San Diego, 1982

Database Machines: An Idea Whose Time has Passed?
A Critique of the Future of Database Machines

Haran Boral
Computer Science Department
Technion - Israel Institute of Technology

David J. DeWitt
Computer Sciences Department
University of Wisconsin - Madison

ABSTRACT

In this paper we take a critical look at the future of the field of database machines. We hypothesize that trends in mass storage technology are making database machines that attempt to exploit a high degree of parallelism to enhance performance an idea whose time has passed.

1. Introduction

In 1979 our colleague David Hsiao wrote an introductory paper [HSIA79] for a special issue of the IEEE Computer Journal on database machines. He titled that article "Database Machines are Coming, Database Machines are Coming". Indeed at that time the future of database machines looked rosy. A large number of research projects were active and several commercial products were on the horizon. Although the designs and assumptions of the projects varied dramatically, the fundamental design objective of each project was to improve access to very large databases.

In this paper we will explore what has happened to database machines in the past four years and will attempt to predict the future of the area. Although we were tempted to title this paper "Database Machines are Dead, Database Machines are Dead", a statement this strong is probably premature. However, we assert that unless some fundamental changes occur in commercially available mass storage technology, the use of massive parallelism or associative memory for reducing the execution time of a single query is definitely an idea whose time has passed.

We will begin by describing in Section 2 the changes in technology that started the database machine revolution. We will then trace the evolution of the field by briefly describing a number of key projects. In Section 3, we will discuss the trends in mass storage and processor technology since 1970 and their effects on the future of database machines. Our assertion is that highly parallel high-performance database machines (of the type described in Section 2) are predicated on the availability of mass storage technologies that have not and probably will not emerge as commercially viable products. In Section 4, we suggest three avenues of research that seem promising for resolving the lack of sufficient mass storage bandwidth. Our conclusions are presented in Section 5.

2. The Desert Blooms

In this section we chronicle the development of database machines during the past twelve years. We have divided the numerous machines that have been proposed into three general classes: processor-per-track designs, processor-per-head designs, and off-the-disk designs. In the following sections we present an overview of each classification and describe several machines belonging to each.

2.1. Processor-per-Track (PPT) Architectures

Database machines were pioneered by Slotnick [SLOT70] who in 1970 formulated the idea of associating processing logic with the read/write heads of a rotating storage device such as a fixed head disk, as shown in Figure 1, in order to process certain search operations "on the fly". The processors are connected to a global data bus onto which they place selected records for transmission to the host processor. Coordination of the operation of the cells is performed by a controlling processor. The basic motivation of Slotnick's design was to be able to search a database directly on the mass storage unit and thus limit the amount of data to be transferred to the host for additional processing. In addition, since an entire database could be searched in one revolution of the mass storage device, the need for

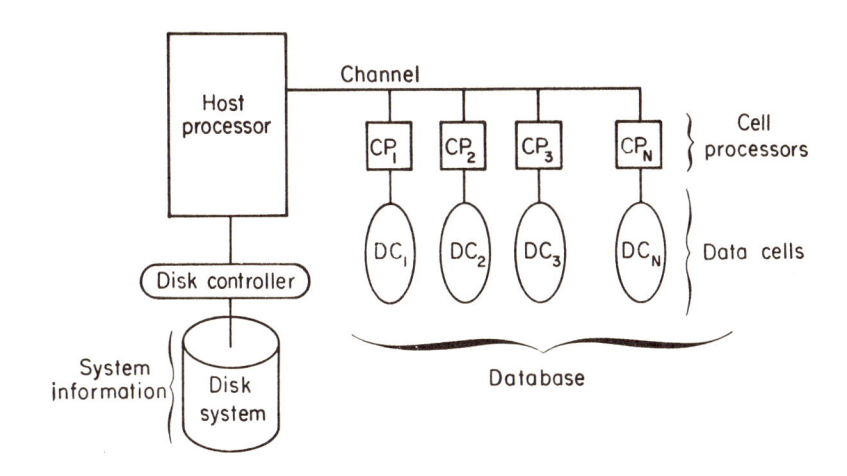

Figure 1

auxiliary storage structures such as indices to enhance performance was eliminated simplifying, considerably, the DBMS software.

Slotnick's ideas were further developed by Parker [PARK71], Minsky [MINS72], and Parhami [PARH72]. Although none of these efforts resulted in a comprehensive proposal for the implementation of a database machine, they served as a source of ideas for subsequent efforts; in particular CASSM, RAP, and RARES which are described briefly below.

2.1.1. CASSM

CASSM was the first complete database machine design. It was designed to support the network, hierarchical, and relational data models. A fixed head disk is used as the storage medium and a simple processing element is associated with each read/write head. The processing elements are controlled by a single processor which is responsible for communication with the host computer(s), distributing instructions to the processors, and collating and processing both intermediate and result relations.

Data items in CASSM are stored as ordered pairs: <attribute name, value>. All data items belonging to a record are stored in a physically contiguous block preceded by record and relation identifiers. Associated with each attribute and each record are a set of mark bits. These bits are used to indicate the results of an operation. Strings are stored only once in the database, separately from the records in which they are values. In these cases the value field of the ordered pair is a pointer to the string

When executing a selection query, a processing element marks tuples belonging to the relation being processed during the first disk revolution. A second revolution is used to search the marked records for the desired attribute and check its value; qualifying attributes are marked. A third revolution is used to output the marked attributes. In the event that the marked attribute is a string, the third revolution is used to chase the pointer in the value field of the marked ordered pair and an additional, fourth, revolution is required to output the marked string. Joins were implemented using a hashing scheme and an auxiliary memory similar to algorithms proposed for the CAFS [BABB79] and LEECH [MGCR76] database machines.

2.1.2. RAP

The RAP [OZKA75, OZKA77] database machine project is also based on a PPT approach in which tuples from a relation are stored bitwise along a track. Only tuples from one relation are allowed on a track, although numerous tracks can be used to store a relation. As in CASSM, a tuple is augmented with a fixed number of mark bits (attributes are not) that serve the same purpose. Processing of a selection operation is similar to CASSM, although it is faster because of the simpler data' structure. Also, the processing elements have the capability of scanning for a number of different values in parallel. Joins are processed as a series of selection sub-queries on the larger relation, using the values of the joining attribute in the smaller relation as the selection criteria (a parallel nested loops algorithm).

2.1.3. RARES

RARES [LIN76], like RAP and CASSM, employs a PPT design utilizing a third storage format. Tuples are stored across tracks in byte parallel fashion. That is, byte 0 of a tuple is stored on track 0; byte 1 of the same tuple is stored in the same position on track 1; and so on. In this orthogonal approach a tuple that is "waiting" to be sent will be distributed over several buffers (a byte in each processing element) whereas in RAP the tuple will reside in a buffer in a single processing element. Thus, RAP would be more likely to be blocked than RARES due to bus contention.

2.1.4. Discussion

Although the PPT designs initially looked attractive, researchers quickly realized that they could not be used for the storage of very large databases (which was the original motivation for database machines). Their fundamental flaw is that a track of data on a magnetic medium was limited in 1970 to about 15,000 bytes [GORS80]. Thus to hold a 150 million byte database (which is not very big), a device with 10,000 tracks and processors would be required. Researchers attacked this problem in three ways. The PPT advocates turned to solid state devices such as bubble memories and charge coupled devices to provide longer tracks. We will address the problems associated with this solution in Section 3. Another group of researchers turned to an approach in which a processor is associated with each read/write head of a moving head disk. We term this approach "processor-per-head". It is discussed in the following section. A third solution investigated was to separate the processors from the storage medium with a large disk cache. The goal of this "off-the-disk" approach was to be able to continue to exploit parallelism to enhance performance while using conventional (and hence cheap) mass storage devices for holding the database. We discuss this approach in more detail below.

2.2. Processor-per-Head Designs

A second class of database machines are those that associate processing logic with each head of a moving-head disk as illustrated in Figure 2. We term this class of machines "processor-per-head" (PPH) machines. In a PPH database machine, data is transferred, in parallel, from the heads to a set of processors. Each processor applies the selection criteria to its incoming data stream and places selected tuples in its output buffer. In such an organization an entire cylinder of a moving head disk is examined in a single revolution (assuming no output bus contention).

2.2.1. Ohio State Data Base Computer (DBC)

The DBC [KANN78, BANE78] project chose the PPH approach as the basis for the design of their "Mass Memory Unit" as PPT devices were not deemed to be cost-effective for the storage of large databases (say more than 10^{10} bytes) [KANN78]. DBC consists of seven functionally different components. Of particular interest are the Mass Memory and Structure Memory components. The mass memory uses several moving head disks, with parallel readout capabilities, to store the database. The heads of the disks are connected, via a switch, to a number of processors which perform search operations.

While an entire cylinder can be searched in one revolution, executing search queries which access data that spans many cylinders in a brute force fashion is not effective [DEWI81]. The DBC designers recognized this fact and incorporated indices into their design. The indices are kept in the Structure Memory. These indices are used to

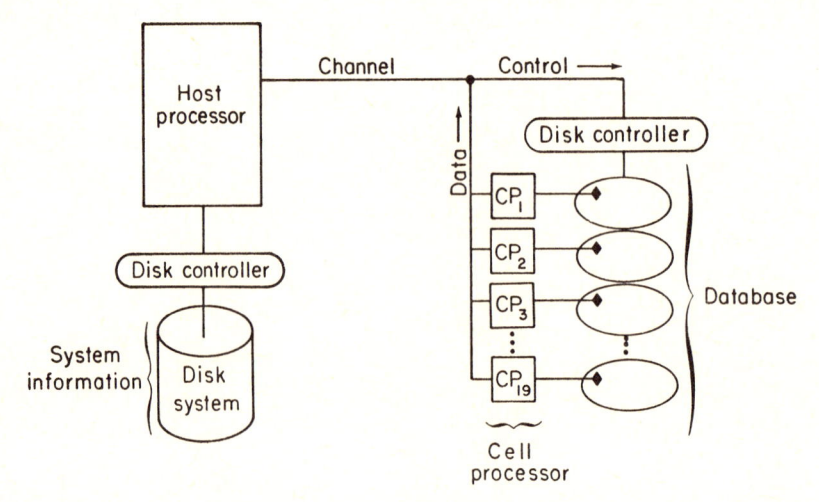

Figure 2

limit the number of cylinders that must be searched when executing a query.

2.2.2. SURE

SURE [LEIL78] uses a moving head disk modified to enable parallel read out from all of the recording surfaces simultaneously. The output is collected into a single high-speed broadcast channel from which it is read by a number of processors. Each processor is a very high-speed pipelined unit with a simple instruction set geared towards searching. A selection query is broken down into as many simple components as possible, each of which is assigned to one of the processors for execution. The actual number of processors used for the execution of a selection query depends on its complexity. Like RARES, SURE is intended to function only as a search processor, perhaps in the context of a database machine or serving a DBMS on a general-purpose computer.

2.2.3. Discussion

In [DEWI81] the performance of a number of alternative database machine architectures were evaluated for a range of different query types. The result of this evaluation indicates that the PPH design provides very good performance when searching a file for those records that satisfy a search condition. When a suitable index was available, a PPH organization with 19 processors (and read/write heads) was never more than a factor of 1.6 slower than a PPT organization with 7676 processors and tracks. Without a suitable index, the PPH organization was approximately a factor of 4 slower.

When, however, this same design was used to process complex queries, such as the relational algebra join operation by repeatedly processing one relation using values from the second relation (the RAP join algorithm), both it and a "generic" PPT design performed significantly slower than a conventional processor. This indicates that the PPH design alone does not provide a suitable level of performance for all relational algebra operations. To solve this problem, the designers of the DBC augmented their original design to include a postprocessing unit for processing complex database operations such as the relational join operator.

2.3. Off-the-Disk Machines

Another solution to the database size problem is to separate the processors from the storage medium with a large disk cache. We term this approach the "off-the-disk" approach. The goal of this approach is to be able to continue to exploit parallelism to enhance performance while using conventional mass storage devices. While all data to be processed must first be moved from mass storage to the disk cache, once the data is there it can be accessed by the processors in parallel (assuming the existence of suitable hardware). Furthermore, intermediate results in processing a query will be placed by the processors in the disk cache and hence be quickly accessible for the subsequent operations in the query.

There is a large number of database machines in this class including RAP.2 [SCHU79], DIRECT [DEWI79], INFOPLEX [MADN79], RDBM [HELL81], and DBMAC [MISS81]. In addition, some database machine designers have designed machines that combine the characteristics of the PPH and "off-the-disk" designs (REPT [SHUL81], HYPERTREE [GOOD81]). As discussed in [DEWI79], such designs look promising if parallel readout disks can be constructed (a point we will return to in Section 3). We will briefly describe DIRECT and RAP.2 in the following sections.

2.3.1. RAP.2

In [SCHU79], Schuster et al describe a virtual RAP machine. In this organization the database resides on some number of conventional mass storage devices. The RAP system consists of a number of cells, each with a pair of tracks. The controller assumes the additional responsibilities of loading the tracks with data to be examined. Each processor can examine only one track at a time. However, while one track is being examined, the second can be loaded.

2.3.2. DIRECT

In this section we describe the architecture of DIRECT. The DIRECT project began after a critical evaluation of several database machine research projects (in particular RAP which in the mid 70´s was the most advanced and best known database machine design) revealed two major shortcomings with each of the proposed designs: the inability to process complex database operations (e.g. joins) efficiently [OZKA77,DEWI81], and the SIMD mode of operation in which only a single instruction from a single query can be executed simultaneously. As shown in [BORA81] a database machine that processes queries in a SIMD mode has a lower transaction throughput than one which processes multiple operations from multiple queries simultaneously. DIRECT was designed to overcome these two shortcomings.

In DIRECT there are some number of processors whose function is to execute selection, projection, join, update, and aggregate operations on the database. These processors are controlled by a processor (termed the back-end controller) which is responsible for distributing instructions and overseeing data transfers to the processors. The database resides on some number of mass storage devices (moving head disks). Each relation is organized as a set of fixed size pages. The disk cache is divided into page frames of the same size. The query processors and disk cache page frames are connected by a cross point switch that has two important capabilities: any number of processors can read the same page simultaneously; and, any two processors can read/write from any two different devices concurrently. This organization permits processors to work in parallel on the same operation or on different operations.

2.3.3. Discussion

Although both the RAP.2 and DIRECT designs appeared promising initially, the research presented in [DEWI81] indicates that when the performance of a DIRECT-like design is compared to that of a conventional computer, increases in parallelism do not result in corresponding decreases in query execution time.

3. The Flowers Wilt

In the previous section we described three classes of database machine architectures: processor-per-track designs, processor-per-head designs, and "off-the-track" designs. In this section we will discuss how recent changes in mass storage technology have either made each of these designs infeasible or of reduced value with present day or near future technology.

Although we realize that all database machines may not fit directly into our classification, we contend that most database designs that <u>utilize parallelism</u> can be represented as a combination of these architectures. Thus, since we have serious doubts about the near term viability of each approach, just patching different approaches together does not resolve the fundamental problem we are facing: <u>current mass storage devices do not provide sufficient I/O bandwidth to justify highly parallel database machines</u>.

The reader should not, however, interpret this statement to mean that we feel that database machines that use limited parallelism (such as the IDM 500 [IDM500] with its database accelerator co-processor) are not viable. On the contrary such database machine designs with 1-3 processors per disk drive look very attractive (see the conclusions of [DEWI81]) and a reasonable design might a collection of such clusters interconnected by a high-speed local network [STON79].

In this section we first discuss the impact of trends in mass storage technology on the processor-per-track, processor-per-head, and off-the-disk database machine designs. Then we briefly discuss trends in processor technology. Finally, we present our interpretation of the compounded effect of these two trends on the future of database machines.

3.1. Trends in Mass Storage Technology

3.1.1. Impact on Processor-per-Track Database Machines

PPT designs were predicated on: 1) associating a processor with every storage cell, and 2) the availability of a sufficient number of storage cells to hold the entire database. Thus, conventional database techniques such as indexing would be never by needed by these designs. Unfortunately, the technologies on which these designs were predicated have either become obsolete or not commercially viable.

Fixed head disks on which the original designs were based are no longer manufactured[1]. Furthermore, storage of entire databases on fixed head disks never has been and never will be cost effective.

The other technologies considered as the basis for the storage cells of the processor-per-track designs were bubble memory and charge-couple-device (CCD) components. Although constructing mass storage devices from either CCD or bubble devices may be academically interesting, at this point in time it does not appear that either technology is likely to become a suitable replacement for moving head disk technology. Since their introduction, the cost/bit of CCD and bubble memory devices has not dropped as rapidly as that of moving head disks or random-access memory components. Although bubble memories are being used in a small niche of the market (mainly non-volatile memory for portable terminals), the state of the art is that Intel sells a board with bubbles that is slower than hard disk and more expensive than RAM.

CCDs have failed to generate a big enough market for parts where the access time did not matter. After their introduction, CCDs never were more than a half generation ahead of RAMs. This meant that if a customer was willing to wait an additional year, he would be able to purchase a RAM chip with the same density for the same price but with an access time of about two orders of magnitude faster. Consequently, most semi-conductor manufacturers have stopped manufacturing both types of components. It is likely that neither of these technologies will ever become cost effective for storing even moderate-sized databases.

---

[1] We are aware that certain models of winchester type disk drives such as the IBM 3380 have a limited number of tracks with fixed read/write heads. These tracks do not, however, store enough data to consider using them as the basis for a database machine.

In conclusion, it appears that processor-per-track database machines have only historical value.

3.1.2. Impact on Processor-per-Head Database Machines

When a parallel-readout disk drive is combined with a simple processor for each read/write head and an indexing mechanism to limit the number of cylinders that must be searched, the result is a database machine that can process *selection* queries at a very high rate [DEWI81]. In addition, when such a design is combined with an off-the-disk design, the performance for processing complex queries is also excellent. Why then is such an architecture not the wave of the future? The problem is that the same changes in magnetic disk technology that have produced constantly increasing disk capacities have made constructing parallel-readout disk drives increasingly more difficult.

To understand why it is difficult to construct a parallel-readout disk, one must reflect on the mechanism used to read/write conventional moving head disks. To minimize costs, all read/write heads are mounted on the same disk arm assembly which is then activated by some form of a linear motor. When the head assembly is moved to a cylinder (i.e. a seek operation), the read/write heads are not properly aligned on their respective tracks and fine adjustment is generally necessary to align the head selected for reading/writing. Due to the effects of thermal expansion of the arm, alignment must take place continuously (even while the track is being read/written). In parallel-readout disks all (or most) read/write heads must be aligned after each seek. If more than one head is to be aligned then the arm's position at any given time instance will most likely not be the optimal position for any one head and the signal received by each head will not be maximal; possibly leading to errors. As disk densities increase, the magnetic spots get smaller, further aggravating the effects discussed above.

Another problem with parallel readout disks is that the error detection and correction logic must be replicated for each head. Although we were not able to obtain precise figures on what part of the cost of a disk the error correction logic represents, we have been lead to understand that it is substantial. Associating error correction logic with each read/write head would contribute significantly to the cost of a disk. As an example, consider the winchester drive in which four of the 16 heads can be read/written at once made by CDC. The storage capacity of the drive is 675 megabytes, transfer rate of 4.84 megabytes/second, cost of $80,000. A drive of comparable storage capacity (484 megabytes) and a transfer rate of about 1.8 megabytes/second costs around $15,000 (Fujistu Eagle).

Thus, while parallel-readout drives were perhaps feasible 5-10 years ago, they are only marginally feasible today (from both technological and cost points of view). As we mentioned above, CDC does have a parallel readout drive with four heads operating in parallel. However, it is not clear whether their new generation of IBM 3380 compatible disks will include a parallel readout version.

Actuating each head with a different mechanical assembly would provide a solution to this problem. But since the linear motor and disk arm assembly with its associated positional sensing circuitry constitutes the major portion of the cost of a conventional disk drive, such a drive would be prohibitively expensive (and extremely bulky!). In addition to the problems of construction, such drives will have higher cost per bit of storage than conventional drives. For some applications (such as feeding data to a Cray-1) the performance benefits probably outweigh the cost disadvantages. For storage of large databases, their cost disadvantage will, in our opinion, make the use of such drives impractical.

In conclusion, although parallel-readout disk drives could form the basis of high performance, highly parallel database machine, changes in disk technology have rendered this approach questionable and other approaches must be developed to provide high bandwidth mass storage devices.

3.1.3. Impact on Off-the-Disk Database Machines

In addition to their effect on PPH designs, increasing disk densities also have had an adverse impact on the performance of off-the-disk database machine designs that utilize parallelism. Consider, for example, the three trends that moving head disk technology has displayed during the last ten years illustrated below in Figures 3, 4, and 5. Figures 3 and 4 illustrate encouraging trends for all computer applications: increased disk capacities (therefore cheaper cost per bit) and increased bandwidth per drive. When we combine the figures to obtain Figure 5 which shows the trend in bandwidth per gigabyte we find that the total bandwidth for a gigabyte of storage has actually decreased with improvements in disk technology from 1970 to 1975. The reason for this phenomenon is that almost every increase in disk capacity was the result of decreasing the distance between adjacent tracks on a surface and not the result of shrinking the distance between bits along a track. Thus, increases in storage capacity per drive were largely due to improvements in the mechanical head positioning technology.

The IBM 3380 caused this trend to change. In the IBM 3380, the capacity of a single track was increased from a typical capacity of about 15,000 bytes to about 45,000 bytes. This increase is due to improvements in head technology that resulted in the shrinking of the area occupied by each bit. Unfortunately, the gains in bandwidth illustrated by the IBM 3380 in Figure 4 (and the corresponding change in direction of the curve in Figure 5) due to increased track capacities are not likely to continue. The 3 megabyte/second bandwidth of the IBM 3380, is difficult for most machines to handle (even on large IBM machines, a special channel is needed to handle these drives). Thus, it is not likely that track capacities will increase further (or

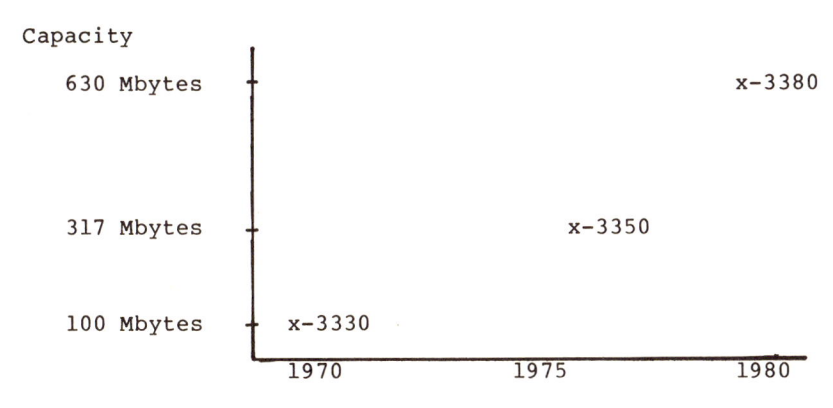

Capacity

630 Mbytes   x-3380

317 Mbytes   x-3350

100 Mbytes   x-3330
          1970   1975   1980

Disk Capacity
Figure 3

Bandwidth

3 Mbytes/Sec   x-3380

                x-3350
1 Mbyte/Sec
          x-3330
          1970   1975   1980

Bandwidth Per Disk Drive
Figure 4

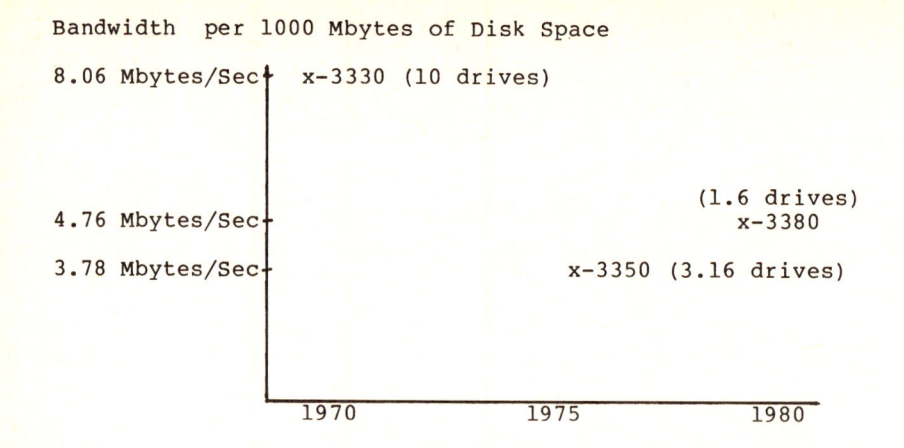

```
Bandwidth  per 1000 Mbytes of Disk Space
8.06 Mbytes/Sec┼ x-3330 (10 drives)



                                          (1.6 drives)
4.76 Mbytes/Sec┼                             x-3380
3.78 Mbytes/Sec┼               x-3350 (3.16 drives)




                 1970           1975          1980
```

Total Available Bandwidth for 1 Billion Bytes of Storage
Figure 5

at least the maximum bandwidth per spindle is likely to remain at the level of the 3380).

What we are saying then is that although the trends illustrated by all three figures seems encouraging, in fact they are not. The improvement in disk storage capacity is due to improvements in mechanical head positioning technology and in head technology itself. Improvements in head technology cause, in addition to increases in disk capacity, a corresponding increase in disk bandwidth. Improvements in mechanical head positioning technology do not affect disk bandwidth. Existing I/O processors cannot handle transfer rates higher than 3 megabytes/second.[2] Undoubtedly this will change over time. However, we believe that several years will pass until this change takes place. In the meantime additional increases in disk capacity will be made through further improvements in head positioning technology. Thus, for a database with a given size, the bandwidth available for access to that database is likely to decrease.

3.2. Trends in Processor Technology

While the capacity of mass storage devices has been growing, "slower" and "slower" conventional microprocessors have been getting faster and faster. In this section we will explore the tasks performed by the processing elements of a database machine and will

---
[2] The Cray-1 and several of the higher-end CDC machines use the parallel readout CDC drive. To handle the high data transfer rate they have had to resort to the use of two I/O processors to control the disk and to ping pong control over the disk between them!

demonstrate that advances in microprocessor technology have eliminated the need for customized database machine processors implemented either through microcode or VLSI.

3.2.1. Description of Major Tasks Performed by the Processing Elements

All the database machine organizations described in the previous section are organized in a two tiered manner: at the top level a single processor that is responsible for communications with the outside world and management of the machine resources; at the bottom level several processing elements are responsible for executing tasks. Practically all of the overhead functions, such as disk arm scheduling and buffer memory management (if there is one in the machine), associated with executing queries, are handled by the controller. The processing elements spend almost none of their time executing any of these overhead tasks. The database machines discussed previously attempt to decrease the execution time of queries through the use of parallelism in the query execution itself not by speeding up the controller's function (an exception is the DBC which uses a form of pipelining to distribute the controller's functions among four or five specialized processors). Since the emphasis in most designs is on the use of parallelism in the lower level we now carefully examine the processing requirements of that level and ignore those of the top level.

The operations supported by most relational database systems, can be divided into two classes according to the time complexity of the algorithms used on a uni-processor system. The first class includes those operations that reference a single relation and require linear time (i.e. they can be processed in a single pass over the relation). The most familiar example is the selection operation that selects those tuples from a relation that satisfy a predicate (e.g. suppliers in "New York").

The second class contains operations that have either one or two input relations and require non-linear time for their execution. An example of an operation in this class that references one relation is the projection operation. Projecting a relation involves first eliminating one or more attributes (columns) of the relation and then eliminating any duplicate tuples that may have been introduced by the first step. Sorting (which requires $O(n\log n)$ time) is the generally accepted way of eliminating the duplicate tuples. The join operation is the most frequently used operation from this class that references two relations. This operation can be viewed as a restricted cross-product of two relations.

For both classes of operations, once a block (page) of data has been retrieved from mass storage to the memory of a database machine, there are three basic operations that must be performed efficiently while executing a query: search operations, moving data from one memory location to another, and indexing operations (pointing at the next tuple/record to be processed).

The operation of searching for a record (tuple) which satisfies certain conditions is used in a variety of relational operations including:

(1) selection - in which the search condition may be arbitrarily complex: name = "Jones" and salary > $10,000 or name = "Smith" and salary = $95,000

(2) join - in which an attribute of one tuple is compared against the attribute of another tuple

(3) projection - duplicate tuples are detected by comparing all attributes of one tuple with all attributes of another.

Moving records from one memory location to another also occurs in a number of database operations including sorting and placing tuples in the result relation of a query. Finally, while searching a block of tuples the task of locating the proper field in the next tuple to be examined is performed frequently and thus should be executed as quickly as possible.

3.2.2. Processing Requirements of these Operations

In a separate paper [BITT83], we report the results of running benchmarks on several database systems. We had hoped to utilize the results of these benchmarks to gather statistics on cpu time per disk access for the different operations. In particular, we were planning to use the Commercial Ingres numbers. However, the numbers we obtained from these benchmarks do not permit separation of cpu time into overhead and processing components. Instead we ran a small subset of the benchmark on the Wisconsin Storage System (WiSS) [CHOU83] running on a VAX 11/750.

A description of WiSS is beyond the scope of this paper. However, a few words are due. WiSS is an extent based file system implemented on top of Unix although bypassing the Unix file system. WiSS consists of several layers that do buffer management, index maintenance, recovery, concurrency control etc. From its inception, in 1981, it was intended to provide faculty and students at Wisconsin with a tool for database research. It has been used as a basis for student projects in database management systems and database machines.

All the major relational operators have been implemented on top of WiSS. Algorithms that rely on sorting, indexing, and other data structures have been implemented. For this paper we ran a small number of experiments trying to measure the amount of cpu time spent per access to disk. We looked at selection and join operations without indexes. The join was implemented using a sort merge algorithm. Selection was implemented using a sequential scan of the relation.

The main result of this effort is that a considerable amount of additional work is required if one is to obtain the kind of numbers we desire. There are numerous factors that contribute to the cpu time measured. Some examples are doing the measurements while other users were using the system, factoring out various overhead costs such as buffer management (not done by the processing elements of a database machine), and disk scheduling.

All tests were run on a 10,000 tuple relation with 182 bytes/tuple. The relation was organized as 4096 byte pages. Tuples were not stored across page boundaries. Pages were full.

Selection operations were evaluated on both 2-byte integer attributes and 52-byte string attributes. Selectivity factors of 1% and 10% were used for each attribute. We found that the average cpu time spent per disk access ranged between a little less than a millisecond to about 2.5 milliseconds.

A 10,000 tuple relation was joined with a 1,000 tuple relation to obtain a 1,000 tuple result relation. We ran the tests with different main memory buffer sizes. The buffer sizes evaluated were 3, 5, 10, 20, 50, and 100 (each buffer could hold a single 4096-byte page). We found that the cpu time time per disk access ranged between 13 and 22 milliseconds. In general, the execution time per disk access increased as the number of buffers available to the sort-merge routine increased (of course, the total execution time decreased).

What is the period of time required to access a page on disk? In the best of cases no seek will be required. Thus total time consists of latency and transfer (about 10 milliseconds on a Fujitsu Eagle disk). On the average the seek time of the Eagle is about 20 milliseconds thus we obtain a figure of 30 milliseconds for the random access case.

The conclusions that can be drawn from these figures are:

(1) A single processor with performance characteristics similar to the VAX 11/750 can process selection queries at the rate the disk delivers data.

(2) Two or three processors would be required to process joins.

3.2.3. Implications

Based on the above arguments, we claim that "off-the-shelf" processing components provide sufficient processing power and that there is no need to implement customized database processors either through microcode or VLSI as has been argued in [KUNG80] and [YAO81] for example.

Although microprogramming is frequently touted as providing orders of magnitude of performance improvement for time critical database operations such as searching and moving strings, we claim that the performance improvements are minimal at best [ATKI73, DEWI76]. For machines without string handling instructions the best improvement one is likely to see is a factor of 2-3. For processors with machine language instructions for processing strings, there is, in general, little or no improvement in performance as such operations are inherently limited by memory bandwidth.

Furthermore, development of customized microcode is a very time consuming process and has the tendency to lock a project into obsolete technology. As an example consider the Braunschweig database machine project RDBM. This project began in 1980. By the end of 1981, the design and initial implementation of the AMD 2901 processor modules was completed and microprogramming of the customized functions was initiated. A year later (December 1982), the microcoding still had not been completed. In fact, for a number of operations, microcoding was abandoned because it was just too time consuming. Although the RDBM may indeed turn out to be relatively fast, we claim that by using "off the shelf" microprocessors and a high level language implementation a machine with equivalent performance could have been constructed. In addition, by utilizing a component such as the Motorola 68000, the performance a database machine can relatively closely track improvements in processor technology. This cannot be accomplished in such a straight-forward fashion if microprogramming is used as an implementation technique.

We also feel that utilizing custom VLSI components as the basis of a database machine will not produce a superior database machine. We have two arguments to support this almost heretical claim. First, since many database operations involve manipulating and moving strings (which are memory intensive operations requiring a high percentage of off-chip accesses), customized VLSI components are not likely to outperform state of the art microprocessors. Second, microprocessors have not only been getting faster but they have also become more sophisticated -- having richer instruction sets and handling a variety of data types, such as floating point numbers and strings, in addition to integers. Examples of such advanced VLSI microprocessors include the HP 9000 product with a 18 megahertz cpu chip containing 450,000 gates, the 16 megahertz Motorola 68020, and the Intel 287.

3.3. Combining the Trends

When one considers the trend of decreasing I/O bandwidth per gigabyte of storage and the increasing performance of off-the-shelf microprocessors, one is forced to conclude that the limiting factor is I/O bandwidth. We are convinced that one needs at most 2 or 3 conventional processors and not tens or hundreds of processors or customized VLSI components to process data at the rate that can be produced by current mass storage technology. Thus, an architecture that blindly uses custom VLSI components or a lot of processors (no matter how they are interconnected) to process data that resides on few standard disk drives will inevitably be I/O bound. Even with IBM 3380 disk drives only several of today's microprocessors are needed (and perhaps only one with the power of a Motorola 68020). Researchers should concentrate their efforts at increasing the I/O bandwidth. In the next section we briefly outline three possible approaches.

4. Making it Rain

We contend that before continuing to explore highly parallel architectures, database machine designers must turn their attention to exploring mechanisms for increasing I/O bandwidth. In addition, it appears that the use of indexing is necessary with ever increasing disk capacities. However, while improving I/O bandwidth is critical, researchers must face reality and figure out how to do it with conventional disk technology. The purpose of a database machine is to improve access to very large databases and users are almost certainly not going to be willing to accept database machines if their performance depends on the utilization of expensive mass storage devices.

One possible approach for improving raw I/O bandwidth is to use unmodified disk drives with a customized disk controller. The basic idea is that instead of trying to read or write all the heads of a single drive in parallel, a number (e.g. 12) of standard drives are attached to a customized controller that has been designed to permit the simultaneous data transfer between the controller and a single head of all drives. This will permit all tracks of a logical cylinder (a logical cylinder is formed by the set of tracks at the same physical location on all the attached drives) to be accessed in parallel. Such a design should provide the same I/O bandwidth as the parallel readout disk while using standard disk drives. Furthermore, by using off-the-shelf drives, one will be able to take advantage of improvements in disk storage technology by simply replacing the set of old drives with new ones.

There are several technical issues to be addressed. Chief is the design of the controller. The controller must coordinate several disks, some of which may be rotating at slightly different speeds. Error handling by the controller also becomes quite tricky. Consider, for example, what happens when one of the drives has a read error. Should all the drives retry the read or just one that had the error? While it might be simplest to have all drives repeat the read, during the retry a different drive may have a read error. Another question warranting attention is if such an organization is utilized in a processor-per-head database machine where should the filtering processors be placed? As part of the controller or between the controller and the other components of the database machine? Finally, how should indexing be incorporated into this mass storage organization? We understand that this approach is being explored by Cray Research as an alternative to using customized parallel-readout disks.

A second approach that appears to be worth exploring is to front end a number of conventional disks with a very large (100-200 megabyte), very fast solid state (RAM) memory.[3] The memory could be used as a disk cache (much in the same way that the CCD memory was used in DIRECT). Data pages could be prefetched from disks in anticipation of their usage, and/or kept in the cache in anticipation of their future usage (as in the case of a sort-merge join). There are a number of open research problems with this approach. The foremost is whether "real" database applications runing in a multi-user environment demonstrate any form of temporal locality. That is, do application programs access different portions of the database in a random fashion or does the working set change gradually over time? The addition of virtual memory to RAP was justified on the notion of temporal locality [SCHU79]. To our knowledge almost no effort has been made to instrument a running database system to determine the extent to which real systems demonstrate locality in their references to the database.[4] If there is a fair degree of locality, then this approach might solve

---

[3] Certain large IBM machines have main memory bandwidths in the 100 megabytes/second range (achieved through a combination of fast memory components, a high degree of interleaving (8 - 16), and a wide path into memory (e.g. 8 bytes at time).

[4] One exception is [RODR]. However, the results of this effort are inconclusive.

the I/O bottleneck. An experiment to determine locality certainly seems to be worthwhile. Other unsolved research problems associated with this approach include: development of replacement strategies that satisfy the needs of a variety of different applications, volatility and the notion of stable storage, and evaluation to see whether this approach will really work for a variety of applications.

Note that IBM has recently announced a disk controller that includes a disk cache that serves as a backup to main memory. The memory management algorithms used for managing the disk cache are different from those used for main memory. For example, data is prefetched from disk. IBM claims that the average access time for a disk with the disk cache is reduced to about 8 or 9 milliseconds from the usual 30-50. Our proposal in the previous paragraph is essentially similar, although specialized for database applications.

Finally, since increased disk densities seem to necessitate the use of indices to reduce the number of cylinders that need to be searched, more research is needed on effective index strategies in a database machine environment. For example, do we need a mechanism as complicated as the Structure Memory of the DBC or will a single fast microprocessor with its own dedicated disk for storage of indices be sufficient?

5. Conclusions

In this paper we have examined the impact in changes of mass storage technology on three different classes of database machines organizations: processor-per-track designs, processor-per-head designs, and off-the-disk designs. We have shown that processor-per-track designs no longer look technically feasible and that increasing magnetic disk capacities have had very a negative impact on the potential of highly parallel database machine designs. We conclude that unless mechanisms for increasing the bandwidth of mass storage devices are found, highly parallel database machine architectures are doomed to extinction.

6. Acknowledgements

We gratefully acknowledge the support of the National Science Foundation under grant MCS82-01870 and the Department of Energy under contract #DE-AC02-81ER10920.

7. References

[ATKI73] Atkins, D., DeWitt, D., and M. Schlansker, "Studies in the Applications of Microprogramming," ISDOS Working Paper No. 97, Dept. of Industrial Engineering and Operations Engineering, University of Michigan, December 1973.

[BABB79] Babb, E. "Implementing a Relational Database by Means of Specialized Hardware," ACM TODS, Vol. 4, No. 1, March 1979.

[BANE78] Banerjee J., R.I. Baum, and D.K. Hsiao, "Concepts and Capabilities of a Database Computer," ACM TODS, Vol. 3, No. 4, Dec. 1978.

[BITT83] Bitton-Friedland D., D.J. DeWitt, and C. Turbyfil, "Can Database Machines Do Better? A Comparative Performance Evaluation," Proceedings of the VLDB Conference, 1983.

[BORA81] Boral H. and D. J. DeWitt, "Processor Allocation Strategies for Multiprocessor Database Machines," ACM Transactions on Database Systems, Vol. 6, No. 2, pp. 227-254, June 1981.

[CHOU83] Chou H. T., D. J. DeWitt, R. H. Katz, and A. Klug "Design and Performance Evaluation of the Wisconsin Storage System," In preparation.

[DEWI76] DeWitt, D.J., "A Machine Independent Approach to the Production of Optimized Horizontal Microcode," Ph.D. Dissertation, University of Michigan, 1976.

[DEWI79] DeWitt, D.J., "DIRECT - A Multiprocessor Organization for Supporting Relational Database Management Systems," IEEE Transactions on Computers, June 1979, pp. 395-406.

[DEWI81] DeWitt, D. J., and P. Hawthorn, "Performance Evaluation of Database Machine Architectures," Invited Paper, 1981 Very Large Database Conference, September, 1981.

[GOOD81] Goodman, J. R., "An Investigation of Multiprocessor Structures and Algorithms for Data Base Management," Electronics Research Laboratory Memorandum No. UCB/ERL M81/33, University of California, Berkeley, May 1981.

[GORS80] Gorsline, G.W., _Computer Organization_, Prentice Hall, 1980.

[HELL81] Hell, W., "RDBM - A Relational Data Base Machine: Architecture and Hardware Design," Proceedings of the 6th Workshop on Computer Architecture for Non-Numeric Processing, June 1981.

[HSIA79] Hsiao, D.K., "Database Machines are Coming, Database Machines are Coming!," Computer, Vol. 12, No. 3, March 1979.

[IDM500] IDM 500 Reference Manual, Britton-Lee Inc., Los Gatos, California.

[KANN78] Kannan, Krishnamurthi, "The Design of a Mass Memory for a Database Computer," Proc. Fifth Annual Symposium on Computer Architecture, Palo Alto, CA. April 1978.

[KUNG80] Kung, H.T. and P.L. Lehman, "Systolic (VLSI) Arrays for Relational Database Operations," Proceedings of the 1980 International Conference on the Management of Data, May 1980, pp. 105-116.

[LEIL78] Leilich H.O., G. Stiege, and H.Ch. Zeidler, "A Search Processor for Data Base Management Systems," Proc. 4th Conference on Very Large Databases, 1978.

[LIN76] Lin, S.C., D.C.P. Smith, and J.M. Smith, "The Design of a Rotating Associative Memory for Relational Database Applications," TODS Vol. 1, No. 1, pages 53 - 75, Mar. 1976.

[MADN79] Madnick, S.E. "The Infoplex Database Computer: Concepts and Directions," Proceedings of the IEEE Computer Conference, Feb. 1979.

[MCGR76] McGregor, D.R., Thomson, R.G., and W.N. Dawson, "High Performance Hardware for Database Systems," in Systems for Large Databases, North Holland, 1976.

[MINS72] Minsky N., "Rotating Storage Devices as Partially Associative Memories," Proc. 1972 FJCC.

[MISS81] Missikoff, M., "An Overview of the project DBMAC for a relational machine," Proceedings of the 6th Workshop on Computer Architecture for Non-Numeric Processing, June 1981.

[OZKA75] Ozkarahan, E.A., S.A. Schuster, and K.C. Smith, "RAP - Associative Processor for Database Management," AFIPS Conference Proceedings, Vol. 44, 1975, pp. 379 - 388.

[OZKA77] Ozkarahan, E.A., Schuster, S.A. and Sevcik, K.C., "Performance Evaluation of a Relational Associative Processor," ACM Transactions on Database Systems, Vol. 2, No.2, June 1977.

[PARH72] Parhami, B., "A Highly Parallel Computing System for Information Retrieval," Proceedings of the Fall Joint Computer Conference, 1972.

[PARK71] Parker, J.L., "A Logic per Track Retrieval System," IFIP Congress, 1971.

[RODR76] Rodriguez-Rosell J., "Empirical Data Reference Behavior in Data Base Systems," Computer Vol. 9, No. 11, November 1976.

[SCHU79] Schuster, S.A., Nguyen, H.B., Ozkarahan, E.A., and K.C. Smith, "RAP.2 - An Associative Processor for Databases and its Applications," IEEE Transactions on Computers, C-28, No. 6, June 1979.

[SLOT70] Slotnik, D.L. "Logic per Track Devices" in Advances in Computers, Vol. 10., Frantz Alt, Ed., Academic Press, New York, 1970, pp. 291 - 296. TODS, Vol 1, No. 3, September 1976.

[STON79] Stonebraker, M. R., "MUFFIN: A Distributed Database Machine," University of California, Electronics Research Laboratory, Memo UCB/ERL m79/28, May, 1979.

[SU75] Su, Stanley Y. W., and G. Jack Lipovski, "CASSM: A Cellular System for Very Large Data Bases", Proceedings of the VLDB Conference, 1975, pages 456 - 472.

[SHUL81] Shultz, R., "A Multiprocessor Computer Architecture for Database Support," Ph.D. Dissertation, Computer Sciences Department, Iowa State University, August, 1981.

[YAO81] Yao, B. and M.M. Tong, "Design of a Two-Dimensional Join Processor Array," Proceedings of the 6th Workshop on Computer Architecture for Non-Numeric Processing, June 1981.

CID: A VLSI DEVICE FOR LISTS INTERSECTION

P. Bertolazzi, M. Missikoff and M. Terranova
IASI - CNR, Viale Manzoni, 30
00185 Roma - ITALY

ABSTRACT

This paper presents a VLSI device for the intersection of lists in a database machine. We show that a better performance can be obtained by partially relaxing the strong constraints on data pipeling characteristic of systolic devices.

The proposed architecture aims to intersect two unsorted lists with high degree of parallelism; moreover particular attention has been payed to maximize the utilization factor of the processors.

1. INTRODUCTION

The intersection of two or more lists is a very common operation in many database systems. In particular, the intersection is a critical operation in the system that use indices and inverted files to speed up the retrieval operation. For example when an interrogation includes two or more conditions on indexed fields of a file, the system will access first the selected indices to extract the lists of pointers corresponding to values that satisfy the required conditions. Successively the qualified lists will be intersected to produce the result list representing the records actually satisfying the original conditions. In relational database systems [1] to each tuple of a relation can be associated a tuple identifier (TID). A TID list can be used to represent in a compact way the intermediate result of a query. Some relational database machines [2,3,4] manage complex data structures with a large use of TIDs to represent not only the intermediate results of a query, but also part of the permanent relations [11]. In both cases each list contains elements without value duplications.

The present work has been carried on in the context of DBMAC project: DBMAC is a relational database machine where the relations are stored as a collection of a fully inverted data sets (called Data Pool [5,6]).

In DBMAC a query is processed accessing first all the Data Pool referred to in the query, extracting the qualified TID sets (one for each DP). Then the TID sets are combined to form the final TID set that represents the solution [13].

Several devices have been proposed that perform lists intersection.

There are devices that require sorted lists to operate [7], some others are more general and can operate also on lists of structured elements (i.e. elements with several attributes).

Very powerful devices are those proposed in [8,10] that appear to be very suitable to be implemented using VLSI technology.

In the next section the characteristics of this class of devices will be described with their principles of operation. Such devices appear to have very good performance when evaluated with the assumption of unlimited parallelism while in the case of limited number of processors the effectiveness can decrease significantly. In section 3 we give a general description of CID both in terms of the general architecture and its operating principles. In section 4 we present the evaluation of CID and we show the improvement we obtain with regards to the architectures presented in section 2. Section 5 presents a more detailed view of the architecture of CID, the layout of the principal circuits and some considerations on the feasibility.

2. SYNCHRONOUS DEVICES

In this section we describe some of the VLSI devices proposed in the literature to perform the intersection between two unsorted lists R and T of cardinality $|R|$ and $|T|$ respectively. The elements of each list have no duplicated values (no replication of TIDs is allowed).

Let T and R be the unsorted lists:

$$T = \{t_i\} \qquad i = 1,\ldots,|T|$$
$$R = \{r_j\} \qquad j = 1,\ldots,|R|$$

the output list, I, is defined follow:

$$I = T \cap R.$$

We define the "hit ratio" a as:

$$a = \frac{|I|}{|T|}.$$

2.1. *The array processor*.

The two dimensional array processor is proposed in [8]. In our case it has $2|T|$ elements arranged in two columns. In the first column (comparison column) the elements are stored and compared; in the second one (result column) the boolean results of successive comparisons of the same element are accumulated.

Each element r_i of R flows downward, followed, in the result column by a logical variable c_i. The elements t of T flow upward in the comparison column so that each t_j encounters all the r_i. Each processor of the comparison column compares t_j and r_i and communicates the result to the right processor which makes the OR with c_i.

In case of limited parallelism the intersection must be performed in several phases. Suppose to have P rows in the array, the list T must be partitioned into $|T|/P$ sublists. Then it is necessary to store one sublist at a time in the array and compare it in parallel with the list R, which flows downward in the device as in the previous case.

The time needed to perform the intersection between a sublist of T and R is given by:

$$T_{IS} = T_{CS} + T_{FR} + T_R$$

where:

T_{CS} is the loading time for the sublist of T. This time is $O(|P|)$.

T_{FR} is the time to obtain the result of the comparison of the first element of R with the elements of the sublist at the output of the circuit. This time is $O(|P|)$.

T_R is the time to obtain the result of the comparison for the last element of R. It is $O(|R|)$.

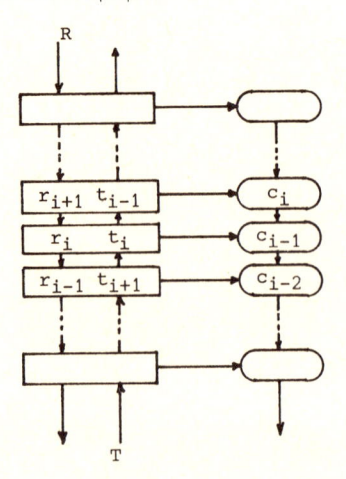

Fig. 2.1: The array processor.

The comparison of each sublist requires $O(P + |R|)$ steps, hence $O(|T|(P + |R|)/P)$ steps are needed to complete the intersection.

2.2. *The tree machine.*

The tree machine, presented in [9,10] is a mirrored binary tree in which each node is a processor and each edge is a wire connecting two processors (see fig. 2.2). The processors of the upper tree, in the case of intersection, are purely devoted to broadcast data. The processors of the lower tree can perform logic operations between boolean values. The leaves of the tree are processors that can perform comparisons.

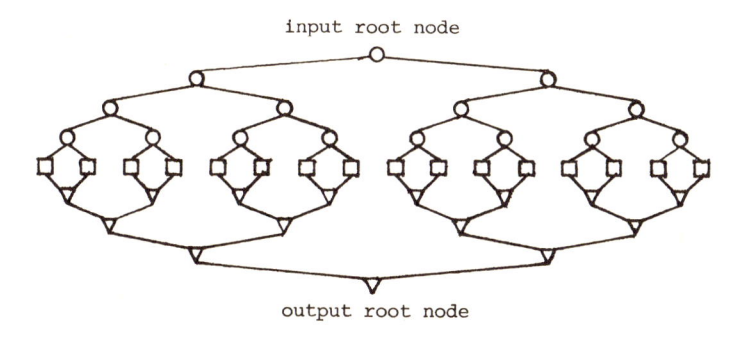

Fig. 2.2: The tree machine.

In our case the tree machine has $|T|$ leaves, in which the list T is stored. The depth of the trees is, consenquently, $\log|T|$.

When T has been stored in the machine, the elements of R are broadcast one after the other from the root through the upper tree to all the leaves; when the $|T|$ copies of the element r_i of R have reached the leaves, $|T|$ comparisons occur in parallel. The results of the $|T|$ comparisons are sent to the nodes of the lower tree, where they are ORed; after $O(\log|T|)$ steps a boolean value is obtained at the root of the tree, which is 1 if the i-th element of R matches at least one element of T.

In case of limited parallelism (a tree machine with P comparison processors: $P < |T|$) an algorithm similar to that illustrated for the array processor with P rows is implemented. The time to perform the intersection of the sublist is given by the following expression:

$$T_{TS} = T_{CS} + T_{FR} + T_R$$

where:

T_{CS} is the time needed to store a sublist of T, which is O(P).

T_{FR} is the time to obtain the result of the comparison of the first element of R with the elements of the sublist. This time is equal to $2\log|P|$.

T_R is the time needed to obtain the result of comparison for the last element of R. This time is O($|R|$).

This time must be multiplied by $|T|/P$ to obtain the total intersection time, that is $O(|T|(P + 2\log P + |R|)/P)$.

3. THE CONTINUOUS INTERSECTION DEVICE: CID.

The device CID has been designed to intersect two TID lists representing intermediate results of a query in DBMAC.

The TID lists that are produced during the operations of DBMAC are essentially of the kind defined in the previous section. In this section we present the base phylosophy of CID and a general view of its architecture.

3.1. *The CID operation.*

The operation of CID has been conceived in order to reduce the idle time of its elements.

We saw in the previous section that the synchronous devices operate in two distinct phases: the load phase in which the device is loaded with one sublist and the compare phase in which the second list is submitted and its elements compared. In CID the load phase is eliminated. The list R continuously rotates while the target list T flows in. The result list I flows out of the device at a rate which is a fraction of the input rate (depending on the hit ratio).

Each processor of CID holds a different element of T while the elements of R are continously shifted among the processors.

A given element t_i resides in a processor until one of the following events occurs:

    i) Match: The processor fetches a r_j equal to t_i it contains. In this case t_i is sent to the output and r_j is destroyed.

    ii) Dead: The processor has unsuccesfully compared t_i with all the elements of R. In this case t_i is destroyed.

In both cases when a processor get rid of t_i it fetches immediately a new element of T.

Notice that for every match the rotating list is shortened, that is the number of elements really contained in R reduces at each rotation of a quantity equal to the number of matches occurred. In the following we indicate as DRC_k (Dynamic R Cardinality) the number of elements that remain in R at k-th rotation.

3.2. *The CID architecture.*

The architecture of the device consists of three sections: Supply Section (SS), Comparison Section (CS) and Drain Section (DS). The figure 3.1 sketches the architecture of a CID having P comparison processors.

Supply Section - It provides to load the processors of the CS with the elements of the target list. It has a binary tree structure to route each element to a different processor.

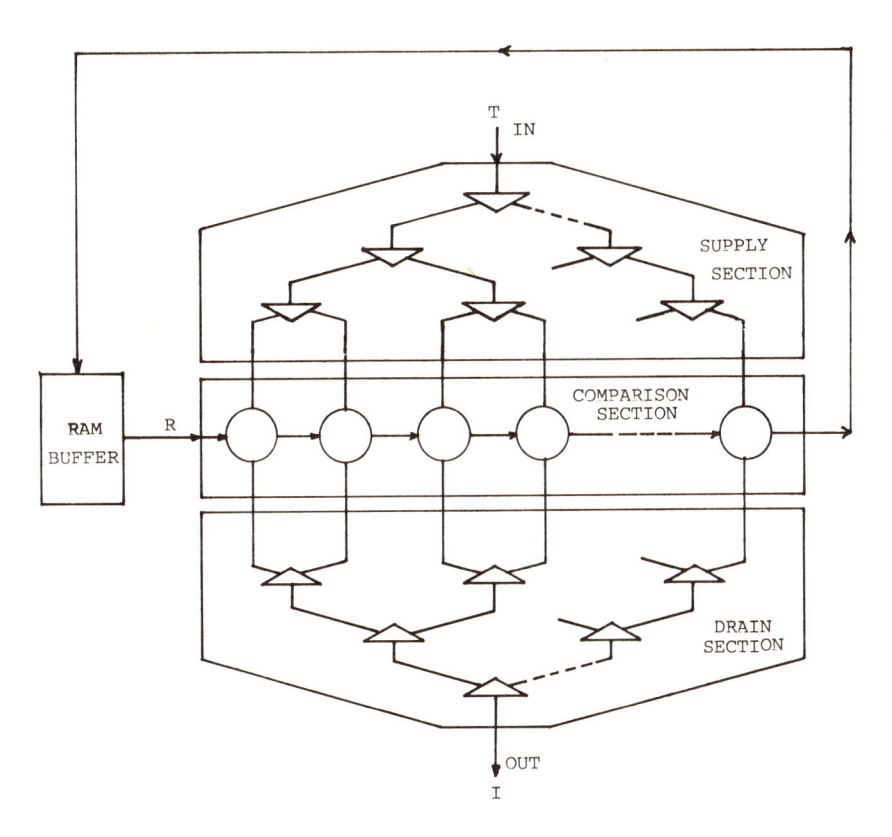

Fig. 3.1: The CID architecture.

Comparison Sections - This section contains a chain of processors (cells) performing the comparison among the elements of the two lists. The beginning of the chain is feed by a RAM buffer containing the list R and the elements r flow through the chain passing from one cell to the next. Each cell holds an element t fed by the SS and compares it with the flowing elements of R. A mismatch causes simply the transfer of r to the next cell; in case of matching the processor transfers the t to the DS, fetches a new t from the SS and passes a null-element (lacuna) to its successor. The lacunas are eliminated in the RAM buffer to which the elements r flowing out of the P chain return; in this way R can be recompacted, causing DRC to decrease.

Drain Section - This section receives the matched elements from the CS and forwards them to the output of the device. It must provide a structure able to reduce as much as possible the problems of congestion that can arise; thus also in this case a binary three structure is used.

To ensure a good performance it is necessary that:
- each time a CS processor requires a new element of T the SS has one ready.
- each time an element matches, the DS is ready to receive it.

When this two conditions are met we can minimize the idle time of the comparison processors.

3.3. *Supply Section operation.*

If the CID has P processors the SS section contains 2P-1 cells. When a comparison cell needs a new element t the SS cells on the path connecting the processor (leaf) to the input (root) behave as a shift register scaling down its contents. If two comparison processors issue a request simultaneously, a complete shift (from the root to the leaf) will be allowed only for one path (primary path). In this case a lacuna will be generated in the cell of the secondary path that is the son of the root of the smallest subtree containing both processors. The lacuna will be filled up with a partial shift from the input to the empty cell in the next cycle.

The figure 3.2 shows an example of generation and filling of a lacuna. When the cells C_1 and C_4 require a new t the path (1,2,4,9) will form the primary path and a complete shift to feed C_1 will occur, while the path to feed C_4 (1,2,5,11) will be broken in 2 and a lacuna will be generated in 5. In the next step a shift through (1,2,5) will fill up the lacuna.

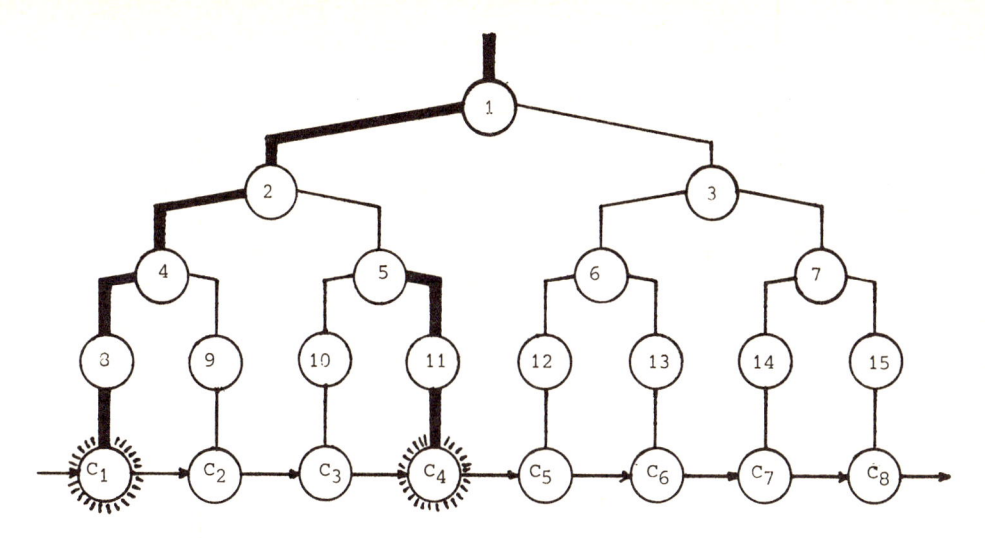

Fig. 3.2: Contention in the SS.

In a more general case it is possible to have in the SS many lacunas that travel from the leaves to the root. At each step a lacuna will be eliminated.

3.4. *Comparison Section operation.*

The Comparison Section operation can be described with the following algorithm:

```
Begin
repeat load t from the SS;
       match <- false;
       count <- 0;
       repeat load r from the predecessor;
              if r = t
              then begin
                   transfer t to the DS;
                   transform r into a lacuna;
                   match <- true
                   end
              else count <- count + 1
       until match or count = DRC
until elements t are finished
end.
```

3.5. *Drain Section operation*.

The Drain Section provides to forward the matched t to the output of the device. It has the structure of a binary tree. The elements t are injected in the leaves and must be carried out to the root.

The DS cell can store a t and, at each step, a non-empty cell transfers its content to its father. In this way a matched t can be carried out in log(P) steps if no contention occurs. The contention arises if and only if more than one element exists in the same level of the output tree, i.e. if and only if more than one t matches simultaneously. In this case one additional step is necessary to output each element after the first. Thus the output of n elements that matches simultaneously requires a number of steps equal to s, where:

$$s = \log(P) + n$$

Note that the output delay introduced by simultaneous matches does not necessarily affects the overall operation time because the DS has an intrinsic buffering capacity.

4. CID PERFORMANCE

To evaluate the performance of CID we consider the mean value of the time required to compute the intersection of a list T, containing |T| elements, and a list R, having |R| elements. We indicate this mean value as MIT (Mean Intersection Time).

To compute the MIT value we consider the mean value of the time required to process a single element t belonging to T. We call this mean value "Mean element Life Time" and indicate it as MLT. MLT is the expected value of the time that an element of T occupies a processor, thus the relationship between MLT and MIT can be expressed as follows:

(1) $$MIT = \frac{MLT |T|}{P}$$

where P is the number of the comparison processors.

The MLT value is given by:

(2) $$MLT = a\, MC + (1 - a)\, DRC$$

where:
- DRC is the mean value of the Dynamic R Cardinality computed from the DRC_k defined in the preceeding section;
- MC is the expected value of the number of comparisons needed to find

the matching element in R, assuming that this element exists;
- a   is the hit ratio.

The preceeding expression is derived considering that an element t has to be compared with all the elements remaining in R if it does not match any of them and the probability of this event is 1-a.

To compute MLT we assume an uniform distribution of values both in R and T. Thus:

(3) $$DRC = |R| - \frac{a}{2}|T|$$

(4) $$MC = \frac{DRC}{2}$$

Note that MC is the mean search time of an element into an unsorted list having length DRC.

The MLT can be expressed as a mapping of the cardinalities of T, R and I by substituting (3) and (4) in (2) and replacing a with $|I|/|T|$. In this way we obtain the following expression that is more suitable to analyze the effects of the operands on the operation time.

(5) $$MLT = |R| + \frac{1}{4}\frac{|I|^2}{|T|} - \frac{1}{2}|I|\left(\frac{|R|}{|T|} + 1\right)$$

The figure 4.1 shows the behaviour of MLT for a given cardinality of T and R varying the cardinality of their intersection. We see that, when $|I|$ increases from 0 to $|R|$, MLT decreases from $|R|$ to $|R|/2$ in a non linear fashion; as far as T is larger than R the curve approximates a straight line. In figure 4.2 MLT is shown as a mapping of $|T|$ assuming $|R|$ and $|I|$ fixed. In this case MLT increases due to the increase of unmatching elements. Note that, due to the (1), the diagram of figure 4.1 applies also to MIT assuming $|T|/P$ as a scaling factor.

The dot lines represents the value of MLT for a tree machine.

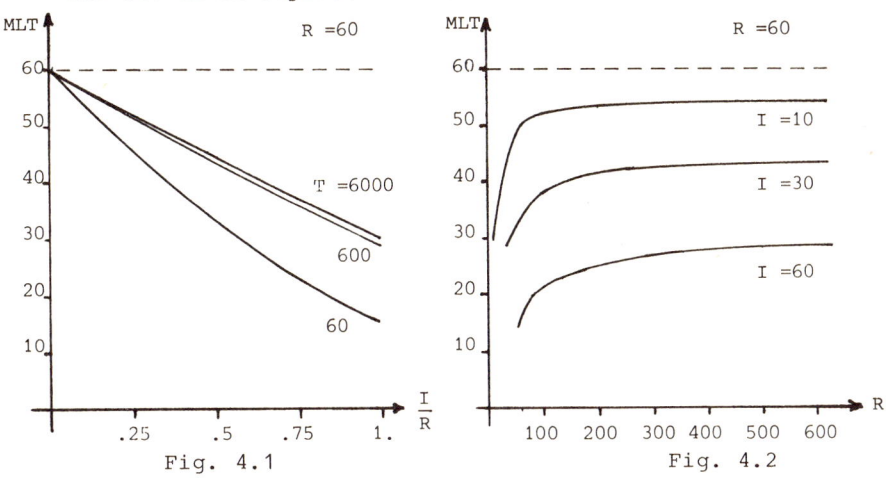

Fig. 4.1

Fig. 4.2

By substituting (5) in (1) we obtain the explicit expression of MIT:

(6) $$\text{MIT} = \frac{1}{P}(|R|\cdot|T| + \frac{1}{4}|I|^2 - \frac{1}{2}|I|(|R| + |T|))$$

From this expression we can see that, given two different sized lists, the choice of the rotating one does not affect the intersection time.

At this point we can compare the CID performance with those of the synchronous devices considered in section 2.

For both the array processor and the tree machine, assuming that the cardinality of the rotating list would be reduced during tne operation, the value of MIT is given by:

(7) $$\text{MIT} = \frac{1}{P}|T|\,\text{DRC}$$

For the CID, from (1), (2), (3) and (4) we obtain:

(8) $$\text{MIT} = \frac{1}{P}|T|\,(1 - \frac{a}{2})\,\text{DRC}$$

In the worst case ($|I| = 0$) (7) and (8) give the same value; this result is obvious because if none element matches we need always $|T|\cdot|R|$ comparisons to terminate the operation. When $|I| > 0$ the value given by (8) is always lower than the value of (7); thus the CID performance is better or equal to those of tree or mesh architectures. The better performance depens essentially on the better utilization factor of the comparison processors of CID: the key feature is the capability of reload a processor when it gets idle after a match. Moreover (7) and (8) do not take into account the device loading and unloading times that are obviously shorter in CID.

5. THE CID IMPLEMENTATION

In designing the implementation of CID we have devoted the main effort in minimizing the number of connection among the cells and in avoiding multiple cell interconnections (necessary when broadcasting needs to take place). In this way we have obtained an implementation structure in which every cell communicates only with their neighbors by means of a few lines; thus the resulting architecture appears very suitable for a VLSI implementation.

To reduce the number of connections between the cells we give the capability to recognize a lacuna to the cells of the SS and DS too. In this way the lacunas can flow among empty cells in the same way as the elements of T; in this way the handshake between the cells can be simplified.

In order to avoid broadcasting we have to overcome two major problems: the communication of the DRC value to each cell of the CS and the signaling of end operation.

The first problem has to be solved by suffixing the R list with an "End Of List" (EOL) mark followed by the DRC value; each comparison processor receives the DRC value at the end of a rotation of R and keeps it until a new DRC arrives; it uses the current DRC value to control the number of comparisons for all the unmatched t supplied before the new DRC.

The termination is detected by recognizing when all the paths from the device input to the device output are empty. To recognize this condition we have defined the "T-path Empty" (TE) signal. Each cell of the device, independently from the section it belongs to, has a "T-path Empty Input" (TEI) and a "T-path Empty Output" (TEO); TEO replies the status of TEI if and only if the cell is empty, otherwise it is held inactive. The SS cells have two TEO outputs that always assume the same value; the DS cells have two TEI inputs that are ANDed to generate the TEO value. The circuit supplying the T list activates the TEI of the root of the SS when it is empty, i.e. when it supplies the last element of T. In this way the TE signal propagates following the last t contained in every path from the input to the output and the TEO of the root of the DS becomes active only when the whole CID is empty.

According to the architecture described in the section 3 the CID can be built using three basic modules:
  1 - Comparison Cell (CC);
  2 - Supply Cell (SC);
  3 - Drain Cell (DC).
In the following we describe the internal architecture of each type of cell.

5.1. *Comparison Cell.*

A block diagram of the CC is shown in figure 5.1. The thin connections represent single wire lines, the wide ones indicate parallel communications. The signals definitions are summarized in the table 5.1.

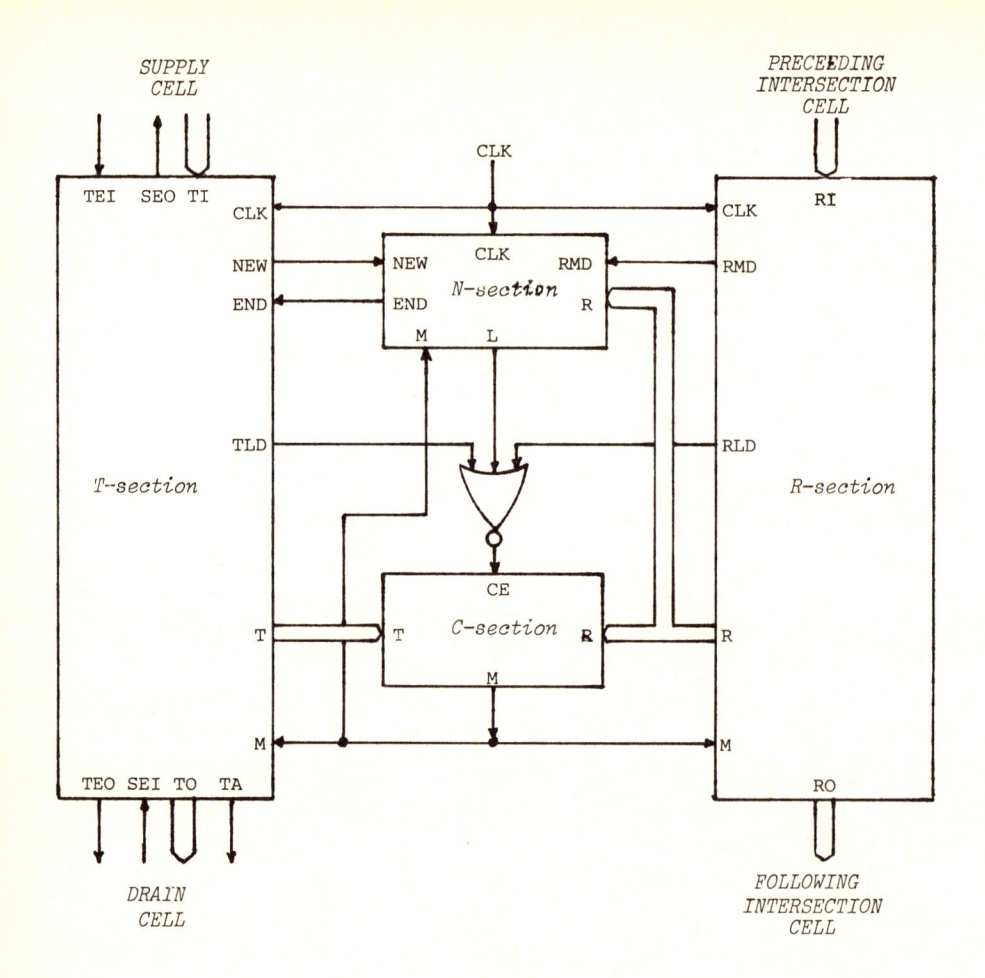

Fig. 5.1: Comparison Cell

RI   element r input
RO   element r output
RMD   EOL mark detect (active when the R-section contains the EOL mark).
RLD   R-lacune detect (active when the R-section contains a lacune).
R   element r value

TI   element t input
SEO   shift enable output (active when the T-section can receive a new element t).
SEI   shift enable input (active when the cell of the DS can receive the element).
TO   element t output
TA   element t available (active when a matched t has to be transferred to the DS).
TLD   T-lacune detect (active when the T-section contains a lacune).
NEW   new element t (active when a new t is loaded in the T-section).
TEI   T-path empty input.
TEO   T-path empty output.
M   match (active when both T and R lines have the same value and CE is active).
CE   comparator enable.
L   load (active during the load of the DRC value in the N-section).
END   end of element t processing (active when the current comparison is the last that has to be performed on the element contained in the T-section).
CLK   clock.

Table 5.1: Signals definitions

The cell is composed by four functional sections:

1) T-section: it stores the element t currently compared. It controls the loading and transfer of the element t according to the signals M and END. The signals TA and SEI controls the transfer of the element to DS.

2) R-section: it stores the element r currently compared, destroying it when a match occurs. It also recognizes the EOL mark and triggers the load of the current DRC value in the N-section by RMD. Receives the match signal to destroy the matched r and generates the RMD to signal the DRC load phase to the N-section.

3) C-section: compares the contents of the T and R sections. The operation is enabled by the CE signal that is active only when both the T and R sections contain a valid element.

4) N-section: counts the number of comparisons performed on the same t, when this number is equal to the current DRC value it signals the end of the processing of an unmatching element.

5.2. *Supply Cell.*

The SC stores an element of T and dispatches it to the son cell that makes a request. Due to the possibility that both the underlying cells make the request at the same time, the SC performs also the arbitration on a fixed priority basis. Note that a more sofisticated arbitration technique can route the elements towards the subtree that contains less elements, but this requires more informations and a more complicated interconnection scheme.

The SC architecture, shown in figure 5.2, is very simple and contains two sections: the L-section and the S-section. The L-section is basically a latch and stores a t element detecting if it is a lacuna. The content of the latch is changed when the previous one is transferred to a son cell. The S-section is a selector that routes the element toward one of the underlying cell. It contains a very simple arbitration logic.

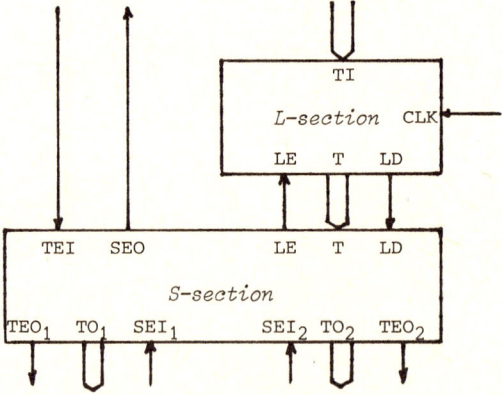

LD   lacuna detect (active when the L-section contains a lacune).
LE   latch enable (active when a new element can be fetched).
    Other signals as in Table 5.1.

Fig. 5.2: Supply Cell

5.3. *Drain Cell*.

The DCs convey the matched elements towards the output. Thus their structure, shown in figure 5.3, is symmetric with respect to the SC. Also in this case a contention problem arises when both the son cells contains an element. Thus also the DS have a fixed priority arbiter.

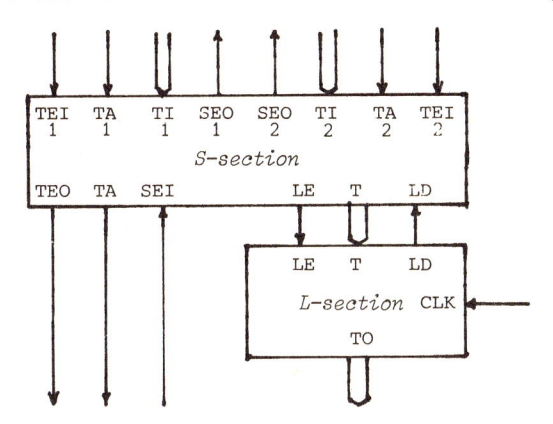

```
     ↓   ↓   ↑   ↑   ↑   ↑   ↓   ↓
    ┌─────────────────────────────┐
    │ TEI  TA  TI  SEO SEO TI  TA  TEI │
    │  1    1   1   1   2   2   2   2  │
    │         S-section           │
    │ TEO  TA  SEI       LE  T  LD │
    └─────────────────────────────┘
           ↓   ↑         ↓  ↑  ↑
                      ┌──────────┐
                      │ LE  T  LD │
                      │L-section CLK │←
                      │    TO     │
                      └──────────┘
                          ↓
```

LD   lacuna detect (active when the L-section contains a lacune).
LE   latch enable (active when a new element can be fetched).
    Other signals as in Table 5.1.

Fig. 5.3.

6. CONCLUSIONS

The list intersection device presented in this paper appeares to be attractive for three major reasons: it can intersect unsorted lists, its performance is better than those of the other parallel intersection devices having a unique input and output, its architecture is based on a few of different units connected in a simple and regular way making the device suitable for a VLSI implementation.

The better performance is due to the fact that each processor is loaded as soon as it becomes available, avoiding any idle state.

The application for which CID has been devised (the DBMAC database machine) refers to lists having no duplicates elements; however CID can operate effectively also with duplicated elements if we do not eliminate the r elements when they match. This is not true for the array processor whose architecture does not allow element replication.

REFERENCES

[1] E.F. Codd "A Relational Model of Data for Large Shared Data Bases", CACM 13 n. 6, June 1970.

[2] D.C.P. Smith and G.M. Smith, "Relational Database Machines", Computer, March 1979.

[3] C.S. Lin, D.C.P. Smith and G.M. Smith "The Design of a Rotating Associative Memory for Relational Database Applications", ACM TODS, vol. 1, n. 1, March 1976.

[4] D.J. De Witt "DIRECT-A Multiprocessor Organization for Supporting Relational Database Management System", IEEE Trans. on Comp., vol. C-28, n. 6, June 1979.

[5] M. Missikoff "RELOB: a Relational Storage System", 1978 ACM/SIGMOD Int. Conf. on Data Management Systems, Milano, June 1978.

[6] M. Missikoff "A Domain Based Internal Schema for Relational Database Machines", 1982 ACM/SIGMOD Int. Conf. on Data Management Systems, Orlando, June 1982.

[7] L.A. Hollaar "A Design for a List Merging Network", IEEE Trans. on Comp., vol. C-28, n. 6, June 1979.

[8] H.T. Kung and P.L. Lehman "Systolic (VLSI) Arrays for Relational Data Base", 1980 ACM/SIGMOD Int. Conf. on Management of Data, Los Angeles, May 1980.

[9] J.L. Bentley and H.T. Kung "A Tree Machine for Searching Problems", Proceedings of 1979 Int. Conf. on Parallel Processing IEEE, August 1979.

[10] S.W. Song "On High Performance VLSI Solution to Database Problems". Technical Report n. CMU-CS-81-130, Carnegie Mellon University, 1981.

[11] M. Missikoff and M. Terranova "The architecture of DBMAC: a Relational Database Computer", Proc. of 2^d Int. Workshop on Database Machines, San Diego, Sept. 1982.

[12] M. Missikoff and M. Scholl "Relational Queries in a Domain Based DBMS", Proc. of ACM/SIGMOD, San Jose, May 1983.

Data Handling and Dedicated Hardware for the Sort Problem

W. TEICH
H.CH. ZEIDLER

Institut fuer Datenverarbeitungsanlagen
Technische Universitaet Braunschweig
Postfach 3329
D-3300 Braunschweig
West-Germany

Abstract

The significance of sorting in the field of data processing is reflected in the trend towards the support of sort operations by hardware specialized for this purpose. The applicable sort algorithms can vary in nature and must always be considered in close conjunction with the access characteristics of the data to be sorted and the possible representations of its sorted order. Three different implementations of special sort components are presented by way of example, whereby the concept of a serial 4-way merge technique is discussed in more detail within the context of the Relational Data Base Machine (RDBM).

1. Introduction

Owing to the trend towards increased cost effectiveness and VLSI technology the application of specialized hardware components in connection with sort operations has been the object of marked attention in recent years. This has not been without its reason, as an optimization of the sort process is desirable from several points of view:

- sorting constitutes a frequently used subordinate operation in systems and user programming,
- sorting can provide both an important elementary operation within data base systems and an auxiliary operation for more complex data base functions,
- sorting involves a heavy loading of the CPU with relatively simple comparison operations, in conjunction with numerous store accesses.

In performing the selection of suitable <u>algorithms</u> for a designed implementation of such specialized sort components, a given system environment for the data to be processed must always be considered. This includes, for example, the <u>data access characteristics</u> (sequential, random or the memory topology features). A further important aspect is the organization of the <u>representation</u> of the sorted order during and at the end of the sort process. This can involve both physical movement of the data and/or a mapping via its lists or address tables.

This article presents some sort units, which have recently been proposed and are nearing prototype completion, and examines them in the light of the above-named criteria.

Finally, the sort processor of the Relational Data Base Machine RDBM is discussed in detail in connection with its system environment.

2. Sorting Algorithms

There are several basic sort procedures (Insertion, Selection, Distribution, Exchange, Enumeration, Merge, etc.) /KNUT 73/. These procedures can also be varied or combined with one another, thus forming optimized procedures as Quicksort, Shell Sort, etc.

In an assessment of such implementations, the number of necessary accesses on the data can in general be considered as forming the essential criterion governing sorting time, leading to time dependencies ranging from $O(n)$ via $O(n\log(n))$ to $O(n^2)$ for n data elements to be sorted. A second assessment criterion is the amount of memory space required for intermediate results. These two characteristics can be traded off against each other, i.e. procedures with low additional memory requirements are slower than ones with high memory overheads.

An optimized procedure is often preferred for a software implementation on a monoprocessor. In contrast, hardware implementations favour relatively clear-cut, simple algorithms, which can be performed very fast in a specialized central processing unit or which can be realized as a set of identical elements ("cells") operating in parallel. Such parallel arrangements can function truly concurrently (e.g. exchange in a cellular array) or operate in a pipeline arrangement on a data stream (enumeration). There are various proposals in which a (necessarily limited) number of units process the total amount of data to be sorted in several "passes".

3. Data Access Characteristics for Sorting

The generally adopted classification of sorting methods into "internal" and "external" sorting arises from the nature of access on the data to be sorted: during internal sorting access is confined to a portion of a main memory, whereas external sorting involves access to files which are held on block-oriented or special storage media such as disks or magnetic tapes. A very clear representation of this is provided by the terms "array sorting" and "file sorting" introduced in /FRIE 81/. Each external sort is, as a rule, preceded by an internal sort in which subsets of the total set to be sorted are each sorted within themselves (presorting).

A data element to be sorted is normally not a single "computer word" but rather a "sort key", having a structure specific to its application. Furthermore this actual part of the element to be sorted (e.g. character string, or numerical value coded in a specific fashion) can have an arbitrary amount of additional information appended to it which, whilst not contributing to the sorting process, must remain attached to its key after the sort is complete for further processing.

For the internal sort the nature of the access to the sort key has a decisive effect on the structure of the sort unit. Those techniques which require random access can be linked to a random access memory, which must be present within a general-purpose computer or a multiprocessor system. Should the innermost loop of a selected algorithm also be given the task of accessing the next portion of data to be read then this access time contributes in its entirety to the sorting time. A configuration with sort units operating in parallel and the requirement for random access to the complete data (shared memory) necessitates the provision of a "multiport memory". If such a component is not originally present in the system then it must be provided as a special memory forming part of the sort hardware, which must be loaded serially before sorting commences. This also applies to shift registers or array arrangements.

4. The Representation of Sort Ordering

4.1. Techniques

The type of representation of sorted ordering should be considered independently of the sorting algorithm itself (Fig. 1). The procedure which comes first to mind is that of producing a <u>physical ordering</u> through continual data movements so that in the memory the complete data is eventually stored in the sort order. A further possibility is that of linking the data via link pointer arrays which are appended to the respective data elements and whose contents are varied during the sort procedure so as to indicate the final sorted order on completion. The transformation of this

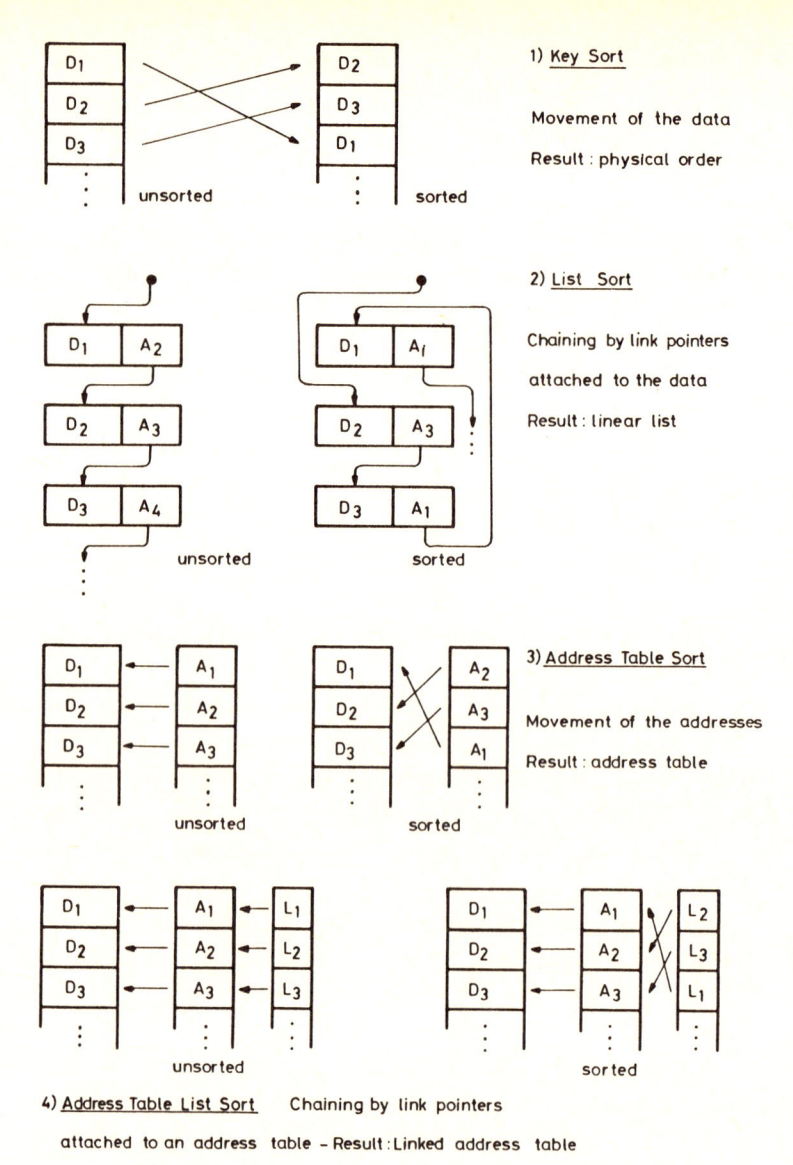

Fig. 1 : Generation and Representation of Sort Ordering

1) **Key Sort**

   Movement of the data

   Result: physical order

2) **List Sort**

   Chaining by link pointers attached to the data

   Result: linear list

3) **Address Table Sort**

   Movement of the addresses

   Result: address table

4) **Address Table List Sort**   Chaining by link pointers attached to an address table – Result: Linked address table

linking into a physical ordering requires, however, an additional read access to the link field of each data element. This technique is referred to as a "list sort". If the address pointer field of the data to be sorted is no longer viewed as an appendage thereto, but held in a separate area of memory then the sorted order can be represented by arranging these pointers in the physical sort order during the sorting process ("address table sort"). This order is then of course governed by the values of the corresponding data elements. The sort result in the data area can then be generated by sequential processing of this address table.

If the two last-named techniques are combined, a configuration is then conceivable in which the address table is no longer physically rearranged. Instead of this, a link field is appended to each address, so that a linking arises which is internal to the address table. Starting from a leading address (anchor), the physical ordering can be produced in the data area, whereby the next data element is given via the link field in the address table. This procedure can thus be termed an "address table list sort".

4.2. Assessment

As already indicated in Section 3, a data element to be sorted can be divided into the sort key, together with further attached satellite information irrelevant in the determination of sorted order. The sort key itself can thereby have a fixed format or be of variable length. A decision in favour of one of the techniques for representing sorted order is strongly dependent on the type of sort keys to be processed.

Physical sorting with continued data movement is always inappropriate if satellite information, irrelevant to the sorting operation itself, constantly has to be moved as well. Relatively long sort keys are also disadvantageous for this type of processing. For a central data memory with random access, the necessary write accesses with the sorted data represent an additional overhead.

In contrast during list sorting, write accesses are only necessary on the link field so that the next question arises as to how -for variable length data elements (free format)- the address field of each data element can be accessed without recourse to additional pointers. This problem could for instance be solved by placing a fixed format address pointer in front of the data. There still remains the principal disadvantage of address information storage in the relatively extensive - and perhaps not very fast - data memory. The address table sort would therefore certainly appear to be a favourable configuration for the processing of freely formatted data or data with satellite information. An address table has a fixed format and can be limited in extent so as to allow fast RAM chips to be used.

If one wishes to reduce the data rearrangement necessary in the address area during the sort process then the address table list sort offers the advantageous feature of internal linking within the address table itself. In this configuration, it is possible to process the relative addresses with reduced length and all internal intermediate status registers necessary for sorting only need to be dimensioned for this size, representing a valuable increase in performance.

During time analysis of the complete sort process, allowance must however be made in all list and address table techniques for address pointer initialization, although applications may arise in which for example an address table is already available in the context of overall system bookkeeping. The data area must be kept consistent during all list and address table techniques, if this area is not to be exclusively allocated to the sorting unit. This fact must in particular be observed for intelligent memories employing paging techniques.

The necessity to provide the result of the sort operation in the form of a physical ordering depends on the further processing which it is to undergo. Provided that the address-data relationship remains consistent, the sorted address table can be used either for the final data transfer into the correct physical order or to provide information for subsequent processing by other specialized processors within a system.

5. Examples of Sort Processor Designs

There is a large number of proposals of sort processor designs; in this context three solutions are introduced as representative examples for specialized sorting hardware which have already been implemented in part or as a prototype model:

- a parallel sorting technique operating by enumeration /YASU 82/

- a parallel sorting technique employing systolic cells /DOHI 82/

- a serial sorting technique using a p-way merge algorithm /LEIL 77/.

The two parallel sorting techniques are designed for implementation in VLSI technology and employ, for a total of n keys to be sorted, n processing cells (Yasuura) and log(n) systolic cells (Dohi). The serial sorting technique is performed on a central, discretely constructed fast processing unit.

5.1. Parallel Technique employing the Enumeration Principle

The enumeration sort is a simple basic technique which determines the position of each sort key in the sorted sequence by counting for each key the number of larger keys in the unsorted sequence. In serial form, the corresponding algorithm has a sorting time of order $O(n^2)$.

The basic idea behind the "parallel enumeration sorting scheme" /YASU 82/ is that of distributing the algorithm over n processing elements which are capable of determining the sorted order in a time dependent on O(n). In terms of the classification introduced in the previous sections, this technique can be ranked among the address table sorting techniques, as the completion of the counting phase leads purely to an address sequence, in this case the relative position of each sort key. The reordering of the data must then be viewed as a further processing phase.

5.1.1. Hardware Implementation

Fig. 2 shows the arrangement of the cells which are linked via central signals and data paths forming a sorter circuit. A dual bus system (input, output) is connected, together with a reset signal to each cell.

After initialization via control signals, this cell arrangement is loaded with data to be sorted so that with every data clock period t a new data word is transferred to the first left-hand cell, whose previous contents are shifted to the next cell to the right. In addition, after i clock pulses at time t(i), the i-th cell is loaded via the "input bus" with the same data element as that currently fed into the leftmost cell in the pipeline, and is thus able to compare this value with the just received contents of the cell to the left. In this way, each cell i counts during the shifting process how many sort-keys are larger than its "own" value loaded at time t(i). The value received from the left is thereby always passed unchanged to the right on the next clock pulse. As soon as the end of the shifted data is indicated by its control signal, the cell i can output its counter state c(i) via the output bus, so that during the course of shifting from left to right a sequence of relative ordering addresses appears at the clock rate 1/t. Fig. 3 shows the block diagram of an individual cell. The contents of the (variable) "shift data registers" and the (constant) "bus data registers" are compared using a comparator. The results of this comparisons are gathered in a counter. A central "control circuit" coordinates the functions of the various modules.

5.1.2. Assessment

The technique illustrated requires an arrangement of n cells for n data to be sorted. A concrete design study using Mead-Conway techniques in NMOS technology led according to the authors to a realizable number of n = 20...30 cells per VLSI chip. The natural limits of the elements within the integrated cell thereby necessitate further measures if the available bit width b of a sort key is exceeded. For this case the authors propose a partitioning technique in which several chips are cascaded.

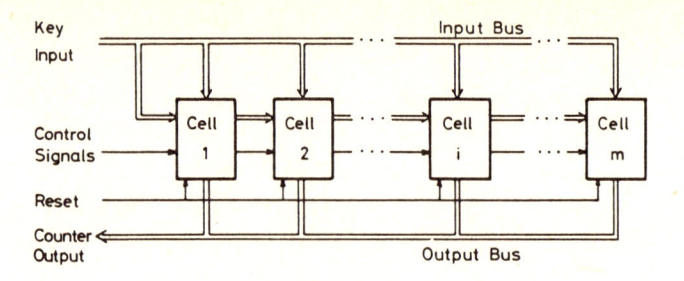

Fig. 2: Parallel Enumeration Sorting Circuit (from /YASU 82/)

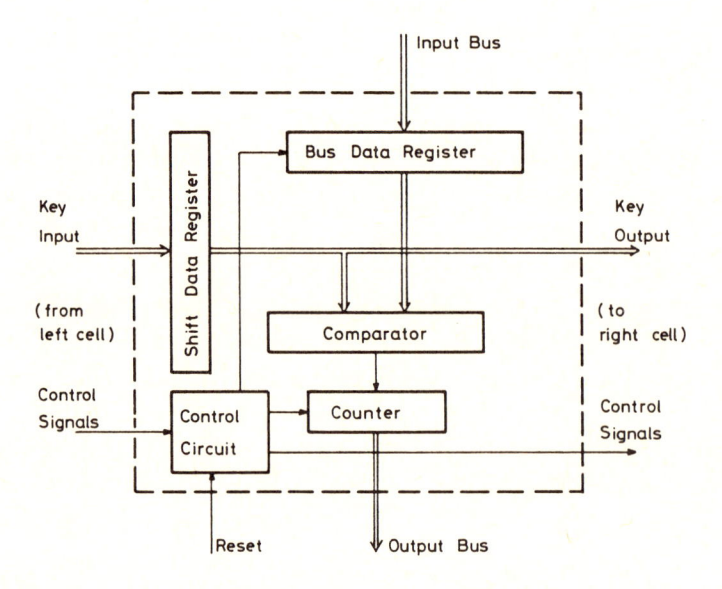

Fig. 3: Block Diagram of the Cell (from /YASU 82/)

All in all, the proposed structure can be viewed as an interesting variation on sorting techniques with sequential access to conventional memories. Within a realistic system environment, however, this structure requires a yet higher degree of integration than this is currently available, despite the relatively simple elementary cell layout within the chip.

5.2. Parallel Merging Technique using Systolic Cell Structures

Elementary 2-way merge processes can be cascaded within a tree structure, leading to the tree arrangement shown in Fig. 4. The resulting sorting principle is termed "tree selection". The sorting speed is thereby determined by the bottleneck in the tree, the final merger at the root of the tree. In each decision process, leading to the output of a sort data element at the tree root, it is replaced by a larger element of the underlying subtree, which is replenished from its underlying subtree and so on, thus enabling the function of all nodes at one level to be replaced by a programmable systolic cell (PSC) with additional memory, leading to the sorter structure proposed by /DOHI 82/ shown in Fig. 5.

5.2.1. Hardware Implementation

Each level of the merger tree is represented as a paired arrangement of a "general purpose" systolic cell, together with a random access memory. For each node, the current valid pair of values (winner and loser) is stored in the level RAM memory, together with a "history bit" necessary for the algorithm. In addition, there are a number of "tag bits" to separate the already sorted data sequences from one another. The increasing number of nodes at each level of the tree arrangement leads to a continuous doubling of the necessary memory space per level from the root to the leaves of the tree. The systolic cell operates in basic cycles whereby the final cycle must be repeated (b+2) times, where b is the number of bytes in the sort key. The level memory contains an autonomous read/write control unit, which can communicate with the attendant systolic cell.

The author quotes a rate of 0.33 Mbyte/s during the sorting of keys with b = 64. The application was simulated for 4 systolic cells (16-way merge) using a PASCAL program. The cell itself is under development at Carnegie-Mellon University in the form of a VLSI chip.

A similar arrangement of "level circuits" with attached "memory banks" ("Sort Engine SOE") is proposed in /TANA 82/ and has been implemented in form of a prototype. These cascadable sort engines use a "Heap Sort" algorithm to process streams of sort keys.

5.2.2. Assessment

The PSC sorter employs the technique of continual data movement during the sorting process and forms a high-performance merge unit with the given dimensions of 17 PSCs and a memory space of 16 Mbytes. In particular, the author's observations regarding

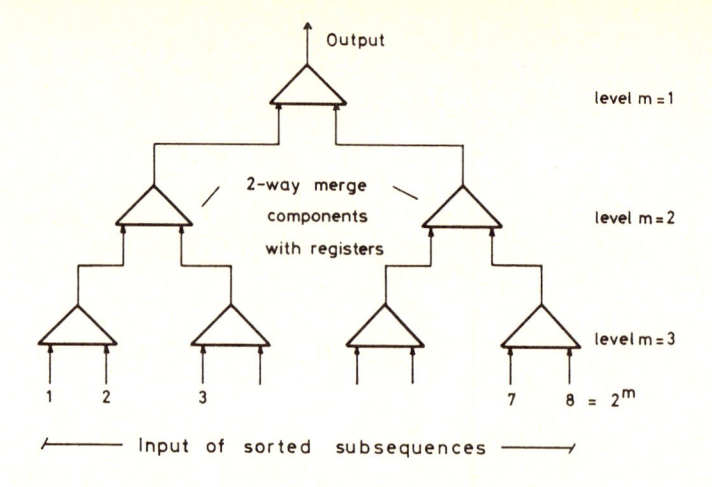

Fig. 4: Tree Selection

Fig. 5: Sorter with a PSC Linear Array (From /DOHI 82/)

the dimensioning of the input buffers at the leaves of the tree in relation to possible disk store chracteristics indicate this structure to be predestined for external sorting. The systolic cells employed are not specialized in their construction for sorting, as they obtain the instructions for the processing of a cycle via their stored microprogram.

5.3. Serial Sorting Technique using a Multiway Merge Principle

Multiway merge sort algorithms require accesses to the data to be sorted of the order $O(n\log(n))$, whereby a quantity of n unsorted keys are processed in $(\log(n)/\log(p))$ passes, if a p-way merger is employed. A typical example of the implementation of the algorithm in a hardware structure is shown in Fig. 6.

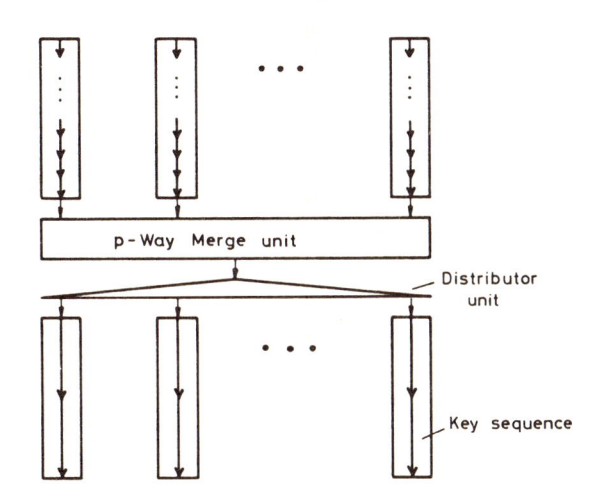

Fig. 6: Functional Principle of a **p**-Way Merger with Shift Registers

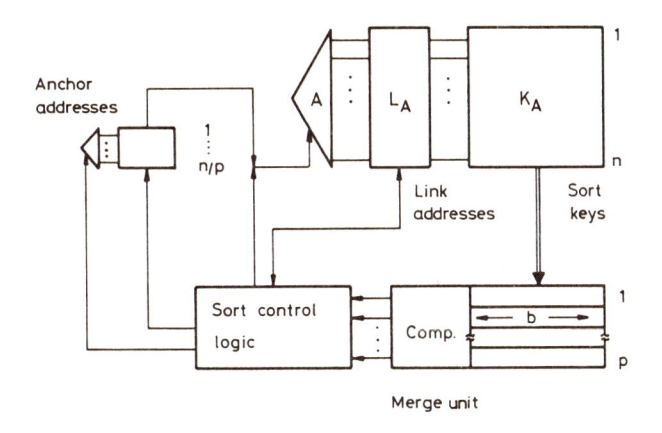

Fig. 7: **p**-Way Merging with Random Access and Address Table

The sort keys held in input shift registers are processed by the merge unit and distributed to output shift registers. The presorted data sequences, for example separated by marker bits, then form the input information for the next merge pass, generating subsequences which are larger by a factor of p. This concept of continual data reordering starting with initially unsorted data proves to be impractical for longer sort keys. In addition, the employment of shift registers for temporary data storage during processing is inconvenient for implementation. The basic idea of a sort unit using the multiway merge principle was therefore developed further to an address table technique with link pointers /TEIC 81/, as shown in Fig.7. Each sort key K(A) is provided with a link field L(A). In the first pass, a sequential stepping through the addresses A allows groups of p keys K(A) to be processed by the merge unit whose ultimate result is the linking of these p keys in sorted order via L(A) to form a string. The anchors of each string thus formed are held in an "anchor memory" for the next pass. After the formation of n/p string subsequences, groups of p anchor addresses are then used to initialize the second pass, leading this time to n/p^2 strings, each of which then contains p^2 sort keys.

5.3.1. Hardware Implementation

The implementation requires read access to data in a separate main memory. Fig. 8 shows the extension of the hardware components to allow data access to a main memory MA, whereby the address table MA(A) and the link field L(A) form the structure necessary to represent the sorted order for the "address table list sort" (see Section 4.1). The maximum number n of entries which can be stored in the address table determines - below the capacity of MA itself - the upper limit to the number of sort keys which can be sorted together during an internal sort. The access to the sort keys in the external main memory is sequential during the first pass, whereas random access is necessary during all subsequent passes. The data are fed to a high-speed merge unit consisting of fast comparators. A sort control logic monitors the course of the linking algorithm.

5.3.2. Assessment

The merge technique using a centralized sort processing unit described in the foregoing sections has been implemented with discrete chip modules in bipolar Schottky technology.

The complete sorting process includes the initial sequential loading of the sort key start addresses, the actual merge passes with a time requirement of $O(n\log(n))$ and the concluding transfer of the sorted key addresses back to the main memory. During the sorting process, only the sort keys themselves are transferred, as access to the satellite information is possible after sorting via the known start addresses. An appropriate structuring of the sort key via special separation characters allow

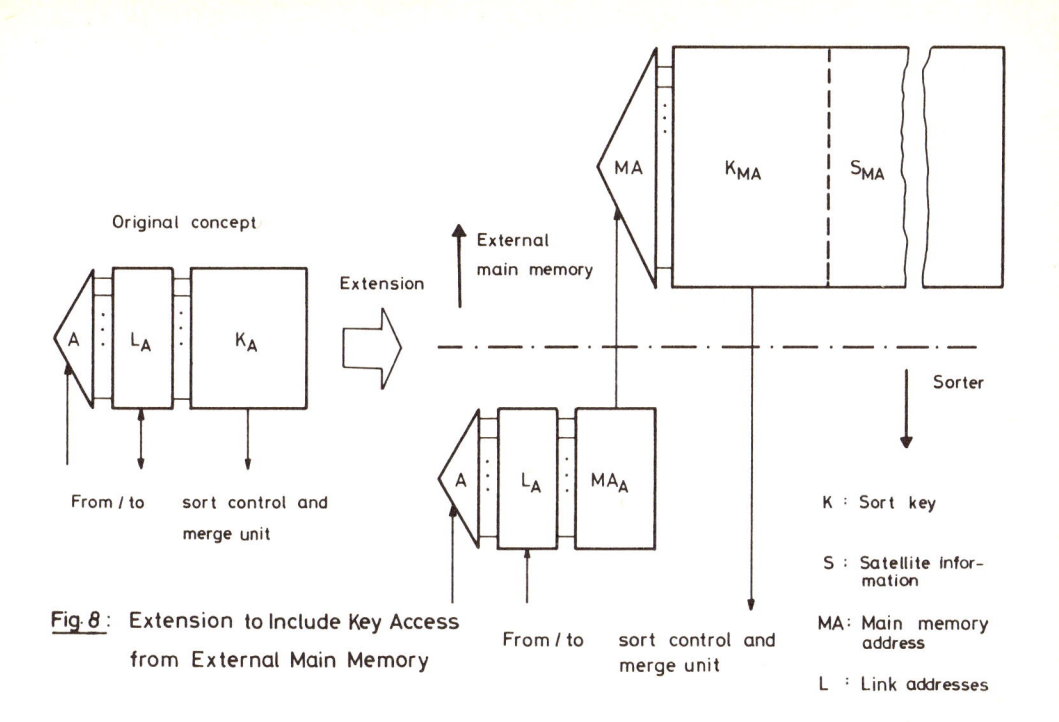

Fig. 8: Extension to Include Key Access from External Main Memory

"multikey sorting" with variable key length to be performed by the intelligent sort control logic.

For the case where several presorted data sequences have already been generated, the sorter structure can assist "external sorting" by performing a merge process on groups of p subblocks from each of the input sequences to form a succession of output blocks, representing the sorted output sequence.

5.4. Overall Assessment

The three hardware implementations of sort techniques given here are not representative of the complete field of already proposed solutions. However, even their limited investigation can indicate certain characteristics which are of significance for the currently technically feasible range of implementations of hardware-assisted sort processes.

The architecture of the "parallel enumeration sorting scheme" provides a VLSI solution which is attractive by virtue of its fast sorting time, whilst only offering simple sort functions through the use of very simple elementary cells. On exceeding hardware-governed limits (internal registers, maximum number of cascadable cells), an unrealistic outlay is incurred for the then necessary additional circuitry. This applies both with regard to variable length sort keys and to external sorting techniques. In contrast, the parallel arrangement of "programmable systolic cells (PSCs)" allows the construction of an efficient merging element for both internal and external sort procedures at a modest outlay in terms of VLSI circuitry. The advantage of individually programmable cell adaption to the particular sorting requirements for the given data formats can thereby be constructively exploited. The fact that only portions of the general-purpose structured PSCs are utilized to perform the sort function lessens the potential attainable efficiency and should also be taken into account.

The serially performed multiway merge algorithm represents centralized, specialized hardware which can be adapted to complex sorting rules for multikey sorting, variable key lengths and various possible different data formats. All data paths in the processing unit are specially geared to their appropriate task and are equally employable in the assistance of external sorting. From a pragmatic standpoint, the realization of this principle allows, by circumventing the (possibly insupportable) VLSI fabrication outlay, the implementation and evaluation of a specialized sort unit within the context of a current project.

6. Sorting with the Relational Data Base Machine RDBM

A sort processor, operating according to the last-named technique, and its functional principle are now examined by way of an example in the context of the Relational Data Base Machine RDBM, currently under development at the Technical University of Braunschweig. As this processor cannot be viewed independently of the system, a summary of the complete RDBM system is initially given.

6.1. Overview of the RDBM

The aim of the research project is the implementation of a backend system which offers enhanced hardware support for the particularly time-consuming operations encountered in data base operations. The machine is based on the concept of a transaction-oriented multiuser system and offers all the features required of a relational data base management system.

The complete system configuration is shown in Fig. 9. The system is controlled by a data base supervisor, implemented on a conventional minicomputer which monitors the various system components, performs those functions not supported by hardware and represents the interface to a host computer. Further principal components are the

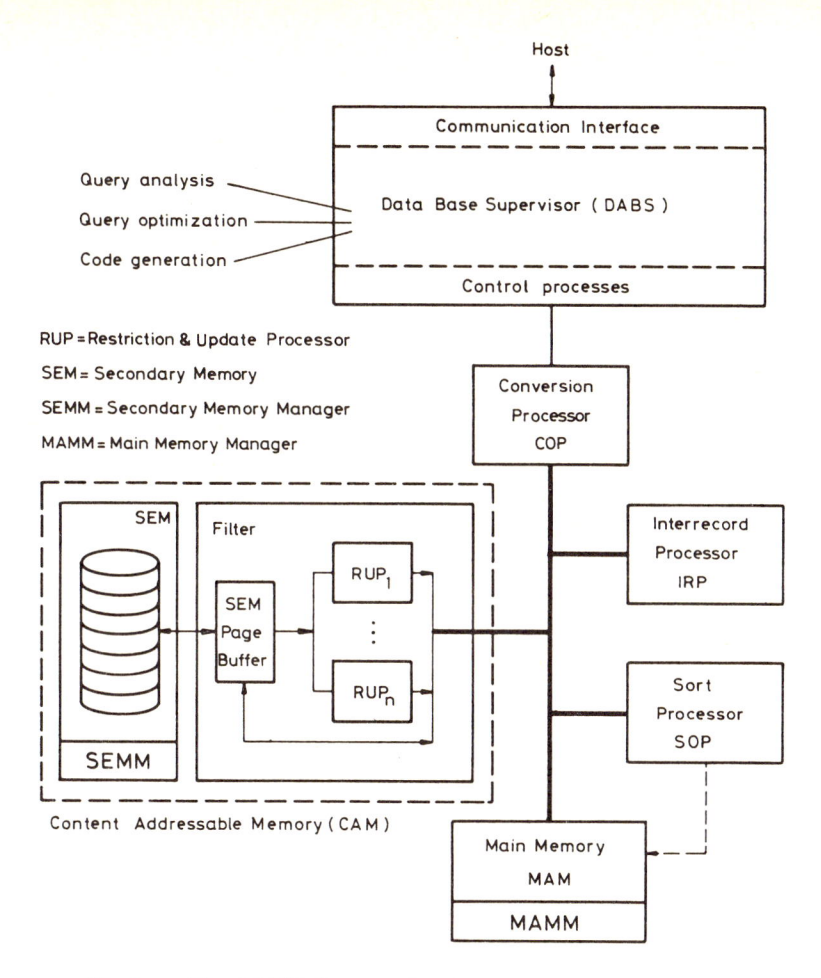

Fig. 9: : The RDBM System Configuration

secondary memory with its own memory manager, which offers the feature of quasi-associative access and an inhomogeneous multiprocessor system with various specialized processors such as data converter, interrecord processor and sort processor. Of particular interest is the intelligent main memory, which is likewise provided with its own memory manager and can be accessed by all processors (shared memory).

A description of the design is given in /AHLL 81/ and a detailed discussion of the complete system is to be found in /SZHL 82/. Therefore we will have only a deeper look at the sort processor. Fig. 10 indicates the data flow during the execution of the complete sort operation, including all those components which are responsible for data storage, data organization and data access. Particular data areas are accessed within the content-addressable secondary memory with the aid of its memory manager

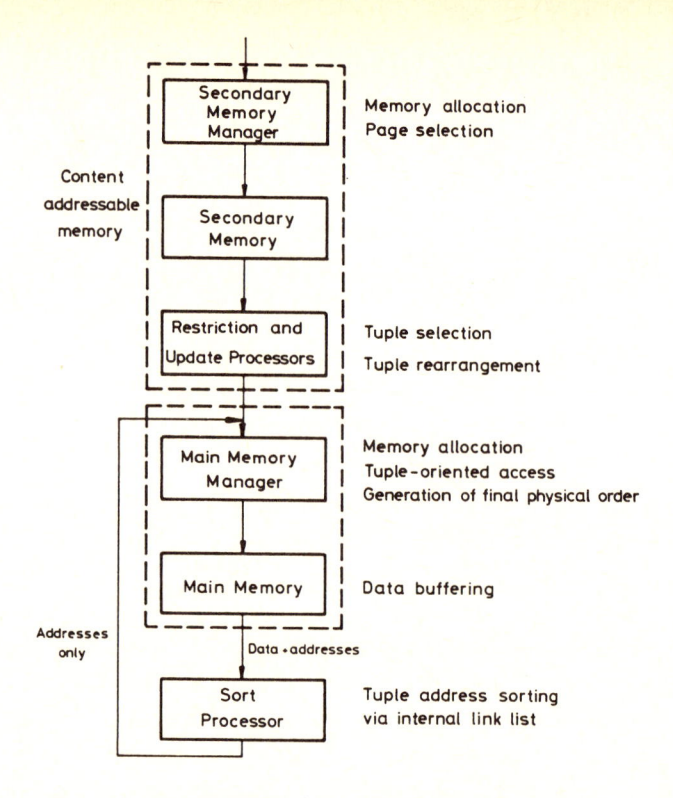

Fig. 10: Execution of Sorting — Data Flow

and passed on for selection and rearrangement of the relevant data to data filters, the so-called restriction and update processors (RUP). The selected information -preprocessed for sorting- is now stored in the main memory with the aid of the main memory manager. The sort processor (SOP) can access the data from there and sort them into the correct order. The result in the form of an address sequence in sorted order will be returned to the main memory manager, which is then able to carry out the physical reordering of the data.

6.2. The Sort Processor

6.2.1. Data Structure, Specification and Environment

In the design of the sort processor, freely formatted tuples, separated by special characters, are assumed. Attributes, also separated by special characters, represent the smallest logical unit recognized during the sort procedure. The length of an attribute is up to 4 Kbytes, with a maximum of 256 attributes per tuple. The data can occur either in the form of ASCII characters (type "string") or as floating point numbers of variable length (type "number") with two BCD digits per byte. Whereas the first type reflects the lexicographical ordering of the binary value of each byte, the numbers must be initially transformed. In general, it should not only be possible to sort complete keys in ascending or descending order but also to allow varying sort orderings for each individual attribute within a tuple. Duplicates should be capable of being ascertained, marked as such and eliminated, if required. The removal of duplicates is particularly useful when performing the relational projection operation.

Regarding the environment, the sort processor forms a self-reliant component within the multiprocessor system and is thus assigned its sorting task (loaded parameters) from the data base supervisor, in which the sort ordering from the various attributes is laid down together with additional parameters. The individual tuples to be sorted are stored external to the sort processor itself, in the main memory.

6.2.2. Sort Algorithm and Interface

Extensive analysis of the various sort algorithms showed that, allowing for all the specified conditions, an address table list sorting algorithm using the merge procedure represents the best design implementation. According to Section 5.3 a 4-way merge reduces the number of passes to $\log(n)/2$. Thus the total number of accesses for comparison on a set of n tuples is $n\log(n)/2$. Each merge operation thereby contains an elementary sorting loop consisting of the following sorting steps. First of all, the largest (or the smallest) of 4 sort keys at the head of the already sorted input strings is determined by an elementary comparison operation. To achieve this, a 4-way comparison hardware unit is employed. In a second step, the address of the selected tuple is linked to the address of its predecessor in the sorted output string via the latter's link adress. The next largest (or smallest) is then accessed from the input string with the aid of link addresses. Should an input string be exhausted, there being no next tuple, the string is blocked off from the current merge process, which is then only carried out among those remaining.

This process is repeated until all four strings have been merged to form a single sorted output string. One commences thereby with strings of one data element in length, leading to sorted strings each of 4 elements after the first merge pass. These strings then form the input strings for the following merge passes, whereby strings of length 16, 64, 256, ... elements are successively generated. A total of 4K keys can be internally sorted, representing the maximum capacity of the address table.

As already mentioned, the tuples to be sorted are held in the main memory of the RDBM. The sort processor requires only a table of the tuple start addresses within this memory. Such a table is generated automatically by the main memory manager during loading and thus already available. It must then be transmitted to the sort processor during its initialization phase. As the addresses only point to the start of a tuple, it must be ensured that the sort key is also to be found at the beginning of the tuple. The address table must remain consistent during processing of the sort, i.e. the relevant memory pages containing the actual tuples must remain locked and available for access during the whole time. Limits to internal sorting are, on the one hand, the maximum number of resident pages in the main memory and, on the other hand, the maximum number of tuple start addresses which can be accomodated at one time by the sort processor.

Both address and data access paths are available as an interface to the main memory. Initially, the already mentioned address table is transmitted via block transfer, after which the actual sort operation can commence. Should parts of a tuple be required then the corresponding address is passed via the address path to the main memory. The data bytes are then received via the data path. At the end of the sort procedure, the table contents are returned via the address bus with the aid of the link addresses, for further processing in the main memory, where the physical reordering of the data can take place. Should the sorting task enable the elimination of duplicates, then the correspondingly marked addresses are suppressed during the address output.

External sorting can be supported by the sort processor using a merge procedure. The processing procedure assumes thereby a situation similar to that just before the last merge pass of an internal sort. Assuming that a number of presorted tuple strings are present as segments in the secondary memory then successive portions of these strings can be transported into the main memory, e.g. in groups of 1K tuples, each equal to one quarter of the maximum sort processor address table capacity. Fig. 11 shows by way of the 4-way merge example the principal course of an external sort. The presorted data blocks with the names a, b, c and d are available as subblocks ai, bi, etc. in the main memory. On demand, a maximum of 1024 tuple start addresses for the

Fig. 11: The External Sort Procedure

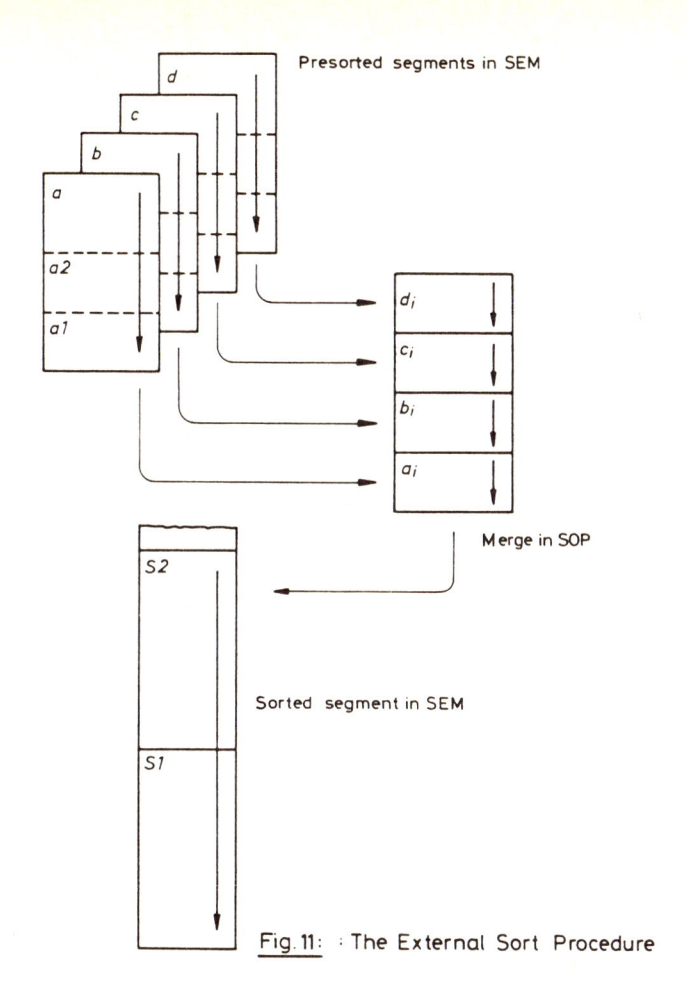

subblocks are transferred to the sort processor address table. The sort linking process can now commence, which then runs in a fashion equivalent to the internal sort until one of the subblocks in the address table is exhausted. Starting from a (single) anchor, all addresses linked up to now in sorted order are returned to the main memory (block S1), thereby freeing at least that part of the address table containing the exhausted subblock for the accomodation of new subsequent addresses from its appropriate block. Only the end of a presorted block actuates the blocking off of an input string from the merge process as already described for internal sorting.

If one employs an appropriate strategy with many merge passes then external sorting can be performed without any limits on the size or number of presorted data sequences. Control of the complete procedure cannot, however, be carried out by the sort processor and must be performed by the data base supervisor, which has access to the various processing elements involved.

6.2.3. Hardware Structure

The universal microprocessor, which is also employed in several other components of the RDBM system, is also used for overall control of the sort processor and to coordinate communication with its environment. However, the sort processor essentially consists of extensive and therefore fast specialized hardware which is housed on seven double Euroboards. This hardware has its own microprogrammed control unit, which performs all phases of the sort algorithm completely autonomously.

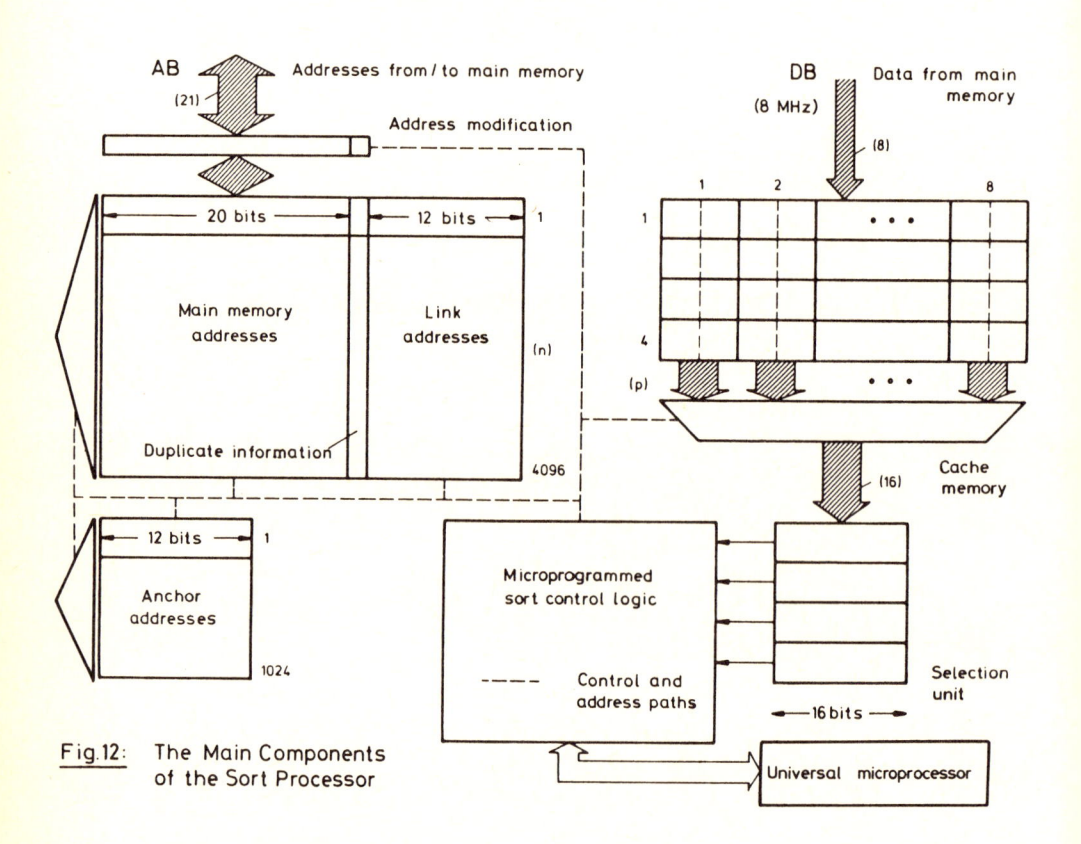

Fig.12: The Main Components of the Sort Processor

The structure of the specialized hardware (Fig. 12) can be broken down into five main components. The <u>address table</u> consists of a store with a 4K x 34bit capacity, which is loaded during the initialization phase with up to 4K tuple (sort key) start addresses. For this purpose, 20 bits are required, corresponding to a memory size of 1Mbyte. In addition, the 12 bit link addresses generated during sorting are also stored here. These are altered during the course of the sort until the final sorted sequence is obtained. One bit per word is also allocated for duplicate marking.

The cache memory with a capacity of 4x16 bytes serves to provide temporary storage for those portions of the four sort keys currently being compared in the merge process. Data can be written to this memory at a speed of 8Mbyte per second. "Number" attributes are transformed on-the-fly during read-in to the cache. The cache can be read out into the 4-way comparison unit in the full width of the comparison window (2 bytes).

The selection unit forms the central core of the sort processor and performs the portions currently under consideration. The actual selection function is carried out by a comparator network in fast Schottky TTL technology.

The microprogrammed control unit is responsible for controlling the sort processor during the task phases of "load", "sort" and "evaluate". It is matched to the processing speed of the sort processor and also contains temporary registers to hold the status of each current sort key.

The anchor memory contains the internal table start addresses of the substrings (anchor addresses) generated during the sort process from the original table provided. For 4K sort keys, 1K anchor addresses are generated in the first pass. The number of the anchor addresses is successively reduced during the sort process until only one anchor address remains, representing a pointer to the first sort key address to be read out in the final sorted sequence. The anchor memory has a capacity of 1K x 13 bits, including a control bit per word.

7. Acknowledgements

The authors gratefully acknowledge the substantial contributions of all the other members of the RDBM-project. Thanks are especially due to John Thornton for his invaluable help in the preparation of the paper.

The research project is funded by the Federal German Ministry for Research and Technology.

8. References

/ AHLL 81 /   Auer, Hell, Leilich, Lie, et al.:
"RDBM- a Relational Data Base Machine",
Inf.Syst., Vol.6, No.2, pp.91-100, 1981

/ DOHI 82 /   Dohi, Y.:
"Sorter using PSC linear Array",
Internal Report, Department of Comp.Sc.,
Carnegie-Mellon Univ., USA, 1982

/ FRIE 82 /   Friedland, D.B.:
"Design, Analysis and Implementation of
Parallel External Sorting Algorithms",
Comp.Sc.Tech.Rep. No.464, University of
Wisconsin-Madison, USA, 1982

/ KNUT 73 /   Knuth, D.E.:
"The Art of Computer Programming", Vol.3,
Addison Wesley, Reading, Mass. 1973

/ LEIL 77 /   Leilich, H.-O.:
"Eine Sortiermaschine", Internal Report DA-77/10,
Institut fuer DV-Anlagen, TU Braunschweig,
W. Germany, 1977

/ SZHL 82 /   Schweppe, Zeidler, Hell, Leilich, et al.:
"RDBM - A Dedicated Multiprocessor System for
Data Base Management", Proc. 2nd Intern.
Workshop on DBM, San Diego, USA, 1982

/ TANA 82 /   Tanaka, Y.:
"A Data Stream Database Machine with Large Capacity",
Proc. 2nd Intern. Workshop on DBM, San Diego, USA, 1982

/ TEIC 81 /   Teich, W.:
"The Sort Processor of the RDBM",
6th Workshop on Comp. Arch. for Non-Numerical Processing,
Hyeres, France, 9.-11.6.1981

/ YASU 82 /   Yasuura, H. et al.:
"The Parallel Enumeration Sorting Scheme for VLSI",
IEEE Trans.Compt. Vol.C-31, pp. 1192-1901, Dec. 1982

IDM-500 WITHIN A MAINFRAME ENVIRONMENT

- Some First Experiences -

Christian Riechmann
FGAN, Forschungsinstitut
für Funk und Mathematik
Königstraße 2, D-5307 Wachtberg

1. Objectives

Starting to implement the connection between the IDM and a mainframe system (SIEMENS 7.561 under BS2000) we had the following objectives:

- to test the possibility of embedding such a DB-backend processor into a real application system environment,

- to learn about the effectiveness of such a supporting backend processor connected to a mainframe system having an operating system overhead of 6000 - 8000 operations per device interrupt,

- to test the ability of the relational user interface to equalize slow communication paths between the access requesting user program and the serving data base handler.

2. Assumptions

We started our implementation in December 1982 with one of the first IDMs in Germany. From the beginning we made two main assumptions concerning this project:

- The host software should be independent of further releases of the underlying operating system.

- The coupling between the IDM and the host computer should use narrow banded communication lines.

Both assumptions differ from those of the project, which GEI, the German OEM-partner of Britton-Lee, started. They are interested in joining both the IDM and the SIEMENS-mainframe as close as possible and use special operating sytem services and a broad banded communication.

The first assumption is self-evident, because we are research oriented. The second one is related to the other research projects in our institute. We are mainly interested in distributed systems expected to be connected by narrow banded communication lines and the support of such systems by special hardware. Another reason is that we plan to do some comparing evaluations with the RDBM of TU-Braunschweig using the X.25 communication protocol.

Therefore we decided to use the RS-232-C I/O-port of the IDM and to use DCAM, which is the official data communication access method of BS2000 to link the host and the backend.

3. Experiences during the Implementation

The communication bore the first problem: The communication protocols of the IDM and those of the host did not fit. The IDM uses its own Britton-Lee-defined protocol, the host system assumes only some of the usual data communication protocols which have been recommended by ISO. In the first version (fig 1) of our implementation this problem was solved by programming a microcomputer system as a gateway processor. Within a later version the IDM-protocol should be implemented within the data communication preprocessor of the host system. Some further problems concerning error detecting techniques arose, when we implemented the host system communication protocol within the gateway processor.

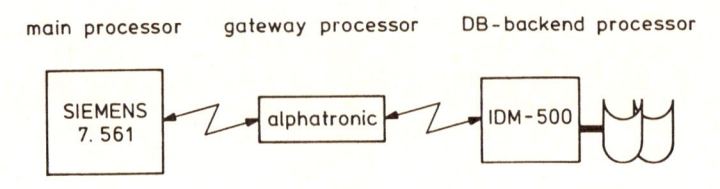

Fig. 1: Version 1 Configuration

We needed 6 man-months for programming the gateway processor. But they could have been saved, if Britton-Lee's I/O-controller would understand "normal", "well defined" and "commonly used" data communication protocols like BSC or X.25 for narrow banded and Ethernet-protocol for broad banded communication. Until now none of these protocols have been announced by Britton-Lee.

Next we had to implement the software for the host-IDM-communication and the support software for user programs. When starting no C-compiler for BS2000 was available. Therefore we could not use software packages written in C. (Meanwhile GEI offers such a compiler.) So we decided to write our own host software package. We used PL/I as implementation language and as host system environment for three reasons:

- PL/I supports the common SIEMENS interface conventions.

- Our "real" application system has a PL/I-interface.

- PL/I offers a certain degree of independency of the operating system.

The IDM-Software-Reference Manual was the only basis for the design and the implementation of the host-software package. This manual gives a rather good guideline, how to implement the host-IDM-communication system, and a description of a user interface language (IDL). From the point of view of modern language design a somewhat more exact definition of the language would be desirable.

Fig 2 shows the concept of our IDM-host-system. We have one BS2000-communication process (IDM-controller), which has driver functions to coordinate and to carry out the message transfer between several IDM-host-userprograms and the IDM. Each of these userprograms has to communicate with the IDM-controller wishing to send or to receive a message to resp. from the IDM. We have implemented some procedures supporting this traffic and guaranteeing its syntactical and semantical correctness.

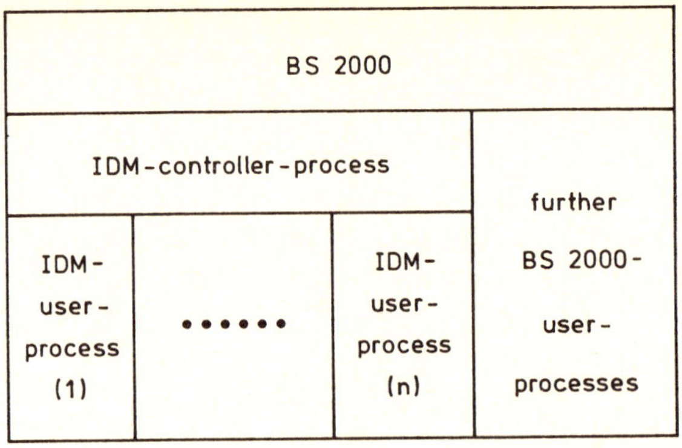

BS 2000			
IDM-controller-process			further BS 2000-user-processes
IDM-user-process (1)	......	IDM-user-process (n)	

Fig. 2: Host Software Stucture

4. Experiences with the IDM-Hardware

We made nearly no experiences concerning the hardware maintenance of the IDM. Because we had no hardware problems since the IDM has been installed. Although the IDM has been used in a laboratory environment and the machine has often been switched on and off, no real and unrecoverable hardware or system failure occurred. The IDM-internal crash/recovery mechanisms seem to work very well.

5. Experiences with the IDM-Software

Up to the date of this paper only limited experiences have been made, concerning the efficiency of the IDM-software. We detected some problems which have to be analysed much deeper. For example there are problems:

- with sorting efficiency (when large relations are sorted),

- with joins (when joining two relations by using attributes, which are indexed on the one relation and not indexed on the other relation),

- with "copying" relations (when using "retrieve into"- or "append"-commands).

Furthermore there seems to be an anomaly concerning the memory size of the IDM. This anomaly has the effect that user tasks need more time using a larger main memory than they need using a smaller one.

But the main problem will be for implementors of user systems with high demands on system security, how to integrate the concept of the isolated IDM-transaction into the concept of the host system transaction. There are no aids to use something like a two-phase-commit-protocol for performing the "end of transaction" handling of the IDM. So the implementors have to try to get system security (integrity) by special IDM-user-system organization. This problem occurs as well in conventional systems, but the solutions are more complicated in the IDM-environment because of its backend concept.

Similar problems will arise, when access control systems of the host and the IDM have to be coordinated consistently.

6. Concluding Remarks and First User Experiences

The actual (May 1983) state of the implementation is

- Version 1 of the gateway processor has just been finished.

- All host software has been coded. Offline testline tests have been completed.

- Some user applications have been defined and programmed.

Since July 1983 the Version-1-system runs and the evaluation tests have been started.

During our first tests we found out that this simple one-to-one gateway implementation is much too slow. The waiting time within a user-program for short write_idm- or read_idm-requests is about 5 to 10 seconds depending on the workload of the host-system. These requests need about 50 bytes to be transferred between user program and IDM.

Although we could not yet locate the exact place within the system where this waiting time comes from, we suppose that most of the time is needed within the data communication subsystem. Therefore our next version will have a much more intelligent gateway processor. Then the number of dialogue steps done by the host will be cut to half.

GEI'S EXPERIENCE WITH BRITTON-LEE'S IDM

Author: Dipl.-Math. Günter Schumacher
          GEI-GESELLSCHAFT FÜR ELEKTRONISCHE
          INFORMATIONSVERARBEITUNG   M. B. H.
          Albert-Einstein-Straße 61
          D-5100 Aachen-Walheim

Introduction

GEI is one of Germany's largest systems and software houses. Employing more than 300 DP professionals and located at about ten major cities in Germany and Switzerland, it offers a wide variety of DP services, including planning and installation of complete hardware/software configurations. A subsidiary in the USA acts as a bridge to the latest American computer technology.

GEI is the exclusive distributor of Britton-Lee's Intelligent Database Machine IDM in Europe's German speaking countries. For testing and demonstration purposes, GEI installed an IDM 500 with serial and parallel host interfaces, 2.5 MB of memory, and one disk controller. Here are some of our experiences with the IDM so far.

General Remarks

Today most DP people know what a database machine is: a dedicated piece of hardware, with special software, performing the functions of a database management system. So did we. Nevertheless it took us a significant amount of time to really get to know and understand what a database machine is most suited for and what it can do for you. It took us several months to discover and fully understand all the capabilities and features of the IDM.

Two aspects of the IDM need to be considered specifically if one wants to determine where to apply the IDM and its benefits:

- The aspect of being a database machine separated from the "host computer" on which the application software is executed. While such things as off-loading parts of the work-load from the host are quite obvious to understand and to judge, others may become visible only in a multi-host configuration.

- the fact that the software inside the IDM is a full implementation of the relational model. Obviously, many of the IDM's valuable features are a consequence of this manufacturing design decision.

In addition, the following issues deserve special attention:

- the performance, i.e. the throughput in terms of operations, transactions, or similar units suitable for measurement. Unfortunately, it is not an easy task to specify a simple method for measuring the performance.

- (from a supplier's point of view:) the effort necessary to install an IDM and to form a host-IDM-disks configuration, the maintainability of the hardware and the software, and the stability of both hardware and software.

Our Own IDM Configuration

Our own IDM configuration used for testing, software development, and demonstration purposes consisted first of just an IDM and a micro computer running CP/M as the host computer. Obviously, this is not a typical configuration nor does it allow large amounts of data to be entered into the IDM. Still it allows you to do almost everything the IDM can do: create databases and relations, store data tuples into the database, create indexes, retrieve and update data, dump and load databases, etc. Even advanced features like pattern matching or defining and using Stored Commands can be used.

Soon afterwards, a VAX was attached to the IDM, first an 11/750, later an 11/730. This eliminated the problem of limited memory and allowed us to do "host-language-programming", i.e. write application programs in ordinary programming languages making use of the IDM services.

A Siemens 7.536 mainframe running under the BS2000 operating system
was connected to the IDM early this year. Both the hardware interface
and the software for this connection were realised by GEI. This gave
us a good opportunity to learn much about the IDM's hardware, software,
and the concepts used inside the IDM.

Functionality of the IDM Software

The functionality of the IDM software is mainly determined by Britton-
Lee's basic decision in favor of the relational model. No attempt will
be made here to discuss the benefits of relational database management.
However, it should be noted that some useful features of the IDM go beyond the relational model, like pattern matching and stored commands.

We could easily verify that the IDM software provides the full relational capabilities, including all types of joins, aggregate functions,
multi-record-update, etc.

Performance

Nothing simple can be said about the performance of a high-sophisti-
cated system like the IDM. Not only is the throughput (whatever this
may be) "application dependent", but there are also many factors that
have significant impact on the time needed to perform certain jobs. Some
of those factors are:

    configuration dependent:
    - the amount of memory within the IDM
    - the number of disk controllers and disk drives
    - special hardware like database accelerator
    - the host interfaces used

    data dependent:
    - the number of relations

- the number of attributes and their sizes
- the number of tuples per relation

application dependent:
- the spreading of data across disks
- indexes
- query and update types
- the number of relations utilised in a query/update

Only a few experiments habe been made varying the above named configuration dependent parameters, except for those tests made with and without the database accelerator (see below).

Also the data dependent parameters normally are a given fact and can only be influenced to a certain extent (e.g. by normalization). However, the application dependent factors can be varied by the database administrator. Tuning may achieve a lot of time saving.

Quite a lot of measurements have been done on the retrieval of data from relations. Obviously, the presence of indexes is a determining factor for the speed of execution and thus for response times. The following table shows some typical execution times (in seconds):

Tuples in the relation	Tuples retrieved	Execution time
20 K	3	0.3
29 K	88	3.3
170 K	6	1.0
260 K	69	1.7
260 K	213	5.7

Typically between 10 and 40 records will be transferred to the host per second. It should be noted that only those records that satisfy the query conditions will be returned to the host. For queries returning only a few records, a basic overhead is needed for the interpretation of the query, thus reducing the records/second rate.

Important is the fact that the records/second rate is roughly independent of the number of tuples in a relation, i.e. it makes no difference whether a relation contains 10K, 100K or a million records. This is a result of the index mechanisms.

In cases where an index cannot be used, qualified retrieves or updates require a complete scan through the relation. We may conclude that execution times are then proportional to the size of the relation. Here are some examples of doing aggregate functions, combined with pattern matching conditions:

Tuples in the relation	Tuples counted	Execution time	
20 K	7,289	62	
20 K	2,374	69	(Pattern matching)

The effect of adding memory to the IDM differs between single user and multi user applications. Adding memory generally improves the response times in the case of a multi user environment. Even in a two-user environment, this normally produces shorter execution times. However, in a single user case, adding memory may slightly decrease the performance. This is due to the increased overhead of larger internal table sizes.

Creation of Indexes

Indexes may be created or destroyed at any time, both by issuing the appropriate command at the screen or from an application program. There are two types of indexes, clustered and non-clustered indexes, each having their own time characteristics.

Here are some figures showing the total time needed to create an index (in minutes):

Number of tuples	Time
29 K	4.8
31 K	6.0
170 K	31
262 K	67

As shown in the following table, the time required to create a clustered index is primarily determined by the total size, i.e. the number of bytes in the relation:

	Rel 1	Rel 2	Rel 3	Rel 4
Number of tuples	180 K	340 K	260 K	140 K
Relation size (Mbytes)	47.8	103	22.8	12.7
Minutes per Ktuples	1.1	1.4	0.48	0.46
Minutes per Megabyte	4.1	4.5	5.5	5.1

The following table indicates non-clustered index creation time is primarily determined by the number of tuples:

	Rel 1	Rel 2	Rel 3	Rel 4
Number of tuples	180 K	340 K	260 K	140 K
Relation size (Mbytes)	47.8	103	22.8	12.7
Minutes per Ktuples	0.28	0.31	0.23	0.21
Minutes per Megabyte	1.1	1.0	2.7	2.4

An index of either type can be created on one or up to fifteen attributes. No significant difference in time can be observed between creating an index on just one attribute or a combination of attributes.

As stated above, the execution time for retrieval and updating greatly depends on the presence of suitable indexes. Since the profile and the nature of queries is application dependent, nobody can accurately anticipate which indexes will produce optimum results. Tests done with a predefined series of queries show that different sets of indexes produce very different results, with particular queries differing by orders of magnitude.

Database Accelerator

All of the above figures were obtained using an IDM 500 without database accelerator.

Several performance comparisons with or without the database accelerator have been done by Britton-Lee. Here are some figures showing the

execution times (in milliseconds) for five different queries on the
same test relation and the improvement factor gained by the database
accelerator:

Query	Execution time without DAC	Execution time with DAC	Improvement Factor
1	2116	300	7.05
2	1816	266	6.83
3	2266	433	5.23
4	50966	33733	1.51
5	5516	4416	1.25

These and other tests show that the improvement factor typically lies
between 2 and 5. Software and hardware tuning currently being done by
Britton-Lee may allow a factor of 10 to be reached.

Stored Commands

The IDM software offers the feature of Stored Commands, being a type of
command macros. Every stored command is a series of one or more retrieve
and/or update commands, as well as special commands like "begin transaction" or "end transaction", with the ability to replace formal parameters by actual values upon executing the stored command.

We must admit that it took us a longer time to really understand and
make use of all benefits of stored commands. Not only are they a means
to shorten command sequences and to reduce execution times (since stored
commands are pre-compiled), they also greatly contribute to data integrity, data consistency, and to data independence.

When it comes to data independence, the relational model in itself is
by far superior to other database models. Using stored commands extensively, one more level of data independence can be achieved. In most
cases, changes in data structure will not affect application programs.
For that reason, in several large software projects in our company, we
decided to use stored commands extensively rather than direct retrieve
or update commands within application programs.

Multi-Host Configurations

As stated before we currently have a multi-host configuration with a Siemens mainframe, a VAX, and several micros attached to our IDM. Some aspects of such a configuration are worth noting.

Firstly: While working with one identical database accessible to all host computers, tasks can be shared among the different hosts. Various functional areas can be supplied with adequate computer resources ranging from a small micro to a large mainframe. Database creation, index creation, etc. can be done in a very convenient way through inexpensive micros. This because each of the host softwares supports the same set of IDM commands. Furthermore, one can use the micro to establish views, define stored commands, and, for example, data protection rules. A mini computer, for example, can be used to load data into the database, therefore using a tape drive attached to it. Application programs doing extensive calculations and number crunching can then be run on a mainframe, again querying the same database.

Secondly: Since we attached host computers of very different architecture and internal structure to one IDM (the hardware adapter and host software for the mainframe being produced at GEI), we were eager to see whether the IDM would be able to serve those very different "clients". One of the fundamental differences was that the VAX used the ASCII code while the mainframe talked EBCDIC. After some problems with EBCDIC pattern matching the IDM talked perfectly to either of them and all hosts could manipulate the same database concurrently without problems.

Interfacing to a New Host

We already mentioned that we realised the connection between a Siemens mainframe and the IDM. On the IDM side the IEEE-488 host interface was used since it provides the speed required for larger data transfers. On the side of the mainframe, we decided to attach the new "intelligent controller" directly to the block multiplexer channel, as would be done for a disk drive. In building the hardware adapter between block MUX and IEEE, we needed the hardware specifications of both devices. Britton-Lee's specs of the host interface and the protocol turned out to be sufficient to do that job in a reasonably short amount of time.

A basic decision facilitating the portation of the necessary host software was taken by Britton-Lee in choosing the programming language "C". Unfortunately, the system software for the mainframe in question contained no C compiler. So GEI took the decision to first implement a C compiler on the mainframe which took us less than three months.

Almost no problems occurred with the portation of the host software itself. However, the attempt to embed the entire software in the mainframe manufacturer's TP monitor turned out to be a tricky task that meanwhile has been fully accomplished.

Hardware Stability

Nothing bad can be said about the stability of Britton-Lee's hardware. After some initial problems with the power supply, the IDM turned out to be very stable and reliable. Changing or adding boards can be done by a layman since there are no preset rules as to which board goes into which slot. The IDM itself determines the addresses and the types of the boards when the system is booted.

Problem Areas

Britton-Lee is constantly improving both the hardware and the software of the IDM. Among things that need to be and will be improved in the software are the following: Evaluation of certain pattern matching conditions, execution of joins of specific types, optimum use of indexes.

A MESSAGE-ORIENTED IMPLEMENTATION OF A MULTI-BACKEND DATABASE
SYSTEM (MDBS)

Richard D. Boyne, David K. Hsiao, Douglas S. Kerr and Ali Orooji
Laboratory for Database Systems Research
Naval Postgraduate School
Monterey, California 93940
USA

Abstract

In this paper we describe the communication mechanisms for a multi-backend database system (MDBS). MDBS is designed to provide for capacity growth and performance enhancement by the addition of more backend minicomputers and associated disks and by the replication of the same software without additional programming. MDBS has been implemented using a permanent process for each major database system function. Further, the processes in a backend are identical to the processes in another backend. The communication functions in MDBS involve interprocess and interbackend mechanisms for control and synchronization. Our primary purpose is to analyze the implementation decisions for the communication mechanism and to describe MDBS from the communications viewpoint.

1. INTRODUCTION

This paper discusses the communication facilities of the Multi-backend Database System (MDBS). The primary design goal of MDBS is to distribute the effort of the database system over several backends, each of which is running identical software [Hsia81a and Hsia81b]. The aim of this design is to allow performance improvement by using additional backends and capacity growth by adding disk drives. To ease the control overhead for the multiple backends and their disk

---

This work was supported by the Office of Naval Research under contract N00014-75-C-0573 and by an equipment grant from the External Research Program of the Digital Equipment Corporation.

R.D. Boyne and A. Orooji are graduate students at Ohio State University. D.S. Kerr is an Associate Professor at Ohio State University. He is on sabbatical at the Naval Postgraduate School.

drives, the entire system is coordinated from one controller computer. To prevent the controller from becoming a bottleneck, the role of the controller is minimized. Instead, the role of the backends is maximized. The resulting machine configuration is shown in Figure 1. The purpose of this paper is to analyze the principles involved in choosing a message-passing implementation and to describe MDBS from the viewpoint of the message-passing system. Details of the implementation may be found in [Boyn83], [He83] and [Hsia83].

1.1. The Primary Characteristics of MDBS

In MDBS, the records within specific attribute-value ranges are grouped into logical clusters. Next, the records of a cluster are spread across the disks of the respective backends. Each cluster of records is known to the system by a specific cluster id. This storage structure, coupled with the replication of system software at each backend, allows the database to be accessed and processed in parallel. When a request for a set of records arrives, it is translated into an equivalent request for a set of clusters. The specific group of records desired are then accessed and processed in parallel by the backends.

In order to locate clusters easily, information allowing us to identify the clusters is stored in a directory. The directory

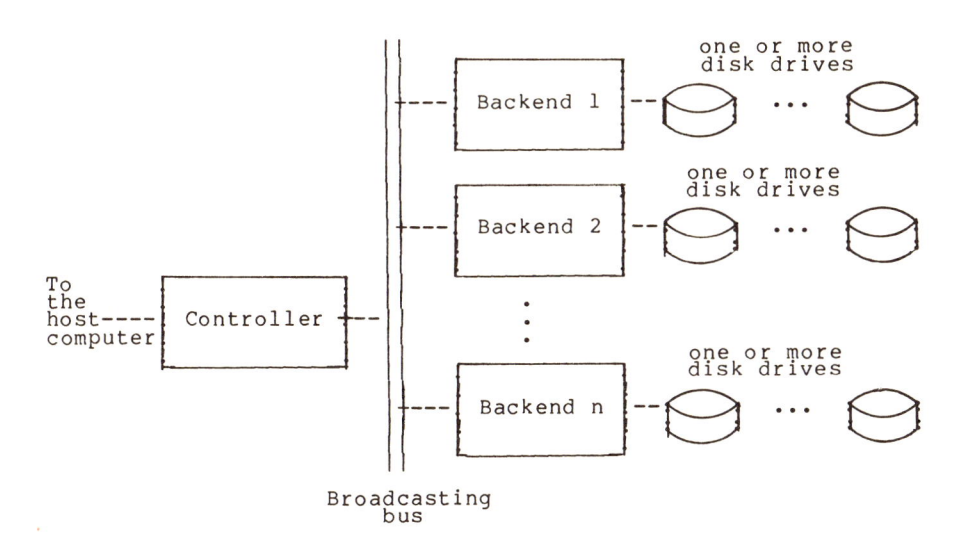

Figure 1. The MDBS Hardware Organization

information consists of descriptor sets and each <u>descriptor</u> is used to specify a range of values that an attribute can have. Every descriptor is identified by a unique <u>descriptor id</u>. A cluster then contains all the records whose attribute values are within the ranges of a particular set of descriptors. For example, assume that the database contains attributes SALARY and CITY. Then possible descriptors for the attributes SALARY and CITY are (10001 <= SALARY <= 15000) and (CITY = Cumberland). A cluster might then contain all records with SALARY between $10,001 and $15,000 and with CITY as Cumberland. To process a database request we must first ascertain which clusters are needed by the request. Then the actual records in those clusters are retrieved. The work of accessing directory information about the database (i.e., descriptor and cluster ids) and retrieving the requested records is done by each backend on its subset of the database (i.e., clustered records on their associated disks).

As MDBS executes, many users may issue requests. The requests of a single user, as well as the requests of multiple users are processed by the backends concurrently. With this design MDBS is a multiple-request-multiple-data-stream system.

1.2. <u>Message-Oriented</u> vs. <u>Procedure-Oriented Approach</u>

Most operating systems supply facilities to support the execution of concurrent processes. These facilities support communication among and synchronization between different processes. Systems developed using multiple processes have generally taken one of two approaches, message-oriented or procedure-oriented, depending on how their designers viewed the concept of a process [Laue79].

In a procedure-oriented system, a process is associated with each user. A synchronizing mechanism based on a lock table would allow processes to cooperate in accessing common data structures within the system. In MDBS, processes would be created for each user and would be deleted as a user's session ended. Access to the database would be controlled by maintaining a common lock table.

In a message-oriented system, each process corresponds to one system function. These processes, then, communicate among themselves by passing messages. For our implementation we would expect to have one process for each MDBS function, directory management, for example. User requests would be passed between processes as messages. The message paths between processes would be fixed for the system and the

MDBS processes would be created at the system start time and would exist until the system is stopped.

Lauer and Needham, [Laue79], have argued that message-oriented systems and procedure-oriented systems are equivalent. That is, we could expect systems implemented using these two methods to be similar in performance and in functionality. Reasons for choosing one of these methods over the other should, therefore, be based on considerations such as the available operating system support and the database system architecture.

1.3. Reasons for Choosing the Message-Oriented Approach

Operating systems are often too general to offer efficient support of database management system operations. Therefore, we look at the amount of work involved to implement either approach. As has been described by Stonebraker [Ston81], we see two major problems with the procedure-oriented approach.

The first problem is that when a process enters a wait state a process switch is necessary in order to execute another process. Considerable effort is required to save the environment of the blocked process and to determine the next process to execute. For the procedure-oriented approach, user processes are created, blocked and destroyed frequently as the priority of the user jobs and duration of the user services vary. There are frequent process switches. For the message-oriented approach, the database system processes are created permanently. These processes do sequence their interactions, but they seldom require blocking. Further, they are never destroyed. Consequently, there are few process switches. Since the procedure-oriented approach causes more process switching than the message-oriented approach, we expect the process-switching overhead to be higher under the procedure-oriented approach.

The second problem associated with the procedure-oriented system is that if the process scheduler deschedules a process while it is in a critical section holding locks on a resource, other processes must wait and be queued up behind the locked resource. An example of this for MDBS would be if several user processes are attempting to update the same cluster. One process (called P in our example) has been given access to the cluster. The other processes will be queued up and waiting for access to the cluster. If process P is descheduled from execution while it is updating the cluster, the other processes will now have to wait indefinitely for they cannot get to access the cluster until process P is scheduled for execution again and completes its updates. Blasgen, [Blas79], called this type of problem the "convoy phenomenon", and developed rules to minimize its occurrence. However, the problem cannot be avoided completely.

In our implementation the real-time operating system RSX-11M is being used on the backends, which are PDP 11/44s and VMS is being used in the controller, which is a VAX 11/780. Both of these operating systems provide the necessary interprocess communication facilities required by MDBS. However, for our use of the operating system processes, we have chosen to use the message-oriented approach.

2. MESSAGE PASSING IN MDBS

In this section we describe briefly the message-passing processes of MDBS. Implementation details may be found in [Boyn83].

2.1. The Process Structure of MDBS

Here we will provide brief functional descriptions of the processes executing in the controller and backends of MDBS. (See Figure 2.) The get and put processes, present in each minicomputer, whether it is a backend or the controller, provide communication services between machines. They are auxiliary processes. We will not describe them as MDBS processes.

The controller has three MDBS processes: request preparation, insert information generation and post processing. The functions of request preparation are those performed on a request before it is sent to all the backends. These functions include the parsing of the user's request. The purpose of the insert information generation process is to aid the backends on an insert request. For example, this process determines which backend should insert a record into the backend's disk. The post processing process collects the responses from all the backends and finishes the computation of any aggregate operations such as the average of the data returned.

The software and hardware of each backend is identical in MDBS; the portion of the database residing on disks of each backend is different. The three MDBS processes in a backend are: directory management, concurrency control, and record processing. The directory management process receives a request from the controller. It determines the clusters needed by the request and generates the

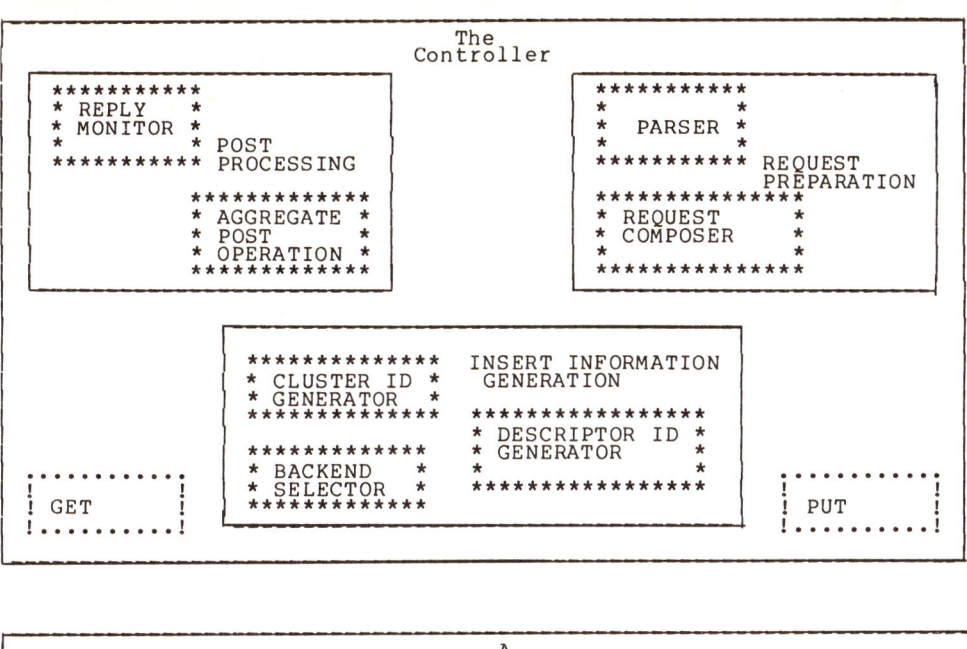

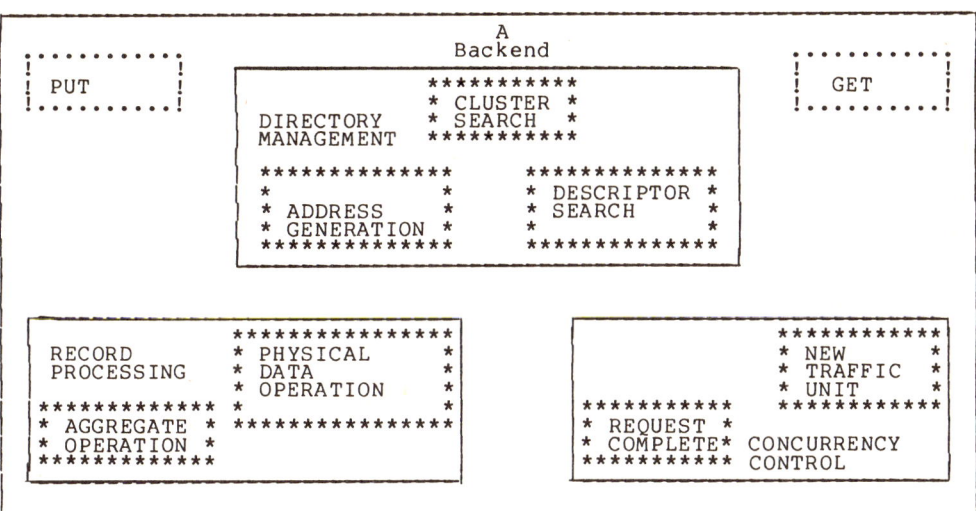

```
┌─────────────────────────────────────────────────────────────────┐
│                            The                                  │
│                         Controller                              │
│  ┌──────────────────────────┐      ┌──────────────────────────┐ │
│  │ **********               │      │ **********               │ │
│  │ * REPLY  *               │      │ *  PARSER *              │ │
│  │ * MONITOR*               │      │ *        *               │ │
│  │ *        * POST          │      │ ********** REQUEST       │ │
│  │ ********** PROCESSING    │      │            PREPARATION   │ │
│  │   **************         │      │   ***************        │ │
│  │   * AGGREGATE  *         │      │   * REQUEST     *        │ │
│  │   * POST       *         │      │   * COMPOSER    *        │ │
│  │   * OPERATION  *         │      │   *             *        │ │
│  │   **************         │      │   ***************        │ │
│  └──────────────────────────┘      └──────────────────────────┘ │
│             ┌─────────────────────────────────────┐             │
│             │ **************  INSERT INFORMATION  │             │
│             │ * CLUSTER ID *  GENERATION          │             │
│             │ * GENERATOR  *                      │             │
│             │ **************  *****************   │             │
│             │                 * DESCRIPTOR ID *   │             │
│             │ **************  * GENERATOR    *    │             │
│             │ * BACKEND    *  *               *   │             │
│ ........... │ * SELECTOR   *  *****************   │ ........... │
│ ! GET     ! │ **************                      │ ! PUT     ! │
│ !.........! └─────────────────────────────────────┘ !.........! │
└─────────────────────────────────────────────────────────────────┘

┌─────────────────────────────────────────────────────────────────┐
│                             A                                   │
│                          Backend                                │
│ ...........   ┌───────────────────────────────────┐ ........... │
│ ! PUT     !   │             **********            │ ! GET     ! │
│ !.........!   │             * CLUSTER *           │ !.........! │
│               │  DIRECTORY  * SEARCH  *           │             │
│               │  MANAGEMENT **********            │             │
│               │  **************   **************  │             │
│               │  *            *   * DESCRIPTOR *  │             │
│               │  * ADDRESS    *   * SEARCH     *  │             │
│               │  * GENERATION *   *            *  │             │
│               │  **************   **************  │             │
│               └───────────────────────────────────┘             │
│  ┌──────────────────────────────┐  ┌──────────────────────────┐ │
│  │              ***************  │  │            ************ │ │
│  │              * PHYSICAL    *  │  │            * NEW      * │ │
│  │   RECORD     * DATA        *  │  │            * TRAFFIC  * │ │
│  │   PROCESSING * OPERATION   *  │  │            * UNIT     * │ │
│  │              *             *  │  │ ********** ************ │ │
│  │ ************ ***************  │  │ * REQUEST *             │ │
│  │ * AGGREGATE*                  │  │ * COMPLETE* CONCURRENCY │ │
│  │ * OPERATION*                  │  │ ********** CONTROL      │ │
│  │ ************                  │  │                         │ │
│  └──────────────────────────────┘  └──────────────────────────┘ │
└─────────────────────────────────────────────────────────────────┘

            Figure 2.  The MDBS Controller and Backend Processes
```

addresses for the clustered records. In record processing, the MDBS process accesses the records on secondary memory and extracts the required information from the retrieved records. The process for concurrency control is used to maintain consistency in the database. That is, it will ensure that concurrent and interleaved execution of the user requests will not produce incorrect results.

2.2. MDBS Message Types

Thirty-one message types are defined in MDBS and one standard message format is used. The standard message format used by MDBS is shown in Figure 3. This same format is used for all message types whether between processes in one machine or between one machine and another. Any message passing between machines will use the get and put processes. For this discussion we will assume these processes without mentioning them. For instance, when the controller sends a message to a backend, we will not mention the two intermediate processes in the message's flow, i.e., the controller-put process and the backend-get process. Figure 4 describes each of the MDBS message types.

These messages can be divided into the following five categories:

    Between host and controller and within the controller.
    Between controller and directory management process
        in the backends.
    From record processing process in the backend to post
        processing and request preparation processes
        in the controller.
    Between directory management processes on different
        backends and between directory management and
        record processing processes within one backend.
    Concurrency control related messages.

Message type	(a numeric code).
Message Sender	(a numeric code).
Message Receiver	(a numeric code).
Message Text	(an alphanumeric field terminated by an end-of-message marker).

Figure 3. The MDBS General Message Format

```
       Process Name                           Path Designation
----------------------------------      ----------------------------------
HOST : HOST MACHINE                     HC: Host to Controller
                                        CH: Controller to Host
REQP : REQUEST PREPARATION              BC: A Backend to the Controller
                                        CB: The Controller to all
IIG  : INSERT INFORMATION GENERATION        Backends
                                        B : Within a Backend
PP   : POST PROCESSING                  BB: One Backend to all other
                                            Backends
DM   : DIRECTORY MANAGEMENT

RECP : RECORD PROCESSING

CC   : CONCURRENCY CONTROL
```

No.	MDBS MESSAGE TYPE	Message Origin	Message Destination	Path Involved
1	TRAFFIC UNIT	HOST	REQP	HC
	RESULTS	PP	HOST	CH
	NUMBER OF REQUESTS IN A TRANSACTION	REQP	PP	C
	AGGREGATE OPERATORS	REQP	PP	C
5	REQUESTS WITH ERRORS	REQP	PP	C
	PARSED TRAFFIC UNIT	REQP	DM	CB
	GENERATED INSERTS COUNT	REQP	DM	CB
	NEW DESCRIPTOR ID	IIG	DM	CB
	BACKEND NUMBER	IIG	DM	CB
10	CLUSTER ID	DM	IIG	BC
	REQUEST FOR NEW DESCRIPTOR ID	DM	IIG	BC
	BACKEND RESULTS FOR A REQUEST	RECP	PP	BC
	BACKEND AGGREGATE OPERATOR RESULTS	RECP	PP	BC
	RECORD THAT HAS CHANGED CLUSTER	RECP	REQP	BC
15	RESULTS OF A RETRIEVE OR FETCH CAUSED BY AN UPDATE	RECP	REQP	BC
	INSERT GENERATION COMPLETE	RECP	REQP	BC
	DESCRIPTOR IDS	DM	DMs	BB
	REQUEST AND DISK ADDRESSES	DM	RECP	B
	CHANGED CLUSTER RESPONSE	DM	RECP	B
20	UPDATED RECORD INSERTED	DM	RECP	B
	FETCH	DM	RECP	B
	ALL GENERATED INSERTS RECEIVED	DM	RECP	B
	OLD AND NEW VALUES OF ATTRIBUTE BEING MODIFIED	RECP	DM	B
	UPDATE REQUEST COMPLETE	RECP	DM	B
25	CLUSTER IDS FOR A TRAFFIC UNIT	DM	CC	B
	FINISHED UPDATE REQUEST ID	DM	CC	B
	CLUSTER CREATED BY AN INSERT REQUEST	DM	CC	B
	CLUSTER CREATED BY AN UPDATE REQUEST	DM	CC	B
	UPDATE WAIT LIST	DM	CC	B
30	REQUEST ID OK TO EXECUTE	CC	DM	B
	REQUEST ID OF A FINISHED REQUEST	RECP	CC	B

Figure 4. The MDBS Message Types

2.3. MDBS Message Definitions

In the following we give short descriptions for messages used in MDBS. The first category of messages are those between the host and the controller and within the controller itself. These messages are shown in Figure 5 and referred by the following description to their parenthesized type numbers.

```
Message type : (1) Traffic Unit
     Source : Host
Destination : Request Preparation
Explanation : The traffic unit represents a single request or
              transaction from a user at the host machine. Each
              traffic unit will be assigned a unique name called
              a request id.


Message type : (2) Results
     Source : Post Processing
Destination : Host
Explanation : Contains the results corresponding to a traffic
              unit after being collected from all the backends
              and aggregated, if necessary, by the controller.
```

```
                    HOST                      HOST
                    /:\                        :
                     : (2) Results             : (1) Traffic Unit
                     :                         :
          ┌──────────:─────────────────────────:──────────────┐
          │               The Controller       :              │
          │          ************              \:/            │
          │          * REPLY    *          ***********        │
          │          * MONITOR  *          *         *        │
          │          *         * POST      * PARSER  *        │
          │          ********* PROCESSING  *         *        │
          │                    <---------- ***********        │
          │                    (3) Number       REQUEST       │
          │                        of          PREPARATION    │
          │          *************  Requests  ***************  │
          │          * AGGREGATE *  (4) Aggre-* REQUEST     *  │
          │          * POST      *    gate    * COMPOSER    *  │
          │          * OPERATION *  Operators *             *  │
          │          *************  (5) Requests ***************│
          │                         with                       │
          │                         Errors                     │
          │                                                    │
          │        *************** INSERT INFORMATION          │
          │        * CLUSTER ID *   GENERATION                 │
          │        * GENERATOR  *                              │
          │        ***************  *****************          │
          │                         * DESCRIPTOR ID *          │
          │        ***************  * GENERATOR    *          │
          │        * BACKEND    *   *****************          │
          │        * SELECTOR   *                              │
          │ ......  ***************                  ......    │
          │ : GET :                                  : PUT :   │
          │ ......                                   ......    │
          └────────────────────────────────────────────────────┘
```

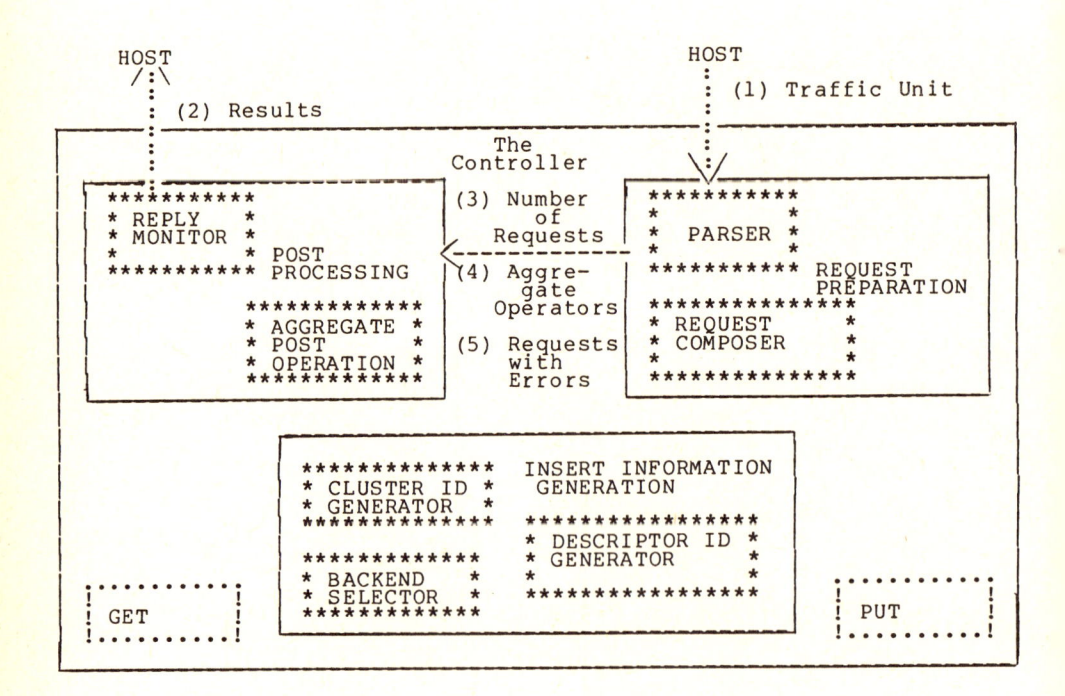

Figure 5. The Host-Controller and Intracontroller Related Messages

```
Message type : (3) Number of Requests in a Transaction
     Source : Request Preparation
Destination : Post Processing
Explanation : Request Preparation sends to Post Processing
              the number of requests in a traffic unit.
              This enables Post Processing to determine whether
              the processing of a traffic unit is complete.


Message type : (4) Aggregate Operators
     Source : Request Preparation
Destination : Post Processing
Explanation : An aggregate operator, such as the average, is
              sent to Post Processing to be used on the results
              of the request coming from the backends.


Message type : (5) Requests with Errors
     Source : Request Preparation
Destination : Post Processing
Explanation : Requests with errors will be found in
              Request Preparation by the Parser
              and sent to Post Processing
              directly.  Post Processing will send
              the requests with errors back to the host.
```

The next category of messages deals with the communication between the controller and the Directory Management process within each backend. These messages can be found in Figure 6.

```
Message type : (6) Parsed Traffic Unit
     Source : Request Preparation
Destination : Directory Management
Explanation : This is the formatted request or transaction sent by
              Request Preparation.


Message type : (7) Generated Inserts Count
     Source : Request Preparation
Destination : Directory Management
Explanation : Request Preparation tells Directory Management the
              total number of inserts that were generated by a
              specific update.


Message type : (8) New Descriptor Id
     Source : Insert Information Generation
Destination : Directory Management
Explanation : This message is a response to the Directory
              Management request for a new descriptor id.


Message type : (9) Backend Number
     Source : Insert Information Generation
Destination : Directory Management
Explanation : This message is used to specify which backend is to
              insert a record.


Message type : (10) Cluster Id
     Source : Directory Management
Destination : Insert Information Generation
Explanation : Directory Management sends a cluster id to Insert
              Information Generation for an insert request.
              Insert Information Generation will decide where to
              do the insert.
```

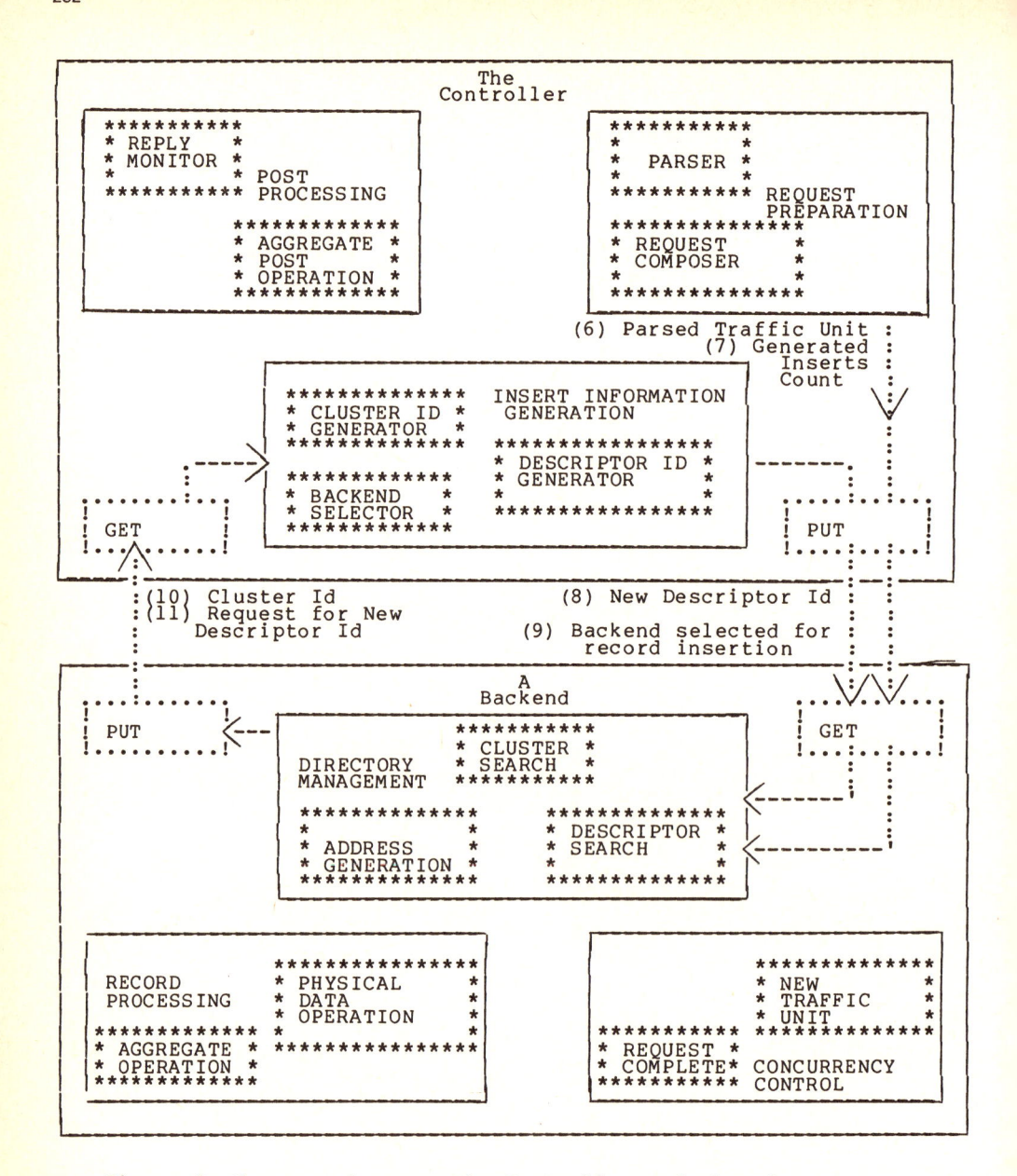

Figure 6. Messages between the Controller and the Directory Management Process

Message type : (11) Request for New Descriptor Id
Source : Directory Management
Destination : Insert Information Generation
Explanation : When Directory Management has found a new descriptor, it is sent to Insert Information Generation to generate an id.

The third category of messages deals with the flow from the Record Processing process in a backend to the Post Processing and Request Preparation processes in the controller. Figure 7 shows the flow of these messages.

Message type : (12) Results of a Request from a Backend
Source : Record Processing
Destination : Post Processing
Explanation : This message contains the results that a specific backend found for a request.

Message type : (13) Aggregate Operator Results from a Backend
Source : Record Processing
Destination : Post Processing
Explanation : When an aggregate operation needs to be done on the retrieved records, each backend will do as much aggregation as possible in the aggregate operation function of Record Processing. This message carries those results to Post Processing.

Message type : (14) Record That Has Changed Cluster
Source : Record Processing
Destination : Request Preparation
Explanation : This message is a record which has changed cluster, Request Preparation will prepare it as an insertion and send it to the backends.

Message type : (15) Results of a Retrieve or Fetch Caused by an Update
Source : Record Processing
Destination : Request Preparation
Explanation : This message carries the information from a retrieve or a fetch back to Request Preparation to complete an update which involved information from the database in specifying the update.

Message type : (16) Insert Generation Complete
Source : Record Processing
Destination : Request Preparation
Explanation : Record Processing notifies Request Preparation that it is done generating inserts for its current update request.

The following descriptions are for messages between Directory Management processes residing on different backends and between Directory Management and Record Processing within a backend. These messages are shown in Figure 8.

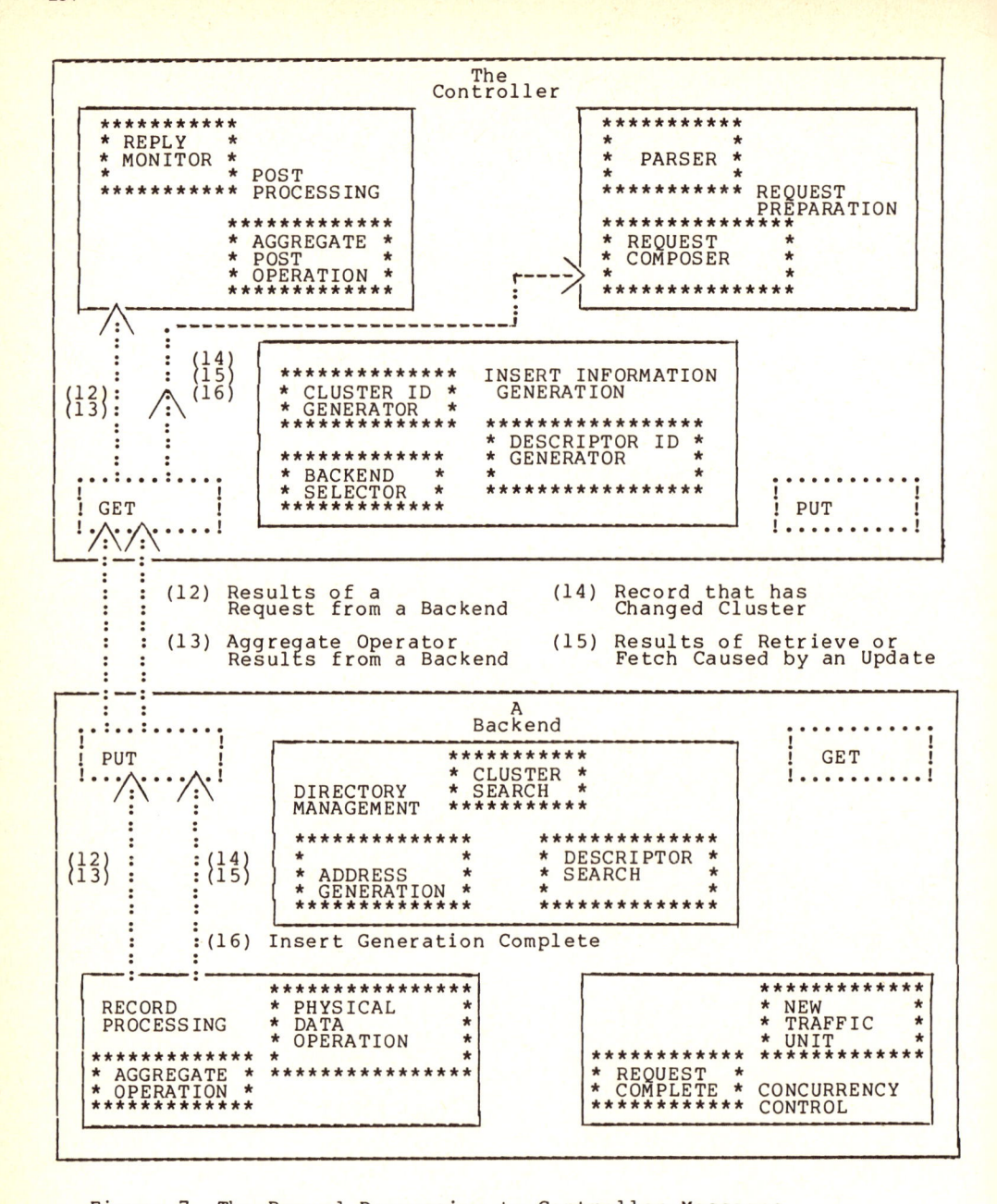

```
+-------------------------------------------------------------------+
|                              The                                  |
|                           Controller                              |
|  **********                          **********                   |
|  * REPLY   *                         *        *                   |
|  * MONITOR *   POST                  * PARSER *                   |
|  *         *   PROCESSING            *        *   REQUEST         |
|  **********                          **********   PREPARATION     |
|          *************                *************              |
|          * AGGREGATE *                * REQUEST   *              |
|          * POST      *                * COMPOSER  *              |
|          * OPERATION *                *           *              |
|          *************                *************              |
|              ^                                                    |
|              |  (14)                                              |
|        (12)  |  (15)    *************   INSERT INFORMATION        |
|        (13)  |  (16)    * CLUSTER ID *  GENERATION                |
|              ^^^        * GENERATOR  *                            |
|                         *************   *****************        |
|                                          * DESCRIPTOR ID *       |
|                         *************    * GENERATOR     *       |
|     ...........        * BACKEND    *    *****************       |
|     ! GET     !        * SELECTOR   *                            |
|     !.........!        *************           ...........       |
|                                                 ! PUT     !       |
|                                                 !.........!       |
+-------------------------------------------------------------------+
        (12) Results of a          (14) Record that has
             Request from a Backend     Changed Cluster
        (13) Aggregate Operator     (15) Results of Retrieve or
             Results from a Backend      Fetch Caused by an Update

+-------------------------------------------------------------------+
|                              A                                    |
|                           Backend                                 |
|   ...........                                       ...........   |
|   ! PUT     !           **********                  ! GET     !   |
|   !.........!           * CLUSTER *                 !.........!   |
|            DIRECTORY    * SEARCH  *                               |
|            MANAGEMENT   **********                                |
|     (12)     (14)    *************    *************              |
|     (13)     (15)    *           *    * DESCRIPTOR*              |
|                      * ADDRESS   *    * SEARCH    *              |
|                      * GENERATION*    *           *              |
|                      *************    *************              |
|         (16) Insert Generation Complete                           |
|                                                                   |
|  *************   *****************      *************            |
|  * RECORD    *   * PHYSICAL       *     * NEW       *            |
|  * PROCESSING*   * DATA           *     * TRAFFIC   *            |
|  *************   * OPERATION      *     * UNIT      *            |
|  *************   *****************     *************            |
|  * AGGREGATE *                          * REQUEST   *            |
|  * OPERATION *                          * COMPLETE  *  CONCURRENCY|
|  *************                          *************  CONTROL    |
+-------------------------------------------------------------------+
```

Figure 7. The Record Processing to Controller Messages

```
<------.(17)    (17) Descriptor Ids from/to Other Backends    :(17)
       :                                                      :
       :                        A                             :
       :                     Backend                          \/
........:....           **********                        ........
! PUT       !<---       * CLUSTER *                       ! GET   !
!...........!   :       * SEARCH  *                       !.......!
                :  DIRECTORY **********
                :  MANAGEMENT
(23) Old and    :  **************        **************
New Values of   :  *            *        * DESCRIPTOR *  <--------:
Attributes      :  *  ADDRESS   *        *  SEARCH    *
Being           :  * GENERATION *        *            *
Modified        :  **************        **************
(24) Update Request  /:\         :  (18) Request and Disk Addresses
      Complete      : :          :  (19) Changed Cluster Response
                    : :          \/ (20) Updated Record Inserted
                    : :             (21) Fetch
                    **************  (22) All Generated Inserts Received
  RECORD            * PHYSICAL   *
  PROCESSING        *  DATA      *                    **************
**************     *  OPERATION *    **********      * NEW TRAFFIC*
* AGGREGATE  *     **************    *REQUEST *      *  UNIT      *
* OPERATION  *                       *COMPLETE*      **************
**************                       **********      CONCURRENCY
                                                     CONTROL
```

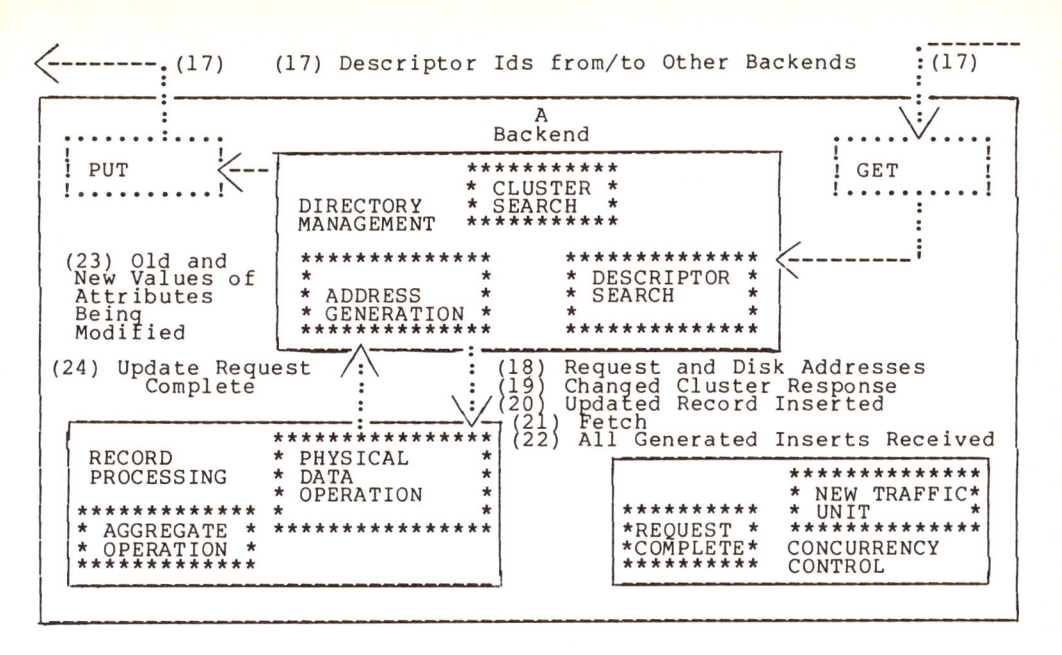

Figure 8. The Backend-Backend Messages for Directory Processing and
         the Intrabackend Messages between Directory Management
         and Record Processing

         Message type : (17) Descriptor Ids
              Source : Directory Management
         Destination : Directory Management (other backends)
         Explanation : This message contains the results of descriptor
                       search by Directory Management.

         Message type : (18) Request and Disk Addresses
              Source : Directory Management
         Destination : Record Processing
         Explanation : This message contains a request and disk addresses
                       for Record Processing, which can then execute the
                       request.

         Message type : (19) Changed Cluster Response
              Source : Directory Management
         Destination : Record Processing
         Explanation : Directory Management uses this message to tell
                       Record Processing whether an updated record has
                       changed cluster.

         Message type : (20) Updated Record Inserted
              Source : Directory Management
         Destination : Record Processing
         Explanation : Directory Management uses this message to tell
                       Record Processing that a record sent to
                       Request Preparation due to an update has been
                       inserted at a backend. Record Processing needs
                       this information to determine whether the
                       processing of the original update is complete.

```
Message type  : (21) Fetch
      Source  : Directory Management
 Destination  : Record Processing
 Explanation  : Fetch is a special retrieval of information for
                Request Preparation due to an update request which
                needs additional information from the database to
                complete the update.

Message type  : (22) All Generated Inserts Received
      Source  : Directory Management
 Destination  : Record Processing
 Explanation  : Directory Management tells Record Processing that
                all inserts generated by an update have been given
                to Record Processing.

Message Type  : (23) Old and New Values of Attribute being Modified
      Source  : Record Processing
 Destination  : Directory Management
 Explanation  : Record Processing uses this message to check
                whether a record that has been updated has changed
                cluster.

Message Type  : (24) Update Request Complete
      Source  : Record Processing
 Destination  : Directory Management
 Explanation  : Record Processing tells Directory Management that
                an entire update request has completed.
```

The last category of messages is the Concurrency Control related messages. These messages pass information between Directory Management, Concurrency Control and Record Processing. These are shown in Figure 9.

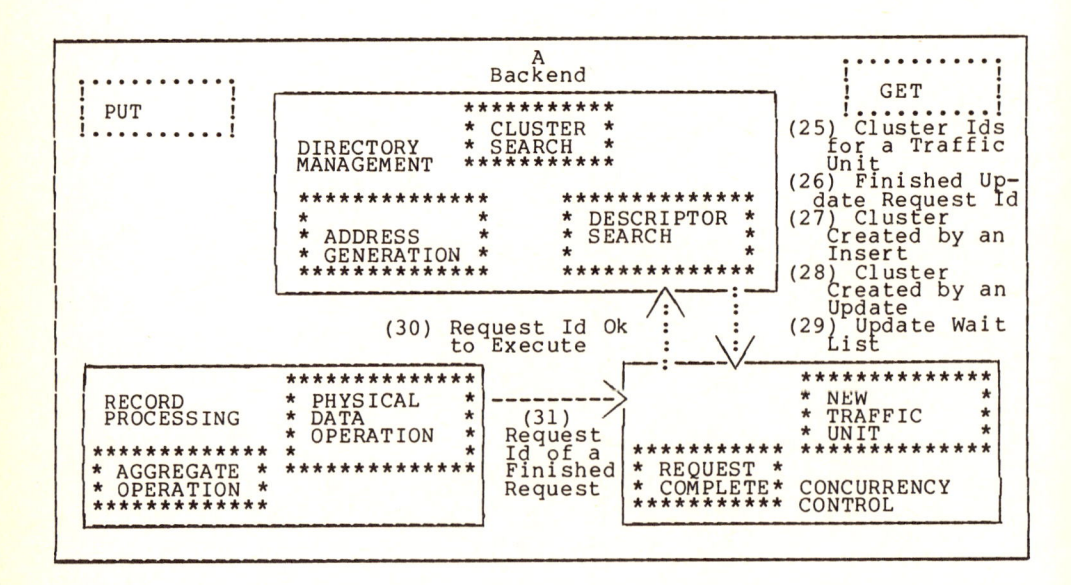

Figure 9. The Intrabackend Messages for Concurrency Control

```
Message Type : (25) Cluster Ids for a Traffic Unit
     Source : Directory Management
Destination : Concurrency Control
Explanation : Concurrency Control takes the cluster ids in this
              message and determines when the requests in the
              traffic unit can execute.


Message Type : (26) Finished Update Request Id
     Source : Directory Management
Destination : Concurrency Control
Explanation : Directory Management tells Concurrency Control that
              an update request has completed execution.


Message Type : (27) Cluster Created by an Insert Request
     Source : Directory Management
Destination : Concurrency Control
Explanation : Directory Management sends to Concurrency Control
              the new cluster id as well as a list of all the
              executing updates which the insert could affect.


Message Type : (28) Cluster Created by an Update Request
     Source : Directory Management
Destination : Concurrency Control
Explanation : Directory Management uses this message to tell
              Concurrency Control to lock a cluster that was
              created by an insert due to an update request.


Message Type : (29) Update Wait List
     Source : Directory Management
Destination : Concurrency Control
Explanation : Directory Management tells Concurrency Control which
              earlier updates (if any) that a new update must
              wait for to complete before it can run.


Message Type : (30) Request Id Ok to Execute
     Source : Concurrency Control
Destination : Directory Management
Explanation : Concurrency Control tells Directory Management
              which request can now execute.


Message Type : (31) Request Id of a Finished Request
     Source : Record Processing
Destination : Concurrency Control
Explanation : Record Processing tells Concurrency Control
              which request has just completed.
```

3. REQUEST EXECUTION IN MDBS - VIEWED VIA MESSAGE PASSING

In this section, we describe the sequence of actions taken by MDBS in executing each of the four types of requests: insert, delete, retrieve and update. The sequence of actions will be described in terms of the types of messages passed between the MDBS processes: Request Preparation (REQP), Insert Information Generation (IIG), Post Processing (PP), Directory Management (DM), Record Processing (RECP) and Concurrency Control (CC). The order in which messages are passed will be denoted alphabetically (e.g., 'a' is first). The digit following the ordering letter will be the message number as shown in Figure 4.

3.1. Sequence of Actions for an Insert Request

The sequence of actions for an insert request is shown in Figure 10. The traffic unit (al) comes into REQP from the host carrying an insert request. REQP sends to PP the number of requests in the transaction (b3). After preparation the formatted request is sent to DM from REQP (c6). From the DM, descriptor ids for the request will be sent to the other backends in the MDBS system (d17). The descriptor ids found by the other backends will then be received by DM (e17). To determine where the insert will occur DM will send the insert cluster id to IIG (f10). Once the backend has been selected, IIG will send the backend number to DM (g9). Concurrency Control must determine if the insert can proceed; therefore, DM will send the insert cluster id to CC (h25). CC will respond to DM with the request id of an executable request (i30). With the go-ahead signal from CC, DM will send RECP the request and its required disk address (j18). After the insert has occurred, RECP will notify CC that the request is done (k31), followed by a message to PP that the transaction has completed (l12). PP will finish the processing by sending a results message to the host (m2).

3.2. Sequence of Actions for a Delete Request

The sequence of actions for a delete request is shown in Figure 11. A traffic unit is sent to REQP from the host containing the delete request (al). REQP notifies PP of the number of requests in the transaction (b3). Next, REQP sends the request down to DM (c6). The descriptor ids for the request are next sent to the other backends from DM (d17). The other backends respond with the descriptor ids they have found (e17). DM will next send the cluster ids to CC to assure the delete can go through (f25). CC responds to DM with the id of the next executable request (g30). Next, RECP receives the addresses and request from DM (h18). After RECP has performed the delete request, it will notify CC that the request is through (i31). PP will then receive a results message from RECP telling it that the request is done (j12). PP will then notify the host with a results message (k2).

3.3. Sequence of Actions for a Retrieve Request with Aggregation

The sequence of actions for a retrieve request is shown in Figure 12. First the retrieve request comes to the controller REQP from the

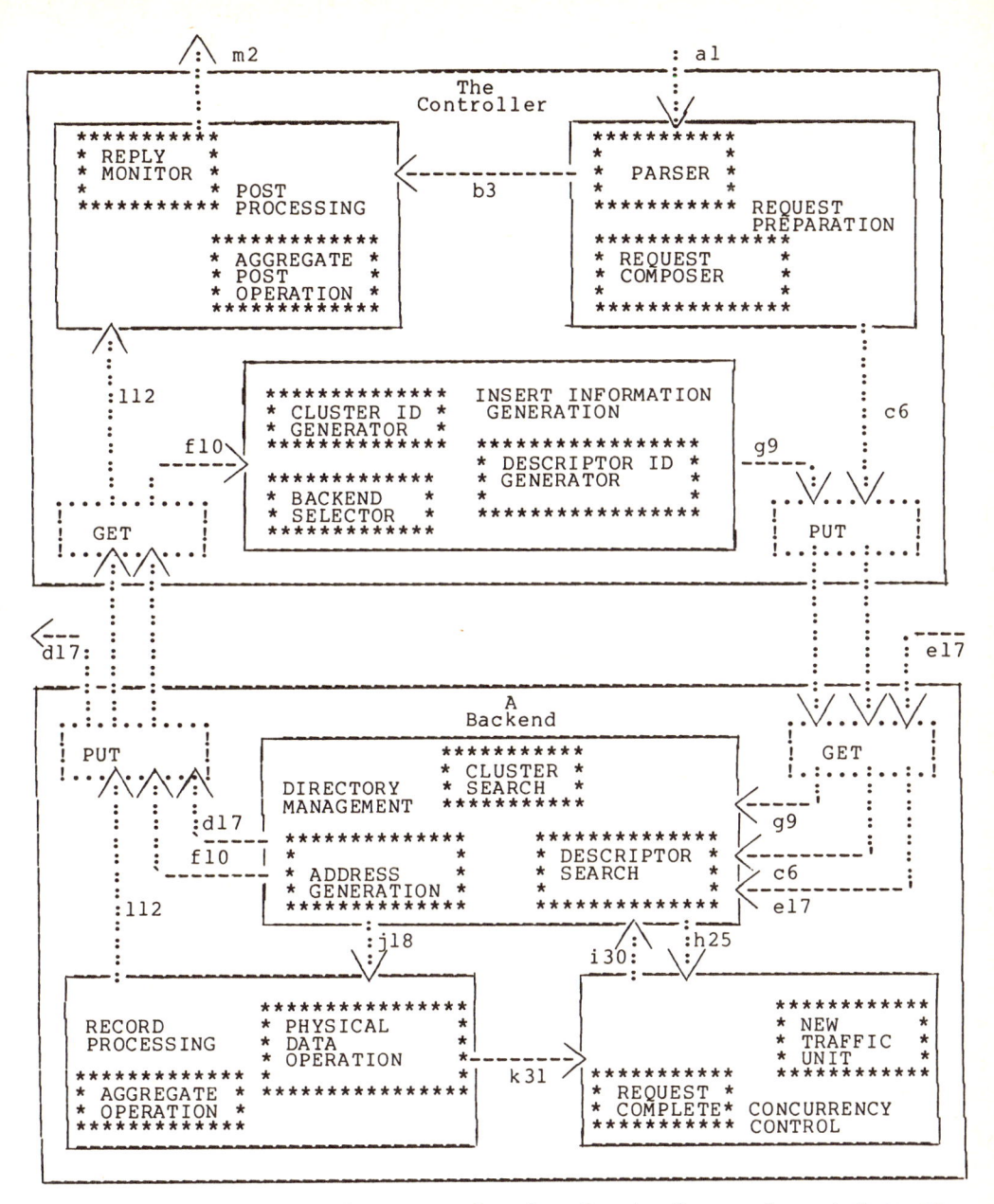

Figure 10. Sequence of Message-Passing Events for an Insert Request

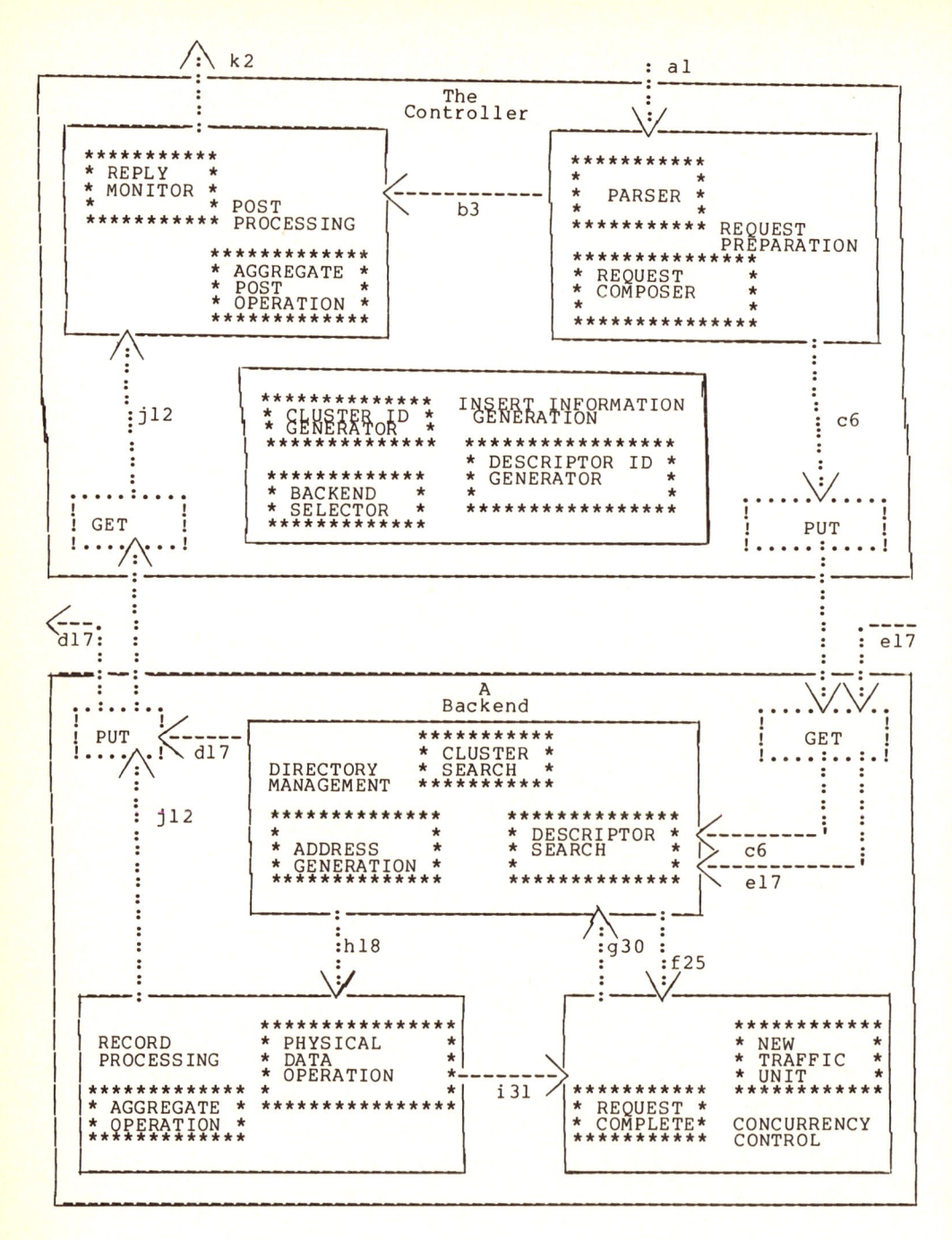

Figure 11. Sequence of Message-Passing Events for a Delete Request

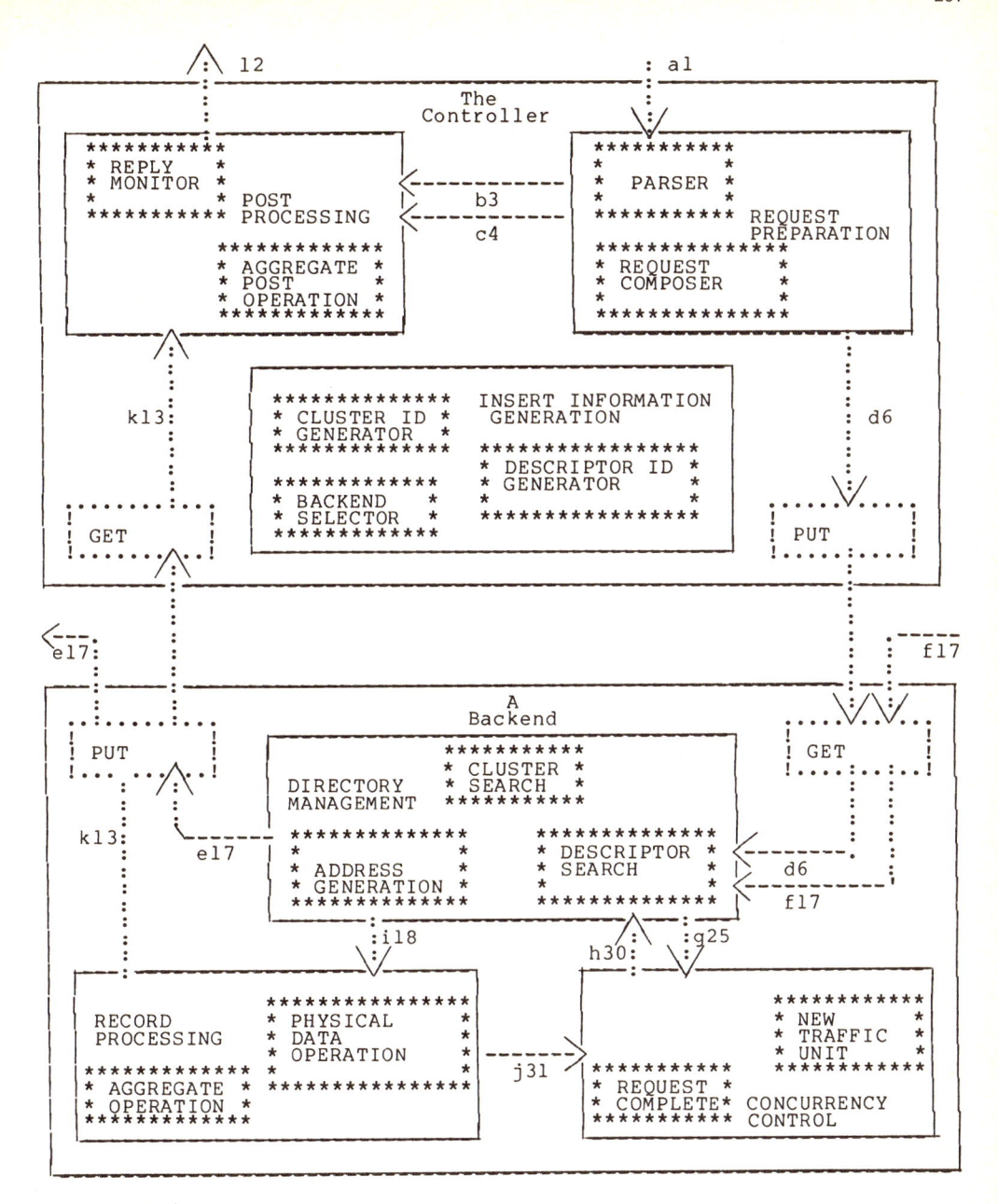

Figure 12. Sequence of Message-Passing Events for a Retrieve Request With an Aggregate Operator

host (a1). REQP sends two messages to PP: the number of requests in the transaction (b3) and the aggregate operator of the request (c4). The third message sent by REQP is the parsed traffic unit which goes to DM in the backends (d6). DM will send the descriptor ids determined from the request to the other backends (e17). The DM processes in the other backends will send their descriptor ids to the DM process residing in this backend (f17). Next, DM will send the cluster ids for the retrieval to CC (g25). CC determines which request can execute next and sends that id to DM (h30). The addresses and the request are sent from DM to RECP for the retrieval (i18). Once the retrieval request has executed properly, RECP will tell CC that the request is done (j31). After the retrieval results have been aggregated within the backend, that result will be sent to PP for further aggregation (k13). When PP is done, the final results will be sent to the host (l2).

3.4. Sequence of Actions for an Update Request Causing an Updated Record to Change Cluster

The sequence of actions for an update request that causes a record to change cluster is shown in Figure 13. Conceptually, this request is processed in two stages, although these stages can overlap. First, after processing the update, it is determined that a record has changed cluster. Then, an insert is generated to store the new record. As in the previous examples we will go through the complete execution of this request.

The first stage begins when the host sends the update request to REQP (a1). REQP follows through by formatting the request and sending PP the number of requests in the transaction (b3). DM also receives a message from REQP, the parsed traffic unit (c6). DM in each backend will exchange descriptor ids with each of the other backends (d17 and e17). DM will send the cluster ids to CC to check if the request can be executed (f25). Directory management will also send CC a list of executing update requests for which this current request must wait to complete execution (g29). Once CC responds to DM that the request can go through (h30), DM will generate the disk addresses and send the request as well as the addresses to RECP (i18). When RECP retrieves the old values of the attribute being modified by the update, it will send these old values and the new values to DM to check for records that have changed cluster (j23). A reply will be sent to RECP from DM stating (for our example) that the update does cause a record to

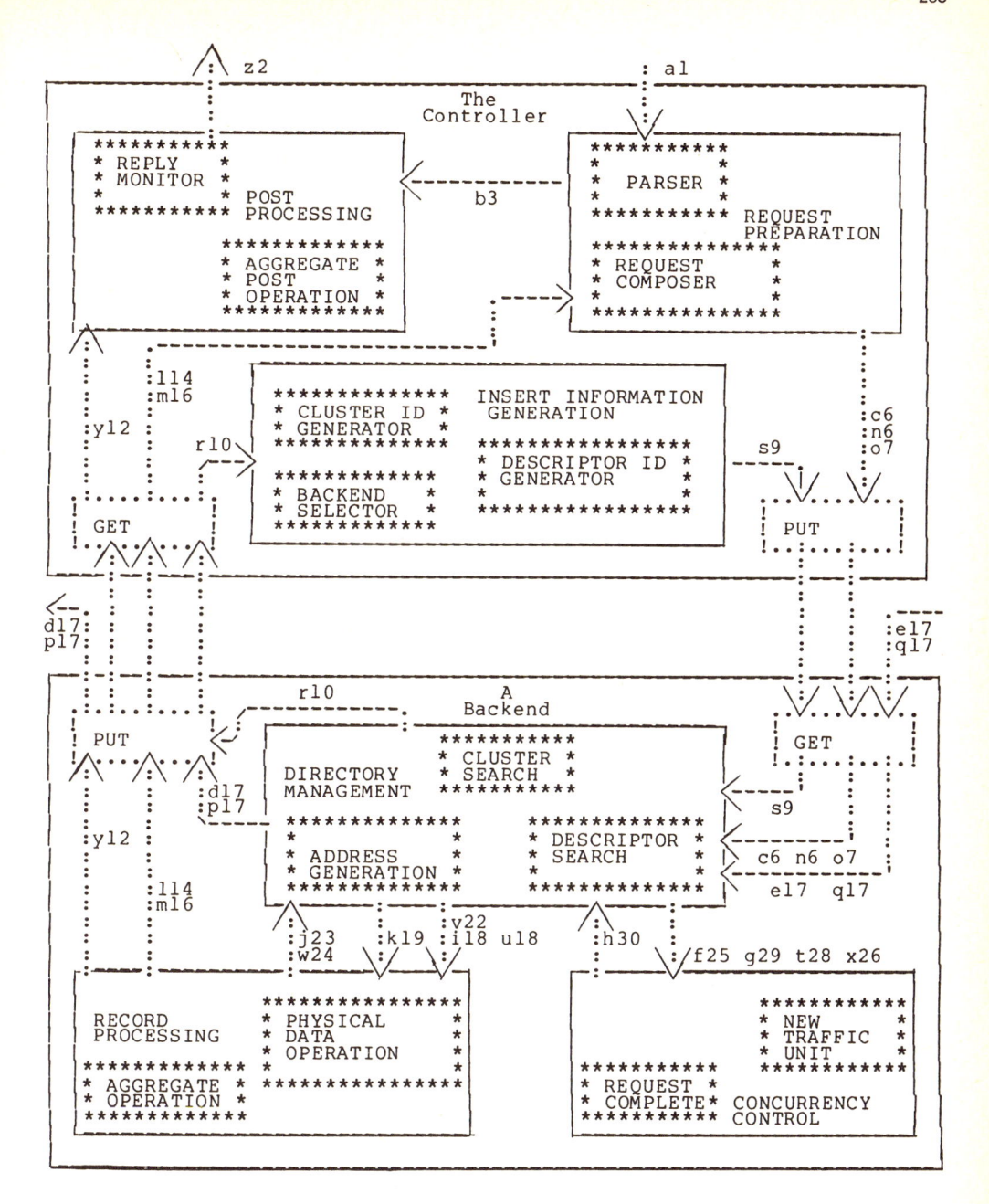

Figure 13. Sequence of Message-Passing Events for an Update Request That Causes a Record to Change Cluster

change cluster (k19). The change of cluster by a record requires an insert, therefore RECP will send the record that has changed cluster to REQP (l14). REQP will then generate an insert request. REQP will count these generated inserts as they come in from the backends for each update request. When RECP is done generating insert requests it will use a message to notify REQP that it is done with this stage of the update (m16). After each backend's RECP has notified REQP that it is through generating inserts, REQP will send a message to DM telling it how many inserts were actually generated by the update (o7).

The second stage of the update request proceeds as an insert request. The backend number and cluster id are determined as in an insert request, and will thus not be described here. The message sequence (n6, p17, q17, n10 and s9) are included in the figure. If this cluster does not already exist, then DM will also send a message to CC to lock this newly defined cluster for the update that caused it to be created (t28). In either case, DM will send the request and the necessary disk address to RECP (u18). RECP cannot begin the insert process until the first stage of the update request is complete. Therefore RECP will hold update generated inserts until DM tells RECP that stage one is complete (v22). Once the inserts are finished, i.e, stage two is complete, RECP will notify DM that it is done with the entire update (w24). Next DM will send CC the finished request id (x26). RECP next sends the results of the update request to PP (y12) and PP notifies the host that the update has completed (z2).

4. CONCLUSION

To summarize our work we can briefly look at three points of interest. They are the process structure of MDBS, the operating systems upon which MDBS is built, and finally the messages themselves.

With our implementation of MDBS, we have shown that a database system with one or more backends can be built on a fairly standard communications model, i.e., the message-oriented approach. We have constructed the system with a fixed number of processes. Each process has well defined message paths for communication with the rest of the processes of the system. These processes provide both intercomputer and intracomputer communications and remain alive from the system startup to the system stop time. More interestingly, all the intercomputer communications are standardized by two processes. Further, all the processes in a backend are identical to all the processes in another backend. In other words, backend processes can be replicated easily on new backend hardware.

Secondly, we can see that the existing operating systems (i.e., VMS and RSX-11M) provide us the basic process mechanism for our communications model. That is, we did not have to duplicate the process mechanism within MDBS in order to implement the database management system functions. Thus, the development work is reduced for the message-passing approach. Instead, the development work is mostly spent on the construction of database system primitives as message-passing processes.

Finally, in looking at the messages defined for our implementation we see the diversity within the scope of our needs for the database system. A message plays two roles. It exists as data which is worked on by the processes as it passes through them. Thus, the database system becomes a data-driven system where different processes relay different results to the other processes with the last process to relay the final result to the host. A message can also serve as a synchronizer which coordinates work being done on a request. Thus, the database system becomes a data-driven system where different data (messages) cause different processes to work on the request.

The fact that 31 message types are currently defined in our system suggests the ease with which message paths can be created. This fact implies two things. First, even for a rather complete database system on a novel hardware configuration, the number of message types and message paths is reasonably small and easy to define. Secondly, should we decide to modify or to expand our implementation, the clear delineations of the processes, the concise definitions of message types and the simple sequences of message paths would make such modifications and expansion straightforward.

Acknowledgements

We would like to thank all of those who have helped us with the design and implementation of the MDBS communication facilities. William Mielke, an undergraduate student, was involved in the early testing of message passing within a backend and of message passing between computers. Two other undergraduate students, Raymond Browder and Jim McKenna, were involved in the design and testing of the message passing mechanisms in the backends and in the controller, respectively.

REFERENCES

[Blas79] Blasgen, M., et al., "The Convoy Phenomenon", *Operating Systems Review*, Vol. 13, 2, April 1979, pp. 20-25.

[Boyn83] Boyne, Richard D., et al., "The Implementation of a Multi-backend Database System (MDBS): Part III - The Message-Oriented Version with Concurrency Control and Secondary-Memory-Based Directory Management," Technical Report, NPS-52-83-003, Naval Postgraduate School, Monterey, California, March, 1983.

[He83] He, X., et al., "The Implementation of a Multi-Backend Database System (MDBS): Part II - The First Prototype MDBS and the Software Engineering Experience," Chapter 11, *Advanced Database Machine Architectures*, Prentice-Hall, August 1983. Also in the Technical Report, NPS-52-82-008, Naval Postgraduate School, Monterey, California, July 1982.

[Hsia81a] Hsiao, D.K. and Menon, M.J., "Design and Analysis of a Multi-Backend Database System for Performance Improvement, Functionality Expansion and Capacity Growth (Part I)," Technical Report, OSU-CISRC-TR-81-7, The Ohio State University, Columbus, Ohio, July 1981.

[Hsia81b] Hsiao, D.K. and Menon, M.J., "Design and Analysis of a Multi-Backend Database System for Performance Improvement, Functionality Expansion and Capacity Growth (Part II)," Technical Report, OSU-CISRC-TR-81-8, The Ohio State University, Columbus, Ohio, August 1981.

[Hsia83] Hsiao, D.K., et al., "The Implementation of a Multi-Backend Database System (MDBS): Part I - Software Engineering Strategies and Efforts Towards a Prototype MDBS," Chapter 10, *Advanced Database Machine Architecture*, Prentice-Hall, August, 1983. Also in the Technical Report, OSU-CISRC-TR-82-1, The Ohio State University, Columbus, Ohio, January 1982.

[Laue79] Lauer, H. and Needham, R., "On the Duality of Operating System Structures," in Proc. Second International Symposium on Operating Systems, IRIA, October 1978, reprinted in *Operating Systems Review*, Vol. 13, No 2, April 1979, pp. 3-19.

[Ston81] Stonebraker, M., "Operating System Support for Database Management," *Communication of the ACM*, Vol. 24, No. 7, July 1981, pp. 412-418.

A PROLOG DATA BASE MACHINE

G. BERGER SABBATEL, J.C. IANESELLI, NGUYEN G.T.
IMAG laboratory. BP 68 38402, St MARTIN D'HERES - FRANCE

ABSTRACT

This paper gives an overall presentation of the OPALE project. This project aims at designing a database machine oriented toward the execution of PROLOG, considered as data description and data manipulation language.

We present the motivations of the project, and an overview of PROLOG language and of its utilization for data bases. We present two important points in the interpretation of PROLOG for data base machine, the parallel execution and the execution of unification on the fly. We then outline the architecture of the machine.

The machine will be distributed, based on the interconnection of 4 types of specialized processors. Each disk is managed and controlled by a dedicated processor, including a sequential filter. The VLSI integration of the main components of the machine is planned.

I. INTRODUCTION:

In this paper, we present the OPALE project [GBS 82, GB2 83], wich aims at designing a database machine oriented toward PROLOG.

PROLOG [WAR 77] is a programming language developed by A. Colmerauer and al [ROU 75]. It is based on first order logic [ROB 65, KOW 74], and deal with applications such as automatic translation, artificial intelligence, data bases [GAL 81, WAR 81], knowledge representation and processing. It operates on tree structured data named terms, and composed of symbols, variables and numbers. The basic operation is the unification, which compares two terms and tries to make them equal by assigning values to the variables. It allows the selection of clause headers, given a goal (predicate to be verified). If it successes, the result is then the list of the susbtitutions made on the variables.

II. PROLOG AND DATA BASES:

PROLOG can be considered as a superset of relational algebra, as every relational operator can be expressed in PROLOG, and additional features are available, such as implicitly defined relations, processing of lists, etc... We will then use directly PROLOG as a data base system, rather than interfacing it with relational data bases, which would create an additional level of translation/interpretation in the system.

We consider two levels of data: the facts (or assertions), similar two the tuples of relations, and the rules which are PROLOG clauses with non-empty bodies. Facts and rules will be separately stored, for access optimization.

Symbolic data will be coded through a dictionnary. The type of every item of data will be explicitly indicated through a one byte descriptor. The clauses (facts and rules) will be sequentially stored. We plan to use an access method derived from compacted lexicographical trees [PLA 82].

III. INTERPRETATION OF PROLOG:

III.1. SEARCH STRATEGY:

The execution of a PROLOG program can be considered as a search in an abstract tree. Classical interpretation, said left to right and depth first, checks one solution at a time. A more efficient strategy for data base accesses will be to globaly process sets of solutions produced by every search (solutions of goals) [CHA 82]. These solutions may, in turn, produce sets of goals (predicates to be verified), which can be globally verified through filtering.

Example:
   C(X,Y) <- C1(X) & C2(Y).
   C1(a).
   C1(b).
   C2(c).
      :

The search on C1 returns two solutions: X<-a and X<-b, which in turn produce two goals: C2(a,Y) and C2(b,Y). These two goals may be searched in a single pass on C2, through sequential filtering.

Some forms of parallelism will be studied for optimizing disk accesses: distribution of search on several disk units, parallel verification of clauses (OR-parallelism), and, in a limited way, parallel verification of independant litterals in a single clause (AND-parallelism) [CON 81].

III.2. UNIFICATION:

The unification must be executed on the fly in most cases. We also want to be able to unify several goals in parallel on the same data flow.

A major difference between PROLOG and relationnal database is the possibility to have variables in the data. The variables can be dependant and define relations between the arguments. Substitutions must then be composed to get a simpler set of substitutions and check its consistency:
example:
   The unification of t(X,Y,X) and t(a,Z,Z) is possible with:
   X<-a; Y<-Z; X<-X; which can be composed, giving:
   X<-a; Y<-a; Z<-a.

The unification can be decomposed in two steps which can be executed in pipe line by two processors:
- The first step compares the terms and transmits substitutions and the body of the filtered clause. It will be executed by a finite state automaton.
- The second step is the composition of the substitutions. Due to the

selection of data by the first step, this may be executed by a microprocessor.

For very complex cases the terms can also be decomposed and the unification is distributed between the filter and other processors.

The possibility of variables in the disk can lead to an explosion in the size of automata, so that they cannot be stored in an acceptable amount of memory:

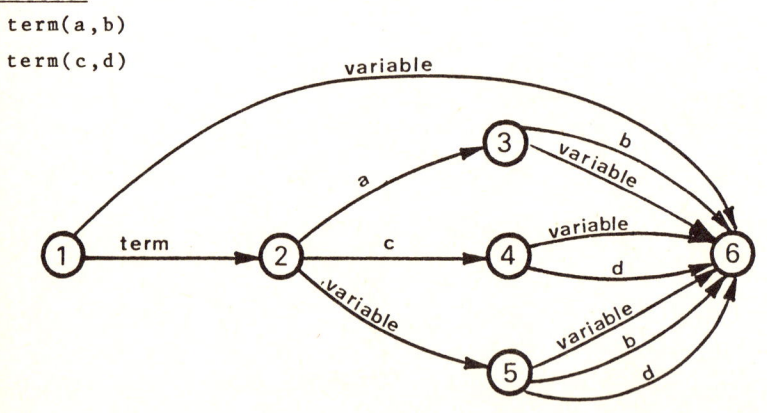

Example:
  term(a,b)
  term(c,d)

For the integration in VLSI of parts of the filter, it seems desirable to distribute the processing between several relatively simple operators, rather than to design a single complex one. The filter can then be decomposed in two automata:
- A lexicographical automaton: it verifies that the data received correspond to the elements of the searched terms. It then transmit a code to the second automaton, called syntaxic automaton. It can be implemented with a finite state automaton [ROH 81]. In the former example, this automaton would recognize terms such that term(c,b), so that its job must be completed by the syntaxic automaton.
- The syntaxic automaton: it checks that the succession of data actualy corresponds to one of the searched terms. It can be implemented by an array of bits.

IV. ARCHITECTURE:

The design of OPALE will provide for fault tolerance, high performances through the use of parallelism, and a great modularity. This lead then to a distributed architecture. VLSI integration of functions such as the filtering is also a feature of the project.

Our design is based on one processor per disk [BOR 81]. We study the possibility of distributing a large data base on mini-disks, allowing an important parallelism, and high performances, even if the disks are slower. This solution can be cost effective, due to the low cost of winchester mini-disks.

IV.2. ARCHITECTURE OF OPALE:

The idea is to dynamically distribute the processing between several types of specialized operators (Fig. IV.1.).

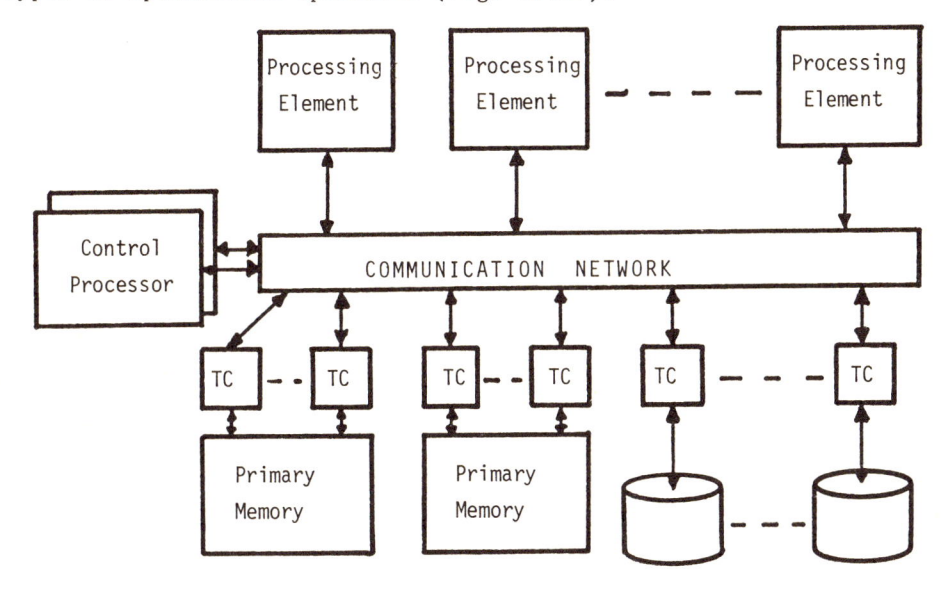

Figure IV.1.

Associated with the disks and the primary memories are the transfer channels (TC), which include a microprocessor and a filter.

The processing elements control the verification of the goals: they execute the parts of the unification not executed by the transfer channels, compile the filtering automata, control the storing of temporary results, manage the verification processes...

The control processors control the exchanges between OPALE and its operating environment (local network or host processor). They will compile the requests and manage the hardware resources of the machine. These functions will be executed by a set of processors.

The requirements of the communication network are: high bandwidth, short distances, modularity, fault tolerance. For a first experimentation, we plan to use a standard multiprocessor bus.

IV.3. DISK PROCESSORS:

They are depicted in figure IV.2.

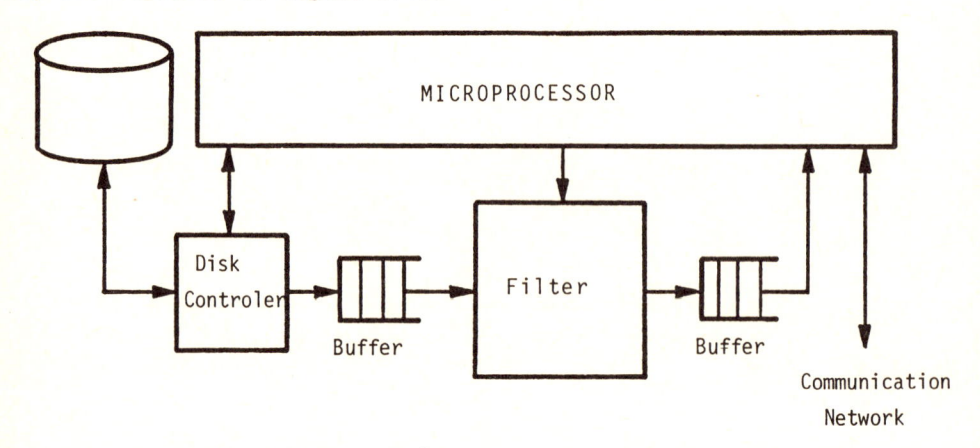

Figure IV.2.

The microprocessor controls the communication with the other processors of the machine, controls the filter and completes its operations.

The filter will be composed of 4 parts (figure IV.3.).

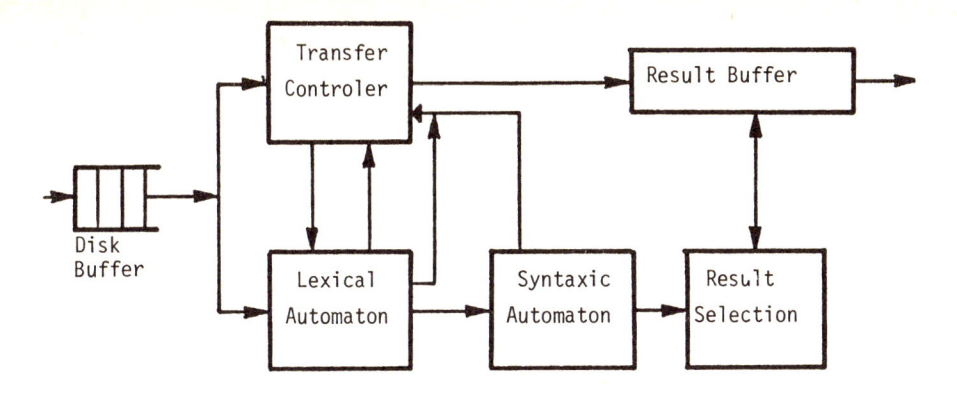

Figure IV.3.

TC (Transfer Controler): it works in parallel with the LA and allows:
- to get data from the input buffer,
- to recognize data structure and decode data types,
- to manage the substitutions and transmit them to the ouput buffer,
- to execute elementary selection operations, such as clause separators search in case of unification fail,
- to reset the lexicographical automaton (LA) at the begining of every clause.

LA (Lexicographical Automaton): it executes a hard-wired dichotomic search. If the received data correspond to a member of searched terms, it sends an address to the SA and sends informations to the TC for the generation of substitutions. If the search fails, it sends an interrupt to the TC.

SA (Syntaxic Automaton): It is composed of a bit array where each column corresponds to a particular goal, and each line correspond to a transition of the LA. A bit is set if the transition is possible for the associated goal. The intersection of the lines addressed by the LA is accumulated in a bit string which indicates the goals which may unify with the received term (Figure IV.4.). If the value of this string becomes zero, then the unification fails, and an interrupt is sent to the TA. A tipical size for the array may be of 256 X 1024 bits, which can be integrated on a single chip.

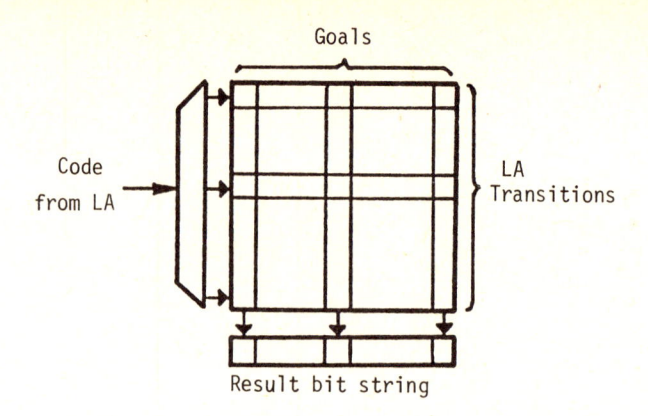

Figure IV.4.

RSO (Result Selection Operator): It manages the output buffer, deletes unusefull data, and send the results to the microprocessor.

Due to this decomposition, only the TC must follow the disk transfer rate. The other modules can work a bit more slowly, as a significant part of the received data is not processed by them. For current technologies, the risk that the disk must wait is negligible, and the performance requirements of the automata is compatible with their integration in VLSI.

V. CONCLUSIONS:

The filter and the data structure are almost completely defined, and the communication system is specified. Researches are curently carried out for the parallel interpretation of PROLOG and for the definition of a data manipulation language based on generalized relational operators.

We are now planning for starting a software simulation. The realization of a hardware prototype will start by the first term of 1984. This realization may last till 1985 for a first step, and parallely, the study of VLSI circuits will start.

VI. REFERENCES:

[BOR 81]   Haran Boral, David J. De Witt, W. Kevin Wilkinson
Performance evaluation of associative disk designs
6th Workshop on comp. arch. for non numeric processing,
june 1981

[CHA 82]   U.S. Chakravarthy, J. Minker, D. Tran
Interfacing predicate logic languages and relationnal
databases
1st int logic programming conference, Marseilles,
september 1982

[CON 81]   J.S. Conery, D.F. Kibler
Parallel interpretation of logic programs
ACM Conf. on functionnal prog. lang. and Comp. arch.
Portsmouth, October 1981.

[EIS 82]   N. Eisinger, S. Kasif, J. Minker
Logic programming: a parallel approach
1st Int. Logic programming conf. Marseilles,
September 1982.

[GAL 81]   H. Gallaire
Impacts of logic on data bases
VLDB 81

[GBS 82]   G. Berger Sabbatel, Nguyen G.T.
Projet OPALE: Motivations et principes pour une machine
bases de données PROLOG
IMAG. RR. 339. December 1982

[KOW 74]   R. Kowalski
Predicate logic as a programming language.
IFIP. 1974

[PLA 82]   D. Plateau
Une structure compacte pour indexer un fichier et son
evaluation.
Séminaire ADI bases de données, Toulouse, november 1982.

[ROB 65]   J.A. Robinson
A machine oriented logic based on the resolution principle
JACM 12, 1, december 1965, pp227-234

[ROH 81]   J. Rohmer
Associative filtering by automata: a key operator for
data base machines

6th Workshop on comp. arch. for non numeric processing,
june 1981

[ROU 75] J. Roussel
PROLOG: manuel de référence et d'utilisation
Rapport, Groupe d'intelligence artificielle,
Université d'Aix Marseille II, 1975

[WAR 77] David H.D. Warren, L.M. Pereira, F. Pereira
PROLOG: the language and its implementation compared
with LISP
ACM symposium on artificial intelligence an programming
language, august 1977

[WAR 81] David H.D. Warren
Efficient processing of interactive relationnal database
queries expressed in logic
VLDB 81

PERFORMANCE EVALUATION OF CONCURRENCY CONTROL ALGORITHMS IN THE SABRE DATABASE COMPUTER

J. Madelaine

SABRE Project
INRIA and Université de Paris VI
INRIA, BP 105, 78153 Le Chesnay Cedex, France

Abstract

This paper compares the performances of two concurrency control algorithms: two-phase locking and timestamp ordering. This is achieved by solving analytically a queuing network which gives response times of the SABRE data base machine. It is shown that locking is better than timestamp ordering when there is a high probability of conflict between transactions. However, if the mean number of requests per transaction is high then timestamp ordering is the better technique; this is improved when the frequency of small transactions increases (i.e. number of requests having a geometrical distribution law).

Key words: Concurrency control, two-phase locking, timestamp ordering, performance evaluation, queuing network.

1- INTRODUCTION

The purpose of this paper is to compare quantitatively the performances of a database machine using two Concurrency Control methods.

Concurrency Control (CC) is that part of the Database Management System which insures that simultaneously executed transactions produce the same results as sequentially executed transactions. In other words, CC makes transaction data sharing completely transparent to the users. Most of the CC methods belong to two classes [BERN81] [GARD81]:
- algorithms based on timestamp ordering (T/O).
- algorithms based on two phase locking (2PL)

The first approach to be considered is basic timestamp ordering [BERN80]. It consists of two steps: (1) ordering and marking transactions before they are executed and (2) verifying that conflicting accesses take place in the originally given order; if two transactions are found out of order, one of these is aborted and restarted later. The second approach avoids conflicts in the locking of data; however, in order to respect the integrity constraints, it turns out to be necessary to restrict the locking rules so that a transaction cannot lock data after it has released a lock on any other data. Thus, locking is two phases: a first phase of locking and a second one of unlocking. Locking may induce a deadlock situation; thus a technique to prevent or detect deadly embraces must be added to get a correct CC method. Two phase locking with deadlock prevention [ROSE78] will be evaluated in this paper. It has been demonstrated that two phase locking with deadlock prevention and basic timestamp ordering work, the problem is to evaluate their performances.

In order to analyse and to compare the performances of two CC algorithms representative of the two general classes, a queuing network wich models an implementation of these methods on the SABRE database machine is studied. The mean response time for a transaction is discussed as a function of the parameters of the transaction set submitted to the system. Analysing a closed network, the first parameter is the total number of users in the system. An important parameter for this study is the probability of a transaction being in conflict with another one when accessing data. This probability depends not only on the number of transactions in the system and on the size of the database, but also on the locality of the accesses. In fact, the conflict probability may be very high with only two transactions in the system in spite of a very large database, if these two transactions access the same data items. That is why the conflict probability will be taken directly as a parameter. Two other parameters influence the response time: the number of requests per transaction and the number of accesses per request. To take into account the distribution laws of these numbers, the model is improved by defining customer classes in the queuing network.

The paper is organised as follows. Section 2 reviews some past work and presents the two studied CC algorithms. The processing of a transaction in the SABRE database machine and its queuing network model are described in section 3. The solving method of the queuing network is exposed in section 4. Finally, results of the comparison of the two CC algorithms are presented in section 5.

2- PROBLEM STATEMENT

The problem is to compare quantitatively the performances of a database system depending on which Concurrency Control algorithm is used: either timestamp ordering or two phase locking with deadlock prevention.

2.1- Past work

Amongst the many studies of CC algorithms evaluation either in quality or quantity, let us first discuss the study of Bernstein and Goodman: "Fundamental Algorithms for Concurrency Control in DDBS" [BERN81]. This work has two parts. The first one is a classification of the various CC methods. The paper identifies 48 different methods which are based either on T/O or 2PL. The second part is a qualitative comparison of the methods in regard to the communication overhead, the local processing overhead, the number of restarts and the blocking behaviour. It comes out with 12 optimal methods including timestamp ordering and two phase locking with deadlock prevention. Note that locking may induce deadlocks, and this event must be ruled out with an appropriate technique: detection or prevention; it appears that the former needs more messages than the latter. In addition, Bernstein and Goodman note that a quantitative evaluation must have a precise environment. The environment of our study will be the SABRE database machine.

Garcia Molina is the author of one of the earliest quantitative analysis of CC algorithms [GARC79]. He models the CC of a Distriduted DBMS with queuing networks. The database is fully duplicated. Solving the queuing networks by simulation and by an analytical method, he concludes that two phase locking with centralized deadlock detection is better than the Thomas's algorithm [THOM79]. These results are observed with transactions having a constant number of accesses and with a low conflict probability.

On the other hand, Ries and Stonebraker studied in "Effects of locking granularity in a DBMS" [RIES77] and "Locking granularity revised" [RIES79] the locking technique by simulation of a centralized DBS. They conclued that a coarse granularity (about 10 granules in the database) is sufficient if each transaction performs many accesses, on the other hand, "small" granules become interesting with "small" transactions. These results are observed with a constant number of accesses per transaction. A similar study made by Irani and Lin [IRAN79] have the same results with an analytical resolution method and a number of accesses per transaction having a geometrical distribution. Potier and Leblanc have also worked on this problem in "Analysis of locking in DBMS" [POTI80]. In this work, they refined the calculation of the conflict probability between transactions. This probability is found in terms of the number of granules in the database, of the number of accesses per transaction and of the number of transactions in the system. The calculation is made under the following restrictive hypothesis: data accesses are uniformely distributed over the whole database.

In our study, we will quantitatively compare two algorithms found optimal by Bernstein and Goodman. To achieve this, the response time of a transaction will be found in terms of the total number of transactions in the system, of the distribution laws of the numbers of requests per transaction and accesses per request, and of the conflict probability between transactions.

2.2- Description of the two studied algorithms

2.2.a- Timestamp ordering (T/O)

This method [BERN80] is based on the definition of an initial order on the transactions: a numerical value, called transaction timestamp, is assigned to each transaction before execution. The T/O algorithm consists in verifying that transactionnal access to data takes place in the order initially assigned to transactions. Actually, it is only necessary to order nonpermutable operations, i.e. the sequences <READ, WRITE>, <WRITE, READ>, <WRITE, WRITE>. To do this, two types of data timestamps are used: SR, the read data timestamp which is the timestamp of the most recent transaction (the transaction whose timestamp has the greatest value) having executed a READ operation, and SW, the write data timestamp which is the timestamp of the last transaction having executed a WRITE operation. When a transaction executes a READ, the scheduler controls the correct sequence of the READ with respect to the last WRITE. When a transaction executes a WRITE, the scheduler controls the correct sequence of the WRITE with respect to the previously executed READ and WRITE. Figure 2.1 depicts the T/O algorithm [GARD81]. Here, d denotes the data accessed by the transaction Ti having transaction timestamp i.

```
Procedure READ (Ti, d)
    if SW(d) <= i then
        "carry out the read"
        SR(d) := max(SR(d), i)
```

```
            else ABORT
         endif
      end READ


      Procedure WRITE (Ti, d)
         if SR(d) <= i then
            if SW(d) <= i then
               "carry out the write"
               SW(d) := i
            endif
         else ABORT
         endif
      end WRITE
```

2.2.b- Two-phase locking with deadlock prevention (2PL)

The locking technique avoids the generation of incorrect schedules of transactions in blocking transactions which attempt to perform conflicting operations on the same data. This technique is derived from the classical operating method for allocating resources to tasks. Thus, various portions of data may be viewed as resources which may therefore be allocated (locked) or deallocated (unlocked) to transactions. However, this method by itself is not sufficient in this situation due to the presence of integrity constraints. In order to enforce them, it is necessary to restrict the locking rules so that a transaction cannot unlock any portion of data until it has locked all the data which it intends to access. This is known as the "two phase restriction" [ESWA76]. Unfortunately the well known deadlock problem now appears because of data locking. To prevent deadlocks, it is possible to define an initial order on the transactions with timestamps and to forbid the waiting of a transaction if the waiting order is not compatible with the predefined order. This is the principle of the DIE-WAIT strategy described by Rosenkrantz [ROSE78]: a transaction may waits only for a younger one; if a transaction is blocked on a lock held by an older one then the blocked transaction is not allowed to wait and it "dies" (it is rolled back).

3- QUEUING NETWORK MODEL.

3.1- Description of the environment.

We model a system made up of three components (figure 3.1):
- a SABRE data base machine,
- a general communication network,
- a set of host terminals.

Transactions are sent by users from their terminals via the communication network and are then processed by the database machine which returns the results to the users.

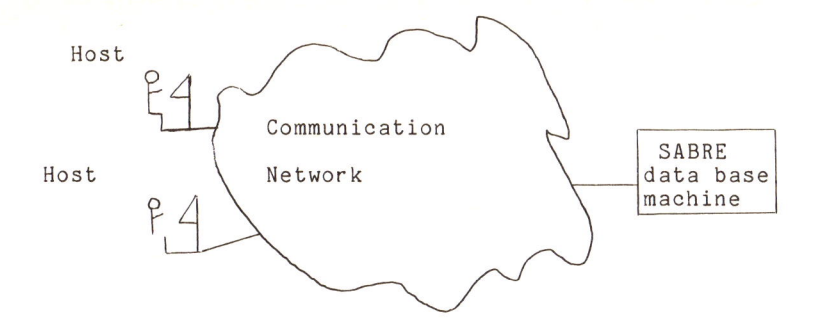

Figure 3.1: Architecture of the system.

The functional architecture of the SABRE database machine is composed of a set of classes of virtual processors. Each processor type is associated with a functional step. The various classes are:
-View and Integrity Processor (VIP) which allows the users to use external views.
-Request Evaluation Processor (REP) which performs the request decomposition and optimisation. It breaks requests into relational algebraic operations.
-Relation Access Processor (RAP) which manages access paths. More precisely, when an insertion of tuples is performed, it determines the partitions where to insert the tuples. When a restriction is performed, it determines which partitions should be scanned.
-Join, Sort and Aggregate Processors (JSP) which perform joins, sorts and compute aggregate functions on partitions. Several join processors generally work in cooperation to carry out efficiently joins and sorts.
-Concurrency Control and Recovery Processor (CRP) which performs concurrency control, two step commitment and manages the update logs.
-Cache Memory Processor (CMP). This processor is responsible for allocating secondary and cache memories.
-Filtering Processor (FIP). These processors perform selection, insertion and deletion of tuples in a partition. They work when possible in flight, during the transfer of data from disk to cache.

3.2- Processing of a transaction

A transaction is defined as a unit which guarantees the data base consistency. It is made of requests decomposed into relational operations (restriction, projection, join, union, ...) leading to data accesses. Figure 3.2 shows the processing of a transaction.

The three components of the system where the actions take place are indicated. The algorithm is composed with an inner loop on each request and an inner loop on each access. The concurrency control leads to three different actions depending on the concurrency control method and on the state of the transactions in the system:
(1) the access to data, if there is no conflict,
(2) the abortion of the whole transaction, followed by a rollback message and the restart of the transaction if there is a severe conflict with rollback,
(3) the waiting of the transaction on a lock before the data access, if there is a conflict without rollback (this event will never happen if the concurrency control method is basic timestamp ordering).
What is called here access to data is the data access itself (reading

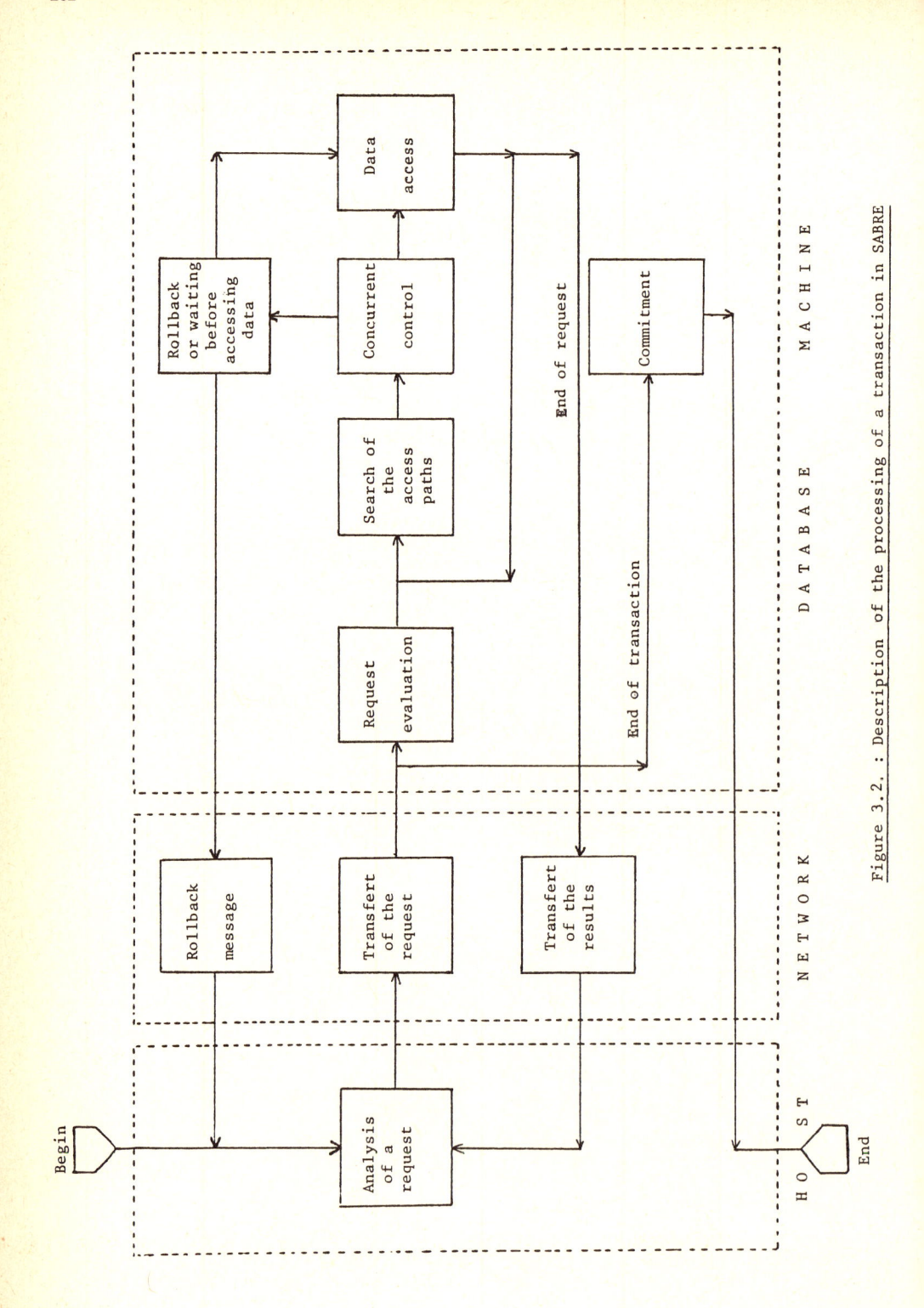

Figure 3.2. : Description of the processing of a transaction in SABRE

or writing) plus the execution of relational operations on the data.
When every request of the transaction has been correctly executed, the
transaction is commited and then ends.

3.3- Queuing network model.

The preceding description leads to the queuing network presented
in figure 3.3. This queuing network models a SABRE database machine
where the virtual processors VIP, REP, RAP and CRP share the same real
processor. We will describe this network and specify:
- the type and the queuing discipline of each station
- the meaning of the queues and their service times
- the transaction in the network.

The type of the different stations in the queuing network is
either Infinite Server (IS) (i.e. delay) or Single Server (SS) with
Processor Sharing as queing discipline. The second type of station
will model processors working in time sharing. The mean response time
of a network composed of stations of these two types depends only on
the mean service times and is independent from the distribution of the
service times. The table portrayed in figure 3.4 sums up the
characteristics of the different queues and stations in the network.
The mean service time of queue 6 is unknown , but can be deduced from
the mean response time. Indeed, the mean waiting time on a lock is
equal to the mean execution time of a transaction, or to the mean
response time divided by the mean number of executions (number of
rollback + 1); successive iterations will then be used to find the
response time (details are given in section 4).

The transitions in the network are defined with the following
probabilities:
PRQ : probability of having another request
PAC : probability of having another access
PC : probability of having a conflict when accessing data
PR : probability of having a rollback given that a conflict occurs.
The first two probabilities determine the loop on each request and on
each access. After the concurrency control (queue 7, three
transitions are possible:
- to queue 3, if there is no conflict (probability 1-PC)
- to queue 8, if there is a conflict and a rollback (probability PC.PR)
- to queue 6, if there is a conflict without a rollback (probability PC(1-PR)).
Both the conflict (PC) and rollback (PR) probabilities depend on both
the concurrency control algorithm and on the set of transactions
submitted to the system. But, on average, conflicts depend on the set
of transactions in the system much more than on the concurrency
method, i.e. we suppose that the conflicts happening for a method and
not for the other balance. This last assumption is valid because a
great variation of PC is needed to induce a significant variation in
the response time for a given method. On the other hand, the rollback
probability (PR), given that a conflict occurs, is 1 in case of
timestamp ordering, because for this method there is rollback as soon
as there is conflict. In case of two phase-locking with deadlock
prevention, if there is conflict, a transaction may wait only for a
younger one. We will assume here that, on the average, there are, for
one given transaction in the system, as many older and younger ones.
So, as a transaction will not be allowed to wait on a lock held by a
younger one (consequently to the deadlock prevention mechanism) the
rollback probability PR is 0.5.

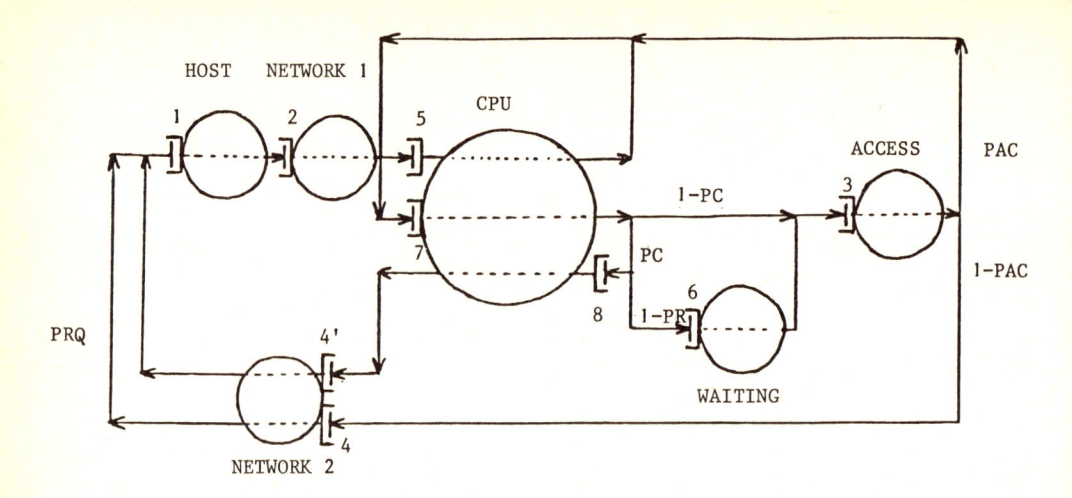

Figure 3.3: Queing network.

Queue label	Meaning	Station	Type	Mean service time
1	User reflexion and query analysis	HOST	IS	30 s
2	Transfer of the query	NETWORK1	IS	0.2 s
3	Data access	ACCESS	SS	1 s
4	Tranfer of results	NETWORK2	IS	2 s
4'	Transfer of a roll-back message	NETWORK2	IS	0.2 s
5	Query evaluation and decomposition	C.P.U.	SS	0.1 s
6	Waiting on a lock	WAITING	IS	?
7	Access path and concurrency control	C.P.U.	SS	0.01 s
8	Transaction Abortion	C.P.U.	SS	0.1 s

Figure 3.4: Characteristics of the queuing network.

A closed network will be used to compare the two conccurrency control algorithms. Indeed, 2PL may block transactions and this increases sensibly the number of customers in an open network and the comparison with T/O is then impossible. Another justification for this choice is that the higher the degree of concurrency, the more important is the concurrency control. Thus, the closed network will modelize a system, each entry point of which is occupied by a user and it will be assumed that any user who exits the system will instantly be replaced by a new one.

4- RESOLUTION METHOD.

The mean response time of a transaction is derived from:
- the conflict probability PC
- the rollback probability PR
- the distribution law of the number of requests per transaction
- the distribution law of the number of accesses per request.

This response time is the result of the Reiser's algorithm: "Mean Value Analysis" (see for example [SAUER81]). In case of 2PL, iterations are necessary to know the mean waiting time which is a function of the total response time. Each station of the queuing network satisfies the hypothesis of the B.C.M.P. theorem [BASK75]. So the network may be replaced by an equivalent network composed of the same stations where each queue has for service time the service time of the old correspondent queue multiplied by the mean number of visits [SAUE81]. To take into account the distribution laws of the numbers of requests per transaction and accesses per request, customer classes are defined in the network. To apply Reiser's algorithm, the mean numbers of visits per queue must be calculated; these numbers will be obtained by adding the numbers of visits per classes. The latter are the solution to a linear equation infinite system, those equations are inferred from class transition probabilities. This section presents the derivation of the numbers of visits and a description of the algorithm used to compute the mean response time.

If the two probabilities PRQ and PAC are independent from the rank of the request or of the access, as it could be understood in section 3.3, the numbers of requests and accesses have a geometrical distribution law. We call rank of a request (respectively access) the serial number of the request (resp. access) in the sequence of requests (resp. accesses) in a transaction (resp. request). To accept other laws, PRQ and PAC must depend on these ranks. To achieve that goal, customers classes are defined in the queues with the quadruplet (n,p,q,a) where:
- n is the label of the queue
- p is the serial number of the execution of a transaction (p equals 1 for a new transaction, 2 if the transaction is restarted, etc.)
- q is the rank of the request
- a is the rank of the access within the request (this rank is set to 0 for queues number 1, 2, 4 and 5 where it is undefined).

Transitions from classe to classe are as follows:

(1,p,q,0)   --->   (2,p,q,0)

(2,p,q,0)   --->   (5,p,q,0)

$(5,p,q,0) \longrightarrow (7,p,q,1)$

$(7,p,q,a) \longrightarrow (8,p,q,a)$ with the probability: PC.PR

$ \longrightarrow (6,p,q,a)$ with the probability: PC(1-PR)

$ \longrightarrow (3,p,q,a)$ with the probability: 1-PC

$(8,p,q,a) \longrightarrow (4',p,q,0)$

$(6,p,q,a) \longrightarrow (3,p,q,a)$

$(3,p,q,a) \longrightarrow (7,p,q,a+1)$ with the probability: PAC^a

$ \longrightarrow (4,p,q,0)$ with the probability: $1-PAC^a$

$(4,p,q,0) \longrightarrow (1,p,q+1,0)$ with the probability: PRQ^q

$ \longrightarrow (1,1,1,0)$ with the probability: $1-PRQ^q$

$(4',p,q,0) \longrightarrow (1,p+1,1,0)$

Let $e(n,p,q,a)$ be the number of visits for the class (n,p,q,a). The set of numbers of visits is solution to linear equations given by the abovementionned transitions. Let us take two examples of the derivation of the equation from a transition. In case of $q>1$, the transition:

$\quad (4,p,q,0) \longrightarrow (1,p,q+1,0)$ with the probability: PRQ^q

becomes:

$\quad (4,p,q-1,0) \longrightarrow (1,p,q,0)$ with the probability: PRQ^q

Hence $\quad e(1,p,q,0) = PRQ^{q-1} \; e(4,p,q-1,0) \quad$ if $q>1$

A second example is given for transition:

$\quad (8,p,q,a) \longrightarrow (4',p,q,0)$

This transition holding whatever a, we get
$$e(4',p,q,0) = \sum_{a>0} e(8,p,q,a)$$

The whole set of transitions gives the following system of linear equations:

(1) if $q>1$

$$e(1,p,q,0) = PRQ^{q-1} \; e(4,p,q-1,0)$$

(1b) if $p>1$

$$e(1,p,1,0) = \sum_{q>0} \sum_{a>0} e(4',p-1,q,a)$$

(1t) $\quad e(1,1,1,0) = \sum_{p>0} \sum_{q>0} (1 - PRQ^q) \; e(4,p,q,0)$

(2) $\quad e(2,p,q,0) = e(1,p,q,0)$

(3)　　$e(3,p,q,a) = (1 - PC)\, e(7,p,q,a) + e(6,p,q,a)$

(4)　　$e(4,p,q,0) = \sum_{a>0} (1 - PAC_a)\, e(3,p,q,a)$

(4')　　$e(4',p,q,0) = \sum_{a>0} e(8,p,q,a)$

(5)　　$e(5,p,q,0) = e(2,p,q,0)$

(6)　　$e(6,p,q,a) = PC\, (1 - PR)\, e(7,p,q,a)$

(7)　　if $a > 1$

$$e(7,p,q,a) = PAC_{a-1}\, e(3,p,q,a-1)$$

(7b)　　$e(7,p,q,1) = e(5,p,q,0)$

(8)　　$e(8,p,q,a) = PC\, PR\, e(7,p,q,a)$

One of the equations of the system is redundant. To have a unique solution to the system, the value of a variable must be set. We will set $e(1,1,1,0)$ to 1 to find the visit number of each class through the whole processing of a transition.
We get, with the substitution method, the solution:

$$e(1,p,q,0) = (1 - T)^{p-1}\, S^{q-1}\, \left(\sum_{k=1}^{q-1} PRQ_k \right)$$

$$e(2,p,q,0) = e(5,p,q,0) = e(1,p,q,0)$$

$$e(7,p,q,a) = (1 - PC.PR)^{a-1}\, \left(\sum_{i=1}^{a-1} PAC_i \right)\, e(1,p,q,0)$$

$$e(3,p,q,a) = (1 - PC.PR)\, e(7,p,q,a)$$

$$e(8,p,q,a) = PC.PR\, e(7,p,q,a)$$

$$e(6,p,q,a) = PC\,(1 - PR)\, e(7,p,q,a)$$

$$e(4',p,q,0) = \sum_{a>0} PC.PR\, e(7,p,q,a)$$

$$e(4,p,q,0) = S\, e(1,p,q,0)$$

Where $S = G_{AC}(1 - PC.PR)$ and $T = G_{RQ}(S)$

with G_{AC} the generating function of the number of accesses

and G_{RQ} the generating function of the number of requests.

Let $E(n)$ be the number of visits for the queue n, then:

$$E(n) = \sum_{p>0} \sum_{q>0} \sum_{a>0} e(n,p,q,a)$$

These numbers reduce to:

$E(1) = \frac{1}{T} \cdot \frac{1-T}{1-S}$ or $\overline{RQ}$ if PC.PR=0

$E(2) = E(4) = E(5) = E(1)$

$E(3) = \frac{1 - PC.PR}{T} \cdot \frac{1 - T}{PC.PR}$ or $\overline{RQ}.\overline{AC}$ if PC.PR=0

$E(7) = \frac{1}{T} \cdot \frac{1 - T}{PC.PR}$ or $PC.\overline{RQ}.\overline{AC}$ if PC.PR=0

$E(8) = \frac{1 - T}{T}$ or 0 if PC.PR=0

Where $\overline{RQ}$ and $\overline{AC}$ are the mean numbers of requests and accesses.

It comes that for a CC method inducing no restart the mean response time is independent from the distribution laws of these last numbers. Of course, such a method does not exist, but T/O will be more sensitive to these distrbution laws than 2PL regarding the performances.

E(8) gives the mean number of restarts and E(8)+1 is the mean number of executions. Hence, the mean waiting time on a lock equals the mean response time divided by E(8)+1. This leads to the following algorithm to compute the mean response time of a transaction:

    Computation of the E(i)

    Computation of the service time of the stations
            of the equivalent network

    If PR=1 then   {T/O is used, no waiting}
        Call the Mean Value Analysis procedure
                {which gives the Response Time}

    Else   {2PL is used}
        Response Time := 1
        repeat
            Previous RT := Response Time
            Call Mean Value Analysis procedure
            Waiting Time := Response Time / (E(8)+1)
            Computation of the new service time of station 8
        until |Previous RT - Response Time|/Response Time < 0.001
    endif

In case of T/O, the result of the algorithm is an exact result, but in case of 2PL, the result is a very good approximation of the response time and need roughly 5 to 10 iterations. Results are presented and analysed in the next section.

5- RESULTS AND CONCLUSION

The mean response time for a transaction is computed with the following parameters:
- the concurrency control method (timestamp ordering or two phase

locking with deadlock prevention)
- the number of transactions in the system (n)
- the probability PC for a transaction to have a conflict while accessing data
- the average and the distribution law of the number of requests per transaction
- the average and the distribution law of the number of accesses per request.
Curves of the response time versus the conflict probability (PC) are presented. After describing the general shape of the curves, results are discussed as a function of the averages and of the distribution laws of the numbers of requests and accesses.

The general shape of the curves is the same for different values of the number (n) of transactions in the system, as it can be seen in figure 5.1 all curves of which correspond to constant numbers of requests and accesses equal to 1. These curves have been drawn with the values given in figure 5.2. Regarding the comparison timestamp ordering versus two phase locking, there is, of course, no difference for small values of PC as concurrency control does not intervene much. On the other hand, for larger values of PC, the curves for T/O have a steep slope. This can be explained by the fact that, in this case, rollbacks are very frequent. For the high values of PC, 2PL is much more satisfactory.

With number of requests and accesses both equal to 1, 2PL is better than T/O whatever the values of the other parameters are (see figure 5.2). If the mean number of requests is greater than 1 then the curves intersect so that in case of a low conflict probability (PC), T/O becomes the best (see figure 5.3). This can be explained by the fact that T/O is more optimistic than 2PL, and therefore, the former behaves well in this case. But, it must be noticed that the differences between the two methods remain small if the distribution laws of the numbers of requests and accesses are constant (a random variable with a constant distribution law take always the same value).

When the distributions of the numbers of requests and accesses follow a geometrical law, T/O becomes significantly better than 2PL. This last result holds even if the mean number of requests equals 1 (see figure 5.4). Intuitively, this could be for two different reasons. Firstly, in case of geometrical distributions, there is a much greater number of "small" transactions than "large" ones (regarding the numbers of requests and accesses) and rollbacks become less frequent and cheaper. Secondly, as 2Pl induces fewer restarts than T/O and as a CC method inducing no restart is independent from the distribution laws of the numbers of requests and accesses (see section 4), the first point yields more profit to T/O than to 2PL.

To sum up, two phase locking with deadlock prevention (2PL) leads to a better response time than timestamp ordering (T/O) if the conflict probability between transactions is high or if the mean numbers of requests and of accesses is small. T/O becomes the best when the mean number of requests and accesses increases and whatever the conflict probability is; this advantage of T/O over 2PL is improved when the frequency of small transactions increases.

ACKNOLEDGEMENTS

I wish to thank G. Gardarin and the other menbers of the SABRE project for their helpful comments.

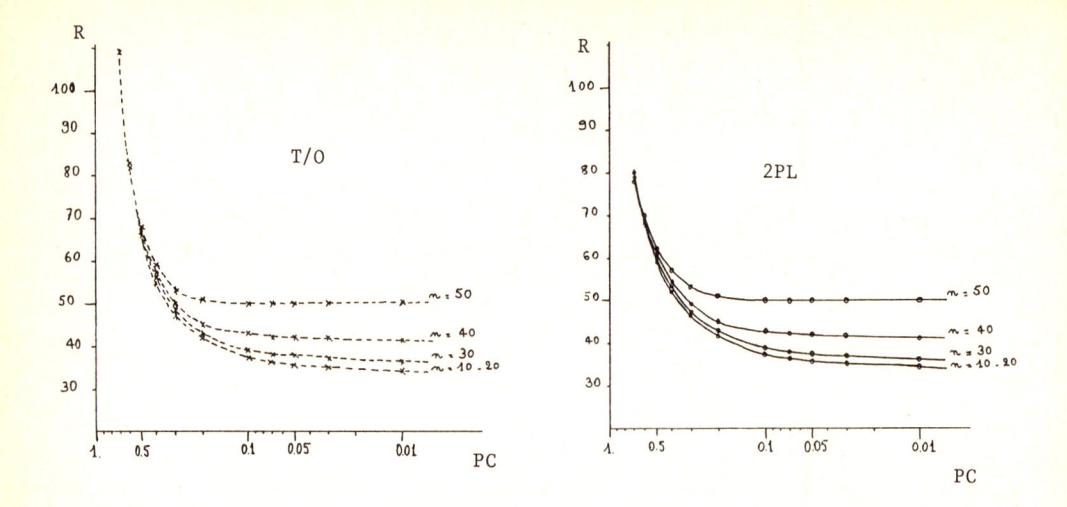

Figure 5.1: Mean response time (R) in seconds versus the conflict probability (PC) with RQ = AC = 1

n PC	10 T/O	10 2PL	20 T/O	20 2PL	30 T/O	30 2PL	40 T/O	40 2PL	50 T/O	50 2PL
0.00	34	34	34	34	36	36	41	41	50	50
0.01	34	34	35	35	37	36	41	41	50	50
0.03	35	35	35	35	37	37	42	42	50	50
0.05	35	35	36	36	38	38	42	42	50	50
0.07	36	36	37	37	38	38	42	42	50	50
0.10	37	37	38	38	39	39	43	43	50	50
0.20	42	41	42	42	43	43	45	45	51	51
0.30	47	46	48	47	48	47	50	49	53	53
0.40	55	52	55	52	56	53	57	54	59	57
0.50	66	59	66	59	66	60	67	61	68	62
0.60	82	67	82	68	82	68	83	69	83	70
0.70	109	78	109	78	109	79	109	79	109	80

Figure 5.2: Mean response time (R) versus the conflict probability (PC) and the number of transactions (n), with RQ = AC = 1

T/O: ----*--*--*--*---   2PL: ————•——•——•——

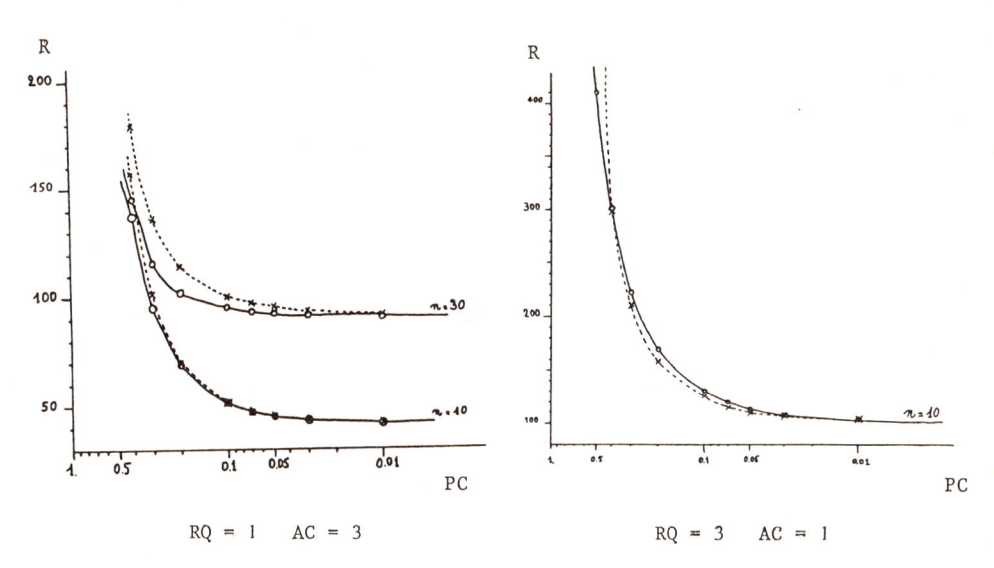

RQ = 1   AC = 3

RQ = 3   AC = 1

Figure 5.3: Mean response time versus the conflict probability with numbers of requests and accesses having a constant distribution law.

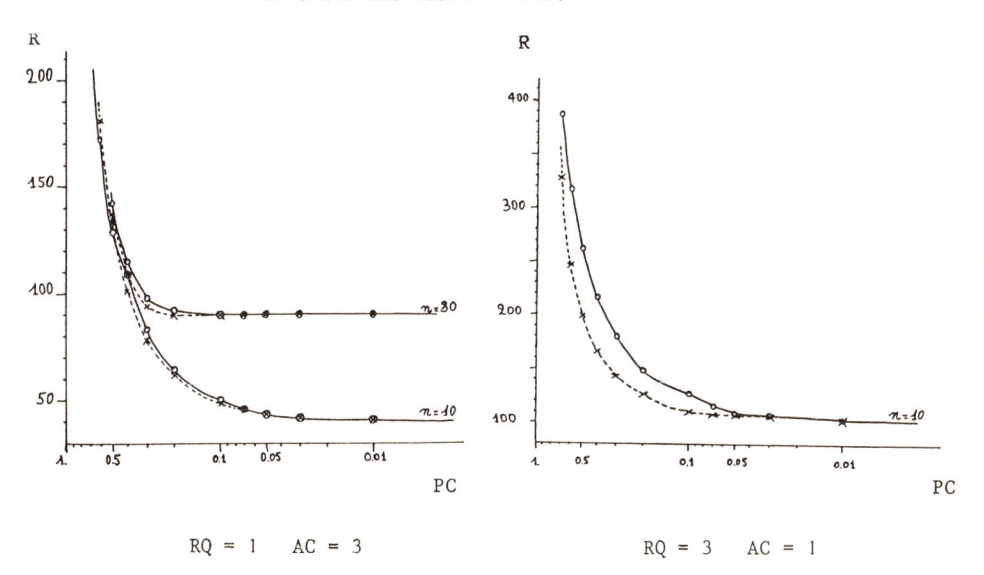

RQ = 1   AC = 3

RQ = 3   AC = 1

Figure 5.4: Mean response time versus the conflict probability with numbers of requests and accesses having a geometrical distribution law.

6- REFERENCES

[BASK75]   Baskett, Chandy, Muntz, Palacios, "Open, closed and mixed networks with different classes of customers", JACM, Vol 22, No 2, P 247-260, April 1975.

[BERN80]   Bernstein P.A., Goodman N., "Timestamp Based Algorithms for Concurrency Control in DDBMS", 6th Very Large Data Bases, Montréal, Oct 1980.

[ESWA76]   Eswaran K.P., Gray J.N., Lorie R.A., Traiger L.L., "The Notion of Consistency and Predicate Locks in a Database System", Comm. of the ACM, Vol 19, No 11, P 624-633, Nov 1976.

[BERN81]   Bernstein P.A., Goodman N., "Concurrency Control in Distributued Database Systems", ACM Computing surveys, Vol 13, No 2, June 1981, P 185-222.

[GARC79]   Garcia Molina H., "Performance of Update Algorithms for Distribued Database", Ph.D. Thesis, Stan.Cs.79.744 Stanford University, June 1979.

[GARD81]   Gardarin G., Melkanoff M., "Concurrency Control Principles in Distributed and Centrelized Databases", Rapport de Recherche INRIA No 113, Jan 1981.

[GARD82]   Gardarin G., Bernadat P., Temmerman N., Valduriez P., Viémont Y., "SABRE: A Relationnal database system for a multi-microprocesssor machine", Proc. of the int. workshop on database machine, San Diego, California, Aug 1982.

[IRAN79]   Irani K.B. and Lin H., "Queing Network models for Concurrent Transaction Processing in a Database System", ACM-SIGMOD, May 1979.

[POTI80]   Potier D. and Leblanc Ph., "Analysis of Locking Policies in Database Management Systems", Communications of the ACM, Vol 23, No 10, Oct 80.

[RIES77]   Ries D.R. and Stonebraker M., "Effect of Locking Granularity in a Database Management System", ACM Transactions on DBS, Vol 2, No 3, p 233-246, Sept 1977.

[RIES79]   Ries D.R. and Stonebraker M., "Locking Granularity Revised", ACM Transactions on DBS, Vol 4, No 2, p 210-227, June 1979.

[ROSE78]   Rosenkrantz D.J., Stearns R.E., Lewis P.W., "System Level Concurrency Control for Distributied Database Systems", ACM TODS, Vol 2, No 3, P 233-246, Sept 1978.

[SAUE81]   Sauer C.H. and Chandy K.M., "Computer systems performance modeling", Prentice-Hall (1981).

[THOM79]   Thomas R.H., "A Majority Consensus Approch to Concurrency Controll for Multiple Copy Databases", ACM TODS, Vol 4, No 2, P 180-209, June 1979.

ADAPTIVE SEGMENTATION SCHEMES FOR LARGE RELATIONAL DATABASE MACHINES

Y. Tanaka
Department of Electrical Engineering
Hokkaido University
Sapporo, 060 Japan

1. INTRODUCTION

The file segmentation is inevitable to cope with large files of information even in the design of database machines if we want to enlarge their capacity. The recent researches on database machines have much improved the processing speed by the introduction of special hardware algorithms for the search and the sort of relations. However, these are the algorithms for the internal processing of relations. In other words, these algorithms can not cope with such a relation whose size is much bigger than the buffer memory size. If a relation has too many tuples to read out all of them from the secondary memory into the primary memory or the buffer memory, the database machine has to divide this relation into a set of smaller segments so that each of them may fit into the primary memory size. If files are segmented arbitrarily, most queries require accesses to all the segments, which severely abates the system performance.

File segmentation schemes are the clustering techniques that appropriately distribute the file records to a set of segments so as to balance and minimize the number of segment accesses necessary to answer various queries. Every segmentation scheme consists of two components, a directory and a set of segments. A directory is a set of rules that specifies how to distribute the file records to a set of segments. It may be represented by a hash function, a table, or a search tree. Every segment has the same finite size, and hence it may possibly overflow.

A segmentation scheme is static if its directory is apriori constructed based on an estimated probability distribution of the record values. The overflow of segments does not change the directory. It is resolved by chaining a new segment to the overflowing segment (Fig. 1 (a)). The increase of the file size may cause the excessive chaining of segments and, hence, it may severely increase the number of necessary segment accesses in the execution of queries. The excessive degradation of performance would need the reorganization of the whole file.

An adaptive segmentation scheme, however, does not presuppose any estimated distribution of the record values. When a segment overflows, the directory is locally rewritten to split the overflowing segment into two new segments so that the records in the old segment may be almost equally distributed to the two new segments (Fig. 1 (b)).

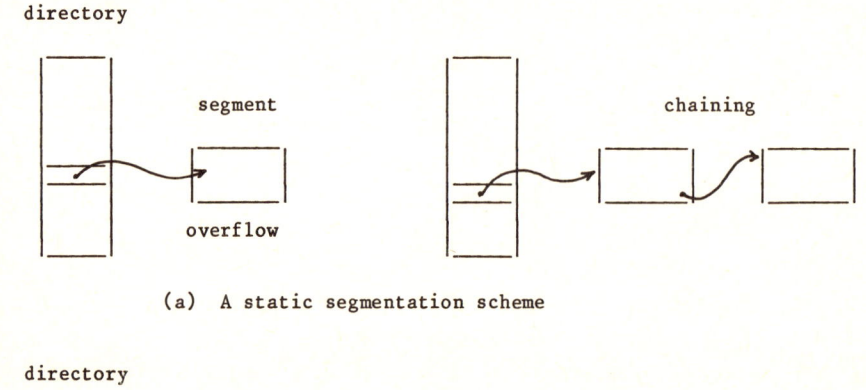

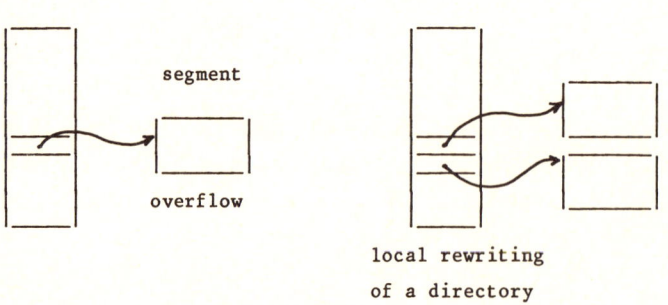

(a) A static segmentation scheme

(b) An adaptive segmentation scheme

Fig. 1 A static segmentation scheme and an adaptive segmentation scheme

A file is said to be relational if it stores a relation defined by E.F. Codd [1]. A primary key of a relational file is an attribute of the relation that uniquely specifies a record in the file. Some query may request a search based on the values of other attributes in the records. Such attributes are denoted by secondary keys. For the retrievals based on the values of a single key attribute, whether it is prime or not, a lot of segmentation schemes have been proposed. Some of them have been practically used and approved. Among them are hashing by an apriori defined function, the B-trees of Bayer and McCreight [2], radix search trees (also known as tries) of Fredkin [3], expandable hashing of Knott [4], dynamic hashing of Larson [5], virtual hashing of Litwin [6], and extendible hashing of Fagin [7]. The first one is a static segmentation scheme, while the others above are dynamic, or adaptive segmentation schemes.

However, segmentation for the retrievals based on the values of multiple secondary key attributes has not been much explored yet. Only several schemes are known as static schemes, and one as an adaptive scheme. Static schemes are essentially classified into two schemes, a combinatorial hashing scheme of Rivest [8] and a balanced filing scheme of Abraham [9]. These schemes are applicable to the restricted cases in which some special relationships hold between the number of segments and the number of secondary keys. Besides, their directories can not be adaptively rewritten.

The extended k-d tree scheme of Chang [10] is the only known adaptive segmentation scheme for the retrievals on multiple secondary key attributes. It is an extension of a k-d tree of Bently [11] that was originally proposed as a search tree whose leaf has a single record. A k-d tree is a binary search tree except that one of the secondary key attributes is assigned to each of its levels. Each internal node splits a set of records into two subsets by the values of the attribute assigned to the level of this node, i.e., the set of the records with the smaller attribute values, and the set of the records with the larger attribute values. The splitting value of the attribute can be arbitrarily chosen at each node.

An extended k-d tree scheme has several disadvantages. The removal of the restriction that the secondary keys used for the segment splitting should be fixed at each level of the tree may decrease the average or the maximum number of segment accesses necessary for query processing. Actually, a k-d tree does not ensure the minimization of either the average or the maximum number of necessary segment accesses. Besides, the scheme does not specify how to analyze the value distribution of records in an overflowing segment in order to determine the splitting value. Generally, an overhead it causes is inevitable.

This paper proposes a new segmentation scheme classified into the same type as an extended k-d tree scheme, namely it falls into the class of adaptive segmentation schemes for the retrievals on multiple secondary key attributes. Its directory is represented by a binary trie whose node is labeled with one of the secondary keys. Different from an extended k-d tree, its node is labeled with an arbitrary secondary key. The splitting of a segment is based upon the value of a certain bit of this attribute value, and hence, it can be arbitrarily chosen either to minimize the average number of segment accesses or to improve the worst case performance. A search of the directory with N segments and its local rewriting need only $O(\log N)$ time on an average for large N. Besides, our segmentation scheme makes the average number of segment accesses necessary for the execution of a relational selection operation no more than $O(N^{(n-1)/n})$, where N and n are respectively the number of records and the number of secondary key attributes.

2. COLORED TRIE SCHEMES FOR RELATIONAL FILES

2.1. Abstract modeling of a relational file segmentation problem

Suppose first that we have a relational file of records each containing n secondary keys, where each secondary key has a fairly large number of possible values. We can map the records whose secondary keys are $(k_0, k_1, \ldots, k_{n-1})$ to the (n*m)-bit number

$$h_0(k_0)h_1(k_1)\ldots h_{n-1}(k_{n-1}),$$

where each h_i is a hash function that maps the values of the (i+1)st secondary key attribute into a set of m-bit values.
The above expression stands for the juxtaposition of n m-bit values.

Now the segmentation of a relational file can be stated in an abstract manner as follows. Suppose that we have a lot of beeds each colored with one of the different colors, $c_0, c_1, \ldots, c_{n-1}$. The set of these colors is denoted by C. A bead with c_i color is referred to as a c_i-bead. Each bead is labeled with an m-bit value. There may be beads with a same color and a same label. A rosary is a string of n beads each having a different color. The c-label of a rosary is defined as the label on its c-bead.

Rosaries are made one by one, choosing an arbitrary label for each color. They are stored in a set of drawers each having a constant capacity. While the number of produced rosaries is less than the capacity of a drawer, they are all stored in a single drawer. If it overflows, the rosaries stored in it are appropriately distributed into two new empty drawers. The old drawer becomes free. The number of drawers used to store rosaries is increased by one.

Suppose that each customer requests a search for all those rosaries with a specified label on a specified color bead. This request is expressed by c=v, where c is the specified color and v is the specified label value. In order to decrease the wait time of the customers, rosaries should have been appropriately distributed into a set of drawers. The wait time is proportional to the number of drawers to be searched. This number varies for various colors and labels. If we desire to minimize the maximum responce time, the maximum number of drawers to be searched should be minimized. If the throughput of services is desired to be maximized, the average number of drawers to be searched should be minimized. In the above metaphorical model of the relational file segmentation, each rosary stands for a relational tuple, or in other words, a record, while each color stands for a secondary key attribute. Each drawer stands for a segment of the relational file and its pull out means the access of the segment.

2.2. A colored binary trie

Initially, only a single drawer is used to store rosaries, and hence its directory has only one entry (Fig. 2 (a)). If an overflow occurs, the rosaries in the drawer should be divided into two classes. They can be divided based upon the values of a certain bit of a certain color label. For this division, we use the most significant bit of some color label. The directory will come to have two entries corresponding to two new drawers that store the two classes. It can be represented as a binary trie with two leaves and a root that is painted with the color whose labels were used as a basis of the division (Fig. 2 (b)). If one of the two drawers overflows again, its contents are further divided into two classes. In general, the division of a cluster can be based upon an arbitrary bit of an arbitrary color label unless this bit has been already used as a basis of another division in the process of having produced this cluster. We use, in every division, the leftmost unused bit of some color label. The directory of drawers that describes the rules of cluster division can be represented as a colored binary trie. It is a binary trie whose each internal node is painted with one of the n colors.

   directory   drawer   directory   drawer

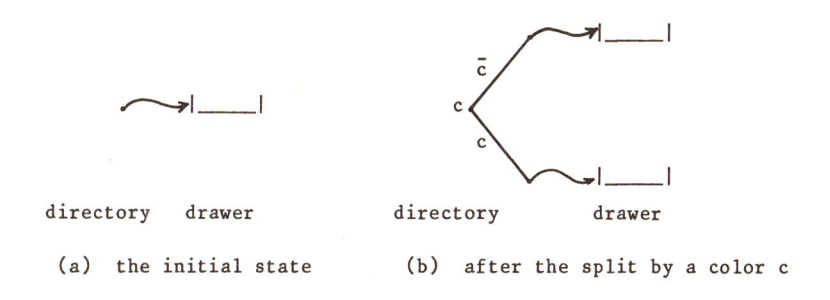

(a) the initial state   (b) after the split by a color c

Fig. 2 The division of the contents of an overflowing drawer based on a bit of the c-labels of rosaries

In a colored binary trie, the left branch from a node colored with c is represented by $\bar{c}$, while the right by c. The concatenation of the representation of branches along the path from the root to any other node uniquely identifies that node in the trie. This identifier is referred to as a node code. For a node code α and each color c, we define the c-code of that node as a bit sequence that is obtained by first deleting all the appearances of c' and $\bar{c}'$ from α for each c' different from c, and then replacing c and $\bar{c}$ respectively with '1' and '0'. The c-code of the node with a node code α is denoted by $c(\alpha)$, while the length of α and that of $c(\alpha)$ are respectively represented by $\rho(\alpha)$ and $\rho(c(\alpha))$. The node α of a colored binary trie stands for the cluster of rosaries whose c-labels begin with $c(\alpha)$ for each color c.

2.3. Access cost

Each customer requests a search for all those rosaries with a specified label on a specified color bead. The processing of such a request first requires a search of a directory for drawers that possibly contains some of the requested rosaries. Then it requires searches of these drawers for all the rosaries of the requested type. The wait time of a customer is approximately proportional to the number of drawers to be searched. Fig. 3 shows an example directory represented by a colored binary trie with three colors, R, G, and B. Segments are denoted by the leaf nodes. They are labeled with the numbering from 1 to 6. Let the search for rosaries with the c-label v be referred to as a 'c=v' search. For the search of R=00...00, it is necessary to pull out three drawers 1, 2, and 3. For R=00...01, a set of necessary drawers is same. Generally, these drawers are necessary and sufficient to search for all the rosaries with the R-labels beginning with 00. These search requests are represented by R=00**...*, where '*' stands for an arbitrary binary value. A search request B=0**...* requires to pull out four drawers, 1, 2, 4, and 5. The number of necessary drawers varies depending on the color c and its label v. This number is denoted by naccess(T, c, v), where T denotes a directory trie.

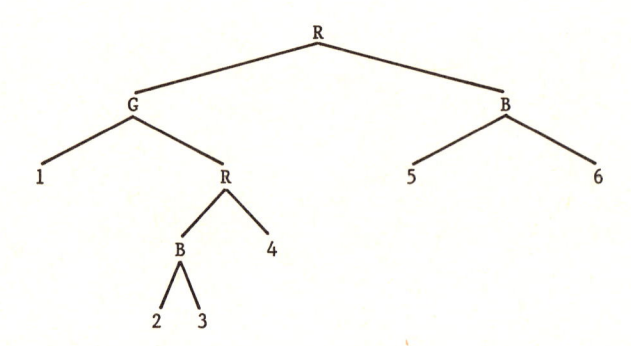

Fig. 3 An example directory represented by a colored binary trie with 3 colors

Let $C_{avg}(T, c)$ and $C_{worst}(T, c)$ respectively denote the average and the maximum number of segment accesses necessary for searches based on the values of the c-label, i.e.,

$$C_{avg}(T, c) = \underset{v \in \{0,1\}^m}{\text{average}} (naccess(T, c, v))$$

$$C_{worst}(T, c) = \underset{v \in \{0,1\}^m}{\max} (naccess(T, c, v)).$$

Two kinds of access costs can be defined:
1. average cost

$$cost^1(T) = \underset{c \in C}{\text{average}} (C_{avg}(T, c)),$$

2. worst cost
$$\text{cost}^2(T) = \max_{c \in C} (\text{Cworst}(T, c)).$$

Suppose that we have a directory T and that one of its drawers overflows. We want to choose the most desirable color to split the overflowing leaf of T so that the result trie may have the least cost. Suppose that the overflow occurs at a leaf with a node code α. Let a trie obtained by splitting this leaf based on the leftmost unused bit of c-label be denoted by new(T, α, c). The most desirable color is formally defined as the one that minimizes the following function of the color variable c;
$$\text{Ccost}^i_{T,\alpha}(c) = \text{cost}^i(\text{new}(T, \alpha, c)).$$
There can be two different schemes corresponding to the two cost functions. The best average scheme minimizes $\text{Ccost}^1_{T,\alpha}(c)$, while the best worst scheme minimizes $\text{Ccost}^2_{T,\alpha}(c)$. The best average scheme results in a good performance throughput, while the best worst scheme improves responce time.

3. ADAPTIVE SEGMENTATION SCHEMES

3.1. Best average scheme

For a colored trie T and an overflowing leaf α, $\text{Ccost}^1_{T,\alpha}(c)$ is calculated as follows.

Theorem 3.1
$$\text{Ccost}^1_{T,\alpha}(c) = \text{cost}^1(T) + (1/n) \sum_{c' \in C} (1/2)^{\rho(c'(\alpha))} - (1/n)(1/2)^{\rho(c(\alpha))}. \tag{1}$$

proof See Appendix A.1.

The first two terms on the right hand side of the equality (1) do not depend on c. Besides, the equality (1) implies that the minimization of $\text{Ccost}^1_{T,\alpha}(c)$ is equivalent to the minimization of $\rho(c(\alpha))$. Therefore, in the best average scheme, the split of a leaf with a node code α should choose a color that minimizes $\rho(c(\alpha))$. Suppose that n colors are $c_0, c_1, \ldots, c_{n-1}$. As a special case of the best average schemes, a scheme is a best average scheme if it selects, for the splitting of a node at the i-th level, the color c_j whose suffix j is congruent to i-1 modulo n. Such a scheme is called a regular best average scheme. We show an example trie in Fig. 4 that is built based on the regular best average scheme. If the node 2 overflows, it will be split by the color 'B'.

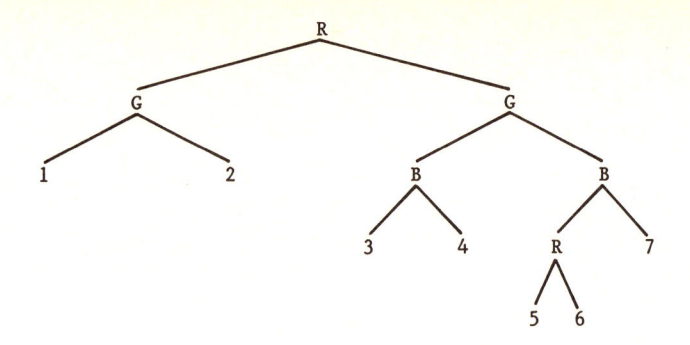

Fig. 4 A colored binary trie with 3 colors that is built based on the best average scheme

3.2 Best worst scheme

When an overflow occurs at some leaf of a colored trie, the best worst scheme splits this leaf by such a color that minimizes $Ccost^2_{T,\alpha}(c)$. If both c' and c'' are different from c then $Cworst(new(T, \alpha, c'), c)$ is equal to $Cworst(new(T, \alpha, c''), c)$. Let c^+ denote a representative of the colors that are different from c. Then the following theorem holds.

Theorem 3.2
If a color c maximizes $Cworst(new(T, \alpha, c^+), c)$ then it minimizes $Ccost^2_{T,\alpha}(c)$.
proof See Appendix A.2.

For each color c, the leaves of a colored trie T can be divided into three classes. The first class consists of those leaves whose node codes do not include c nor $\bar{c}$. A subtree of T that consists of these leaves is denoted by T/c. The second class consists of such leaves whose each node code has $\bar{c}$ that is not preceded by c. A subtree of T consisting of these leaves is denoted by $T|\bar{c}$. Each of the remaining leaves has a node code that has c before any appearances of $\bar{c}$ in it. A subtree consisting of these remaining leaves is denoted by $T|c$. An example of a trie T, and its $T|\bar{c}$, $T|c$ and T/c are shown in Fig. 5. Then $Cworst(T, c)$ is recursively calculated as follows.

Theorem 3.3

$$Cworst(T, c) = card(leaves(T/c)) + \max(Cworst(T|\bar{c}, c), Cworst(T|c, c)), \quad (2)$$

where leaves(T) denotes a set of the leaves of T while card(S) denotes the cardinality of a set S.
proof See Appendix A.3.

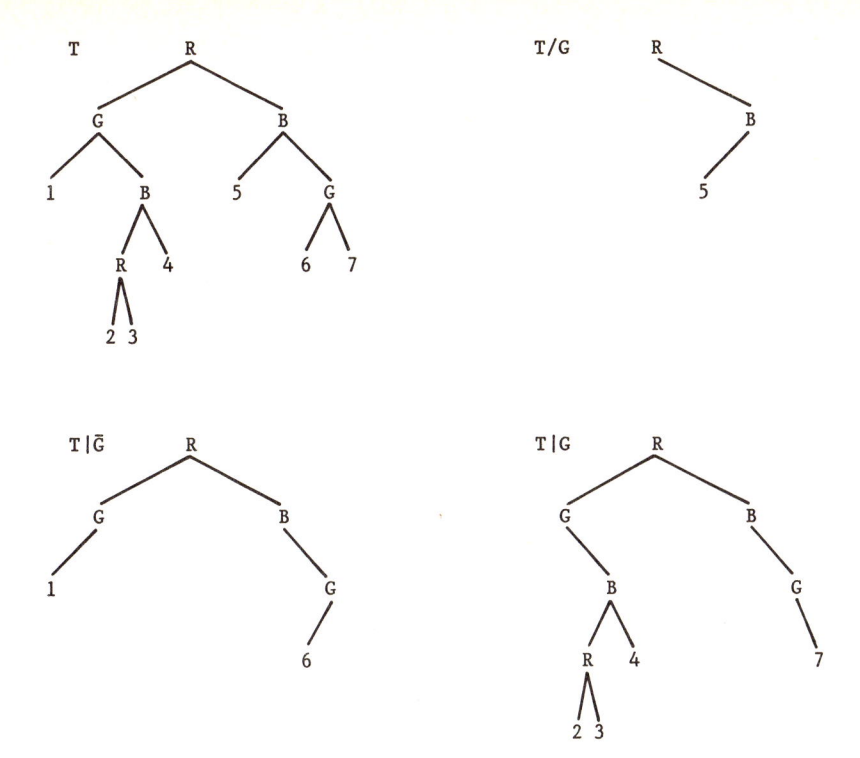

Fig. 5 An example of a colored trie, and its T/G, T|Ḡ, and T|G

For each finite binary sequence over {0,1}, let $T|_v^c$ denote
$$((...((T|v_1)|v_2)...)|v_{k-1})|v_k,$$
where k is the length of v, and v_i is c (, $\bar{c}$) if the i-th bit of v is 1 (, 0). We define a set P(v) for a finite binary sequence v as a set of prefixes of v, i.e.,
$$P(v) = \{ u \mid \text{there exists } u' \text{ in } \{0,1\}^*, \text{ and } u \circ u' = v \}.$$
Let $L_c(v)$ and $W_c(v)$ be defined as
$$L_c(v) = \text{card}(\text{leaves}((T|_v^c)/c)),$$
$$W_c(v) = \text{Cworst}(T|_v^c, c).$$
The number $L_c(v)$ denote the number of those leaves whose node code α satisfies c(α)=v. Then they satisfy the following relation;
$$W_c(v) = L_c(v) + \max (W_c(v \circ 0), W_c(v \circ 1)). \qquad (3)$$
This can be obtained by substituting $T|_v^c$ for T in the equality given by Theorem 3.3. Let S_c be
$$S_c = \{ c(\alpha) \mid \alpha \in \text{leaves}(T) \},$$
and S∘{0,1} denote
$$S \circ \{0,1\} = \{a \circ 0, a \circ 1 \mid a \in S \}.$$

The algorithm for the best worst scheme is stated as follows.

Algorithm

1. Compute Cworst(new(T, α, c⁺), c) for each c.

Let $L_c^\alpha(v)$ and $W_c^\alpha(v)$ be defined as

$L_c^\alpha(v) = \text{card}(\text{leaves}(\text{new}(T, \alpha, c^+)|_v^c/c))$,

$W_c^\alpha(v) = \text{Cworst}(\text{new}(T, \alpha, c^+)|_v^c, c)$.

Then $W_c^\alpha(\epsilon)$ is Cworst(new(T, α, c⁺), c), where ε denotes an empty string. Since new(T, α, c⁺)$|_v^c$ is T$|_v^c$ for any v∉P(c(α)), $L_c^\alpha(v)$ and $W_c^\alpha(v)$ are equal to $L_c(v)$ and $W_c(v)$ for such v. For v∈P(c(α)), $L_c(v)$ and $W_c(v)$ may have to be updated. Since the leaf α is also a leaf of T$|_{c(\alpha)}^c$, and α is split into two leaves by a color different from c, the number of leaves of new(T, α, c⁺)$|_{c(\alpha)}^c$ increases from that of T$|_{c(\alpha)}^c$, by one. Therefore, $L_c^\alpha(v)$ is

$L_c^\alpha(v) = $ if v=c(α) then $L_c(v)+1$
    else $L_c(v)$.

From the equality (3) and the definitions of $W_c^\alpha(v)$ and $L_c^\alpha(v)$, $W_c^\alpha(v)$ is

$W_c^\alpha(v) = L_c^\alpha(v) + \max(W_c^\alpha(v\circ 0), W_c^\alpha(v\circ 1))$.

If v equals c(α) then the following equalities hold;

$L_c^\alpha(v) = L_c(v)+1$,

$W_c^\alpha(v\circ 0) = W_c^\alpha(v\circ 1) = 0$.

Therefore, it holds that

$W_c^\alpha(v) = $ if v=c(α) then $W_c(v)+1$
    else $L_c(v)+\max(W_c^\alpha(v\circ 0), W_c^\alpha(v\circ 1))$.

Since $W_c^\alpha(v)$ equals $W_c(v)$ if v is not a prefix of c(α), the following equality is obtained;

$W_c^\alpha(v) = $ if v=c(α) then $W_c(v)+1$
    elseif v∉P(c(α)) then $W_c(v)$
    else $L_c(v)+\max(W_c^\alpha(v\circ 0), W_c^\alpha(v\circ 1))$.

Now we will further examine the case when v is a prefix of c(α). Since v∘0 and v∘1 can not simultaneously be prefixes of c(α), only one of $W_c^\alpha(v\circ 0)$ and $W_c^\alpha(v\circ 1)$ needs further computation. Assume that v∘0 is a prefix of c(α), and that $W_c(v\circ 1)$ is greater than $W_c(v\circ 0)$. Since $W_c^\alpha(v)$ is greater than $W_c(v)$ by one at most, $W_c^\alpha(v\circ 0)$ is no more than $W_c(v\circ 0)+1$. Therefore, it holds that

$W_c(v\circ 1) = W_c^\alpha(v\circ 1)$

$\leq \max(W_c^\alpha(v\circ 1), W_c^\alpha(v\circ 0))$

$\leq \max(W_c(v\circ 1), W_c(v\circ 0)+1)$

$\leq W_c(v\circ 1)$.

This implies that

$W_c(v\circ 1) = \max(W_c^\alpha(v\circ 1), W_c^\alpha(v\circ 0))$.

Similarly, if v∘1 is a prefix of c(α) and $W_c(v\circ 0)$ is greater than $W_c(v\circ 1)$, then it can be proved that

$$W_c(v \circ 0) = \max(W_c^\alpha(v \circ 0), W_c^\alpha(v \circ 1)).$$

Therefore, the computation of $W_c^\alpha(\epsilon)$ can be recursively performed by the following formula;

$W_c^\alpha(v) = $ if $v = c(\alpha)$ then $W_c(v) + 1$
    elseif $v \not\in P(c(\alpha))$ then $W_c(v)$
    else for $b \in \{0,1\}$ such that $v \circ b \in P(c(\alpha))$
        if $W_c(v \circ \bar{b}) \geq W_c(v \circ b) + 1$
            then $W_c(v)$
            else $L_c(v) + W_c^\alpha(v \circ b)$. (4)

The number of steps necessary for the computation of $W_c^\alpha(v)$ is proportional to the length of $c(\alpha)$. Therefore, the total number of steps necessary to compute $W_c(v)$ for n different colors is proportional to

$$\sum_c \rho(c(\alpha)) = \rho(\alpha),$$

which is bounded by the height of the colored trie.

2. Choose a color c that maximizes Cworst(new(T, α, c⁺), c).

Since Cworst(new(T, α, c⁺), c) is $W_c(\epsilon)$, what we have to do is to find out a color that maximizes $W_c(\epsilon)$. If there are more than one candidates, choose one that minimizes $\rho(c(\alpha))$.

3. Split the overflowing node by the selected color c_0, and update $L_c(v)$ and $W_c(v)$ for each c and $v \in P(c(\alpha))$.

For any c different from c_0, and any $v \in P(c(\alpha))$,
    $L_c^{new}(v) \leftarrow L_c^\alpha(v)$,
    $W_c^{new}(v) \leftarrow W_c^\alpha(v)$.

For $c = c_0$,
    $S_c^{new} \leftarrow (S_c - \{c(\alpha)\}) \cup \{c(\alpha) \circ 0, c(\alpha) \circ 1\}$,
    $L_c^{new}(v) \leftarrow$ if $v = c(\alpha)$ then $L_c(v) - 1$
                elseif $v = c(\alpha) \circ 0$ or $v = c(\alpha) \circ 1$
                    then $L_c(v) + 1$
                    else $L_c(v)$.
    $W_c^{new}(v) \leftarrow$ if $v \in S_c^{new} \circ \{0,1\}$ then 0
                elseif $v \not\in P(c(\alpha))$
                    then $W_c(v)$
                    else $L_c^{new}(v) + \max(W_c^{new}(v \circ 0), W_c^{new}(v \circ 1))$.

Because of the same reason, the number of steps necessary for the update of $L_c(v)$ and $W_c(v)$ is proportional to the length of $c(\alpha)$. Therefore, the total number of steps necessary to update $L_c(v)$ and $W_c(v)$ for all the different colors is proportional to $\rho(\alpha)$, which is bounded by the height of the colored trie.

For each $v \in \{c(\alpha) | \alpha$ is a node in T.$\}$, let $T_c(v)$ be a tree defined recursively as follows. Its root is labeled with a pair $(W_c(v) - L_c(v), L_c(v))$ (= $(\max(W_c(v \circ 0), W_c(v \circ 1)), L_c(v))$). Its left and right subtrees are respectively defined as $T_c(v \circ 0)$

and $T_c(v \circ 1)$. For $v \notin \{c(\alpha) | \alpha$ is a node on $T.\}$, $T_c(v)$ is considered empty. Fig. 6 (a) shows an example colored trie and its corresponding $T_c(\epsilon)$ for each color c. The overflowing node is indicated by an arrow. For the selection of a color that minimizes $Ccost^2_{T,\alpha}(c)$, the value of $Cworst(new(T, \alpha, c^+), c)$ is computed for each c, which is shown in (b). Its computation process for c=R is shown in (c). In this case, G is selected. For each c, the change of $T_c(\epsilon)$ by the splitting is shown in (d), and the computation process for c=G is shown in (e).

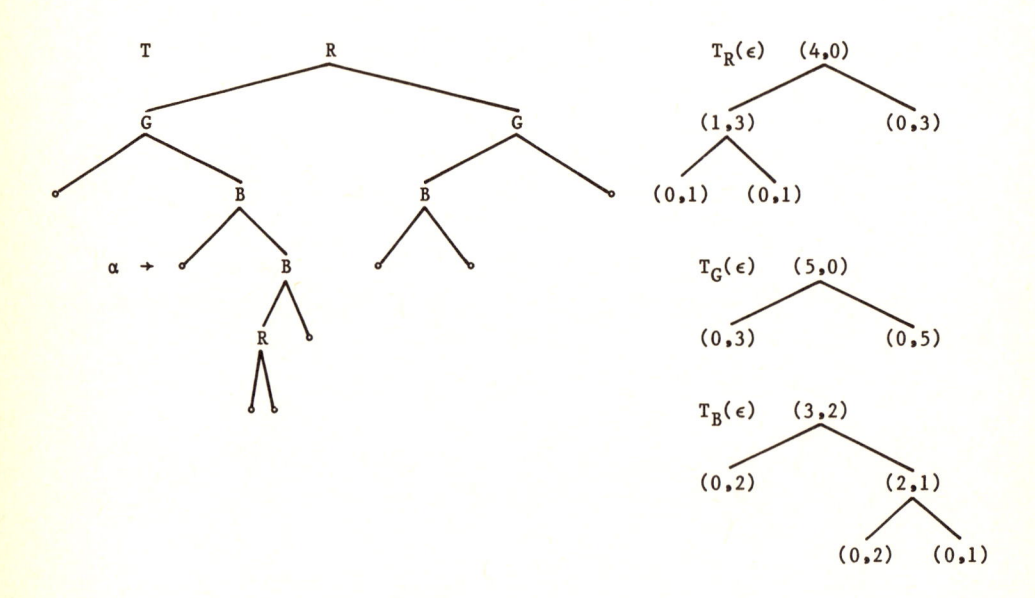

(a) a colored trie and its $T_c(\epsilon)$'s

	R	G	B
$Cworst(new(T, \alpha, c^+), c)$	5	6	5

(b) selection of a color that minimizes $Ccost^2_{T,\alpha}(c)$

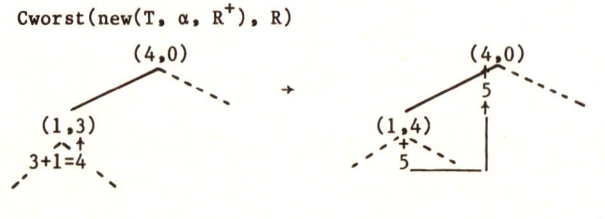

(c) The computation process of $Cworst(new(T, \alpha, c^+), c)$

Fig. 6 The splitting of an overflowing segment based on the best worst scheme (continued)

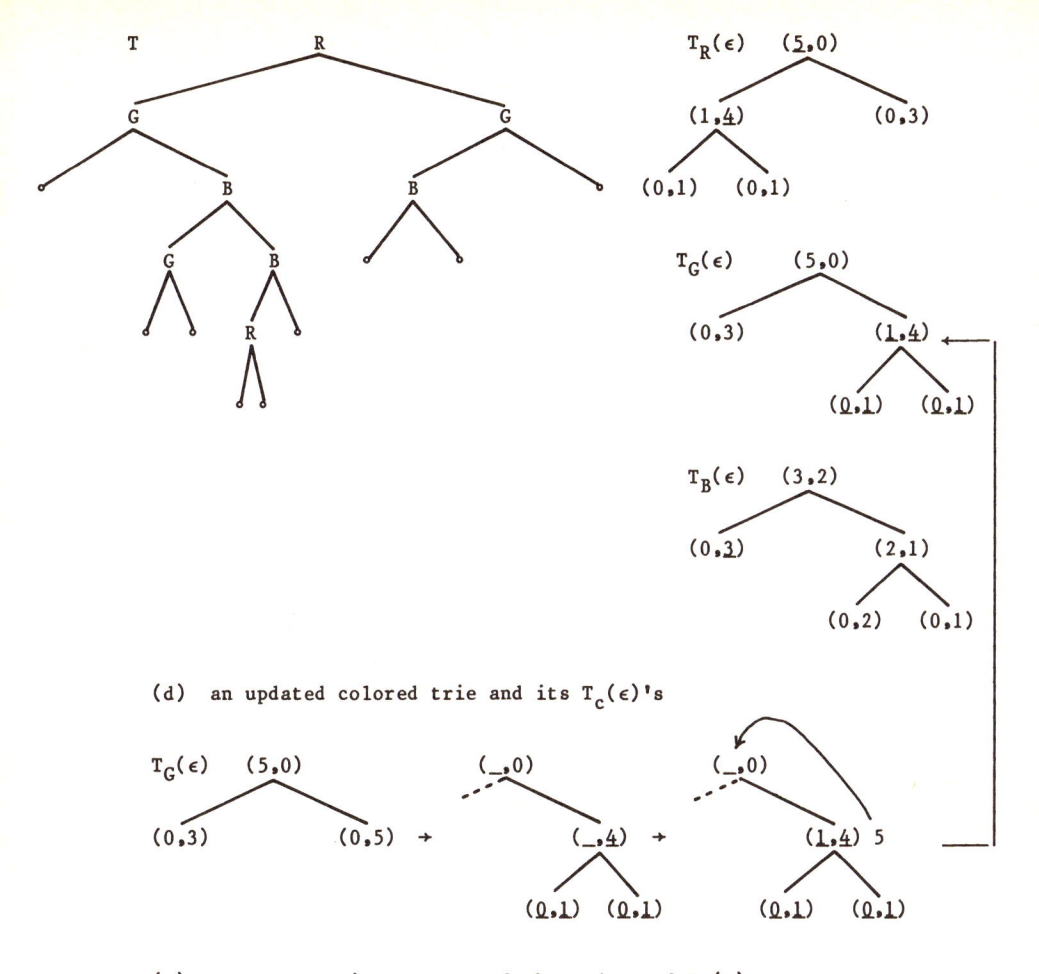

(d) an updated colored trie and its $T_c(\epsilon)$'s

(e) The computation process of the update of $T_G(\epsilon)$

Fig. 6 The splitting of an overflowing segment based on the best worst scheme

4. ANALYSIS OF COLORED BINARY TRIES

4.1. Theoretical analysis

It is well known that the average height of a randomly constructed binary tree with N external nodes is $2*\ln(N-1) \doteq 1.386 \log_2(N-1)$ [12]. Since a colored binary trie is also a binary tree, the average height of randomly constructed colored binary tries with N leaves is also $1.386 \log_2(N-1)$.

For the regular best average scheme, we can get a fairly good lower bound and a upper bound of $\text{cost}^1(T)$.

Theorem 4.1

Let N and n be the number of rosaries and the number of different colors. The regular best average scheme makes $cost^1(T)$ as
$$cost^1(T) \leq 2^{(n+1)/n} N^{(n-1)/n}.$$
This bound is independent from whether the label values on rosaries are uniformly distributed or not.

proof See Appendix A.4.

Theorem 4.2

Let N and n be the number of rosaries and the number of different colors. The regular best average scheme makes $cost^1(T)$ as
$$cost^1(T) \geq \frac{A(1+A^{N-2}-2A^{N-1})}{4(1-A)} \qquad (N \leq n*m),$$
$$cost^1(T) \geq \frac{A(1+A^{n*m-2}-2A^{n*m-1})}{4(1-A)} \doteq \frac{A}{4(1-A)} \qquad (N \geq n*m),$$
where A equals $(1/2)^{1/n}$ and m is the maximum bit length of the labels. Especially, if the label values on rosaries are uniformly distributed, $cost^1(T)$ is bounded as
$$cost^1(T) \geq N^{(n-1)/n}.$$
proof See Appendix A.5.

4.2. Experimental analysis

The experimental analysis by computer simulations has shown desirable features of these proposed schemes.

In the best average scheme, the loading factor of a segment is about 70 %, which does not depend on the size of segments, the number of different colors, nor the distribution of the label values on rosaries. Theoretically, if the label values on rosaries are uniformly distributed, the lower bound of $cost^1(T)$ becomes $N^{(n-1)/n}$, which can not be crossed by any segmentation scheme regardless of whether it is static or adaptive. Fig. 7 (a) shows the simulated values of $cost^1(T)$ in the case of the best average scheme together with the theoretical lower bound. The two curves coincide almost everywhere. The average cost $cost^1(T)$ is almost independent from the distribution of the label values on rosaries. However, the worst cost $cost^2(T)$ seriously depends on how the distribution of the label values deviates from uniform distribution.

For a trie constructed by the best worst scheme, both the average cost $cost^1(T)$ and the worst cost $cost^2(T)$ are almost independent from the value distribution (Fig. 7 (b)). Besides, the difference between $cost^1(T)$ and $cost^2(T)$ is very small. The loading factor of a segment is almost same as in the case of the best average scheme.

It is worth mentioning that our computer simulations have shown the fact that

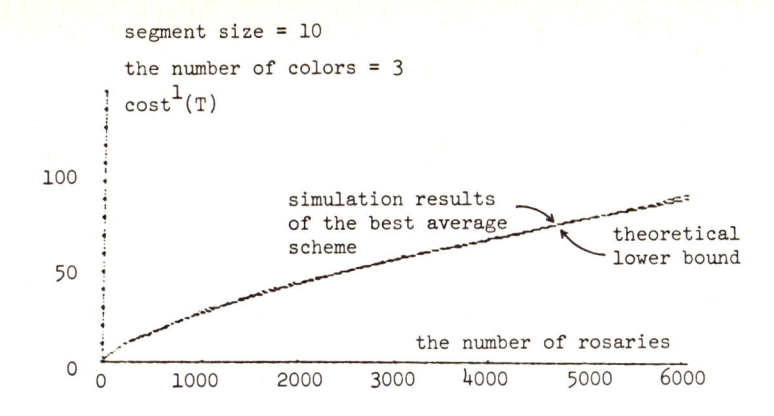

(a) the simulated average number of segment accesses in the best average scheme together with its theoretical lower bound
(The loading factor is assumed to be 70 % in the computation of the theoretical lower bound.)

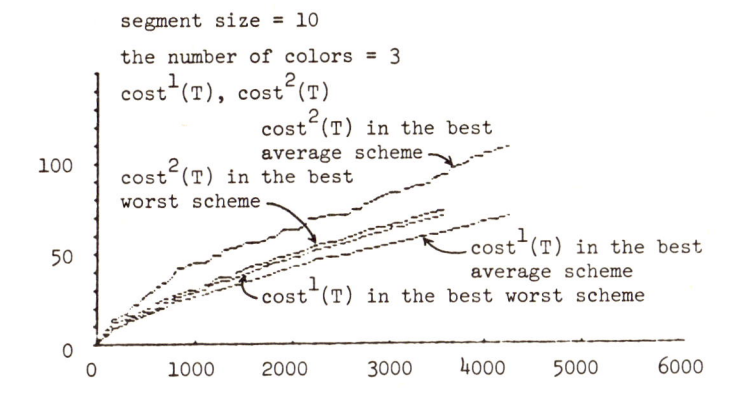

(b) the comparison of the two schemes, the best average scheme and the best worst scheme, in the case in which record values are uniformly distributed

Fig. 7 The experimental analysis of the proposed segmentation schemes

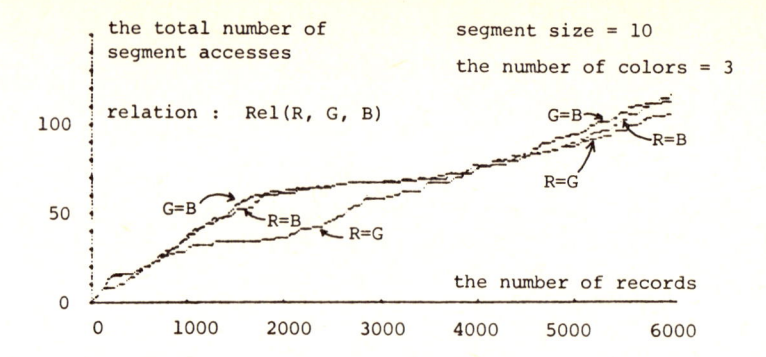

(a) The total number of segment accesses necessary for the processing of a restriction operation in the case of the best average scheme.

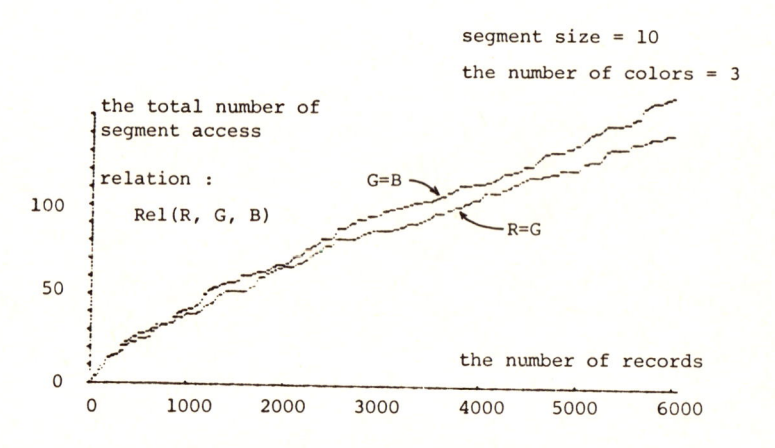

(b) The total number of segment accesses necessary for the processing of a restriction operation in the case of the best worst scheme.

Fig. 8 The improvement of the file access cost in the processing of a restriction operation by using our new adaptive segmentation schemes.

both the average cost $cost^1(T)$ in the best average scheme and the worst cost $cost^2(T)$ in the best worst scheme are almost independent from the distribution of label values on rosaries.

The two cost functions above correspond to the average and the maximum number of segment accesses necessary for the processing of a selection operation on a relation, such as R[A='v'], where R, A, and v are respectively a relation, an attribute of R, and an attribute value of A. We have also simulated our file segmentation schemes to know the number of necessary segment accesses in the processing of a restriction operation on a relation, such as R[A=B], where A and B are two different attributes of a relation R (Fig. 8). The figure shows that the access cost of restriction operations is mostly similar to the cost of selection operations. Although our schemes are designed to decrease the access cost of selection operations, they have also shown a remarkable improvement in the access cost of restriction operations.

5. CONCLUSION

We have proposed new adaptive segmentation schemes for the retrievals on secondary keys. They have the following advantageous features.

1. It is completely adaptive, and has no restrictions on the number of segments and of attributes.
2. It can be arbitrarily chosen either to minimize the average number of segment accesses or to improve the worst case performance. This property is different from an extended k-d tree scheme, which can minimize only the average. Besides, the minimization in an extended k-d tree scheme is performed under the restriction that the node splitting at each level uses a same secondary key. Our new scheme assumes no such restrictions.
3. A search of the directory for N segments and its local rewriting need only $O(\log N)$ time on an average for large N. Especially, if the values of the secondary keys are independently and uniformly distributed, these operations need no more than $O(\log N)$ time for large N.
4. The regular best average scheme makes the average number of segment accesses necessary for the processing of a relational selection operation no more than $O(N^{(n-1)/n})$, where N and n are respectively the number of relational records and the number of secondary key attributes. On the other hand, it is proved that, if the record values are uniformly distributed, no segmentation scheme can make this file access cost less than $O(N^{(n-1)/n})$, whether it is static or adaptive.

The computer simulations have shown various desirable features of these schemes. Among them, the following features are worth mentioning.

1. The loading factor is about 70 %, which is fairly good.
2. In the best average scheme, the expected number of segment acesses necessary for the processing of a relational selection operation almost coincides with the lower bound of the average cost, and it is almost independent from the distribution of record values.
3. In the best worst scheme, the responce time of the processing of a relational selection operation is almost independent from the distribution of record values. Besides, the maximum number of segment accesses becomes very close to the expected number of segment accesses. In other words, the best worst scheme results in very small variance of the number of necessary segment accesses in the processing of various selection queries
4. In the proposed schemes, the number of segment accesses necessary for the processing of a relational restriction operation is approximately same as in the case of a selection operation.

All of these desirable features of our schemes shows their applicability to the practical relational files and also to the large relational database machines.

Acknowledgement

The author wishes to express his thanks to Prof. R. Tagawa of Hokkaido University for his support on this research, and my student Mr. N. Mori for his help in the computer simulations.

REFERENCES

[1] Codd, E.F., 'A relational model for large shared data banks,' Comm. ACM, Vol. 13 No. 6, 1970, pp. 377-387.
[2] Bayer, R. and E. McCreight, 'Organization and maintenance of large unordered indices,' Acta Informatica, Vol. 1 Fasc. 3, 1972, pp. 173-189.
[3] Fredkin, E., 'TRIE memory,' CACM, Vol. 3 NO. 9, 1960, pp. 490-499.
[4] Knott, G.D., 'Expandable open addressing hash table storage and retrieval,' Proc. ACM SIGFIDET Workshop on Data Description, Access and Control, 1971, pp. 186-206.
[5] Larson, P., 'Dynamic hashing,' BIT, Vol. 18, 1978, pp. 184-201.
[6] Litwin, W., 'Virtual hashing: A dynamically changing hashing,' Proc. Very Large Data Bases Conf. Berlin, 1978, pp. 517-523.
[7] Fagin, R., J. Nievergelt, N. Pippenger, and H.R. Strong, 'Extendible hashing—a fast access method for dynamic files,' ACM Transaction on Database Systems, Vol. 4 No. 3, 1979, pp. 315-344.
[8] Rivest, R.L., 'Partial-match retrieval algorithm,' SIAM J. Comput., Vol. 5 No. 1, 1976, pp. 19-50.

[9] Abraham, C.T., S.P. Ghosh, and D.K. Ray-Chaudhuri, 'File organization schemes based on finite geometries,' Information and Control, Vol. 12, 1968, pp. 143-163.

[10] Chang, J., and K. Fu, 'Extended k-d tree database organization: A dynamic multiattribute clustering method,' IEEE Trans. Software Engineering, Vol. SE-7, No. 3, 1981, pp. 284-290.

[11] Bentley, J.L., 'Multi-dimensional binary search trees used for associative searching,' Comm. ACM, Vol. 18, 1975.

[12] Knuth, D.E., The Art of Computer Programming, Vol. 3 / Sorting and Searching, Addison-Wesley, 1973, p. 427.

[13] Tanaka, Y., 'Adaptive segmentation schemes for relational files,' Information Society of Japan, Tech. Rep. on Software Theory, No. 4-5, 1983.

APPENDIX

A.1. Proof of Theorem 3.1.

For a colored trie T, let $L(T)$ and $R(T)$ denote the left subtrie and the right subtrie of its root, and $C(T)$ be a color of its root. Then the following equalities hold.

Lemma A.1

$$Cavg(T, c) = \text{if } T \text{ has only one node then } 1$$
$$\text{else}$$
$$(1-(1/2)\Delta(c, C(T)))$$
$$*(Cavg(L(T), c)+Cavg(R(T), c)), \quad (A.1)$$
$$\text{where}$$
$$\Delta(c, c') = 1 \text{ if } c=c',$$
$$0 \text{ otherwise.}$$

proof

If T has only one node, then the equality holds. Assume that T has more than one nodes. If $c \neq C(T)$ then $Cavg(T, c)$ is

$$Cavg(T, c) = (1/2)^m (\sum_{v \in \{0,1\}^m} naccess(T, c, v))$$

$$= (1/2)^m (\sum_{v \in \{0,1\}^m} (naccess(L(T), c, v)$$
$$+naccess(R(T), c, v)))$$

$$= Cavg(L(T), c) + Cavg(R(T), c).$$

Otherwise, c equals to $C(T)$ and, hence, $Cavg(T, c)$ is

$$Cavg(T, c) = (1/2)^m (\sum_{v \in \{0,1\}^{m-1}} naccess(L(T), c, v)$$

$$+ \sum_{v \in \{0,1\}^{m-1}} naccess(R(T), c, v)). \quad (A.2)$$

Since $naccess(L(T), c, v)$ equals to $naccess(L(T), c, v \circ 0)$ and also to $naccess(L(T), c, v \circ 1)$, the first sum in (A.2) becomes

$$(1/2)(\sum_{v \in \{0,1\}^{m-1}} naccess(L(T), c, v \circ 0)$$

$$+ \sum_{v \in \{0,1\}^{m-1}} naccess(L(T), c, v \circ 1))$$

$$= (1/2) \sum_{v \in \{0,1\}^m} naccess(L(T), c, v)$$

$$= (1/2) Cavg(L(T), c).$$

Similarly, the second sum in (A.2) becomes

$$\sum_{v \in \{0,1\}^{m-1}} naccess(R(T), c, v) = (1/2) Cavg(R(T), c).$$

Both cases can be summarized as shown in this lemma. Q.E.D.

Theorem A.2

Let $leaves(T)$ denote a set of node codes of leaves in T. Then $Cavg(T, c)$ is

$$Cavg(T, c) = \sum_{\alpha \in leaves(T)} (1/2)^{\rho(c(\alpha))}. \quad (A.3)$$

proof

This is proved by a mathematical induction on the number of leaves in T. If the number of leaves in T is one, then α is an empty string, and hence $\rho(c(\alpha))$ is zero for any c. Therefore, the right hand side of (A.3) becomes one for any c, which is consistent with the definition of $Cavg(T, c)$. Suppose that the theorem holds for every trie that has less than N leaves. Let T be a trie with N leaves. From (A.1), $Cavg(T, c)$ is

$$Cavg(T, c)$$
$$= (1-(1/2)\Delta(c, C(T)))*(Cavg(L(T), c) + Cavg(R(T), c)).$$

Since each of L(T) and R(T) has less than N leaves, this equality can be changed to

$$Cavg(T, c)$$
$$= (1-(1/2)\Delta(c, C(T)))$$
$$*(\sum_{\alpha \in leaves(L(T))} (1/2)^{\rho(c(\alpha))} + \sum_{\alpha \in leaves(R(T))} (1/2)^{\rho(c(\alpha))}). \quad (A.4)$$

The set of leaves of T is clustered into two subsets;

$$leaves(T)$$
$$= \{\overline{C(T)} \circ \alpha \mid \alpha \in leaves(L(T))\}$$
$$\cup \{C(T) \circ \alpha \mid \alpha \in leaves(R(T))\},$$

where $c \circ \alpha$ denotes a concatenation of c and α. Besides, the following relation holds;

$$\rho(c(\overline{C(T)} \circ \alpha)) = \rho(c(C(T) \circ \alpha)) = \rho(c(\alpha)) + \Delta(c, C(T)).$$

Therefore, (A.4) becomes

$$(1-(1/2)\Delta(c, C(T)))$$
$$*(\sum_{\alpha \in leaves(L(T))} (1/2)^{\rho(c(\overline{C(T)} \circ \alpha)) - \Delta(c, C(T))}$$
$$+ \sum_{\alpha \in leaves(R(T))} (1/2)^{\rho(c(C(T) \circ \alpha)) - \Delta(c, C(T))}$$
$$= (1-(1/2)\Delta(c, C(T)))*(\sum_{\alpha' \in leaves(T)} (1/2)^{\rho(c(\alpha'))})*2^{\Delta(c, C(T))}$$

$$= \sum_{\alpha' \in \text{leaves}(T)} (1/2)^{\rho(c(\alpha'))}.$$

Therefore, the theorem also holds for T. This completes the proof. Q.E.D.

Lemma A.3
$$C_{avg}(\text{new}(T, \alpha, c), c') = C_{avg}(T, c') + (1-\Delta(c, c'))(1/2)^{\rho(c'(\alpha))}. \tag{A.5}$$

proof

From Theorem A.2, $C_{avg}(\text{new}(T, \alpha, c), c')$ is
$$C_{avg}(\text{new}(T, \alpha, c), c') = \sum_{\alpha \in \text{leaves}(\text{new}(T, \alpha, c))} (1/2)^{\rho(c'(\alpha))}. \tag{A.6}$$

Since it holds that
$$\text{leaves}(\text{new}(T, \alpha, c)) = (\text{leaves}(T) - \{\alpha\}) \cup \{\alpha \circ \bar{c}, \alpha \circ c\},$$
and that
$$\rho(c'(\alpha \circ \bar{c})) = \rho(c'(\alpha \circ c)) = \rho(c'(\alpha)) + \Delta(c, c'),$$
the equality (A.6) becomes
$$\sum_{\alpha' \in \text{leaves}(T)} (1/2)^{\rho(c'(\alpha'))} - (1/2)^{\rho(c'(\alpha))} + 2(1/2)^{\rho(c'(\alpha)) + \Delta(c, c')}$$
$$= C_{avg}(T, c') + (1-\Delta(c, c'))(1/2)^{\rho(c'(\alpha))}. \quad \text{Q.E.D.}$$

Now the computation of $\text{Ccost}^1_{T,\alpha}(c)$ is an easy task, since it holds from Lemma A.3 that

$\text{Ccost}^1_{T,\alpha}(c)$
$= \underset{c' \in C}{\text{average}}(C_{avg}(\text{new}(T, \alpha, c), c'))$
$= (1/n)\underset{c' \in C}{\sum}(C_{avg}(T, c') + (1-\Delta(c, c'))(1/2)^{\rho(c'(\alpha))})$
$= \text{cost}^1(T) + (1/n)\underset{c' \in C}{\sum}(1/2)^{\rho(c'(\alpha))} - (1/n)(1/2)^{\rho(c(\alpha))}.$

A.2. Proof of Theorem 3.2.

Lemma A.4

Each color satisfies the following relation;
$$C_{worst}(\text{new}(T, \alpha, c), c) \leq C_{worst}(\text{new}(T, \alpha, c^+), c),$$
where c^+ denotes a representative of the colors that are different from c.

proof

For each $v \in \{0,1\}^m$, it holds that
$$\text{naccess}(\text{new}(T, \alpha, c), c, v) = \text{naccess}(T, c, v).$$
Since the cost of the new trie is more than the old trie, it holds that
$$C_{worst}(\text{new}(T, \alpha, c^+), c) \geq C_{worst}(T, c)$$
$$= \max_{v \in \{0,1\}^m} \text{naccess}(T, c, v)$$
$$= \max_{v \in \{0,1\}^m} \text{naccess}(\text{new}(T, \alpha, c), c, v)$$
$$= C_{worst}(\text{new}(T, \alpha, c), c),$$
which proves the lemma. Q.E.D.

Assume that c maximizes $Cworst(new(T, \alpha, c^+), c)$. From the definition, $Ccost^2_{T,\alpha}(c)$ is

$$Ccost^2_{T,\alpha}(c) = \max_{c' \in C} Cworst(new(T, \alpha, c), c')$$

$$= \max (\max_{c' \in C-\{c\}} Cworst(new(T, \alpha, c), c'),$$

$$Cworst(new(T, \alpha, c), c)).$$

From Lemma A.4, this becomes

$$Ccost^2_{T,\alpha}(c) \leq \max (\max_{c' \in C-\{c\}} Cworst(new(T, \alpha, c'^+), c'),$$

$$Cworst(new(T, \alpha, c^+), c))$$

$$= \max_{c' \in C} Cworst(new(T, \alpha, c'^+), c').$$

$$\leq Cworst(new(T, \alpha, c^+), c). \tag{A.7}$$

Let c' be different from c. Then the followings hold.

$$Ccost^2_{T,\alpha}(c') = \max_{c'' \in C} Cworst(new(T, \alpha, c'), c'')$$

$$= \max (\max_{c'' \in C-\{c'\}} Cworst(new(T, \alpha, c'), c''),$$

$$Cworst(new(T, \alpha, c'), c'))$$

$$\geq Cworst(new(T, \alpha, c^+), c). \tag{A.8}$$

From (A.7) and (A.8), it holds that

$$Ccost^2_{T,\alpha}(c') \geq Ccost^2_{T,\alpha}(c).$$

Therefore, c minimizes $Ccost^2_{T,\alpha}(c)$. Q.E.D.

A.3. Proof of Theorem 3.3.

From the definition of $Cworst(T, c)$, it becomes

$$Cworst(T, c) = \max (\max_{v \in \{0,1\}^m} naccess(T, c, 0 \circ v),$$

$$\max_{v \in \{0,1\}^m} naccess(T, c, 1 \circ v)). \tag{A.9}$$

Consider a search specified as '$c = 0 \circ v$'. The search fails in $T|\bar{c}$, while all the leaves in T/c satisfy this search condition. Therefore, the following equality holds.

$$\max_{v \in \{0,1\}^{m-1}} naccess(T, c, 0 \circ v)$$

$$= card(leaves(T/c)) + \max_{v \in \{0,1\}^{m-1}} naccess(T|\bar{c}, c, 0 \circ v).$$

Since a leaf with a node code α does not belong to $T|\bar{c}$ if $c(\alpha)$ begins with '1', the subtree $T|\bar{c}$ satisfies

$$\max_{v \in \{0,1\}^{m-1}} naccess(T|\bar{c}, c, 1 \circ v) = 0.$$

Therefore, the followings hold.

$$\max_{v \in \{0,1\}^{m-1}} naccess(T, c, 0 \circ v)$$

$$= card(leaves(T/c)) + \max_{v \in \{0,1\}^{m-1}} naccess(T|\bar{c}, c, 0 \circ v)$$

$$= \text{card}(\text{leaves}(T/c))$$
$$+ \max \ (\max_{v \in \{0,1\}^{m-1}} \text{naccess}(T|\bar{c}, c, 0 \circ v),$$
$$\max_{v \in \{0,1\}^{m-1}} \text{naccess}(T|c, c, 1 \circ v) \ )$$
$$= \text{card}(\text{leaves}(T/c)) + \max_{v \in \{0,1\}^m} \text{naccess}(T|\bar{c}, c, v)$$
$$= \text{card}(\text{leaves}(T/c)) + \text{Cworst}(T|\bar{c}, c) \tag{A.10}$$

The substitution of (A.10) and the similar result for $\max(\text{naccess}(T, c, 1 \circ v))$ in (A.9) proves the theorem.

A.4. Proof of Theorem 4.1.

From its definition and Theorem A.2, $\text{cost}^1(T)$ is
$$\text{cost}^1(T) = (1/n) \sum_{c \in C} \text{Cavg}(T, c)$$
$$= (1/n) \sum_{c, \alpha} (1/2)^{\rho(c(\alpha))}.$$

Let $\rho_1(\alpha)$ and $\rho_2(\alpha)$ be defined as
$$\rho(\alpha) = n * \rho_1(\alpha) + \rho_2(\alpha), \quad 0 \le \rho_2(\alpha) \le n-1,$$

where n is the number of colors. Since the regular best average scheme selects, for the splitting of a node at the i-th level, the color c_j whose suffix j is congruent to i-1 modulo n, there are $n - \rho_2(\alpha)$ colors whose $\rho(c(\alpha))$ is $\rho_1(\alpha)$, and $\rho_2(\alpha)$ colors whose $\rho(c(\alpha))$ is $\rho_1(\alpha)+1$. Therefore, $\text{cost}^1(T)$ is

$$\text{cost}^1(T) = (1/n) \sum_\alpha ((n-\rho_2(\alpha))(1/2)^{\rho_1(\alpha)} + \rho_2(\alpha)(1/2)^{\rho_1(\alpha)+1})$$
$$\le (1/n) \sum_\alpha n * (1/2)^{\rho_1(\alpha)}$$
$$\le \sum_\alpha (1/2)^{(\rho(\alpha)/n)-1}$$
$$= 2 \sum_\alpha ((1/2)^{1/n})^{\rho(\alpha)}$$
$$= 2 \sum_\alpha A^{\rho(\alpha)}, \tag{A.11}$$

where A is defined as
$$A = (1/2)^{1/n} > 1/2.$$

The value of
$$\sum_\alpha A^{\rho(\alpha)} \tag{A.12}$$

varies for different shapes of colored tries. What we want to obtain is the maximum value of this sum. For each leaf α, $\rho(\alpha)$ is the level of this node in the trie T. Let α_1 and α_2 be brother leaves at the bottom level of T, α_0 their parent node, and α_3 a leaf at the heighest level of T (Fig. A.1 (a)). Let T' be a trie obtained by first removing α_1 and α_2 and then splitting α_3 into two new leaves α_4 and α_5 (Fig. A.1 (b)).

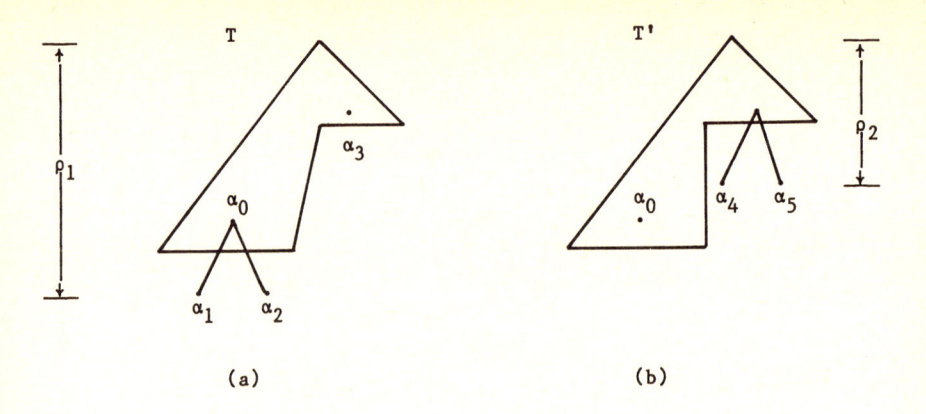

Fig. A.1 Comparison of $cost^1(T)$ between the two colored tries

The value of (A.12) changes as
$$\sum_{\alpha \in leaves(T')} A^{\rho(\alpha)}$$
$$= \sum_{\alpha \in leaves(T)} A^{\rho(\alpha)} - A^{\rho(\alpha_1)} - A^{\rho(\alpha_2)} + A^{\rho(\alpha_0)} + A^{\rho(\alpha_4)} + A^{\rho(\alpha_5)} - A^{\rho(\alpha_3)}.$$

Let $\rho(\alpha_1)$ (= $\rho(\alpha_2)$) be ρ_1 and $\rho(\alpha_4)$ (= $\rho(\alpha_5)$) be ρ_2. From the assumption, ρ_1 is greater than ρ_2. Then above value becomes
$$\sum_{\alpha \in leaves(T')} A^{\rho(\alpha)} = \sum_{\alpha \in leaves(T)} A^{\rho(\alpha)} + (2A-1)(A^{(\rho_2-1)} - A^{(\rho_1-1)})$$

Since $1/2 < A < 1$, it holds that
$$\sum_{\alpha \in leaves(T')} A^{\rho(\alpha)} > \sum_{\alpha \in leaves(T)} A^{\rho(\alpha)}.$$

Therefore, the value of sum $A^{\rho(\alpha)}$ becomes maximum when the difference among the leaf levels is no more than one. The height of such a trie is $\lceil \log_2 N \rceil$. Hence, for each leaf α, $\rho(\alpha)$ is
$$\rho(\alpha) \geq \lceil \log_2 N \rceil - 1 \geq \log_2 N - 1.$$

Therefore, it holds that
$$\text{sum } A^{\rho(\alpha)} \leq N * A^{\log_2 N - 1}$$
$$= (N/A) * A^{\log_2 N}$$
$$= (N/A) * (1/2)^{(\log_2 N)/n}$$
$$= (1/A) * N^{(n-1)/n}. \quad (A.13)$$

From (A.11) and (A.13), $cost^1(T)$ is
$$cost^1(T) \leq (2/A) * N^{(n-1)/n} = 2^{(n+1)/n} N^{(n-1)/n}. \quad \text{Q.E.D.}$$

A.5. Proof of Theorem 4.2

As was shown in Appendix A.4, $cost^1(T)$ is
$$cost^1(T) = (1/n) \sum_{c,\alpha} (1/2)^{\rho(c(\alpha))}$$

$$= (1/n) \sum_{c,\alpha} ((n-\rho_2(\alpha))(1/2)^{\rho_1(\alpha)} + \rho_2(\alpha)(1/2)^{\rho_1(\alpha)+1})$$

$$\geq (1/n) \sum_{\alpha} n*(1/2)^{\rho_1(\alpha)+1}$$

$$= (1/n) \sum_{\alpha} n*(1/2)^{\lfloor \rho(\alpha)/n \rfloor + 1}$$

$$\geq (1/n) \sum_{\alpha} n*(1/2)^{\rho(\alpha)/n + 1}$$

$$= (1/2) \sum_{\alpha} ((1/2)^{1/n})^{\rho(\alpha)}$$

$$= (1/2) \sum_{\alpha} A^{\rho(\alpha)},$$

where $A = (1/2)^{1/n}$. By the same reason discussed in Appendix A.4, sum $A^{\rho(\alpha)}$ becomes minimum for a linear trie as shown in Fig. A.2. However, from the definition of rosaries, the height of the trie should be no more than n*m, where m is the number of colors and m is the maximum bit length of the binary representation of the label values.

Therefore, if N≤n*m, it holds

$$\text{sum } A^{\rho(\alpha)} \geq A + A^2 + \ldots + A^{N-1}$$

$$= \frac{A(1 + A^{N-2} - 2A^{N-1})}{2(1-A)},$$

and, hence,

$$\text{cost}^1(T) \geq \frac{A(1+A^{N-2}+A^{N-1})}{2(1-A)}.$$

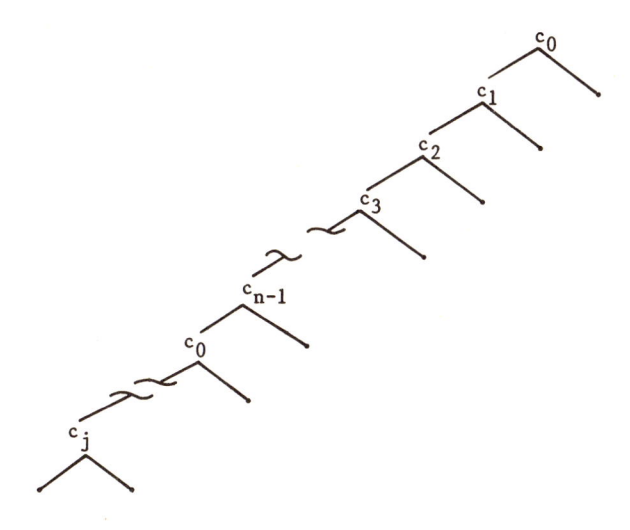

Fig. A.2 A linear colored trie obtained by the regular best average scheme

Assume that $N \geq n*m$. Consider the splitting of a leaf at some level ρ of the linear trie in Fig. A.2. Let the resultant trie be T'. Then it holds that

$$\sum_{\alpha \in leaveas(T')} A^{\rho(\alpha)} = \sum_{\alpha \in leaves(T)} A^{\rho(\alpha)} - A^\rho + 2*A^{\rho+1}$$

$$= \sum_{\alpha \in leaves(T)} A^{\rho(\alpha)} + A^\rho*(2A-1).$$

Since $A > (1/2)$, it holds that

$$\sum_{\alpha \in leaves(T')} A^{\rho(\alpha)} \geq \sum_{\alpha \in leaves(T)} A^{\rho(\alpha)}.$$

Therefore, $cost^1(T)$ satisfies

$$cost^1(T) \geq \frac{A(1 + A^{n*m-2} - 2A^{n*m-1})}{2(1-A)}.$$

Generally, $n*m$ is large enough to approximate the lower bound of $cost^1(T)$ as

$$cost^1(T) \geq A/(2(1-A)).$$

Assume that the label values on rosaries are uniformly distributed. When N is the n-th power of some integer M, it is well known that the static segmentation obtained by the division of a set of labels on each color into M equal size subets attains the minimum value M^{n-1} of $cost^1(T)$. If N is not the n-th power of any integer, this minimum value can not be attained. Therefore, $cost^1(T)$ satisfies

$$cost^1(T) \geq N^{(n-1)/n}.$$

Q.E.D.

QUERYING AND FILTERING FORMATTED FILES

S. Abiteboul(+) M-O. Cordier(x), S.Gamerman(+x), A. Verroust(+)

INTRODUCTION

More and more database machines are using the so-called technique of "filtering on the fly" [BRS]. The underlying idea is the fast processing of sequential files. The main theme of the present paper is to propose a simple model (formatted file) to represent information of (possibly) sequential nature, and simple query languages to access this information. It turns out that our formalism highlights the close relationship between file filtering and formal language translation. This leads to the other theme of the paper, that is the presentation of some filters and a description of their respective powers.

Organizationally, the paper is divided as follows. In Section I, the notion of formatted file is formalized, and the associated semantic briefly discussed. Section II introduces a language to express Yes/No queries on a file, and Section III presents a device to answer them. In Section IV, a very powerful language to express filtering from a file is exhibited, and it is shown that it involves inherent nondeterminism. In Section V, a more restricted filtering language is presented, as well as a device to implement it. Finally, Section VI discusses the implementation in the Verso machine [B+] of a filter for some restricted formats.

In the following, we assume standard knowledge of the Foundations of formal languages such as in [HU].

(x) Laboratoire de Recherche en Informatique, Université de Paris Sud, Orsay
(+) Institut National de Recherche en Informatique et Automatique, Rocquencourt

I FORMATTED FILES

In this section, we formalize the notion of formatted file using regular expressions. The semantics associated with a given format is briefly discussed.

We shall assume throughout the existence of a set of abstract elements called the attributes, and for each attribute A a set Dom(A), called the domain of A. To simplify the discussion, we shall assume that the attributes are defined on disjoint domains, i.e. Dom(A) $\neq$ Dom(B) for each A and B, A $\neq$ B. (To state it in a different way, each value is "tagged" by the name of the corresponding attribute.)

Using the attributes, we define the formats.

Definition: A format is a regular expression over a set of attributes. (See Figures 1.1 and 1.2.)

The regular expressions are used to define the underlying structure of a file which we call "skeleton".

Definition: For each format F, a file skeleton of format F is a word of the language F. (See Figures 1.1 and 1.2.)

We are now ready to define the formatted files.

Definition: Given a file skeleton w of format F, a file of format F is obtained by replacing in w each occurence of an attribute A by a value in Dom(A). (See Figures 1.1 and 1.2.)

Format F: (Class Student*)*

Skeleton: Class Student   Student Class   Class Student

File: Music Vittorio   Dona Comp-Sci Danse   Dona

                Figure 1.1

Format G: (Name ((Male Mil_Pos) + (Female Maiden_Name)))*

Skeleton: Name   Male Mil_Pos Name Female Maiden_Name

File: Vittorio male soldier Dona female   Risi

                Figure 1.2

In this example, Male and Female have one-element domains ({male} and {female}, respectively).

It is possible to associate a very strong semantic to the three operations used to obtain the formats:

Concatenation: Let f, f´ be two files of format F and F´, respectively. Then the concatenation of f and f´ is a file of format FF´. Very similar constructs appear in programming languages (Pascal record) and databases (aggregation [SS]).

Sum: Let F, F´ be two formats. Then a file of formats F + F´ is either a file of format F or a file of format F´. This operation has also analogues in programming languages (Pascal variant record) and databases (generalization [SS]).

Kleene closure (star): Let $f_1, \ldots f_n (n \geq 0)$ be files of format F. Then $f_1 \ldots f_n$ is a file of format F*. This allows us to represent a (possibly empty) sequence of files. This operation has no exact analogue in databases although the notion of sequence is closely related to the concept of sets of objects. Indeed, several papers [AG, DGK, SK] have pointed the need to introduce sequencing in the relational model either to improve the implementation (index) or to provide a better user interface (relation browser).

It is interesting to note that concatenation, sum and sets form the basis of a database model, namely the Format Model [HY]. We conclude this section by three examples. The first two indicate how formatted files can serve to implement database models. The last one emphasizes the representation of incomplete information by formatted files.

Example 1 - Relational model [C] -

Let R(A,B) be a relation schema. Then the relation can clearly be stored on a file of format (AB)*.

Example 2 - Hierarchical model [IMS] -

Consider the hierarchy containing some office numbers, and for each office (1) the names of the employees in this office and (2) the numbers of all the telephones in this office. Then this hierarchy can be represented by a file of format (office_number(employee_name)*(telephone_number)*)*

Example 3 - Incomplete information -

In the file in Figure 1.1, there is no known student in the computer science class. However it is still possible to keep track of the existence of that class.

In the file in Figure 1.2, a male person has no maiden name. The attribute maiden name is not applicable for that person. (We assume that a person appears at most once in the file. We shall come back to this notion of constraint further on.)

II A LANGUAGE TO EXPRESS Y/N QUERIES ON FILES

We present a simple language to express Y/N queries on files. Intuitively, the query is going to be a pattern and the answer to the query is yes if the file has the given pattern.

To define the query language, we need two auxiliary concepts, namely "elementary condition" over an attribute, and "query frame". We first introduce the elementary condition.

Definition : Let A be an attribute and a in Dom(A). An elementary condition is one of the following:

(1) A, A=a, A≠a, (by definition every value in Dom(A) satisfies the simple condition A)

(2) A<a, A>a, A≤a, A≥a (if Dom(A) is ordered)

Then a condition on A is built inductively from elementary conditions using disjunctions or conjunctions. (For instance, (A<17) OR (A>20 AND A<25).)

We next introduce the concept of "query format".

Definition: Let F be a format. A query format (over F) is a regular expression G over the same set of attributes. (See Figure 2.1) Intuitively, the query format provides the underlying structure for a query.

Now we have:

Definition : Let F be a format and G a query format over F. A (formatted file) Y/N query (over F) is obtained by replacing each occurence of an attribute in G by a condition on that attribute.

    Format: (C (S G*)*)*

     (C for class, S for student and G for grade)

    Query format: (C (S G*)*)* (C (S G G G*)*)(C (S G*)*)*

    Query q: (C (S G*)*)* (C (S G$\leq$5 G$\geq$15 G*)*)(C (S G*)*)*

Figure 2.1

Figure 2.1 gives an example of such a query. The intuitive meaning of Q is " Does there exists a class in which all students have their first grade in that class smaller than 5 and their second grade larger than 15 ?".

We now give an informal definition of the semantics of a Y/N query.

Definition: Let f be a file of format F and q a Y/N query on F. Then

   (1) q(f)= yes if f "matches" the pattern q, and
   (2) q(f)= no otherwise.

Not surprisingly, the tools that we are going to use to answer Y/N queries (see Section IV) are typical pattern matching tools, i.e., finite state machines.

To conclude this section, we present three examples of Y/N queries on the files of format (C (S G*)*)*.

   (1) Is Vittorio taking a music class ?
   (C (S G*)*)*(C= music (S G*)*(S= Vittorio G*)(S G*)*)(C (S G*)*)*

   (2) Is Vittorio taking all music classes ?
   ((C≠ music (S G*)*)* + (C= music (S G*)*(S= Vittorio G*)(S G*)*))*

   (3) Is Vittorio taking only music classes ?
   ((C ≠ music (S≠Vittorio G*)*) + (C= music (S G*)*))*

Note that in (2), if there is no music class, the answer is yes and in (3), if Vittorio isn't taking any class the answer is also yes. It may seem complicated to express queries in this langage. However, the use of regular expressions allows to specify very intricate queries even when the sequential nature of the file is considered. Furthermore, such langages present the advantage over other possible langages to have an intimately tied device, that is, the finite state machine.

III ANSWERING Y/N QUERIES BY PATTERN RECOGNITION

In this section, we show how to answer a Y/N query on file using the essential tool of syntactic pattern recognition, that is a finite state device.

Given a query q and a file f, q(f)= yes if f matches the pattern associated with q. The key difference with classical pattern matching is that the value domains may be infinite. We process as follows:

(1) The Y/N query q is translated into a regular expression t(q), and

(2) a scanner s is constructed which transforms the file f into a word s(f) over a finite alphabet.

The main result of this section is that q(f)= yes if and only if s(f) belongs to t(q):

```
            f  (such that q(f)= yes)      q
            |                              |
         s  |                              | t
            |                              |
            V                              V
           s(f)      (belongs to)        t(q)
```

We first define the translation from q to t(q).

Lets take first an example

Example 3.1:

Let Q: (C (S G*)*)*(C (S G$\leq$5 G<15 G*)*)(C (S G*)*

Let $\pi_G = \{\pi_1, \pi_2, \pi_3\}$ where
$\pi_1 = [0,5[$, $\pi_2 = [5,15[$, and $\pi_3 = [15,20]$

(Dom(G) is supposed to be [0,20]) Let C, S, G_1, G_2, G_3 be some attributes. (Intuitively, G_1, G_2, G_3, resp, are associated with π_1, π_2, π_3, resp.)

then we replace in q

(1) C by C ,

(2) S by S ,

(3) G by $G_1 + G_2 + G_3$,

(4) G$\leq$5 by G_1 ,

(5) G<15 by $G_1 + G_2$,

and we obtain t(Q) = (C (S ($G_1+G_2+G_3$)*)*)*
(C (S G_1 (G_1+G_2)($G_1+G_2+G_3$)*)*)
(C (S ($G_1+G_2+G_3$)*)*)*

In the general case we have:

Notation 3.1: Let A be an attribute and $\mathcal{L}_A$ the set of conditions on A appearing in q. Let $\pi_A = \{\pi_A^1, \pi_A^2, \ldots, \pi_A^{n(A)}\}$ be the partition of Dom(A) defined by:

for each x, y in Dom(A), x and y belong to the same block of the partition iff they satisfy the same conditions in $\mathcal{L}_A$.

For each attribute A in the query, we associate to $\pi_A^1, \ldots, \pi_A^{n(A)}$ some attributes A_1, A_2, ... $A_{n(A)}$ such that each A_i has a one-element domain, say Dom(A_i)={a_i}.

Then t(q) is obtained by replacing in q each condition C over some attribute A by

$$\sum \{A_i \mid \forall x \in \pi_A^i, \; x \text{ satisfies } C\}.$$

The query q has been tranlated into a regular expression t(q). Now a scanner s is defined which tranforms the file into a word over the same alphabet than t(q).

Notation 3.2 : Let q be a query. Let $\pi_A = \{\pi_A^1, \ldots, \pi_A^{n(A)}\}$ and $A_1, A_2, \ldots A_{n(A)}$ be like in Notation 3.1 for each A appearing in q. Then the scanner s associated with q is defined by:
for each B appearing in q and x in Dom(B), $s(x) = b_i$ iff x is in π_B^i

The definition of s is extended to files in the obvious way:
$s(f) = s(x)s(y)s(z)\ldots$ if $f = xyz\ldots$

Example 3.1 (continued) The scanner s for the query q is defined by

$s(x) = c$ for each x in Dom(C)

$s(x) = s$ for each x in Dom(S)

for each x in Dom(G)

$\quad s(x) = g_1$ if $x < 5$

$\quad s(x) = g_2$ if $5 \leq x < 15$

$\quad s(x) = g_3$ if $x \geq 15$

Note that for each file f of format (C (S G*)*)*, s(f) is a word of the regular language (C (S ($G_1 + G_2 + G_3$)*)*)*.

We now state without proof the following result:

Theorem : Let q be a Y/N query, t(q) its translation and s the associated scanner. Then for each file f,

$$q(f) = \text{yes iff } s(f) \text{ is in } t(q).$$

The process of answering a Y/N query q can thus be split into two phases :

(a) compilation : the scanner s is constructed and a finite automata for t(q) is built.

(b) execution : the finite automata analyses the file using s as a preprocessor.

A diagram for this recognition is shown in Figure 3.2

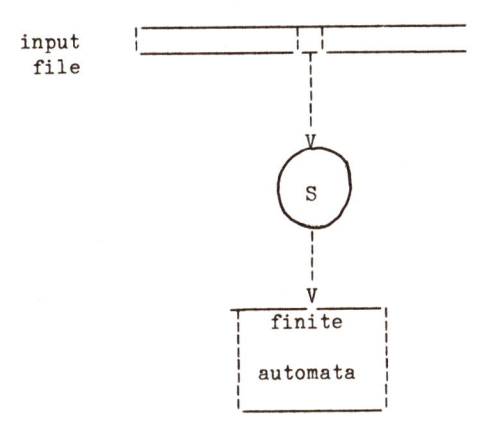

Figure 3.2

It is probably possible to obtain faster machines by allowing the scanner to be modified during execution depending on the automata state.(Indeed a similar type of technique is used in the Verso machine.) It is still an open problem whether the gain in scanning time is worth the time spent loading various versions of the scanner.

To conclude this section, let us remark that Y/N query can be used to check whether a file has format G, it suffices to ask the query G. (By definition a format G is also a query.)

IV FILTERING LANGUAGE

In this section, we present a very powerful language to express "filtering" of a formatted file. We show that it can lead to ambiguity , and that the corresponding processes are inherently nondeterministic.

We start by the definition of "formatted file query"

Definition: A (formatted file) query is a trivial Y/N query in which some attribute occurences are marked. (In the present paper marked attributes will be underlined.)

(A trivial query over F is a Y/N query which gives a yes answer for each file of format F)

Intuitively, marked attributes indicate the information which is extracted from the file whereas nonmarked attributes indicate the information which is not kept. To illustrate this concept, two examples are given:

Example 4.1: "Give Vittorio's courses and grades"

((C (S≠Vittorio G*)*)*(C̲ ((S≠Vittorio G*)*(S=Vittorio G̲*)*)*)*

Example 4.2:   "Give, for each class, the name of a student (if there is one) whose grades in that class are all larger than 10"

((C (S G*)*(S̲ (G>10)*)(S G*)*)*(C (S G*(G<10)G*)*)*)*

Thus, given a file of format F and q a formatted file query, filtering f by q consists in matching f with the pattern associated with q and, during this process, extracting the information corresponding to marked attributes in q.

It should be noted in Example 4.2 that the filter allows one to ask ambiguous questions. Indeed if f is the file "Guitar Vittorio 12 15 Donatella 13", then "Vittorio" and "Donatella" are two possible answers.

In Section III, the automata tied directly with a Y/N query is nondeterministic. However, an equivalent deterministic automata can clearly be constructed. In the filtering case, an output device must be added. As emphasised by the following example, the handling of such a device makes the answering process inherently nondeterministic.

Example 4.3: Let F be the format ((A* B*)C)* and q the query

((A̲* B*)C≥0 + (A* B̲*)C<0)*

This query is not ambiguous in the sense that the answer on any file is unique. (Keep the A-values if $C \geq 0$ and the B-values otherwise.) However, the criteria to decide whether to keep the A or B values comes too late for a deterministic finite state machine to know what to write while reading (A* B*).

V IMPLEMENTING SIMPLE QUERIES

In the previous section, the notion of formatted file query was introduced, and it was shown that this concept involves inherent nondeterminism. The purpose of this section is to exhibit a large subclass, namely the "simple queries", of these queries which can be processed sequentially in a totally deterministic way.

In order to define the simple queries, we introduce the function FIRST. The function FIRST takes a Y/N query as its argument and returns the set of values which can appear at the beginning of a file accepted by the query.

Definition: For each Y/N query q, FIRST(q) is defined as follows

(1) If C is a condition on some attribute A, then FIRST(C)= $\{x \text{ in Dom}(A) \mid x \text{ satisfies } C\}$;

(2) FIRST(q*)= FIRST(q)$\cup\{\$\}$;

(3) FIRST(qq´)= FIRST(q) if $\$ \notin$ FIRST(q), and FIRST(qq´)= $\{$FIRST(q) - $\{\$\}\} \cup$ FIRST(q´) otherwise; and

(4) FIRST(q+q´)= FIRST(q)∪FIRST(q´)

(In the definition, $ is a special symbol such that $ isn't in Dom(A) for each A. Then $ is in FIRST(q) iff the empty file is accepted by q.)

For instance, FIRST(AB*)= Dom(A)

and FIRST((AB*)*)= Dom(A)∪{$}

Now we have:

Definition: A simple Y/N query is a Y/N query such that

(a) If qq´ appears in the Y/N query, either $ is not in FIRST(q) or FIRST(q)∩FIRST(q´)= ∅; and

(b) If q+q´ appears in the Y/N query, then FIRST(q)∩FIRST(q´)⊆{$}.

A simple query is a query associated with a simple Y/N query.

Intuitively, Condition (a), resp. (b), removes the nondeterminism introduced by the concatenation, resp. sum. It should be noted that, although FIRST(q) may be an infinite set, it is the union of a finite number of domain intervals. Therefore it can easily be checked whether a given Y/N query satisfies (a) and (b). For instance,

((C=music (SG>10*)*)* (C≠music (SG*)*)*)* is simple; and

(C(SG*)*)* (C (S G≤5 G≥15 G*)*) (C(SG*)*)* is not simple.

It turns out that simple queries can easily be checked by a device, namely the simple filter, that we describe now. The simple filter ressembles the finite state machine described in Section 3 except that it has an output tape. (See Figure 5.1.). Depending on the state of the automata, the scanner has the choice to copy or not a complete value from the input tape on the output tape or to ignore it.

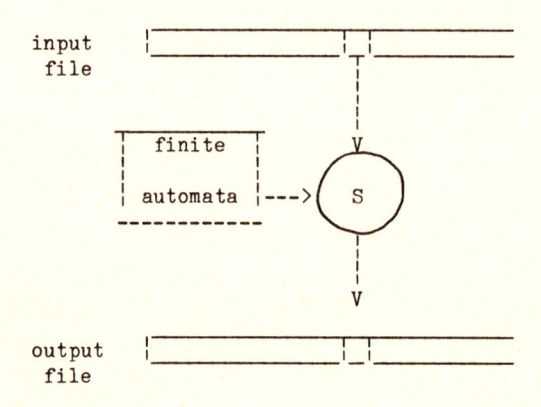

```
input     |_____|_|_____|
file                        | |
                            |T|
                            | |
                            |V|
         ┌─────────────┐    
         | finite      |    ╭───╮
         |             |───>|   |
         | automata    |    | S |
         └─────────────┘    ╰───╯
                            | |
                            |V|
                            | |
output    |_____|_|_____|
file
```

Figure 5.1

We state without proof a result relating simple queries and simple filters. (The proof can be deduced very simply from well-known results of language theory.)

Theorem: For each simple query q, there exists a simple filter which outputs q(f) on input f.

VI AN EXAMPLE : THE VERSO MACHINE

The formats used in Verso [BRS] form a particular subset of the file formats.

Definition: For each string of attributes X, X* is a Verso format. For each string of attributes X, and Verso formats $F_1,...,F_n$ for some n, $(X\ F_1\ ...F_n)^*$ is a Verso format.

For instance, (A B(C D)* E*)* and (A(B C*)*)* are Verso formats whereas A(B C*)* or A*B are not.

The query language in Verso is very different to the query languages previously presented in this paper in the sense that it isn't "format oriented" but rather "logic oriented". The queries are of the form

$$(F \mid c_1 \wedge ... \wedge c_p)\ [X]$$

where each c_i is a condition on some attribute of the format. In the query, X is the set of attributes which must be extracted. (See [BRS] for a precise definition.) It turns out that the set of Verso queries is a subset of the set of formatted file queries:

Theorem: For each Verso query, there exists an equivalent formatted file query (i.e. a formatted file query which gives the same answer).

Proof: The proof is straightforward and consists in the construction of the equivalent query.

Example 6.2: Consider the compacted format (C (S G*)*)* and the query:

"Give the name of the student who got a grade larger than 15 in the Computer Science class".

The corresponding Verso query is:

(R ¦ C=Comp_Science ∧ G>15)[S]

and the formatted query:

(C≠Comp_Science (S G*)*)*

((C=Comp_Science (S (G≤15)*)*((S (G≤15)*(G>15)G*) (S (G≤15)*)*)*)

(C≠Comp_Science (S G*)*)*

Although Verso queries are much simpler than general formatted file queries, their sequential computation involves also inherent nondeterminism. In [BRS], some conditions are given on Verso queries so that they can be computed without backtrack on the input file. However, the Verso filter handles a stack of output addresses, and allows backtracking on the output file. It is clear that the Verso filter can be formally represented by a pushdown transducer with the addition of the scanner used in Section III. (See Figure 6.1)

```
        input    |_____|
        file                       |
                                   |
                 _____       |
                |  finite   |      V
                |           |    _____
                |  automata |-->(  S  )
                 -----------     -----
                                   |
                                   |
                                   V
        output   |_____|
        stack
```

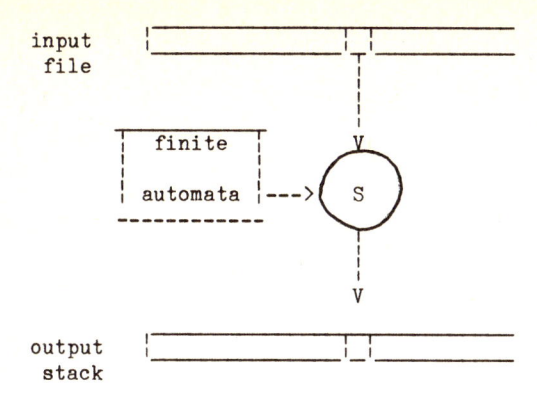

Figure 6.1

Indeed, it would be interesting to characterize classes of queries that can be answered with such device.

ACKNOWLEDGEMENT

We would like to thank all the participants to the third French-Italian workshop on Databases. Special thanks are also due to the La Luna "Maitre d'Hotel" for his very warm support.

REFERENCES

[AG] Abiteboul, S., and S. Ginsburg, "Tuple Sequences and Indexes," Univ. of South. Cal., Technical Report, #83-205

[BRS] Bancilhon, F., P. Richard and M. Scholl, "On Line Processing of Compacted Relations", Proc. of VLDB (1982)

[B+] Bancilhon & al, "Verso: A Relational Back End Data Base Machine," Proc. of the International Workshop on Database Machines, San Diego, (1982)

[C] Codd, E.F., "A Relational Model of Data for Large Shared data banks," Communications ACM Vol. 13, #6, (1970)

[DKG] Dayal, U., N. Goodman and R.H. Katz, "An Extended Relational Algebra with Control over Duplicate Elimination," Proc. of ACM Symp. on Princ. of Databases Sys., (1982)

[HY] Hull, R. and C.K. Yap, "The Format Model: A Theory of Database Organization," Proc. of ACM Symp. on Princ. of Databases Sys., (1982)

[HU] Hopcroft, J.E., and J.D. Ullman, "Formal Languages and Their Relation to Automata", Reading, Mass.: Addison-Wesley, (1969)

[IMS] Information Management System/360 Version 2 General Information Manual, IBM Form #GH20-0765

[SK] Stonebraker, M. and J. Kalash, "TIMBER: A Sophisticated Relation Browser," Proc. VLDB (1982)

[SS] Smith, J.M., and D.C.P. Smith, "Database Abstractions: Aggregation and Generalization," ACM Trans. on Database Sys., (1977)

ON THE USE OF A DATABASE MACHINE FOR FUZZY QUERYING

P. Bosc, A. Chauffaut, G. Hamon
I.R.I.S.A.
Campus de Beaulieu
35042 RENNES Cédex - France

INTRODUCTION

Presently at the IRISA, we work on a system for the automatic management of classified advertisements called HAVANE. The basic idea is to enable a user to submit his advertisement by means of the usual language employed in the newspapers and to be offered a set of "matching" advertisements from a database.

The system involves two main components. The first one deals with the understanding of advertisements expressed in somewhat of a natural language. The end of this step is achieved when the user agrees on a paraphrase proposed by the system to summarize its understanding of the advertisement. This point will not be detailed later in this note. The second component concerns the retrieval of "matching" advertisements out of a database, ie those satisfying the need of the user. The retrieving process must verify several constraints to be credible :
- it will most of the time concern a large amount of advertisements
- it must be efficient and the response time must be short
- the number of returned responses must be neither too big nor too narrow, so that the result is managable and useful for the user.

These requirements -especially the third-, are not specific to HAVANE. They are also valid for other applications aimed at the help for a choice based on fuzzy criteria. These features imply a capability of adaptation of the retrieving process.

We shall first describe what kind of query the user implicitely addresses to the HAVANE system. This will lead to the notion of fuzzy query and we shall talk about the functions to include into a DBMS in order to allow fuzzy querying. Then, we focus on the example of classified advertisements and give some features of a database machine architecture aimed at fuzzy querying.

FUZZY QUERIES

When looking at the retrieving process of HAVANE, we guess that the query to solve may be expressed by some sentence like :

(1) *find about n advertisements as close as possible to* 'given advertisement describing a need'.

This formulation may be generalized to other kinds of objects -document retrieval for instance-, what would be :

(2) *find about n objects as close as possible to* 'description of a given object'.

Such expressions lead to the notion of fuzzy queries. With usual DBMS, the query is precise and the answer corresponds exactly to the query. In our case, the system will have to adapt the interpretation of fuzzy terms contained in the query, in order to confine the volume of resulting objects around n.

Fuzzyness is situated at two levels in (2) :
- how to interpret fuzzy terms involved in the quoted expression 'description of a given object', like : *around* x, y *maxium*, *very long*, *not too large*, *reasonable* price.
- even if the description is precise, how to translate the words *as close as possible*. For instance, if we consider the advertisement
  house 5 rooms to sell 70000 dollars located at Palo
  it seems reasonable to deliver advertisements of potential purchasers involving elements slightly different from the previous -for example four rooms only, located in the neighbourhood of Palo, and so on-.

It is worthy to notice that the use of fuzzy terms, like adjectives and adverbs especially, would be a matter of course if we imagined the interrogation of databases by means of a really natural language. For example, we could express some queries such as
   find persons who are reasonably paid, use to practise jogging and are more than 35
involving both fuzzy and precise conditions.

OUR APPROACH

Rather than make a specific system for HAVANE, we prefer a more general solution which is expected to be utilizable in a larger scale. The basic principle is to design a DBMS architecture providing the capability of fuzzy querying on non fuzzy databases in a first time.

Moreover, we think that more or less dedicated interfaces should be in charge of user language aspects (conviviality and understanding particularly). One of their roles would be to generate a fuzzy query intended for the extended DBMS. In order to answer to these queries, two aspects must be developed :
- definition of a language allowing the formulation of fuzzy queries. It constitutes the target language for the interfaces mentioned above
- extension of the conceptual and/or external schemas in order to state the fuzzy words or functions utilizable for a given view and their interpretation in terms of usual computations or comparisons.

In addition, let us say that another important point of view concerns the performances of such a DBMS. As we shall see below, it is necessary to use efficient implementation techniques so that we could guarantee both a good amount of results and an acceptable response time.

SOME POSSIBLE INTERPRETATIONS IN THE CONTEXT OF CLASSIFIED ADVERTISEMENTS

We now come back to the particular case of HAVANE to illustrate the basic problems encountered and the reason why we propose a database machine approach.

In HAVANE, two points are to be solved : a) the semantics of the expression as close as possible and b) the calibration of the selected advertisements. These two aspects are strongly connected but basically different.

The first way of doing is to define a boolean function f answering whether or not two advertisements are close. Since a single function fails with respect to point b), we may define several embedded functions f_i corresponding to tolerance levels, ie for any couple of advertisements A and D

$$f_i(A,d) = \underline{true} \Rightarrow f_j(A,D) = \underline{true} \;\forall i > j$$

It is to notice that this solution does not necessarily succeed in the calibration since at level l the number of response may be too little and too important at level l+1. Moreover, if p embedded functions are specified, we may have up to p passes. However, the use of secondary indexes is theoretically possible for those f_i involving conditions which are equivalent to the predicate linked to the index. This case occurs when a function f_i is written f_i^1 and ... and f_i^m and one (or several) f_i^j is answered using an index. If no index is utilizable, the retrieval process will require up to p sequential scans of the base what may be unacceptable.

To avoid this situation, a close solution is to define a function g(A,D) delivering an integer $\varepsilon[1,p]$ which is the strongest tolerance level satisfied by the couple A,D. Using an appropriate queue management, the result obtained by the previous method will be reached in exactly one sequential scan of the base.

These two methods are likely practicable but they present drawbacks, especially a bad control of the calibration and some lack of efficiency and generality of the processings. Consequently, we decided to investigate a third way which is expected to be more general and efficient.

PROXIMITY, FUZZY SETS THEORY AND FILTERING

In this way we shall try to associate the fuzzy set theory and programmable filtering technology. We have to find "how to do" and to evoluate our different solutions.

We plan to investigate the fuzzy sets theory and to use the "grade of membership" notion to represent the proximity of two advertisements.

Let us remember you that the fuzzy function gives us, for each member of a set, a number belonging to the [0,1] interval. This number represents the compatibility of this member with the criteria attached to this function.

For example :

F = <u>tall person</u>   {French people} ———> [0,1]
F(P-140) = 0   F(P-150) = 0,4
F(P-160) = 0,6   F(P-190) = 1

The fuzzy algebra gives us basic function to calculate the proximity on one criteria and the operations to do when multiple criterias are combined into a complex expression.

For instance if h(A,D) is written as h_1 and h_2 and ... and h_q where h_i applies to subsets of attributes of both A and D the fuzzy set theory suggests to take h as $\min_i(h_i)$.

So we don't want to discuss on the fuzzy set theory but the use its present known results to build our fuzzy querying processor.

The interest of this kind of function resides first in primitivity of h compare to f and g, and then in the case to deliver any desired number n of responses. This only needs one scan of the base and requires to keep at all times the n advertisements causing the highest values of h.

As we have to compute fuzzy function of each tuple of the base we think that the filtering technology will give us the best efficiency.

In the last example we could implement h by means of a programmable filter composed of either one, or several processors working in parallel. We may imagine the schema :

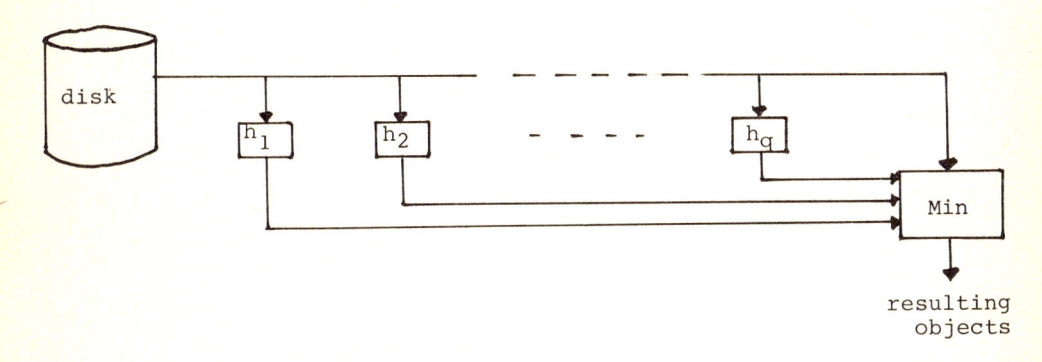

[Diagram: disk connected to parallel processors h_1, h_2, ..., h_q, feeding into a Min block producing resulting objects]

where each elementary processor performs one of the h_i's and a special processor uses the partial result of each h_i to compute the total proximity of the current advertisement coming from the disk against the user's advertisement and deals with calibration. In this work we have to compare the different possible architectures, their complexity and their efficiency before to do our choice for a realisation.

CONCLUSION

We have briefly presented an architecture allowing high level user languages, especially fuzzy querying. We sketched out a way of interpretation of fuzzy queries based on fuzzy set theory. It requires the whole scan of the database and is thus thought to be implemented by means of a specialized filter. We first intend to build such a filter for a particular system managing classified advertisements and then extend our work to a more general DBMS.

Relational Database Systems

Analysis and Comparison

Editors: **J. W. Schmidt, M. L. Brodie**
1983. XV, 618 pages. ISBN 3-540-12032-7

Contents:
Introduction. – Features of Relational Database Systems. – Analysis of Relational Database Management Systems. – Feature Summaries and Comparisons. – References.

The book is the most comprehensive and detailed analysis of existing relational database management systems to date. It presents a generic characterization of an RDBMS independently of specific RDBMSs) in terms of:

- relational database constituents
- relational functional capabilities
- definition, generation and administration facilities
- interfaces and DBMS architecture
- operational aspects

These features are then used as a common basis to analyse fourteen of the most important existing RDBMSs. The fourteen systems analyses are then compared, in a tabular format, with respect to the features, and system feature summaries are presented.
The book is introduced by a foreword written by Dr. E. F. Codd, the inventor of the relational approach to databases.
The book is intended to assist the reader in developing a detailed understanding of the Relational Data Model, Relational Database Managment Systems, and the state-of-the-art in relational DBMS technology. It provides a comprehensive check list of features with which to evaluate RDBMSs or DBMSs in general.

Springer-Verlag
Berlin
Heidelberg
New York
Tokyo